D1307574

Desktop Applications for
Microsoft®
Visual Basic® 6.0
MCSD
Training Kit

Microsoft Press

PUBLISHED BY
Microsoft Press
A Division of Microsoft Corporation
One Microsoft Way
Redmond, Washington 98052-6399

Copyright © 1999 by Microsoft Corporation

Library of Congress Cataloging-in-Publication Data
Desktop Applications for Microsoft Visual Basic 6.0 MCSD Training Kit.
      p. cm.
   ISBN 0-7356-0620-X
    1. Electronic data processing personnel--Certification.
   2. Microsoft software--Examinations--Study guides. 3. Microsoft
Visual BASIC. I. Microsoft Corporation.
   QA76.3.M329   1999
   005.26'8--dc21   99-13775
                                               CIP

Printed and bound in the United States of America.

2 3 4 5 6 7 8 9   QMQM   4 3 2 1 0 9

Distributed in Canada by ITP Nelson, a division of Thomson Canada Limited.

A CIP catalogue record for this book is available from the British Library.

Microsoft Press books are available through booksellers and distributors worldwide. For further information about international editions, contact your local Microsoft Corporation office or contact Microsoft Press International directly at fax (425) 936-7329. Visit our Web site at mspress.microsoft.com.

Acquisitions Editor: Eric Stroo
Project Editor: Victoria Thulman

Contents

About This Book

Welcome to Desktop Applications for Microsoft Visual Basic 6.0 MCSD Training Kit. By completing the lessons and associated exercises in this course, you will acquire the knowledge and skills necessary to develop solutions using Visual Basic 6.0.

This book also addresses the objectives of the Microsoft Designing and Implementing Desktop Applications with Microsoft® Visual Basic® 6.0 (70-176) exam. This self-paced course provides content that supports the skills measured by this exam.

Note For more information on becoming a Microsoft Certified Solutions Developer, see the section titled "The Microsoft Certified Professional Program" later in this chapter.

Each chapter in this book is divided into lessons. Most lessons include hands-on procedures that allow you to practice or demonstrate a particular concept or skill. Each chapter ends with a short summary of all chapter lessons, a hands-on lab, and a set of review questions to test your knowledge of the chapter material.

The "Getting Started" section of this chapter provides important setup instructions that describe the hardware and software requirements to complete the exercises in this course. Read through this section thoroughly before you start the lessons.

Intended Audience

This course is designed for students interested in developing Visual Basic solutions at an intermediate level. This includes developing desktop applications that conform to the Microsoft Solution Framework. More complex topics, such as creating class modules and ActiveX controls, are included in this course.

Prerequisites

Before beginning this self-paced course, you should be able to:

- Create a simple application using Visual Basic.
- Describe the relationship between controls and events.
- Describe the purpose and use of basic controls and menus in a Visual Basic application.
- View and understand a simple hypertext markup language (HTML) page.
- Create and work with Word documents, Excel worksheets, and Access databases.

Getting Started

This self-paced training course contains hands-on procedures to help you learn about Visual Basic. To complete the exercises, your computer must meet the following hardware and software requirements.

Hardware Requirements

All hardware should be on the Microsoft Windows 98 or Microsoft Windows NT Hardware Compatibility List.

Computer/ Processor	PC with a 486DX, 66MHz or higher processor; Pentium or higher processor recommended
Memory	16 MB of RAM for Windows 95 or later (32 MB recommended); 24 MB for Windows NT 4.0 (32 MB recommended)
Hard Disk	VB6.0: 76MB typical;94MB maximum
	IE: 43MB typical;59MB maximum
	MSDN: 57MB typical;493MB maximum
	Windows NT 4.0 Option Pack: 20MB Windows 95 or later;200MB Windows NT 4.0
Drive	CD-ROM drive
Display	VGA or higher-resolution monitor; Super VGA recommended
Operating System	Microsoft Windows 95 or later operating system or Microsoft Windows NT operating system version 4.0 with Service Pack 3 or later
Peripheral/ Miscellaneous	Microsoft Internet Explorer 4.01 Service Pack 1
	Microsoft Mouse or compatible pointing device
	A sound card and speakers or headphones for the multimedia clips

Software Requirements

The following software is required to complete the procedures in this course:

- Visual Basic 6, Professional Edition
- Visual SourceSafe
- Microsoft Word 97
- Microsoft Excel 97

Course Overview

This self-paced course combines text, graphics, hands-on procedures, multimedia presentations, and review questions to teach you about Visual Basic. The course is designed for you to work through the book from beginning to end, but you can choose a customized track and complete only the sections that interest you. If you choose to customize your study, see the "Before You Begin" section in each chapter for important information regarding prerequisites.

The self-paced training book is divided into the following chapters:

- "About This Book" contains a self-paced training overview and introduces the components of this book. Read this section thoroughly to get the greatest educational value from this self-paced training and to plan which lessons you will complete.
- Chapter 1, "Planning the Design of an Application," describes the elements of designing a Visual Basic application in relation to Microsoft design concepts. This chapter explains the issues that you should consider in planning your design. After working through the chapter, you will be able to describe these elements and their relationship to the Microsoft Solution Framework.
- Chapter 2, "Creating the User Interface," describes the elements of the interface and the steps you take in creating it. It explains navigation features, menus, buttons, labels, and controls. After completing the lessons in this chapter, you will be able to explain the role of each of these elements and incorporate them in your application.
- Chapter 3, "Validating and Processing User Input," explains how to manage user input, including input validation techniques. At the end of this chapter, you will be able to perform field and form-level validation, and design forms and controls based on input.
- Chapter 4, "Using the Debugging Tools," describes the types of errors you may encounter and the process of debugging the application. After completing the lesson in this chapter, you will be able to use the various debugging tools such as setting break points and creating watch expressions.
- Chapter 5, "Implementing Error Handling," explains how to incorporate error handling techniques in your application. After you have completed the lessons

in this chapter, you will be able to build applications with inline, procedural, and centralized error handling.

- Chapter 6, "Introduction to Class Modules," explains how to design, create, and use class modules in a Visual Basic application. It also includes an explanation of the Class Builder. After completing the lessons in this chapter, you will be able to use class modules in your application.

- Chapter 7, "Introduction to ActiveX Data Objects (ADO)," explains the ActiveX Data Objects architecture and the use of the ActiveX Data Control. After you have completed the lessons in this chapter, you will be able to implement fundamental database connectivity in a Visual Basic application.

- Chapter 8, "Developing Solutions Using ADO," explains the ADO Object Model and how it differs from the ActiveX Data Control introduced in Chapter 7. After you have completed the lessons in this chapter, you will be able to implement advanced database functionality using ADO objects in a Visual Basic application.

- Chapter 9, "Connecting to COM Servers," describes the role of COM clients and COM servers. This chapter explains how to use your application to connect to servers and other applications that support COM. After completing the lessons in this chapter, you will be able to develop COM client applications that connect to external COM servers such as Microsoft Word.

- Chapter 10, "Creating and Managing COM Components," explains ActiveX Controls, Active DLLs, ActiveX EXEs, and ActiveX Documents. After completing the lessons in this module, you will be able to create a COM component and debug a COM client.

- Chapter 11, "Creating Internet Applications," explains how to create applications on the Internet or a corporate intranet. This chapter includes Dynamic HTML (DHTML) applications, ActiveX documents, and Internet Information Server (IIS) applications. After you complete the lessons in this chapter, you will be able to use the DHTML Page Designer, create an ActiveX document, and create and use IIS WebClasses.

- Chapter 12, "Packaging and Deploying an Application," provides details on incorporating Help files for your application. This chapter also discusses compiler options and the issues involved in distributing your application, including the use of the Package and Deployment Wizard. At the end of this chapter, you will be able to distribute your application via disk, Web or network.

Features of This Book

- Each chapter opens with a "Before You Begin" section, which prepares you for completing the chapter.

- Each chapter is divided into lessons. Most lessons include hands-on exercises that allow you to practice an associated skill or procedure. Some lessons also contain references to animations included on the student CD-ROM that further explain conceptual material.

- Most lessons contain procedures that give you an opportunity to use the skills presented or explore the part of the application described in the lesson. All procedures are identified with an arrow symbol at the left margin.

- Many lessons also contain Practices that allow you to try the new procedure on your own. The icon shown in the left margin identifies the Practices.

- Each lesson ends with a short Lesson Summary of the material presented. Each chapter also has a Summary that covers all lessons in the chapter.

- The Review section at the end of the chapter lets you test what you have learned in the lesson. The icon shown in the left margin identifies the Reviews.

- The Appendix, "Questions and Answers," located at the end of this book, contains all of the book's lab and review questions and corresponding answers.

- The Glossary contains key terms and definitions used in the course.

Conventions Used in This Book

Before you start any of the lessons, it is important that you understand the terms and notational conventions used in this book.

Notational Conventions

- *Italic* in syntax statements indicates placeholders for variable information. *Italic* is also used for book titles.

- Names of files and folders appear in Title Caps. Unless otherwise indicated, you can use all lowercase letters when you type a file name in a dialog box or at a command prompt.

- File name extensions appear in all lowercase.

- Names of folders appear in initial caps. Unless otherwise indicated, you can use all lowercase letters when you type a folder name in a dialog box or at a command prompt.

- Acronyms appear in all uppercase.

- Monospace type represents code samples, examples of screen text, or entries that you might type at a command prompt or in initialization files.

- Square brackets [ ] are used in syntax statements to enclose optional items. For example, [*filename*] in command syntax indicates that you can choose to type a file name with the command. Type only the information within the brackets, not the brackets themselves.

- Braces { } are used in syntax statements to enclose required items. Type only the information within the braces, not the braces themselves.

Keyboard Conventions

- A plus sign (+) between two key names means that you must press those keys at the same time. For example, "Press ALT+TAB" means that you hold down ALT while you press TAB.

- A comma (,) between two or more key names means that you must press each of the keys consecutively, not together. For example, "Press ALT, F, X" means that you press and release each key in sequence. "Press ALT+W, L" means that you first press ALT and W together, and then release them and press L.

- You can choose menu commands with the keyboard. Press the ALT key to activate the menu bar, and then sequentially press the keys that correspond to the highlighted or underlined letter of the menu name and the command name. For some commands, you can also press a key combination listed in the menu.

- You can select or clear check boxes or option buttons in dialog boxes with the keyboard. Press the ALT key, and then press the key that corresponds to the underlined letter of the option name. Or you can press TAB until the option is highlighted, and then press the spacebar to select or clear the check box or option button.

- You can cancel the display of a dialog box by pressing the ESC key.

About The CD-ROM

The Supplemental Course Material compact disc contains multimedia presentations, as well as files used in hands-on exercises.

Using the Lab Exercises

The Supplemental Course Material compact disc contains files required to perform the hands-on lab exercises. These files must first be copied onto your hard disk using the setup program located on the CD-ROM.

Using the Multimedia Presentations

The multimedia presentations supplement some of the key concepts covered in the book. You should view these presentations when suggested, and then use them as a review tool while you work through the material. The animations are denoted with the icon that appears in the left margin below.

To play the animation, open the Animations folder on the student CD-ROM, and double-click on the appropriate file. The animation contains controls that can start, pause, and stop the animations, control the volume, and toggle on or off the sound and associated text.

Also Included on the Supplemental CD-ROM

Two additional features on this disc will assist you in this course.

Self-Test Software Visual Basic 6.0 Sample Exam

Install this sample exam from Self-Test Software to experience a sample certification exam. Designed in accordance with the actual Microsoft certification exam, this sample includes questions to help you assess your understanding of the materials presented in this book. Each question includes feedback with an associated course reference so you can review the material presented. Be sure to visit the STS web site at www.selftestsoftware.com for a complete list of available practice exams.

"Learn Visual Basic 6.0 Now" Multimedia Course

Also included is the Microsoft Press multimedia course, "Learn Visual Basic 6.0 Now." Designed to teach programming fundamentals, it is the perfect companion to this book. Use "Learn Visual Basic 6.0 Now" to increase your understanding of the basic concepts of developing applications using the Visual Basic programming language. If you do not meet all the prerequisites for this course, or just want to refresh your fundamental skills, consider using "Learn Visual Basic 6.0 Now" before starting the lessons presented in this book.

Using this Book to Prepare for Certification

Where to Find Specific Skills in This Book

The following tables provide a list of the skills measured on the certification exam Designing and Implementing Desktop Applications with Microsoft® Visual Basic® 6.0. The tables provide the skill, and where in this book you will find the lesson relating to that skill.

Note Exam skills are subject to change without prior notice and at the sole discretion of Microsoft.

Deriving the Physical Design

Skill Being Measured	Location in Book
Assess the potential impact of the logical design on performance, maintainability, extensibility, and availability.	Chapter 1, Lesson 1
Design Visual Basic components to access data from a database.	Chapter 10, Lesson 2
Design the properties, methods, and events of components.	Chapter 6, Lesson 3

Establishing the Development Environment

Skill Being Measured	Location in Book
Establish the environment for source-code version control	Chapter 1, Lesson 3

Creating User Services

Skill Being Measured	Location in Book
Implement navigational design.	
Dynamically modify the appearance of a menu.	Chapter 2, Lesson 4
Add a pop-up menu to an application.	Chapter 2, Lesson 4
Create an application that adds and deletes menus at run time.	Chapter 2, Lesson 4
Add controls to forms.	Chapter 2, Lesson 3
Set properties for controls.	Chapter 2, Lesson 3
Assign code to a control to respond to an event.	Chapter 3, Lesson 3
Create data input forms and dialog boxes.	
Display and manipulate data by using custom controls. Controls include TreeView, ListView, ImageList, Toolbar, and StatusBar.	Chapter 2, Lesson 3
Create an application that adds and deletes controls at run time.	Chapter 2, Lesson 3

Skill Being Measured	Location in Book
Use the Controls collection to manipulate controls at run time.	Chapter 2, Lesson 3
Use the Forms collection to manipulate forms at run time.	Chapter 2, Lesson 2
Write code that validates user input.	
Create an application that verifies data entered at the field level and the form level by a user.	Chapter 3, Lessons 2,3
Create an application that enables or disables controls based on input in fields.	Chapter 3, Lesson 2
Write code that processes data entered on a form.	
Given a scenario, add code to the appropriate form event. Events include Initialize, Terminate, Load, Unload, QueryUnload, Activate, and Deactivate.	Chapter 2, Lesson 2
Add an ActiveX control to the toolbox.	Chapter 2, Lesson 3
Create a Web page by using the DHTML Page Designer to dynamically change attributes of elements, change content, change styles, and position elements.	Chapter 11, Lesson 1
Use data binding to display and manipulate data from a data source.	Chapter 7, Lesson 4
Instantiate and invoke a COM component.	
Create a Visual Basic client application that uses a COM component.	Chapter 10, Lessons 2,3
Create a Visual Basic application that handles events from a COM component.	Chapter 6, Lesson 3
Create callback procedures to enable asynchronous processing between COM components and Visual Basic client applications.	Chapter 9, Lesson 3
Implement online user assistance in a desktop application.	
Set appropriate properties to enable user assistance. Help properties include HelpFile, HelpContextID, and WhatsThisHelp.	Chapter 12, Lesson 1
Create HTML Help for an application.	Chapter 12, Lesson 1
Implement messages from a server component to a user interface.	Chapter 9, Lesson 3
Implement error handling for the user interface in desktop applications.	
Identify and trap run-time errors.	Chapter 5, Lesson 2
Handle inline errors.	Chapter 5, Lesson 3

Creating and Managing COM Components

Skill Being Measured	Location in Book
Create a COM component that implements business rules or logic. Components include DLLs, ActiveX controls, and active documents.	Chapter 10, Lessons 2,3
Create ActiveX controls.	
Create an ActiveX control that exposes properties.	Chapter 10, Lesson 2
Use control events to save and load persistent properties.	Chapter 10, Lesson2
Test and debug an ActiveX control.	Chapter 10, Lesson 2
Create and enable property pages for an ActiveX control.	Chapter 10, Lesson 2
Enable the data-binding capabilities of an ActiveX control.	Chapter 10, Lesson 2
Create an ActiveX control that is a data source.	Chapter 10, Lesson 2
Create an active document.	
Use code within an active document to interact with a container application.	Chapter 11, Lesson 2
Navigate to other active documents.	Chapter 11, Lesson 2
Debug a COM client written in Visual Basic.	Chapter 10, Lesson 3
Compile a project with class modules into a COM component.	
Implement an object model within a COM component.	Chapter 6, Lesson 4
Set properties to control the instancing of a class within a COM component.	Chapter 10, Lesson 3
Use Visual Component Manager to manage components.	Ch 10, Lesson 4
Register and unregister a COM component.	Chapter 9, Lesson 1

Creating Data Services

Skill Being Measured	Location in Book
Access and manipulate a data source by using ADO and the ADO Data control.	Chapter 7, Lessons 4,5

Testing the Solution

Skill Being Measured	Location in Book
Given a scenario, select the appropriate compiler options.	Chapter 12, Lesson 2
Control an application by using conditional compilation.	Chapter 12, Lesson 2
Set watch expressions during program execution.	Chapter 4, Lesson 2
Monitor the values of expressions and variables by using the Immediate window.	
Use the Immediate window to check or change values.	Chapter 4, Lesson 2
Use the Locals window to check or change values.	Chapter 4, Lesson 2

Skill Being Measured	Location in Book
Implement project groups to support the development and debugging process.	
Debug DLLs in process.	Chapter 10, Lesson 3
Test and debug a control in process.	Chapter 10, Lesson 2
Given a scenario, define the scope of a watch variable.	Chapter 4, Lesson 2

Deploying an Application

Skill Being Measured	Location in Book
Use the Package and Deployment Wizard to create a setup program that installs a desktop application, registers the COM components, and allows for uninstall.	Chapter 12, Lesson 3
Plan and implement floppy disk-based deployment or compact disc-based deployment for a desktop application.	Chapter 12, Lesson 3
Plan and implement Web-based deployment for a desktop application.	Chapter 12, Lesson 3
Plan and implement network-based deployment for a desktop application.	Chapter 12, Lesson 3

Maintaining and Supporting an Application

Skill Being Measured	Location in Book
Fix errors, and take measures to prevent future errors.	Chapter 5, Lessons 1,2,3

The Microsoft Certified Professional Program

The Microsoft Certified Professional (MCP) program provides the best method to prove your command of current Microsoft products and technologies. Microsoft, an industry leader in certification, is on the forefront of testing methodology. Our exams and corresponding certifications are developed to validate your mastery of critical competencies as you design and develop, or implement and support, solutions with Microsoft products and technologies. Computer professionals who become Microsoft certified are recognized as experts and are sought after industry-wide.

The Microsoft Certified Professional program offers five certifications, based on specific areas of technical expertise:

- *Microsoft Certified Professional (MCP).* Demonstrated in-depth knowledge of at least one Microsoft operating system. Candidates may pass additional Microsoft certification exams to further qualify their skills with Microsoft BackOffice products, development tools, or desktop programs.

- *Microsoft Certified Professional - Specialist: Internet.* MCPs with a specialty in the Internet are qualified to plan security, install and configure server products, manage server resources, extend servers to run CGI scripts or ISAPI scripts, monitor and analyze performance, and troubleshoot problems.

- *Microsoft Certified Systems Engineer (MCSE).* Qualified to effectively plan, implement, maintain, and support information systems in a wide range of computing environments with Microsoft Windows 98, Microsoft Windows NT, and the Microsoft BackOffice integrated family of server software.

- *Microsoft Certified Solution Developer (MCSD).* Qualified to design and develop custom business solutions with Microsoft development tools, technologies, and platforms, including Microsoft Office and Microsoft BackOffice.

- *Microsoft Certified Trainer (MCT).* Instructionally and technically qualified to deliver Microsoft Official Curriculum through a Microsoft Authorized Technical Education Center (ATEC).

Microsoft Certification Benefits

Microsoft certification, one of the most comprehensive certification programs available for assessing and maintaining software-related skills, is a valuable measure of an individual's knowledge and expertise. Microsoft certification is awarded to individuals who have successfully demonstrated their ability to perform specific tasks and implement solutions with Microsoft products. Not only does this provide an objective measure for employers to consider; it also provides guidance for what an individual should know to be proficient. And as with any skills-assessment and benchmarking measure, certification brings a variety of benefits: to the individual, and to employers and organizations.

Technical Support

Every effort has been made to ensure the accuracy of this book and the contents of the companion disc. If you have comments, questions, or ideas regarding this book or the companion disc, please send them to Microsoft Press using either of the following methods:

E-mail:

tkinput@microsoft.com

Postal Mail:

Microsoft Press
Attn: Windows Architecture Training for Developers Editor
One Microsoft Way
Redmond, WA 98052-6399

Microsoft Press provides corrections for books through the World Wide Web at the following address:

http://mspress.microsoft.com/support/

Please note that product support is not offered through the above mail addresses. For further information regarding Microsoft software support options, please connect to http://www.microsoft.com/support/ or call Microsoft Support Network Sales at (800) 936-3500.

About the Authors

This course was developed for Microsoft Press by Training Associates, Inc. an Arizona-based corporation founded in 1995. Training Associates has developed a number of MCSD and MCSE-related courses for Microsoft. These include traditional instructor-led courses, self-paced kits, and computer-based (CD-ROM) multimedia titles. In addition, Training Associates offers complete conversion services for existing courses that will be used in an online training environment.

As a Microsoft Certified Technical Education Center (CTEC), Training Associates is one of the first Microsoft-approved online training organizations. Training Associates has delivered courses to thousands of students worldwide that are interested in obtaining all levels of Microsoft certification (MOUS, MCSD, and MCSE). All Training Associates' online instructors and authors are Microsoft Certified Trainers with both traditional classroom and online training experience.

In addition to developing technical curriculum and delivering online instruction, Training Associates has also created the edCenter online learning system. This Web-based, client/server application can be used by training organizations that want to deliver curriculum via a local network or over the Internet. edCenter has been designed to support all forms of technical and non-technical curriculum.

For more information about the products or services offered by Training Associates, please contact us at:

- E-mail: curriculum@trainingassociates.com
- Web site: www.trainingassociates.com

Training Associates' staff who developed this course include:

Project Lead	Dave Perkovich, MCSD, MCT
Instructional Designer	Marilyn Holmlund, M. Ed.
Subject Matter Experts	Sean Chase, MCSD, MCT
	Bruce Hatch, MCSD, MCT
	Brian Larson, MCT
Technical Writer	Wendy Bellows
Video Writer	Tracey Clark, MCSE, MCT
Graphic Artist	Stephanie Lewis
Production Support	Jim Croasman, M. S.

C H A P T E R   1

Planning the Design of an Application

About This Chapter

In this chapter, you will learn about the elements of designing a Visual Basic application using Microsoft design concepts. You will study the issues that you should consider in planning your design. In addition, you will learn about source code control using a library management system called Visual Source Safe.

Before You Begin

To complete the lessons in this chapter, there are no prerequisites.

Lesson 1: Using the Microsoft Solutions Framework

The Microsoft Solutions Framework (MSF) is a development framework produced by Microsoft Consulting Services (MCS). It is based on Microsoft's internal development methodology. MSF also includes the practices of hundreds of MCS corporate clients. Consider applying some or all of these concepts as you plan a multi-developer project.

This lesson explains the features of MSF and how they relate to planning Visual Basic applications.

After this lesson you will be able to:

- Describe the elements of the Microsoft Solutions Framework.
- Explain the role of the Microsoft Solutions Framework in the design and development process.

Estimated lesson time: 30 minutes

Overview of Microsoft Solutions Framework

MSF is a suite of models, principles, and guides for building and deploying software. It is a collection of best practices used by the Microsoft product groups and Microsoft Consulting Services.

MSF helps organizations merge business and technology objectives, reduce the life cycle costs of using new technology, and successfully deploy Microsoft technologies to streamline business processes. MSF exposes critical risks, important planning assumptions, and key interdependencies that are required to successfully plan, build, and manage a technology infrastructure or a business solution. It contains tangible resources, guides, and practices.

By utilizing experience from Microsoft's software development endeavors, MSF helps you to:

- Speed up development cycles.
- Lower the cost of owning technology.
- Improve execution of planned events.
- Improve reaction to unplanned events.
- Create scalable, reliable technology solutions.
- Improve core information technology competencies.

Microsoft Solutions Framework Models

MSF implements models that contribute to the software development cycle. MSF clarifies the relationship between a company's business objectives and the technology solutions to meet those objectives. As a whole, the MSF models interrelate. For example, the Team Model provides accountability for project tasks; use the Process Model when decisions need to be made.

Each model and its purpose is listed in the following table:

Model	Description
Team Model	Defines a team of peers working in interdependent and cooperating roles.
Process Model	Helps your team establish guidelines for planning and controlling results-oriented projects based on project scope, the resources available, and the schedule.
Application Model	Helps your team design distributed applications that take optimum advantage of component reuse.
Enterprise Architecture Model	Supports decisions relating to the information, applications, and technology needed to support a business. It is the key to successful long-term use of new technologies.
Solutions Design Model	Shows how applications must be designed from a user and business perspective (as opposed to the ideal streamlined development proposed in the Application Model).
Infrastructure Model	Establishes MSF principles for managing the people, processes, and technology that support networks in a large enterprise.
Total Cost of Ownership Model	Supports the process of assessing, improving, and managing information technology costs and maximizing value.

The Solutions Design Model

In this course, you will focus on key areas of the Solutions Design Model and the design phases involved in the model. Because software development is a creative and complex process, you can apply MSF's Solution Design Model to software development.

The Solutions Design Model provides a step-by-step strategy for designing business-oriented solutions driven by a specific business need. This model ties together the Application, Team, and Process Models, and lets the information system staff focus resources where they can produce the most value.

This model ties together solutions development and business objectives in two key ways:

- Solutions are driven from the context of the business, which is an essential consideration when developing workflow applications.

- End users are brought in to address usability early on to minimize help desk incidents. Also, information systems professionals are brought in to attempt to solve end user concerns without changing the infrastructure.

The Application, Team, and Process Models help planners identify all business and technical requirements of an application up front, so that resources can be assigned more effectively. Together, these models help organizations recognize the similarities between the process of designing software and the complex process of designing a building. This is why Microsoft gives the title Architect to experts in software design.

You can think of these three perspectives on design—the Application, Team, and Process Models—as convenient points along a continuum that help you apply a particular set of techniques and tools, and address the needs of a particular audience. These perspectives describe the design process in a more focused way. At any given point, you can revisit portions of your design. Design is a continuing process of incremental refinement.

Design Phases of the Solution Design Model

The information-system design process is evolutionary. A good analogy of software design is the design of a building. A building design has three phases: the first is an architect's sketches, the second is architectural plans, and the third is the addition of detail to the plans to make adjustments for the physical environment of the building. This last phase also includes the technology and materials available to construct the building. The following describes this analogy to software design:

- Conceptual design

  The architect's initial sketches provide a view of the building for the client and may contain elements such as floor plans, cutaways, and other figures. This view corresponds to the conceptual design for a software development project, which starts with understanding what the user really needs to do, and then expands to creating a clear set of objectives that capture this understanding.

- Logical design

  The second phase in the architectural process combines the client's view with the architect's view and knowledge. The architect uses detailed drawings to communicate with contractors and other parties involved in the construction of the building. This phase corresponds to the logical design phase in a software development process, in which you lay out the structure of the solution and provide a basis for physical design. As a developer, logical design is important to creating the appropriate solution in the physical design phase. The logical design phase is covered in detail in Lesson 2.

- Physical design

  The architect draws up the plans for the builder. These plans include details for construction activities, and even finer details for individual subcontractors. This phase corresponds to an application designer's physical design in the software development process.

Goals of Conceptual Design

Conceptual design facilitates complete and accurate requirements by involving business sponsors, users, managers, and constituencies. The goal of conceptual design is to understand what the users do and to identify business needs. This process includes:

- Determining the problem that you are trying to solve.
- Determining the needs, and technological capabilities, of the business and users.
- Describing the desired, future state of the work.
- Deciding if there is value in upgrading an existing solution.

In conceptual design, team members present scenarios to enhance understanding and express the problems and visions for the future state of the solution. The purpose of scenarios is to think of the solution in the business environment, and answer the who, what, when, why, and how questions.

Much of conceptual design is an analysis activity that leads to determining which processes and activities will go into the new system, how the needs of those processes and activities will be met, and what the user's experience will be of those activities.

Goals of Logical Design

Logical design activities are integrated directly with the resulting scenarios from conceptual design, and provide the basis for Physical design. Logical design describes the organization of the elements that make up the solution and how they interact. You assemble the elements for optimum efficiency, performance, and reuse. In Lesson 2, you will learn more about using logical design when planning an application.

Goals of Physical Design

Physical design describes a solution in a way that allows developers to construct the solution. Physical design communicates the necessary details of the solution, including organization, structure, technology, and relationships between elements that you will use to create the solution.

Your Role as a Developer

Business problems are generally identified and direction established at a high organizational level—for example, strategic management. As a software developer, your role in conceptual design is usually limited at best. For this reason, the conceptual design phase is not discussed further in this course.

Developers are involved not only in the physical design of a solution, which involves creating flow charts, pseudo-code, and object models, but also in logical design. Because logical design provides a basis for physical design, it is important to include developers. Work on the logical design phase will overlap with work on the physical design in an iterative process. This allows development team members to incrementally optimize a system and improve its operation.

The logical design process must promote a greater understanding of the solution by the project team. This is the primary consideration when determining the level of detail that should be included in the design. If too little detail is included, the team runs the risk of missing relevant interactions. If too much detail is included, the design may become overly complicated.

Logical Design Tasks

A technically correct project is not effective if it does not address the stated problems. Conceptual design is all about solving the right problem; you determine the solution based on the description of the business and the users. In logical design, you determine a logical organization for the solution. This provides a coherent view of the entire project. Logical design should encompass the following characteristics:

- Technological independence

  Logical design should be as independent of physical implementations as possible. Nevertheless, certain physical constraints or opportunities should be considered in logical design in order to validate whether the design can be implemented. Purely technology-dependent decisions should be made later, in the physical design phase.

- Reduced complexity

  The primary purpose of logical design is to manage complexity. Complexity leads to incomplete understanding, which leads to confusion, which leads to poorly specified and inadequate designs.The key to managing complexity is organizing the solution and suppressing unnecessary details.

- Focus on structure

  The goal in logical design is to lay out the elements in the system, describe how they are connected, and define what can be done with each of them. Logical design describes how the system accomodates each scenario created in conceptual design. Every feature and activity described in each scenario should be addressed by at least one element in the logical design.

The Logical Design Process

You start the logical design process by defining the major modules of the system. A module represents some collection of processes that work together to accomplish a task. You must specify each element, the functions of each of these elements, and how each element interacts with other elements. The output includes:

- Core functional areas and elements that are of concern.
- Activities and functions of those areas.
- Connections between areas.

An architect's drawings contain detailed views of all rooms in a house, how they are laid out, and how they are connected. The architect determines the physical layout by the function and proximity of the activities that occur, which achieves ease-of-use and efficiency. Likewise, in logical design, designers need to determine the functional areas, the services and connections from one module to the next.

As illustrated in Figure 1.1, the house has a subset consisting of three rooms: Kitchen, Dining Room, and Pantry. For each room and any connections to other rooms, you define what functions and activities will take place. On a larger scale, a system could be a hotel. The hotel consists of areas such as the front desk, housekeeping, food services, reservations, and security. Each of these areas can probably be broken down into individual subsystems and applications of the overall hotel system. For example, in this course you will create a hotel reservation system by completing the lab in each chapter. This hotel reservation system could be a subsystem within a hotel system.

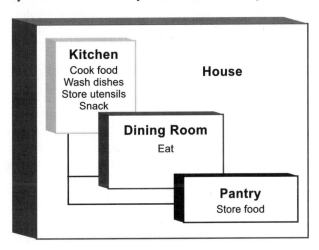

Figure 1.1 Functional modules example

Lesson Summary

The Microsoft Solutions Framework (MSF) is a suite of models, principles, and guides for building and deploying software. MSF is a collection of best practices used by the Microsoft product groups and Microsoft Consulting Services.

The MSF implements the following models that contribute to the software development cycle:

- Team Model

  The Team Model defines a team of peers working in interdependent and cooperating roles.

- Process Model

  The Process Model helps your team establish guidelines for planning and controlling results-oriented projects based on their scope, the resources available, and the schedule.

- Application Model

  The Application Model helps your team design distributed applications that take optimum advantage of component reuse. Together, the Team and Process models form the core of the MSF discipline as it relates to development and infrastructure projects.

- Enterprise Architecture Model

  The key to successful long-term use of new technologies is the Enterprise Architecture Model. This model supports decisions relating to the information, applications, and technology needed to support a business.

- Solutions Design Model

  The Solutions Design Model shows how applications must be designed from a user and business perspective (as opposed to the ideal streamlined development proposed in the Application Model).

- Infrastructure Model

  To establish MSF principles for managing the people, processes, and technology that support networks in a large enterprise, use the Infrastructure Model.

- Total Cost of Ownership Model

  The Total Cost of Ownership Model is a process for assessing, improving, and managing information technology costs and maximizing value.

In this course, you will focus on key areas of the Solutions Design Model and the design phases involved in the model. Because software development is a creative and complex process, you can apply MSF's Solution Design Model to software development. The Solution Design Model has three phases:

1. Conceptual design

    This phase gives you an understanding of what the user really needs to do, and creates a clear set of objectives that capture this understanding.

2. Logical design

    In this phase, you lay out the structure of the solution, and provide a basis for physical design. As a developer, logical design is important for creating the appropriate solution in the physical design phase.

3. Physical design

    The physical design represents the solution from the developer's perspective. It defines the solutions' components, services, and technologies.

Sometimes developers participate only in the physical design of a solution. However, logical design should not be neglected; because it provides a basis for physical design, it plays an important role in software development. In logical design, you determine a logical organization for the solution. This provides a coherent view of the entire project. You start the logical design process by defining the major modules of the system. A module represents some collection of processes that work together to accomplish a task. You must specify each element, its responsibilities, and how it interacts with other elements.

Lesson 2: Designing a System Architecture

The system architecture is an important feature in application design since it defines how elements in the application interact and what functionality each element provides. The three types of system (or application) architecture are:

- Single-tier (or monolithic)
- Two-tier
- Multi-tier

In this course, you will focus on creating single-tier and two-tier applications. Multi-tier applications can be implemented using multiple computers across a network. This type of application is referred to as a distributed application, or *n-tier application*. An n-tier application represents a special instance of a three-tier application, in which one or more of the tiers are separated into additional tiers, providing better scalability. What you learn about three-tier application design and implementation can be extended to an n-tier design.

After this lesson you will be able to:

- Describe the three main types of system architecture.
- Explain the difference between single-tier, two-tier, and multi-tier applications.
- Describe the three conceptual service types in an application.

Estimated lesson time: 15 minutes

Understanding Application Structure

A typical application that interacts with a user, from spreadsheets on personal computers to accounts payable systems on mainframes, consists of three elements: presentation, application logic, and data services. Each of these elements (or services) has its own attributes, as the following table shows:

Service Type	Service Attribute
Presentation	Presentation of information and functionality, navigation, and protection of user interface consistency and integrity.
Application Logic	Shared business policies, generation of business information from data, and protection of business integrity.
Data Services	Definition of data, storage and retrieval of persistent data, and protection of data integrity.

Presentation, also known as the user interface (UI), focuses on interacting with the user. In Visual Basic, this would be the forms and controls that the user interacts with.

Application logic, or business rules, perform calculations and determine the flow of the application. Business rules encompass those practices and policies that define a corporation's behavior. Business rules are constraints, usually self-imposed, that companies use to help them operate in their particular business environment. Business rules often define a baseline for application requirements and provide guidance to the developer. In practical terms, these business rules are goals that developers strive to meet for their applications.

Data services manage information by storing data and providing data-related functionality. For example, a SQL Server running on a Windows NT Server computer would be a data service.

Single-tier Applications

In a single-tier application, only one layer supports the user interface, business rules, and data services. Only one application or application element processes all three of these services. The data itself can be physically stored in any location, such as on a server. However, the functionality for accessing the data is part of the application.

An example of a single-tier application is Microsoft Excel, where the user interface and business rules are combined in the application. The business rules include calculating totals, spell check, and other mathematical functions. In addition, the routines that access and save the Excel application files are part of the same application layer as the user interface and business rules. Traditional mainframe applications are also single-tier (monolithic) but are shared among multiple clients.

Two-tier Applications

Two-tier, or standard client/server applications, group presentation and application logic components on the client machine and access a shared data source using a network connection. In a two-tier application, the user interface and business rules are a single layer that runs on the client computer. Separate applications, such as SQL Server or Oracle database servers, provide the data services. This scenario is often used in client/server applications, such as in a Visual Basic application that calls a SQL Server stored procedure to provide data to the application. The Visual Basic application is one layer, and the SQL Server data services is another layer. The code for the user interface and business rules would not necessarily have to be within the same project; the Visual Basic application could call a dynamic-link library (DLL) that accesses data. In this scenario, the user interface and business rules are a single layer; however, the business rules are stored in the DLL This is the type of system architecture you will design in this course.

Two-tier applications work well in department-scale applications with modest numbers of users (under 100), a single database, and secure, fast networking. For example, a two-tier application would be a good solution for a workgroup whose function is to enter product orders. Another example is a design department that shares one set of designs within its group of engineers.

Multi-tier Applications

In multi-tier architectures, presentation, application logic, and data elements are conceptually separated. Presentation components manage user interaction and request application services by calling middle-tier components. Application components perform business logic and make requests to databases.

With multi-tier applications, the client only provides one layer: the user interface. The business rules are performed on a system in between the user interface and the data storage system. This allows the user interface, business rules, and database to reside separately, as illustrated in Figure 1.2.

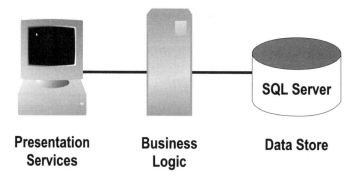

Presentation   Business   Data Store
Services   Logic

Figure 1.2 User interface, business rules, and database reside separately

The benefit of this model is that business rules are centralized and can be updated and maintained easily. The presentation layer does practically no work beyond interacting with the user. In a multi-tier application, the client does not directly access a data storage system. The separation of presentation, business rules, and data services allows you to modify any layer of the system without having to change the other two (or more) layers. This significantly reduces the need to maintain clients. In a small, 10-person system, this is not too much of a problem. But when the number of clients reaches hundreds or thousands, the cost of updating business rules and application logic can be significant. Another advantage to using a multi-tier model is that you improve code reusability. Code that you write for business logic in one application can be reused on other servers within different applications.

Developing a Multi-tier System

When developing a multi-tier system, you can build intelligent clients with business rules that have been compiled into stand-alone DLLs. These DLLs can be written in Visual Basic and reside on a server. The client, DLL, and database constitute a service in a multi-tier system. If you view applications as being separated into presentation, business rules, and data services, you can build each application as a set of features or services that are used to fill consumer requests. When you model an application as a collection of discrete services, its features and functionality can be packaged for reuse, shared among multiple applications, and distributed across network boundaries.

Lesson Summary

A typical application consists of three elements: presentation, application logic, and data. Presentation, also known as the user interface (UI), focuses on interacting with the user. Business rules, or application logic, perform calculations and determine the flow of the application. Data elements manage information by storing data and providing data-related services.

Applications can be single-tier, two-tier, or multi-tier:

- Single-tier (monolithic)

  In a single-tier application, only one application processes the presentation, application logic, and data service elements.

- Two-tier

  In a two-tier application, the user interface and business rules form a single layer that runs on the client computer. However, data services are performed by a separate application such as SQL Server or Oracle database servers. Two-tier applications work well in departmental-scale applications with modest numbers of users (under 100), a single database, and secure, fast networking.

- Multi-tier

  In multi-tier architectures, presentation, application logic, and data elements are conceptually separated. Presentation components manage user interaction and request application services by calling middle-tier components. Application components perform business logic and make requests to databases. In a multi-tier application, the client does not directly access a data storage system. The separation of presentation, business rules, and data services allows for any layer of the system to be modified without having to change the other layers; this significantly reduces the need to maintain clients. In Visual Basic, you can compile business rules into DLLs that reside on a server.

Lesson 3: Using Visual SourceSafe

Software development in a team environment introduces concerns such as tracking file usage and loss of critical information, such as code, documents, data, etc. These concerns can detract and delay the development process. Microsoft Visual Source Safe (VSS), which is a version control system for team development of software applications, is a viable solution that lets you effectively manage project files. Version control systems track and store changes to a file so that developers can review a file's history, return to earlier versions of a file, and develop programs concurrently.

Visual Basic provides complete integration with VSS. This integration is included with the Professional and Enterprise Editions of Visual Basic. Although you can use Visual SourceSafe to mange software projects, you can also use it as version control software for all types of files including Word documents, Excel spreadsheets, text, graphics, and binary files.

After this lesson you will be able to:

- State the advantages of using Visual SourceSafe.
- Explain the installation options of Visual SourceSafe's main components.
- Explain the use of commonly used commands.

Estimated lesson time: 15 minutes

Overview of Visual SourceSafe

With version control systems, you use a database to track, organize, and manage projects. These projects are a unit of organization, like a folder, and can contain various kinds of files, including code, graphics and documentation. You can create a VSS project to group together related files. For example, you can create a project in VSS to store a Visual Basic project file. All .frm, .vbp, .cls, .bas, and other files from your Visual Basic project can be included in the VSS project folder. VSS functions in a similar way as Windows Explorer in that project files can be organized into folders and subfolders. In addition, a single file can be shared among multiple projects within VSS.

Using VSS as your version control software offers several advantages:

- VSS maintains multiple versions of a file, including a record of the changes to the file from version to version. Using reverse delta technology, VSS has to store changes made to the file only when the file is checked in. (You check files out to work on them and then check the files back into VSS when you're not working on them.) This allows VSS to use disk space efficiently.

- Only one person at a time can modify a file. This prevents accidental replacement of another user's changes. (Your SourceSafe administrator can change this default to allow multiple, simultaneous file check-outs.)
- VSS can archive and track old versions of source code and other files. These files can be retrieved if necessary.
- You can see the history of a source control project through the History command in the development environment. This tells you when the latest changes were made, by whom the changes were made, and what happened to the item each time it was checked in, starting from the time the item was first created.

Practice: Adding Visual SourceSafe to Visual Basic

In this practice you will integrate Visual SourceSafe into a Visual Basic project.

➤ **To use Visual SourceSafe in Visual Basic**

1. Start Visual Basic.
2. On the **New Project** dialog box, click **Standard EXE,** then click **Open.**
3. On the **Add-ins** menu, click **Add-in Manager.**

   The **Add-in Manager** dialog box appears.
4. Click the **Source Code Control** add-in, then click the **Loaded/Unloaded** check box.

   The word **Loaded** appears to the right of the add-in.
5. Click **OK** to close the **Add In** Manager dialog box.

Visual SourceSafe Components

Visual SourceSafe consists of two components: the Visual SourceSafe Explorer (the user interface) and the Visual SourceSafe Database.

The Visual SourceSafe Explorer is the client component of VSS that is installed on each user's computer. It is the user's interface with the files stored in the Visual SourceSafe Database. It is similar to Windows Explorer in that its window is made up of two panes. The project's folder structure is on the left and the files listed in the selected folder on the right. The menu bar and toolbar allow the user to check files in and out of VSS easily.

The Visual SourceSafe Database is the central repository where master copies, history, project structures, and user information are stored. The Visual SourceSafe Database is installed on a server computer so that each client can access files stored in VSS. A project is always stored within one database. A database can house multiple projects, and multiple Visual SourceSafe databases can exist to store multiple projects.

Managing Files in VSS

Visual SourceSafe uses several commands to move files from the VSS database to the user's working directory. Common commands are Check Out, Check In, Undo Check Out, and Get Latest Version.

Check Out

The Check Out command copies one or more selected files from the current project in VSS into your current working directory so that you can modify them. You must have permission to use a file in VSS before you can check it out. The administrator sets file permissions in VSS. When you check out a file, a check mark appears to the left of the filename in the Visual Basic Project window, as shown in Figure 1.3.

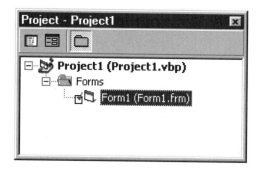

Figure 1.3 Files checked out in the Visual Basic Project Explorer

Check In

When you finish editing the file, check it in to Visual SourceSafe using the Check In command. Checking in the file copies the modified file from your folder into Visual SourceSafe's database, making your changes accessible to other users. However, Visual SourceSafe stores all the changes that have been made to the file—the most recent copy is always available, but previous versions can be retrieved as well. Visual SourceSafe's reverse delta technology ensures that all versions of a file are available while minimizing use of disk space.

Undo Check Out

The Undo Check Out command cancels a Check Out operation. Any changes you made are lost. You must have a file checked out to use this command.

Get Latest Version

When you want to view a file or project, but not modify it, use the Get Latest Version command. Get Latest Version copies the file or project from the current project into a local folder referred to as the working folder. The file placed in your working folder is read-only, and any modifications you make are not saved in the VSS project.

Reusing Visual SourceSafe Files

In Visual SourceSafe you can reuse files within the same project or with other projects. Some of the commands used to reuse these files are Share, Branch, and Merge.

To see a demonstration, run the Chap01.exe animation located in the Animations folder on the Supplemental Course Materials CD-ROM that accompanies this book.

Sharing

In VSS, one file can be shared among multiple projects. Changes to the file from one project are automatically seen by other projects sharing the file. To share a file, you create a share link between two projects. The file is then in two (or more) projects at the same time. When you check in the file to any one of the projects, your changes are automatically updated in all of the linked files.

➤ **To share a file between multiple projects**

1. In Visual SourceSafe, open the folder that will hold the shared file.

2. On the **SourceSafe** menu, click **Share...**

   The **Share With** dialog box appears.

3. Click the file that you wish to share, then click **Share**.

   The shared file is added to the open folder. The icon to the left of the filename indicates that it is a shared file.

4. Click **Close**.

➤ **To display a list of all projects that share a specific file**

1. In the VSS Explorer, click the filename.

2. On the **File** menu, click **Properties...**

   The **Properties** dialog box appears.

3. Click the **Links** tab to view the names of projects that share the file.

Branching

VSS allows you to share files between projects; normally when you do this, only one version of the file exists. However, you might want to create a copy of the file for a customized version of an application that you create. For example, if you develop software in which code for each customer is the same, but you need to create a custom version of the software for a particular customer, you can use the VSS branching feature. Branching duplicates files from one project and uses the duplicates to create a new version of the project. These duplicate files can be altered without affecting the original version of the files.

➤ **To branch a project file**

1. In Visual SourceSafe, click the shared file you want to branch.

2. On the **SourceSafe** menu, click **Branch...**

   The **Branch** dialog box appears.

3. Type in a comment, then click **OK**.

   The icon to the left of the filename changed to a normal icon.

Merging

Merging is the process of combining differences in two or more changed copies of a file into a single, new version of the file. In VSS, a merge can occur in three different circumstances:

1. Using multiple checkouts

   If multiple users have checked out a file, the first user simply checks in the file. Subsequent users also check in the file, but their changes are merged with all other users' changes, and VSS retains all the modifications.

2. Explicitly merging previously branched files

   When file branches are merged back into one of the branched projects, VSS takes the changes made along one line of the project and merges the changes with the other line.

3. Using Get Latest Version

   VSS will allow you to merge the differences between an existing local copy of a file and the most up-to-date version of the file saved in the VSS database by using the Get Lastest Version command.

When a merge occurs, VSS takes the file(s) with differences, compares the differences to the original file, and then creates a resulting file containing all the changes. For example, if you check in a file that causes a merge, the file on your hard disk and the file in the project are combined into a resultant file containing both sets of changes.

➤ **To merge branched files**

1. In VSS Explorer, click the shared file you want to branch.

2. On the **SourceSafe** menu click **Merge Branches...**

   The **Merge To** dialog box appears.

3. Click the project into which you want to merge your file.

   The **Versions** column shows the version numbers you will be merging.

4. Click **Merge**.

Using Administration Tools

The Visual SourceSafe Administrator is an easy way to preserve project data. Backing up project files takes only moments, but provides many benefits to both the server and the Visual SourceSafe application. For example, if your original files are damaged or lost, you can restore them from these archived files.

New to Visual SourceSafe 6.0 is the ability to archive and restore databases from the VSS Administrator wizard. In previous versions, all archiving and restoring was done from the command line. The VSS Administrator can open databases, archive information, and restore data from archived files.

Opening SourceSafe Databases

The VSS Administrator can manage multiple databases. Before you can archive or restore a database, it must be open in the VSS Administrator.

➤ **To open a database**

1. Open the **VSS Administrator**.

2. On the **Users** menu, click **Open SourceSafe Database...**

   The **Open SourceSafe Database** dialog box appears.

3. Click the name of the database to open in the list.

4. Click **Open** on the **Open SourceSafe Database** dialog box.

Note If the database is not in the list, click the **Browse** button. Navigate to the srcsafe.ini file for an existing VSS database, then click the srcsafe.ini file. Click **Open** to add the database to the list.

Archiving Projects

Archiving databases lets you:

- Save disk space on the VSS database server.
- Transport files and projects between VSS databases, keeping the history information intact.
- Back up all or part of the VSS database to a compressed file.

➤ **To archive a database**

1. Open **VSS Administrator**.
2. Open the database containing the information to be archived.
3. On the **Archive** menu, click **Archive Projects...**

    The **Archive Wizard** appears.
4. Click the names of the project(s) you want to archive.
5. Click **OK**, and then click **Next**.

    Step 2 appears.
6. Specify how you want the project to be archived:

    - **Save data to file**—this overwrites existing files.
    - **Save data to file, then delete the data from the database to save space**—this overwrites existing files.
    - **Delete data permanently**—the **Archive** check box is disabled.
7. Click **Next**.

    Step 3 appears.
8. Specify the version of the data you'd like archived.

    - To archive by version number, type the number in the **Version** box.
    - To archive by label, type **L** followed by the label string.
    - To archive by date, type **D** followed by a date string--for example, D11/26/98.
9. Click **Finish**.

Lesson Summary

Microsoft Visual Source Safe (VSS) is a version control system for team development of software applications that provides the following advantages:

- VSS can maintain multiple versions of a file, including a record of changes.
- VSS can archive and track old versions of files.
- Only one person at a time can modify a file. This prevents accidental changes and deletions.
- Projects with multiple development platforms can have one code base.
- Code modules can be reused.

VSS has two components:

- VSS Explorer is the client application used to access VSS files; it is similar to Windows Explorer.
- VSS Database is the central repository of master copies, history, project structure, and user information. All files related to one project are always contained within a single database. The VSS Database is stored on a server computer to allow clients to access the files stored in VSS.

Use VSS commands to access and manage project files:

- Check Out lets you work offline on the master file. Other users cannot change the master file when it is checked out.
- Check In returns a file to the database when it has been edited under the Check Out command. Your changes will appear in the master file.
- Undo Check Out cancels a Check Out command without any changes.
- Get Latest Version lets you work offline on a file, but you cannot save changes to the master file in the database.
- Other VSS features include the capability to share a file between projects, archive files, and restore files.

Summary

Using the Microsoft Solutions Framework

The Microsoft Solutions Framework (MSF) is a suite of models, principles, guides and best practices for building and deploying software. It implements several models that contribute to the software development cycle.

The Solutions Design Model, emphasized in this course, has three phases:

- Conceptual design includes the users' requirements as stated in objectives. A developer typically has little input in this phase.

- Logical design includes a structure layout for the solution and is the basis for the next phase. A developer's role is important in this phase.

- Physical design includes the solution in terms of the components, services and technologies. This requires a low-level design by the developer.

Logical design begins with defining the major modules of the system. Each module is a collection of processes that work together to accomplish a task. Logical design specifies the individual elements, their functions, and their interaction with other elements.

Designing a System Architecture

A typical application consists of three services:

- Presentation interface supports the user's interaction with the application.

- Business rules, also called application logic, performs calculations and determines the flow of the application.

- Data services manage data storage and related services.

Applications are grouped by tier or level:

- A single-tier application such as Microsoft Excel has only one layer to process all three of the above services.

- A two-tier application runs the user interface and business rules on the client, and the data services on a separate server.

- A multi-tier application runs each service on a separate system. The user interface is the only service run on the client. This simplifies application update and maintenance.

Using Visual SourceSafe

Microsoft Visual SourceSafe (VSS) is a version control system for team development of software applications. It supports maintenance of multiple versions, a record of changes, and sharing and reuse of code modules. It also prevents accidental overwriting of changes.

The VSS components are VSS Explorer, a user interface similar to Windows Explorer, and VSS Database, the central repository of projects and files.

Several VSS commands control access and manage files. The most common commands are Check Out, Check In, and Get Latest Version.

Lab: Using the Microsoft Solutions Framework

This lab reiterates the role of the Microsoft Solutions Framework (MSF) in planning your Visual Basic application. It also includes a brief overview of the application you will develop throughout the labs in this course.

Estimated lesson time: 10 minutes

Microsoft Solutions Framework

The Microsoft Solutions Framework is a development framework produced by Microsoft Consulting Services (MCS). It is based on Microsoft's internal development methodology, and is a collection of best practices used by the Microsoft product groups and Microsoft Consulting Services. You can use MSF concepts as you plan a multi-developer project.

1. What are the benefits of implementing MSF?

2. What are the models implemented in MSF? What are their purposes?

3. What are the three design phases of the solution design model? What tasks are accomplished in these phases?

The Chateau St. Mark Hotel Reservation System

Throughout this course, you will create a cumulative lab based on a fictitious hotel reservation system. By the end of all the labs, you will have created:

- A complete user interface for the hotel reservation system.
- Validation functions and subroutines to ensure accurate data.
- Class modules from which objects can be created based on guests and reservations.

You will also have performed these functions in creating this application:

- Store and retrieve data for the reservation system from a database used ADO technology.
- Implement ActiveX components to construct a sound solution.
- Provide help to users of the hotel reservation system.
- Compile and deploy your solution using Visual Basic tools.

Using the Supplemental Course Material Lab Files

The CD-ROM that accompanies this course has several files for your use. By default, these files are copied to your local hard drive in the \Labs folder. Each lab is in a separate subfolder, for example Lab 1 is in \Labs\Lab01. In each of these folders are two additional subfolders, \Partial and \Solution.

The Partial folder contains the applications as it looks at the beginning of the lab.

The Solution folder contains a completed version of the lab solution. This project has had each step applied and can be used to review the completed lab.

- The recommended procedure is to build the hotel reservation in the order presented by each lab. Follow the labs in numerical order. Save your work and use it in the next lab to continue building the reservation system.
- If you do not create the reservation application, you can start with the project in the \Labs\Lab*n*\Partial folder. It lets you begin each lab from the appropriate starting point.
- You should check your work against the \Labs\Lab*n*\Solution project after you complete each lab.

Viewing the Chateau St. Mark Hotel Solution

If you would like a preview of the overall lab solution that you will create, open the Visual Basic project file (.vbp) located in the \Labs\Lab01\Solution directory.

➤ **To view lab solution code**

1. Open the Hotelres.vbp file located in the \Labs\Lab01\Solution directory.

   In this lab, there are no coding steps to follow. So, you will use the project in the Solution folder for review.

2. Double-click the **frmReservations** form object in the **Project Explorer**.

   This opens the form designer for the main user interface of the Chateau St. Mark hotel lab solution.

3. Double-click the form to open the Visual Basic code window.

   In the Visual Basic code window, you can view the various event procedures that perform tasks in the user interface. You can view code for any other object in the Project Explorer by double-clicking it and opening the Visual Basic code Window.

4. Double-click the class modules in the Visual Basic Project Explorer to view the code that performs check-in, check-out, and cancellation services for guests of the hotel.

Review

The following questions are intended to reinforce key information presented in this chapter. If you are unable to answer a question, review the appropriate lesson and then try the question again. Answers to the questions can be found in the Appendix, "Questions and Answers," located at the back of this book.

1. What is the Microsoft Solutions Framework?

2. Which MSF Model directly focuses on software development?

3. What is an example of a single-tier application?

4. When is a two-tier application most effective?

5. What are three ways to install Visual SourceSafe?

6. What are some of the commands used in Visual SourceSafe to reuse files and how are they used?

C H A P T E R   2

Creating the User Interface

About This Chapter

This chapter provides information on design and usability principles you should consider when planning a user interface. It discusses the actual development of the interface, including forms and controls and the role of menus.

Before You Begin

To complete the lessons in this chapter, there are no prerequisites.

Lesson 1: User Interface Design Principles

The user interface is the link between your audience and the capabilities of your application. This lesson presents guidelines for developing user-friendly, productive, and manageable user interfaces.

The primary users of an application are called the *target audience*. With a working knowledge of these users, designing the user interface will be simple. A well-designed user interface makes it easy for your audience to learn and to use your application. A poorly designed interface, on the other hand, can result in confusion, frustration, and even lack of use as well as increased training time and costs.

Basic design principles such as composition and color apply to a computer screen just as they do to a sheet of paper or a canvas. You don't need to be an artist to create an effective user interface, but if you apply basic principles, your interface will be easy to use, and the code behind the interface will be more efficient. The way you initially design the interface has a direct impact on the way you create the underlying code.

When creating a Visual Basic application, the form is the basic element of the user interface. Controls and menus are then added to the form to provide specific functionality. Although Visual Basic allows you to quickly develop an interface, a little planning can make a big difference. Consider drafting your forms on paper first, determining which controls and menus are needed, the relative importance of the different elements, and the relationships between them.

After this lesson you will be able to:

- Describe the importance of the user interface.

- Explain the roles of forms, controls, and menus in the user interface.

- Explain the significance of the basic design principles of composition and color.

- Explain the use of images, icons, and fonts in interface design.

Estimated lesson time: 30 minutes

Composition

Composition is the layout, or look and feel, of an application. It not only influences aesthetic appeal; it also has a tremendous impact on the usability of your application. Composition includes such factors as:

- Simplicity
- Positioning of controls
- Consistency
- Affordances
- White space

Simplicity

Perhaps the most important principle of composition is simplicity. When it comes to application design, if the interface looks difficult, it probably is. A little forethought can help create an interface that looks, and is, simple to use. Also, from an aesthetic standpoint, a clean, simple design is always preferable.

A common pitfall in interface design is to try to model your interface after real-world objects. Imagine, for instance, that you were asked to create an application for completing insurance forms. A natural reaction would be to design an interface that exactly duplicates the paper form on screen. This creates several problems: the shape and dimensions of a paper form are different than those of the screen; duplicating a form limits you to text boxes and check boxes, which offers no real benefit to the user.

You are better off designing your own interface. By creating groupings of fields and using a tabbed interface, or several linked forms, you can logically present the information. You can also use additional controls, such as a list box preloaded with choices, to reduce the amount of typing required of the user. This reduces the chance of data entry errors made by users.

Providing defaults can sometimes simplify an application. If nine out of ten users select USA as their country, make the country USA the default rather than forcing the user to make a choice each time. Be sure to provide an option to override the default. Implementing wizards can also help to simplify complex or infrequent tasks.

The best test of simplicity is to observe your application in use. If a typical user can't accomplish a desired task without assistance, a redesign may be in order.

Positioning of Controls

In most interface designs, not all controls are of equal importance. Careful design can ensure that the essential controls are readily apparent to the user. Important or frequently accessed controls should be given a position of prominence; less important controls should be relegated to less prominent locations.

In most languages, the user reads from left to right and from the top to the bottom of a page. The same holds true for a computer screen. Most users' eyes will be drawn to the upper left portion of the screen first, so the most important control should go there. For example, if the information on a form is related to a customer, the name field should appear where it will be seen first—in the upper left corner. Buttons, such as OK or Next, should generally be placed in the lower right portion of the screen because users normally won't access these items until they have finished working with the form.

Another design consideration is to group information logically according to function or relationship. Buttons for navigating a database, for example, should be grouped together because their functions are related. Fields for name and address are generally grouped together, as they are closely related. In many cases, you can use the Frame control to help reinforce the relationships between controls. Figure 2.1 illustrates the grouping of controls that interact with a database.

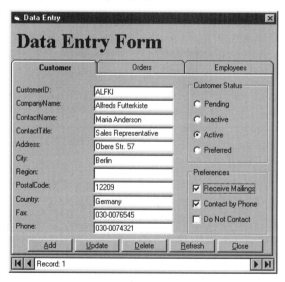

Figure 2.1 A logical grouping of controls on a form

Consistency

Consistency, or sameness, is a key consideration in user interface design. Keeping a similar design or "look" throughout your application enhances usability. A lack of consistency in the user interface can be confusing and make an application seem chaotic and disorganized, possibly even causing the user to doubt the reliability of it. Consistency across applications is also advisable; conforming to the look and feel of existing client applications, such as Microsoft Word, helps to reduce training costs for the organization.

For visual consistency, establish the design strategy and style conventions before you begin development. Design elements such as the types of controls, standards for size and grouping of controls, and font choices should be established in advance. You can create prototypes of possible designs to help you make design decisions.

The wide variety of controls available in Visual Basic makes it tempting to use them all. Avoid this temptation; choose a subset of controls that best fit your particular application. Whereas list box, combo box, grid, and tree controls can all be used to present lists of information, it's best to be consistent and choose a single style when possible.

Also, try to use controls appropriately. While a text box control can be used to display a title or a caption, a Label control is usually more appropriate for this purpose. Be consistent in setting the properties for your controls. For example, if you use a white background color for editable text in one place, don't use gray in another place unless there's a good reason.

Consistency between different forms in your application is important for usability. If you use a gray background and three-dimensional effects on one form and a white background on another, the forms will appear to be unrelated. Choose a style and remain consistent throughout your application, even if it means redesigning some features.

Affordances

Affordances are visual clues to the function of a user interface. Although the term may be unfamiliar, examples of affordances are all around you. A handgrip on a bicycle has depressions where you place your fingers. This affordance makes the use obvious. Push buttons, knobs, and light switches are all affordances—just by looking at them you can understand their purpose.

A user interface also makes use of affordances. For instance, the three-dimensional effects used on command buttons make them inviting to click. If you designed a command button with a flat border, the user might not understand that the button is a command button. Flat buttons might be appropriate in some cases, such as in games or in multimedia applications.

Text boxes provide a sort of affordance. For example, users expect that a box with a border and a white background will contain editable text. While you can display a text box with no border (BorderStyle = 0), doing so will make the box look like a label, and it won't necessarily be obvious to the user that the control is editable.

White Space

Including white space in your user interface can help to emphasize elements and improve usability. White space doesn't necessarily have to be white; it refers to the use of blank space between and around controls on a form. Too many controls on a form can lead to a cluttered interface, making it difficult to find an individual field or control. You need to incorporate white space in your design to emphasize particular elements.

Consistent spacing between controls and alignment of vertical and horizontal elements can make your design more usable as well. Just as text in a magazine is arranged in orderly columns with even spacing between lines, an orderly interface makes your interface easy to read. Visual Basic provides several tools that make it easy to adjust the spacing, alignment, and size of controls: Align, Make Same Size, Horizontal Spacing, Vertical Spacing, and Center in Form commands can all be found under the Format menu.

Color

The use of color in your interface can add visual appeal, but color can be easily overused. Color, like the other design principles, can be a problem if not carefully considered in your initial design.

Preference for colors varies widely; the user's taste may not be the same as your own. Color can also evoke strong emotions. If you're designing for international audiences, certain colors may have cultural significance.

Small amounts of contrasting color can be used effectively to emphasize or draw attention to an important area. You should try to limit the number of colors in an application and maintain a consistent color scheme.

Another consideration is color blindness. Many people, for example, are unable to tell the difference between different combinations of primary colors such as red and green. To someone with this condition, red text on a green background would be invisible. For the same reason, you should not use color to indicate the relative importance of elements in your application.

Images and Icons

The use of pictures and icons add visual interest to your application—but, as with all interface elements, careful design is essential. Images can convey information efficiently without the need for text, but images are often perceived differently by different people. So consider the cultural significance of images. Many programs use a picture of a rural-style mailbox with a flag to represent mail functions. This is primarily an American icon; users in other countries or cultures may not recognize it as a mailbox.

Icons that appear on a toolbar can represent various functions within the application. In designing toolbar icons, look at other applications to see what standards have already been established. For example, many applications use a sheet of paper with a folded corner to represent the New File command, a black X to represent delete, a picture of a printer to print, and the picture of a floppy disk for the save command (see Figure 2.2). There may be other metaphors for these functions, but representing them differently could confuse the user.

Figure 2.2 Example of icons on a toolbar

In designing your own icons and images, try to keep them simple. Complex pictures with a lot of colors don't degrade well when displayed as a 16-by-16 pixel toolbar icon, or when displayed at high screen resolutions.

Fonts

Fonts are also an important part of your user interface. They often communicate important information to the user. Certain fonts can be easily read at different resolutions and on different types of monitors. Choose one or two simple fonts such as Arial or Times New Roman. Script and other decorative fonts often look better in print than on the screen; they can also be difficult to read at smaller point sizes.

Menus

Menus and toolbars provide a structured and accessible organization for the commands and tools contained in your applications. Proper planning and design of menus and toolbars ensures that users will understand the purpose and features of your application. Users often browse menus before looking elsewhere for information about your application. If your menus are well designed, users can organize their understanding of the application by developing a mental model based on the menu organization and content alone. The Visual Basic Menu Editor lets you create menus that enhance the quality of your applications.

Each part of a Visual Basic application can have its own menu system or set of menus. Consistency across applications holds true for menus. Keep the same look and feel of existing client application menus (such as MS Word) and control the menu structure as users navigate through the application. Dynamically enabling, checking, or adding menus facilitates movement throughout the application without a loss of control. How to create a menu system is discussed in Lesson 4.

Lesson Summary

Interface design is important for two reasons:

- Users can quickly understand and learn applications that have a well-designed interface, thus saving training time and costs as well as encouraging use of the application.
- Programming is easier with a properly designed interface.

A good application begins with a carefully planned design and attention to the following principles:

- Simplicity:
  - Be original.
  - Don't just copy paper forms.
  - Make the most common choices defaults.
- Positioning of controls:
  - Importance of each control,
  - Relationship between controls
  - Order of use of controls
- Consistency: fewer, carefully chosen controls; standardized color, font, size; and similarity of groupings.
- Affordances: choose what the average user would expect for buttons, toolbar icons, etc.
- Color and images: keep the user in mind, especially cultural issues.
- Images and icons: consider the user's expectations.
- Choosing fonts: simplicity and consistency.
- Menus: well-planned commands and tools.

Lesson 2: Managing Forms

Forms are the basic element of the user interface in a Visual Basic application. They provide a framework you can use throughout your application to give a consistent look and feel. Differences in user interface design and behavior from one application to another, or within one application, can result in increased training and support costs. In a corporate environment, enforcing a consistent user interface across all of your applications can help reduce those costs.

As your application becomes more complex, you will need to add additional forms to the project. Understanding the capabilities of forms can also aid in the development process of your program.

After this lesson you will be able to:

- State the role of forms in an application.
- Explain how to add forms to a project and set up the startup form.
- Explain the purpose of form events.
- Explain the differences between the four form methods.
- Explain the attributes of a forms collection.

Estimated lesson time: 45 minutes

Adding a Form to a Project

Forms serve as a window that you customize to design the interface of your application. When you create a new Standard EXE project, Visual Basic provides one default form. As your application becomes more complex, you will need to add additional forms. You can then add controls, graphics, and pictures to the form to create the look you want. Each form in your application has its own form designer window.

➤ **To add a new form to the project**

1. On the Project menu, click Add Form.

   The **Add Form** dialog box appears.

2. Click **Form**, and then click **Open**.

   A new form is added to the project and appears in the Visual Basic environment.

Setting the Startup Form

Visual Basic uses the first form in a project as the default startup form. However, as you add new forms to a project, you may need to change this default. Visual Basic's Project Properties allow you to specify the startup form. The form name selected in Startup Object will be the form which first appears when the application is run.

➤ **To change the startup form**

1. On the **Project** menu, click *ProjectName* Properties.

    The **Project Properties** dialog box appears.

2. In the **Startup Object** drop-down list box, click the name of the form you want to set as the default startup form and click **OK**.

Note The Startup Object list may contain other options depending on the project type.

Using Form Events

After adding the necessary forms to your project and setting the startup form, you must determine which events to use. Forms are code modules that contain procedures called *events*. Events respond to system or user input by running whatever code you have placed in the particular event. One example is the Click event, which runs whenever the mouse is clicked on the form. When an event is called to execute its code, the request is often referred to as *firing* or *triggering* the event.

In some cases, Windows passes parameters to an event. For example, the MouseUp event receives four parameters from Windows, as in the following example:

```
Private Sub Form_MouseUp(Button As Integer, _
    Shift As Integer, X As Single, Y As Single)

End Sub
```

Note Sometimes you may want to call an event procedures from the application code itself. However, this is possible only if no parameters have to be passed.

You can use many types of form events. Depending on how you use a form, some of these events may not fire, while others will always fire. Form events are generally triggered in this order:

- Initialize
- Load
- Activate
- Deactivate
- QueryUnload
- Unload
- Terminate

Initialize

The Initialize event is typically used to prepare an application for use. Variables are assigned to initial values, and controls may be moved or resized to accommodate initialization data.

The Initialize event occurs when an application creates an instance of a form, but before the form is loaded or displayed. However, the Initialize event will fire only once during the life of the application. In order to have the Initialize event fire again, you must exit and restart the application. Therefore, if you have code that needs to run more than once, you will want to use a different event. The following examples fire the Initialize event:

```
frmMyForm.show
```

or

```
Load frmMyForm
```

The Initialize event also occurs when you set or return a property or apply a method that is defined in a form module. For example, suppose you've defined a general procedure named ListNames within the frmCustomer form. To run this procedure from another module, you must qualify it with the name of the form module. Qualifying the procedure with the name of the form creates an instance of the form, and the Initialize event occurs. The following example shows how to qualify a procedure with the name of the form in which it resides:

```
FrmCustomer.ListNames
```

Form-level variables are variables that are recognized by all procedures within that form's module. Once these variables are initialized, they are maintained while the application is running, even if the form is unloaded. If the form is redisplayed, the Initialize event will not trigger again.

Load

The Load event is used to perform actions that need to occur prior to the form being displayed. It is also used to assign default values to the form and its controls.

The Load event occurs each time that a form is loaded into memory. The first time that a form is loaded, the Load event is fired after the Initialize event. A form's Load event can run multiple times during an application's life. Load fires when a form starts as the result of the Load statement, Show statement, or when a reference is made to an unloaded form's properties, methods, or controls. This example shows how to fill a ComboBox's default values during the Load event:

```
Private Sub Form_Load ()
    'Add items to list
    Combo1.AddItem "Mozart"
    Combo1.AddItem "Beethoven"
    Combo1.AddItem "Rock 'n Roll"
    Combo1.AddItem "Reggae"
    'Set default selection
    Combo1.ListIndex = 2
End Sub
```

Activate/Deactivate

When the user moves between two or more forms, you can use the Activate and Deactivate events to define the forms' behavior.

The Activate event fires when the form receives focus from another form within the same project. This event fires only when the form is visible. For example, a form loaded using the Load statement isn't visible unless you use the Show method, or set the form's Visible property to True. The Activate event fires before the GotFocus event.

Deactivate fires when the form loses focus to another form. This event fires after the LostFocus event.

Both the Activate and Deactivate events fire only when focus is changing within the same application. If you click a different application and then return to the Visual Basic program, neither event fires.

QueryUnload

The QueryUnload event is useful when you need to know how the user is closing the form.

The QueryUnload event occurs before the form's Unload event. QueryUnload has an additional feature compared to the Unload event. The UnloadMode argument tells you how the form was closed and allows the cancellation of the event. Some things that may cause the QueryUnload event are:

- The user chooses the Close command from the Control menu on the form.
- The Unload statement is invoked from code.
- The current Microsoft Windows operating environment session is ending.
- The Microsoft Windows Task Manager is closing the application.
- An MDI child form is closing because the MDI form is closing.

To stop the form from unloading, set the Cancel argument to True. For example:

```
Private Sub Form_QueryUnload(Cancel As Integer, _
    UnloadMode As Integer)
    'How was the form closed
    If UnloadMode <> vbFormCode Then
        MsgBox "Use the Exit button to close the form"
        Cancel = True    'The form remains open
    End If
End Sub
```

Unload

The Unload event occurs before the Terminate event. Use the Unload event procedure to verify that the form should be unloaded or to specify actions that take place when unloading the form. You can also include form-level validation code needed for closing the form or saving data to a file. You can add the End statement to this event to verify that all forms have been unloaded before ending the application.

Setting Cancel to any nonzero value prevents the form from being removed, but doesn't stop other events, such as exiting from the Microsoft Windows operating environment. Use the QueryUnload event to stop Windows from shutting down.

Terminate

The Terminate fires when all references to an instance of a Form are removed from memory. To remove the form's variables from memory and free the form's system resources, set the form equal to Nothing. For example:

```
Set frmMyForm = Nothing
```

For all objects except classes, the Terminate event occurs after the Unload event. The Terminate event will not fire if the instance of the form or class is removed from memory because the application terminated abnormally. For example, if your system crashes before removing all existing instances of the class or form from memory, the Terminate event will not fire for that class or form.

Using Form Methods

A *method* performs an action on an object. Understanding the form methods that Visual Basic provides enables you to develop an application that efficiently utilizes computer resources, such as memory and processing speed. These are the methods that you can use to manage forms in Visual Basic:

- Load
- Unload
- Hide
- Show

It is essential that you take into account the systems on which your application will be running in the early stages of the design process. Computer limitations may effect the way in which forms are handled. For example, for slower computers, you might choose to load some of the forms during the start of your application. Once they are loaded into memory, you can use the Show and Hide methods to display the forms as needed.

Load

The Load statement initializes and loads the form into memory without displaying the form on the user's screen. Any reference to a form automatically loads the form's resources, if they are not already loaded. The following example loads the form MyForm into memory but does not display it:

```
Load frmMyForm
```

Unload

Unload removes a form from memory. Unloading a form may be necessary to free system resources, or to reset form properties to their original values. The Me statement can be used to refer to the current form in code. The following examples show two ways to unload the form MyForm from memory:

```
Unload frmMyForm
```

or

```
Unload Me
```

Hide

Hide removes a form from the screen without removing it from memory. A hidden form's controls are not accessible to the user, but they are available to the running Visual Basic application. When a form is hidden, the user cannot interact with the application until all code in the event procedure that caused the form to be hidden has finished executing.

If the form is not already loaded into memory when the Hide method is called, the Hide method loads the form but doesn't display it. The following examples show two ways to hide the form MyForm from the users without losing the form values:

```
frmMyForm.Hide
```

or

```
Me.Hide
```

Show

The Show method includes an implied Load; this means that if the specified form is not already loaded when the Show method is called, Visual Basic automatically loads the form into memory and then displays it to the user. The Show method displays forms either modally or modelessly. A modal window or dialog box requires the user to take some action before the focus can change to another form. A modeless window or dialog box does not require user action before the focus can change to another form. The default argument for the Show method is modeless.

When Show displays a modeless form, subsequent code is executed as it is encountered. When Show displays a modal form, no subsequent code is executed until the form is hidden or unloaded. When Show displays a modal form, no input, such as a keyboard or a mouse click, can occur except to controls on the modal form; the program must hide or unload the modal form, usually in response to some user action, before input to another form can occur. Although other forms in your application are disabled when a modal form is displayed, other applications are not. Here is an example of how the Show method is used:

```
frmResults.Show vbModal
```

Figure 2.3 illustrates the actions of the four form events:

- The Show method loads the form and then displays it to the screen.
- The Hide method removes the form from the screen and retains its values in memory.
- The Load method initializes and loads the form into memory without displaying it.
- The Unload method removes the form from the screen and from memory.

Method	Hard Drive	Memory	Screen	Sample Code
Show				Me.Show vbModal frmMyForm.Show
Hide				Me.Hide frmMyForm.Hide
Load				Load frmMyForm
UnLoad				Unload Me Unload frmMyForm

Figure 2.3 Using methods to manage forms

Using the Forms Collection

In Visual Basic, a collection is a grouping of related objects. There are many types of collections in Visual Basic. A project can have a collection of forms and a form can have a collection of controls. Some collections are created automatically by Visual Basic, such as when you load forms or controls into your application. You can also create collections of your own using the Collection object.

Collections have an object called an enumerator that you can use to keep track of the items in a collection. Enumeration is the process of navigating through a collection. For example, you can enumerate the Forms collection to set or return the values of properties of individual forms in the collection.

The Forms collection has a single property: Count. The Forms collection is indexed beginning with zero. If you refer to a form by its index, the first form is Forms(0), the second form is Forms(1), and so on. You can refer to an individual Form object in the Forms collection either by referring to the form by name, or by referring to its index within the collection. You can then use the Name property of each individual form variable object to return the name of a form. You can also enumerate the Forms collection to set or return the values of properties of individual forms in the collection.

Sometimes you may need to loop through, sometimes called *enumerate*, all of the forms in your application. You can use the For...Next and the For Each...Next statements to enumerate the items in a collection. You do not need to know the number of items in the collection to use these statements. The following example loops through the Forms collection using a For...Next statement:

```
Dim i As Integer
For i = 0 To Forms.Count - 1
    MsgBox "Form '" & Forms(i).Name & "' is open."
Next i
```

The following is the syntax used for the For Each...Next statement:

```
For Each element In group
    element.property = expression
    '[statements]
Next element
```

The following example shows enumerating the Forms collection using a For Each...Next statement:

```
Dim frm As Form
'Loop through Forms collection.
For Each frm In Forms
    'Enumerate Controls collection of each form.
    MsgBox "Form '" & Frm.Name & "' is open."
Next frm
```

Lesson Summary

Forms are the basic element of the user interface in Visual Basic. It is important to manage an application's forms carefully to enhance usability and also to facilitate development of the application. By default, Visual Basic uses the first form as the project's startup form. However, you can specify any form in the project as the startup form.

Form events are private procedures; they are fired in response to user actions such as clicking the mouse or pressing a key on the keyboard. Some common form events are:

- Initialize
- Load
- Activate
- Deactivate
- QueryUnload
- Unload
- Terminate

Depending on how you want to display or hide a form, you will need to use the following methods:

- Load
- Unload
- Hide
- Show

The forms collection is a grouping of loaded forms. You can refer to the individual forms in a collection by their names or by their index within the collection. If you do not know which form to access, or need to step through all the forms, you can loop through the collection. This process is called enumeration.

Lesson 3: Using Controls

Controls (also referred to as ActiveX controls) are the second element of the user interface. They are graphical tools used to create and/or enhance the functionality of an application. The Visual Basic toolbox includes several controls. Some controls are useful for working with large amounts of data contained in an external database. Other controls can be used to access the Windows file system. Like forms, each control has properties, methods and events that you can use for a specific purpose in the user interface.

This lesson provides information on using controls when building a user interface.

After this lesson you will be able to:

- Define the role of controls in Visual Basic.
- Explain the difference between standard controls, custom controls, and inherent objects.
- Describe the process for adding controls to the Visual Basic toolbox, including the role of the Components dialog box.
- State the advantages of control arrays.
- Explain three ways to create control arrays.
- Describe the purpose and procedure for creating controls dynamically.
- Explain the value of four particularly useful custom controls.

Estimated lesson time: 45 minutes

Working with Controls

There are two categories of ActiveX controls, inherent and custom. The Visual Basic toolbox includes inherent controls, sometimes called standard controls, by default. This includes controls such as the command button and text box. Custom controls are optional. You must add them to the toolbox before you can use them in a project.

ActiveX controls are available for almost any function imaginable. These controls are contained in files that have an .ocx extension. ActiveX controls, like forms, contain properties, methods, and events. The Professional and Enterprise editions of Visual Basic let you build your own custom controls.

Note Controls with the .vbx filename extension use older technology and are found in applications written in earlier versions of Visual Basic. When Visual Basic opens a project containing a .vbx control, it replaces the .vbx control with an .ocx control, but only if an .ocx version of the control is available.

Adding Custom Controls

Some custom controls are included with Visual Basic and others are available from third-party vendors. To use these controls in a project, select them in the Components dialog box (see Figure 2.4) and add them to the Visual Basic toolbox.

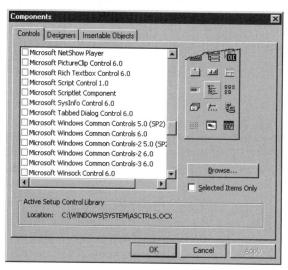

Figure 2.4 The Components dialog box

If the control you want is not listed in the Components dialog box, it means that the control is not registered on your computer. You must first install it using the vendor's installation program. It will then appear in the Components dialog box and you can add it to a project. After you add a control to a project, or instantiate it, the control remains a part of the project's workspace. The control cannot be removed from the toolbox until it is removed from the application. When you open a different project, the toolbox appears as it was prior to adding the ActiveX control.

➤ **To add an ActiveX control to a project's toolbox**

1. On the **Project** menu, click **Components**.

   You can also right-click on the toolbox and click **Components**.

   The **Components** dialog box appears; the **Controls** tab is the default.

2. Click the check box to the left of the name of the appropriate control.

3. Click **OK** to close the **Components** dialog box.

   The new control appears in the toolbox.

➤ **To add an ActiveX control to the Components dialog box**

1. In the **Components** dialog box, click the **Browse** button.

   The **Add ActiveX Control** dialog box appears.

2. Locate and open the control you want by searching directories for files with an .ocx filename extension.

3. Add an ActiveX control to the list of available controls.

   The new control appears in the **Components** dialog box.

After you add the control to the toolbox, you can add it to your form. You can then set properties for the control. Setting the Name property of a control is important because it determines how you refer to the control in code. You should follow standard naming conventions when naming a control. For more information on this topic, search for "Visual Basic Coding Conventions" in the MSDN Online Help.

Removing Controls

Be sure to remove any unused controls in a project. When you package your application for distribution, Visual Basic will not verify that all controls listed in the Components dialog box are required by the application. If you fail to remove unused controls, they will be included in the setup files. This makes the distribution size larger and adds unnecessary overhead to the application. You cannot remove a control from the toolbox if an instance of that control is used on any form in the project.

➤ **To remove a control from a project**

1. On the **Project** menu, click **Components**.

   You can also right-click on the toolbox and click **Components**.

   The **Components** dialog box appears.

2. Clear the check box next to each control you want to remove.

3. Click **OK** to close the **Components** dialog box.

   The control icons are removed from the toolbox.

Setting Control Properties

You can set Control properties at design time or at run time. Properties set at design time allow the developer to set default values used in the application. To set these properties, you can use the Properties window, which is illustrated in Figure 2.5. You can set properties for a single control or for multiple controls.

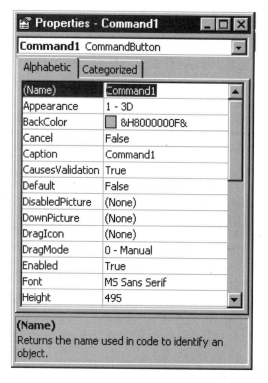

Figure 2.5 The Properties window

▶ **To set control properties at design time**

1. Right-click a control and click Properties, or left-click the control and click F4.

2. Type the value in the appropriate property box.

▶ **To set properties for multiple controls at design time**

1. Click and drag the mouse over the controls you want to select, or click **CTRL+SHIFT** and click the controls.

   The **Properties** window displays those properties that are common to the selected controls.

2. Type the value in the appropriate property's box.

Note When you work with properties for multiple controls, any change you make to a property applies to all of the controls.

You can also set control properties at run time. This allows you to programmatically control objects as the application is running. Use the following syntax to set control properties at run time:

objectname.property = expression

The following example sets the Font.Bold property to True for the txtData text box:

```
txtData.Font.Bold = True      'Set text to bold.
```

The following example sets the Text property of the text box txtData:

```
txtData.Text = "Hello World" 'Set value of text.
```

Some controls have default properties. This allows you to omit the property name when you set the control's default property. For example, the default property of a text box is the Text property. The default property of a label is the Caption property.

The following code sets the default Text and Caption properties for a text box and a Label control:

```
txtData = "Set the Text property of this text box"
lblData = "Set the Caption property of this label"
```

Note For consistency and readability, always include the object's property name.

Using Control Arrays

Microsoft Visual Basic 6.0 provides several additional tools that help you create efficient and flexible applications. One of these is the control array, a group of controls that share the same name, type, and event procedures. However, elements of a control array retain their individual property settings. For example, you can use the Index, Caption, or Tag properties to distinguish one control from another. Figure 2.6 shows an example of a form containing a control array.

A control array has at least one element with an Index property that is greater than or equal to zero. The Index can grow to a maximum of 32,767 elements if your system resources and memory permit. Its size also depends on how much memory and Windows resources each control requires. Common uses for control arrays include menu controls and option button groupings.

Control arrays offer three advantages:

- Control arrays allow you to add new controls at run time. This is the most significant advantage. It is especially useful when you do not know how many controls you will need at run time. Adding controls at run time is also more fficient because you use fewer resources than you would by adding multiple controls at design time. Controls added at run time are often called dynamic controls.

- Each new element you add to a control array inherits the common event procedures of the array. This can facilitate development.

- Controls in a control array can share code. For example, if your form has several text boxes that receive a date value, a control array can be set up so that all of the text boxes share the same validation code.

Note Visual Basic limits you to 254 control names on a form. Each control array counts once toward this limit.

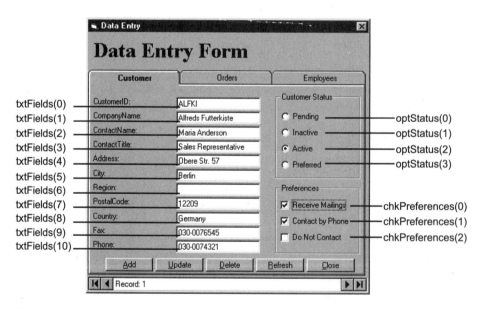

Figure 2.6 Control array

Creating Control Arrays at Design Time

You can create control arrays at design time in three ways:

- Give two controls the same name. They must be the same type.
- Copy and paste a control.
- Set the Index property by using the Properties window.

Visual Basic automatically creates a control array and gives these controls the index values.

➤ To create a control array at design time

1. Add the first control to a form and set the initial properties that all the controls in the control array will share.

2. Set the Name property for the control.

3. Do one of the following:

   - Click the control, copy it, then paste it on the form.
   - Place two controls of the same type on a form. Set the Name property of the second control to the name selected for the first control.
   - Click **Yes** when Visual Basic asks if you want to create a control array.

4. Repeat Step 3 until all controls have been added to the form.

Coding a Control Array

You refer to a control with the following syntax:

controlname(index)

You specify the index of a control when you create it. For example, when the control chkPreferences(2) recognizes the Click event, Visual Basic invokes the event procedure chkPreferences_Click and passes the index value 2 as an argument. The following code demonstrates using the Select Case statement to evaluate the index value passed to the chkPreferences_Click procedure. The Index value determines which box the user selected to display the appropriate message box:

```
Private Sub chkPreferences_Click(Index As Integer)
    If chkPreferences(Index).Value = vbChecked Then
        Select Case Index
            Case 0
                MsgBox "You will be notified by mail"
            Case 1
                MsgBox "You will be notified by phone"
            Case 2
                MsgBox "You will not be notified"
        End Select
    End If
End Sub
```

Creating Controls at Run Time

Visual Basic lets you create controls at run time. This gives you the flexibility to customize the interface according to the needs of the user. The Load statement and Add method are used to create controls dynamically.

Adding Controls with the Load Statement

Once a control array is established, the Load statement copies all the property settings except Visible, Index, and TabIndex from the lowest existing element in the array. When you want to display a control, set the Visible property to True.

If you try to load a control that already exists, a run-time error will occur.

In the following example, the code creates a new text box every time the user clicks the cmdAddTextBox button:

```
Private Sub cmdAddTextBox_Click ( )
    Dim intNextVal As Integer

    'Find the next available Index (indexes begin with 0)
    intNextVal = txtArray( ).Count
    'Add the new text box to the form
    Load txtArray(intNextVal)
    'Position the text box on the form
    txtArray(intNextVal).Top = txtArray(intNextVal - 1).Top + 400
    'By default the control is not visible
    txtArray(intNextVal).Visible = True
End Sub
```

Removing Controls with the Unload Statement

If you have dynamically created controls, you can use the Unload statement to remove these controls. If you try to unload a control that was created at design time or that has already been unloaded, a run-time error occurs. In the following code, each time the user clicks the cmdRemoveTextBox button, the textbox index is checked. If this control was created at run time, it is removed from the form:

```
Private Sub cmdRemoveTextBox_Click ()
    Dim intTopIndex As Integer

    'The variable holds the top index value
    intTopIndex = txtArray().Count - 1
    'Do not remove the original control with index 0
    If intTopIndex > 0 Then
        'Remove the control
        Unload txtArray(intTopIndex)
    End If
End Sub
```

Practice: Using Controls Arrays

In this practice you will create control arrays, add controls to your form at run time using the Load statement, and remove them with the Unload statement.

To see a demonstration, run the Chap02.exe animation located in the Animations folder on the Supplemental Course Materials CD-ROM that accompanies this book.

➤ To add control arrays to a form

1. Open a new **Standard EXE** project.

2. Add three CommandButton controls and one TextBox control to **Form1**.

3. Set the properties for the controls as specified in the following table:

Control	Property	Value
Command1	Name	CmdButtons
	Caption	&Add Textbox
Command2	Name	CmdButtons
	Caption	&Remove Textbox
Command3	Name	cmdButtons
	Caption	&Close
Text1	Name	txtData
	Index	0

4. Click **Yes** when Visual Basic asks if you want to create a control array.

Figure 2.7 illustrates the form layout.

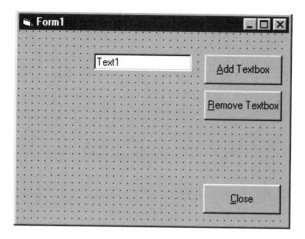

Figure 2.7 Practice form layout

➤ **To add code to a control array**

1. Open the Click event for any of the command buttons.

    The following Event procedure appears.

    ```
    Private Sub cmdButtons_Click( Index As Integer )

    End Sub
    ```

    The Index argument between parentheses indicates that the command button is part of a control array. Use this argument to determine which control was clicked.

2. Add the following code to the cmdButton's_Click event:

    ```
    Dim intNextVal As Integer, intTopIndex As Integer

    Select Case Index
        Case 0  'Add textbox button
            intNextVal = txtData().Count
            'Limit 5 controls on the form
            If intNextVal < 5 Then
                Load txtData(intNextVal)
                txtData(intNextVal).Top = _
                    txtData(intNextVal - 1).Top + 400
                txtData(intNextVal).Visible = True
            End If

        Case 1  'Remove textbox button
    ```

```
        intTopIndex = txtData().Count - 1
        'Remove all but the original control from the form
        If intTopIndex > 0 Then
            Unload txtData(intTopIndex)
        End If

    Case 2  'Close the form
            Unload Me
End Select
```

3. On the **File** menu, click **Save**.

   Save your form as frmControlArrays and your project file as ControlArrays to the \Practice\Ch02 folder.

4. Test your application.

Adding Controls Using the Add Method

Visual Basic 6.0 has the capability to add controls dynamically without using a control array. The Add method lets you add controls to an application at run time. This gives you greater flexibility because you can create new controls during run time and avoid the overhead of design-time controls. The following example uses the Add method to dynamically add a command button to the form frmCustomers:

```
Private Sub Form_Load()
    frmCustomers.Controls.Add "VB.CommandButton", "cmdObj1", Frame1
    With frmCustomers!cmdObj1
        .Visible = True
        .Width = 2000
        .Caption = "Dynamic Button"
    End With
End Sub
```

Note The preceding code uses an exclamation mark (!) as a syntax element. You can also use standard collection syntax such as frmCustomers.Controls("cmdObj1") to reference the control. For more information on the Add method, search for "What's New in Controls" in the MSDN Online Help.

Using the Controls Collection

Visual Basic provides an array that contains all the controls on a form. This array is known as the Controls collection. The Controls collection has one property, Count, which returns the number of controls on the form.

There are two ways to identify a control in the Controls collection. You can reference its index value or its name as shown in the following example:

```
Controls(1).Top
Controls("cmdObject1").Top
```

You can use the Controls collection to perform an action on a group of controls, such as changing a particular property value for several controls. You can use the TypeOf keyword with the If statement, or the TypeName function to determine the type of a control in the Controls collection. In the following code, Visual Basic scans the Controls collection, identifies all text boxes, then sets the font size to 12:

```
Sub cmdChangeFont_Click()
    Dim i As Integer
    For i = 0 To Controls.Count - 1
        If TypeOf Controls(i) Is TextBox Then
            Controls(i).FontSize = 12
        End If
    Next I
End Sub
```

You can also use the For Each statement to loop through collections:

```
Dim ctl As Control
For Each ctl In Controls
    If TypeName(ctl) = "TextBox" Then
        ctl.Text=""
    End If
Next ctl
```

Practice: Using the Add Method with a Controls Collection

In this practice you will dynamically add a label to the form using the Add method. You will also navigate through the Controls collection and clear all of the text boxes.

➤ **To add a label using the Add method**

1. Open a new **Standard EXE** project.

2. Add the following code to the **Form_Load** event:

```
Form1.Controls.Add "VB.Label", "lblTitle", Form1
With Form1!lblTitle
    .Visible = True
    .Top = 0
    .Left = 0
    .Width = 4000
    .Height = 500
    .Font.Size = 18
    .Caption = "This is a Dynamic label!"
End With
```

This code dynamically adds, sizes, and positions a new label in the top left corner of the form. The new label will have the caption, "This is a Dynamic label!"

3. Save and test your application.

    Save your form as frmControls and your project as ControlsCollection to the \Practice\Ch02 folder. Figure 2.8 illustrates the practice form at run time.

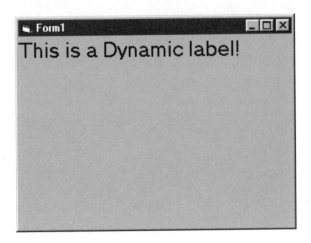

Figure 2.8 Results of the practice form

➤ **To navigate the Controls collection**

1. Add a CommandButton control to the form.

2. Set the Name property to **cmdClear** and the Caption property to **&ClearForm**.

3. Add two textboxes to the form.

    Figure 2.9 illustrates the form.

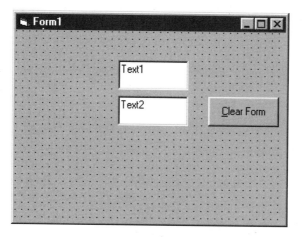

Figure 2.9 Appearance of the practice form

4. Declare an object variable in the **cmdClear_Click** event that will hold the value of the current control:

```
Dim ctl As Control
```

5. Add the following code to the **cmdButtons_Click** event:

```
For Each ctl In Controls
    If TypeOf ctl Is TextBox Then
        ctl.Text = ""
    End If
Next ctl
```

6. Save and test your application.

Enhancing the User Interface

Additional ActiveX controls are included with the Professional and Enterprise editions of Visual Basic. These controls increase functionality and can dramatically enhance the user interface. Some examples of these ActiveX controls, which are shown in Figure 2.10, are: ImageList, TreeView, ListView, ToolBar, and Status Bar.

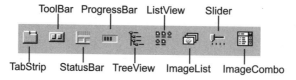

Figure 2.10 Controls added using the Windows Common Controls 6.0

Note These controls are part of a group of ActiveX controls that are found in the mscomctl.ocx file. To use these controls in your application, add this file to the project.

ImageList

The ImageList control is a storehouse for images. It contains a collection of ListImage objects, each of which can be referred to by its index or key. It is a companion control in that it acts as a central repository to supply images to other controls. The ImageList's companion control is any control that can display an image's Picture object, or it is one of the Windows Common Controls specifically designed to bind to the ImageList control. These Common Controls include the ListView, ToolBar, TabStrip, Header, ImageCombo, and TreeView.

Other controls must be bound to the ImageList control to access the stored images:

- For the ListView control, set the Icons and SmallIcons properties to ImageList controls.
- For the TreeView, TabStrip, ImageCombo, and Toolbar controls, set the ImageList property to an ImageList control.

At design time, you can add images using the Images tab of the ImageList Control Property Pages dialog box, shown in Figure 2.11. The ImageList is not visible to the user interface at run time, but you can dynamically add images using the Add method for the ListImages collection.

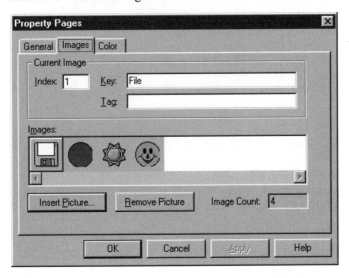

Figure 2.11 ImageList Control Property Pages dialog box

TreeView

A TreeView control displays a hierarchical list of Node objects, each of which consists of a label and an optional bitmap. You typically use a TreeView to display the headings in a document, the entries in an index, the files and directories on a disk, or any other kind of information that might be useful displayed as a hierarchy. Figure 2.12 illustrates the Window Explorer, an example of the TreeView control.

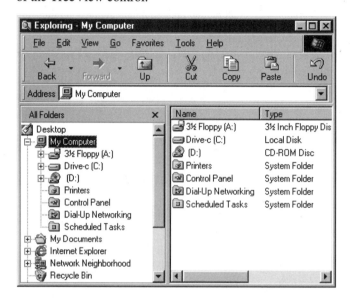

Figure 2.12 The Windows Explorer, which is a TreeView control

After you create a TreeView control, you can add, remove, arrange, and otherwise manipulate Node objects by setting properties and invoking methods. You can programmatically expand and collapse Node objects to display or hide all child nodes. The following example creates a TreeView control; Figure 2.13 shows the results of the code on the TreeView control:

```
Dim nodTreeView As Node

'Set the style.
TreeView1.Style = tvwTreelinesPlusMinusText

'Add the root node with key M1 and Caption January
Set nodTreeView = TreeView1.Nodes.Add(, , "M1", "January")

'Add Child (Week1) and Sub Child Nodes(Monday,Tuesday...)
Set nodTreeView = TreeView1.Nodes.Add("M1", tvwChild, "W1", "Week1")
Set nodTreeView = TreeView1.Nodes.Add("W1", tvwChild, "W1WD1", "Monday")
Set nodTreeView = TreeView1.Nodes.Add("W1", tvwChild, "W1WD2", _
    "Tuesday")
```

```
Set nodTreeView = TreeView1.Nodes.Add("M1", tvwChild, "W2", "Week2")
Set nodTreeView = TreeView1.Nodes.Add("W2", tvwChild, "W2WD1", "Monday")
Set nodTreeView = TreeView1.Nodes.Add("W2", tvwChild, "W2WD2", _
    "Tuesday")

Set nodTreeView = TreeView1.Nodes.Add("M1", tvwChild, "W3", "Week3")
Set nodTreeView = TreeView1.Nodes.Add("W3", tvwChild, "W3WD1", "Monday")
Set nodTreeView = TreeView1.Nodes.Add("W3", tvwChild, "W3WD2", _
    "Tuesday")

Set nodTreeView = TreeView1.Nodes.Add("M1", tvwChild, "W4", "Week4")
Set nodTreeView = TreeView1.Nodes.Add("W4", tvwChild, "W4WD1", "Monday")
Set nodTreeView = TreeView1.Nodes.Add("W4", tvwChild, "W4WD2", _
    "Tuesday")
```

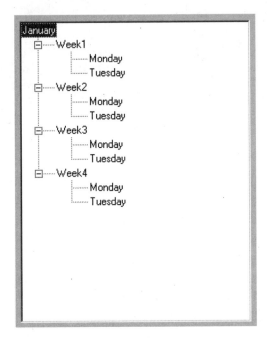

Figure 2.13 Example of the TreeView control

The TreeView control includes three primary events: Collapse, Expand, and NodeClick. An example of the NodeClick event is:

```
Private Sub TreeView1_NodeClick(ByVal Node As MSComctlLib.Node)
    'Place the selected nodes text into a label control
    lblNodeClicked.Caption = Node.Text
End Sub
```

Note The TreeView control uses the ImageList control, specified by the ImageList property, to store the bitmaps and icons that are displayed in Node objects. A TreeView control can use only one ImageList at a time.

ListView

The ListView control displays items, called ListItem objects, in one of four different views: Large (standard) icons, Small icons, List, and Report.

You can arrange items into columns with or without column headings. You can also display accompanying icons and text.

The View property determines which view the control uses to display the items in the list. You can also control whether the labels associated with items in the list wrap to more than one line using the LabelWrap property. Use the Sorted property to determine how the data is organized. In addition, you can manage how items in the list are sorted and how selected items appear. The following example fills a ListView control:

```
Dim itmX As ListItem

'Set the view to report.
ListView1.View = lvwReport
ListView1.Sorted = True

'Add ColumnHeaders and set their width.
ListView1.ColumnHeaders.Add , , "Product", ListView1.Width / 3
ListView1.ColumnHeaders.Add , , "Description", ListView1.Width / 3
ListView1.ColumnHeaders.Add , , "Price", ListView1.Width / 3

'Add the items and sub items to the list.
Set itmX = ListView1.ListItems.Add(, , "Tires")
'Sub items appear in the middle column.
itmX.SubItems(1) = "Radial"
'Set the third column value
itmX.SubItems(2) = "$100.00"

'Add a new item and sub items to the list.
Set itmX = ListView1.ListItems.Add(, , "Engine")
itmX.SubItems(1) = "Rebuild"
itmX.SubItems(2) = "$2,000.00"
```

```
'Add a new item and sub items to the list.
Set itmX = ListView1.ListItems.Add(, , "Seats")
itmX.SubItems(1) = "Bucket"
itmX.SubItems(2) = "$800.00"

'Add a new item and sub items to the list.
Set itmX = ListView1.ListItems.Add(, , "Paint")
itmX.SubItems(1) = "2 Coats"
itmX.SubItems(2) = "$550.00"
```

The ListView control uses several events to handle user actions. The following is an example of the ItemClick event:

```
Private Sub ListView1_ItemClick(ByVal Item As MSComctlLib.ListItem)
    'Display the selected row's data to a label control.
    lblLastItemClicked.Caption = Item.Text & ", " & _
        Item.ListSubItems(1).Text & ", " & Item.ListSubItems(2).Text
End Sub
```

ToolBar

A ToolBar control contains a collection of Button objects. A toolbar typically contains buttons that correspond to items in an application's menu. This provides a graphic interface for the user to access the most frequently used functions and commands.

The ToolBar control lets you create toolbars by adding Button objects to a Buttons collection. Each Button object can have optional text, an image, or both, supplied by an associated ImageList control. For each Button object, you display an image on a button with the Image property, or display text with the Caption property, or both. At design time, you can add Button objects to the control using the Properties Page of the ToolBar control. At run time, you can add or remove buttons from the Buttons collection with the Add and Remove methods. Figure 2.14 illustrates the use of a toolbar on a form.

Figure 2.14 Toolbar on a form

The toolbar buttons share the same event. The buttons can be identified by their Key or Index properties. For example:

```
Private Sub tlbDataEntry_ButtonClick(ByVal Button As MSComctlLib.Button)
    Select Case Button.Index
        Case 1
            'Navigate back a record.
        Case 2
            'Navigate forward a record.
        Case 3
            'Used a separator.
        Case 4
            'Save the record.
        Case 5
            'Activate help.
    End Select
End Sub
```

StatusBar

A StatusBar control provides a window, usually at the bottom of a parent form, through which an application can display status data. A StatusBar control consists of up to 16 Panel objects that are contained in a Panels collection. Each Panel object can contain text and/or a picture. Properties that control the appearance of individual panels include Width, Alignment (of text and pictures), and Bevel. Additionally, you can use one of seven values of the Style property to automatically display common data such as date, time, and keyboard states. Figure 2.15 illustrates a status bar.

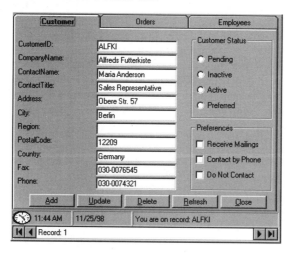

Figure 2.15 Form with StatusBar control

At design time, you can create panels and customize their appearance by setting values in the Panel tab of the Properties Page of the StatusBar control. At run time, the Panel objects can be reconfigured to reflect different functions depending on the state of the application.

To change the text that appears in a status bar panel, set the Text property of one of the panels in the StatusBar control. The following code displays the Customer ID in the third pane of the StatusBar that was shown in Figure 2.15:

```
staDataEntry.Panels(1).Text = "You are on record: " & txtFields(0).Text
```

If the status bar contains only one pane (the Style property is set to sbrSimple), you can set the text using the SimpleText property. For example:

```
staDataEntry.SimpleText = "Processing, please wait..."
```

One of the events the StatusBar uses is the PanelClick event. It is generated when a click occurs on a StatusBar control's Panel object. When the StatusBar control's Style property is set to Simple style, panels are hidden and the PanelClick event is not generated.

You can use a reference to the Panel object to set properties for that panel. For example, the following code resets the Bevel property of a clicked Panel:

```
Private Sub staDataEntry_PanelClick(ByVal Panel As MSComctlLib.Panel)
    'Determine the key property of the panel clicked
    Select Case Panel.Key
        Case "time"
            Panel.Bevel = sbrRaised
            '[statements]
        Case "date"
            Panel.Bevel = sbrRaised
            '[statements]
        Case "record"
            Panel.Bevel = sbrRaised
            '[statements]
    End Select
    MsgBox "The panel's index is: " & Panel.Index
End Sub
```

Lesson Summary

Inherent (standard) controls, such as the text box and command button, are included in the Visual Basic toolbox.

Custom controls have an .ocx extension and are optional. They are available from three sources:

- Visual Basic
- The Professional and Enterprise editions
- Third-party developers

To use custom controls in a project, add them to the toolbox. If they are not registered on your system, add them first to the Components dialog box.

You can set control properties at design time; doing so establishes default values. You can also set the properties at run time; this controls objects as the application runs.

A control array is a group of controls that share the same name, type, and event procedures, but retain individual properties. Control arrays allow you to add controls to an application at run time. This minimizes the use of system resources.

Custom controls that are especially useful include:

- ListView
- ImageList
- ToolBar
- StatusBar

Lesson 4: Using Menus

Menus provide a structured way for users to access the commands and tools contained in an application. Proper planning and design of menus and toolbars is essential and ensures proper functionality and accessibility of your application to users.

After this lesson you will be able to:

- Explain the importance of menus in interface design.
- Describe the process of creating a menu using the Menu Editor, including separator bars, and access and shortcut keys.
- Describe the process for creating a pop-up menu.
- Explain how to enable or disable a menu control.
- Explain how to display a check mark on a menu.
- Explain how to make menu items invisible.
- Explain how to use a control array to add menu controls at run time.

Estimated lesson time: 30 minutes

Creating Menus at Design Time

Well-designed menus help users understand and use your application. With the Visual Basic Menu Editor, you can create menus that enhance the quality of your applications.

Using the Menu Editor

The Menu Editor (see Figure 2.16) lets you do the following:

- Create new menus and menu bars.
- Add new commands to existing menus.
- Modify menu properties.

Note Menu properties can also be set in the Properties window. To access the Properties window, press F4 and click the name of the menu item from the drop-down Object list box.

A menu control has many properties such as Name, Caption, and Index.

- The Name property identifies the menu control in code.
- The Index property identifies controls that share the same name.
- The Description property is the text that appears on the menu bar at run time.

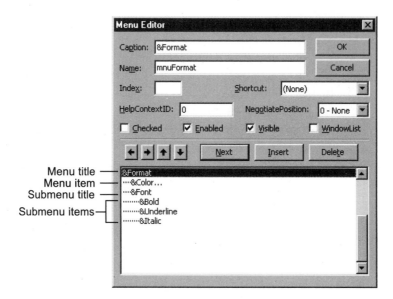

Menu title
Menu item
Submenu title
Submenu items

Figure 2.16 The Menu Editor window

The lower portion of the Menu Editor window lists all the menu controls for the current form, as illustrated in Figure 2.16. Select a menu item from the list box to edit the properties for that item.

The position of the menu control in the menu control list box determines whether the control is a menu title, a menu item, a submenu title, or a submenu item:

- A menu control that appears flush left in the list box displays on the menu bar as a menu title; Figure 2.17 illustrates the menu's appearance.

- A menu control that is indented once in the list box displays on the menu when the user clicks the menu title.

- An indented menu control, followed by menu controls that are further indented, becomes a submenu title. Menu controls indented below the submenu title become items of that submenu.

Figure 2.17 Displaying your menus

➤ **To create menu controls in the Menu Editor**

1. Click the form.

2. On the **Tools** menu, click **Menu Editor,** or click the **Menu Editor** button on the toolbar.

3. In the **Caption** text box, enter the text for the first menu's title. This title will appear on the menu bar.

Note   Using an ampersand (&) in the caption enables access keys in a menu item.

---

4. In the **Name** text box, enter the name that you will use to refer to the menu control in code.

5. Click the left or right arrow button to decrease or increase, respectively, the indentation level of the control.

6. Set the other properties as necessary.

Note   You can do this in the Menu Editor or, later, in the Properties window.

---

7. Click **Next** to create another menu control, or click **Insert** to add a menu control between existing controls.

8. When you have created all the menu controls for the form, click **OK** to close the **Menu Editor**.

Note   Click the up arrow and down arrow buttons to move the item in the existing menu structure.

Separating Menu Items

A separator bar is a horizontal line between items on a menu. You can use a hyphen (-) as the Caption property for a menu control to create a separator bar. On menus that contain multiple items, you can use separator bars to divide items into logical groups.

In the following example, the File menu uses a separator bar between the Close and Exit commands to divide the menu items into two separate groups, as illustrated in Figure 2.18.

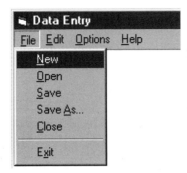

Figure 2.18 Menu separators

➤ **To create a separator bar in the Menu Editor**

1. Click **Insert** to insert a menu item between the menu items you want to separate.

2. If necessary, click the right arrow button to indent the new menu item to the same level as the menu items it will separate.

3. Enter a hyphen (-) in the **Caption** text box.

4. Set the **Name** property.

5. Click **OK** to close the **Menu Editor**.

Note Although separator bars are created as menu items, they do not respond to the Click event, and users cannot choose them. A menu item cannot be a separator bar if it is a menu title, has submenu items, is checked or disabled, or has a shortcut key.

Menu Access and Shortcut Keys

You can improve keyboard access to menu items by defining access keys and shortcut keys.

Access Keys

Access keys allow the user to open a menu by pressing the ALT key and typing a designated letter. When a menu is open, the user can choose a command by pressing the letter (the access key) assigned to it. For example, ALT+E opens the Edit menu, and P selects the Paste menu item. An access-key assignment appears as an underlined letter in the menu control's caption, as illustrated in Figure 2.18.

➤ **To assign an access key to a menu control in the Menu Editor**

1. Click the menu item that you want to assign an access key.

2. In the **Caption** box, enter an ampersand (**&**) in front of the desired letter for the access key.

Note Do not use duplicate access keys on menus. If you use the same access key for more than one menu item, the key will not work. For example, if C is the access key for both Cut and Copy, when you select the Edit menu and press C, the Copy command will be selected, but the application will not carry out the command until the user presses ENTER. The Cut command cannot be selected with an access key.

Shortcut Keys

Shortcut keys run a menu item immediately when pressed. Frequently used menu items may be assigned a keyboard shortcut. The shortcut provides a single-step method of keyboard access. Without a shortcut, you must press ALT, a menu title access character, and then a menu item access character. Shortcut key assignments include function key and control key combinations, such as CTRL+F1 or CTRL+A. Shortcut keys appear on the menu to the right of the corresponding menu item, as shown in Figure 2.19.

Figure 2.19 Using shortcut keys

➤ **To assign a shortcut key to a menu item**

1. Open the **Menu Editor** and click the menu item.

2. Select the name of a function key or key combination in the **Shortcut** combo box.

3. To remove a shortcut key assignment, click **(none)** from the top of the list.

Note When a shortcut key is added to a menu item, the shortcut keys appear automatically on the menu. Therefore, you do not have to enter CTRL+key in the Caption box of the Menu Editor.

Creating Pop-up Menus

Pop-up menus are a convenient way to provide access to common, contextual commands. You can use the PopupMenu method to display a Menu created in the Menu Editor. This method displays a pop-up menu on top of a form or control at the current mouse location. The menu can also be displayed at specified coordinates. If a menu has at least one menu item, it can be displayed as a pop-up menu at run time.

The following example displays a pop-up menu at the cursor location when the user clicks the right mouse button on a form.

➤ **Creating Pop-upMenus**

1. Create a form that includes a menu control named **mnuFile**, with at least one submenu.

2. Add the following code to the Form_MouseDown event.

```
Private Sub Form_MouseDown (Button As Integer, _
        Shift As, X As Single, Y As Single)
    If Button = vbRightButton Then
        PopupMenu mnuFile
    End If
End Sub
```

The PopupMenu method displays the mnuFile menu when the user right clicks the form.

Modifying Menus at Run Time

The menus that you create at design time can respond dynamically to run-time conditions. For example, if a menu item action becomes inappropriate at some point, you can disable that menu item to prevent users from selecting it. You can also use a check mark next to a menu item that indicates which command was last selected. Other menu control features described in this section include code that makes a menu item visible or invisible and that adds or deletes menu items. You can also dynamically add menu items if you have a menu control array. This is described in "Adding Menu Controls at Run Time," later in this lesson.

Enabling and Disabling Menu Commands

All menu controls have an Enabled property. When this property is set to False, the menu is disabled and does not respond to user actions, and shortcut key access is disabled. A disabled menu control appears dimmed to the user. For example, the following statement disables the Paste menu item on the Edit menu:

```
mnuEditPaste.Enabled = False
```

Disabling a menu title disables the entire menu and the user will not be able to activate that menu. For example, the following code will disable the entire Edit menu:

```
mnuEdit.Enabled = False
```

Displaying a Check Mark on a Menu Item

Use the Checked property to place a check mark next to a menu item. This tells the user the status of an on/off condition. To use this feature, set the initial value of the Checked property in the Menu Editor by selecting the check box labeled Checked. To add or remove a check mark from a menu control at run time, set its Checked property from code. For example, the following code demonstrates using the Checked property:

```
Private Sub mnuOptions_Click ()
    'Set the state of the check mark based on
    'the property's current value.
    mnuOptionsToolbar.Checked = Not mnuOptionsToolbar.Checked
End Sub
```

Making Menu Items Invisible

In the Menu Editor, click the Visible check box to set the initial value of the Visible property for a menu control. To make a menu item visible or invisible at run time, set its Visible property from code. For example, the following code demonstrates adding and removing a menu by assigning a value to the menu's Visible property:

```
mnuFile.Visible = True    'Make the menu visible.
mnuFile.Visible = False   'Make the menu invisible.
```

When a menu item is invisible, the rest of the items in the menu move up to fill the empty space. If the item is on the main menu bar, the rest of the items move left to fill the space.

Note Making a menu item invisible removes it from the menu bar. If the menu title's Visible property is set to False, all submenus on that menu will also be unavailable to the user.

Using a Menu Control Array

In Lesson 3 you worked with control arrays. You can also create a menu control array. A menu is defined as a menu control array when each submenu item shares the same name. When submenu items share the same name, they must each have a unique Index property. The items in a menu control array don't have to be contiguous (for example, 2, 3, 4), but they must be in ascending order according to their location on the menu. Figure 2.20 illustrates using the Menu Editor and menu control arrays.

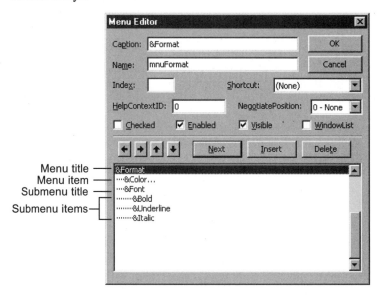

Figure 2.20 The Menu Editor window

Adding Menu Items at Run Time

For example, you can add menu items dynamically to display the path names of the most recently opened files. You must use a menu control array to create a menu item at run time. Because the menu item is assigned a value for the Index property at design time, it automatically becomes an element of the array even though no other elements have been created.

➤ **To create a menu control array in the Menu Editor**

1. Click the form.

2. From the **Tools** menu, click **Menu Editor**, or click the **Menu Editor** button on the toolbar.

3. In the **Caption** text box, type the text for the first menu title that you want appearing on the menu bar.

   The menu title text appears in the menu control list box.

4. In the **Name** text box, type the name that you will use to refer to the menu control in code. Leave the **Index** box empty.

5. At the next indentation level, create the menu item that will become the first element in the array by setting its **Caption** and **Name**.

6. Set the **Index** for the first element in the array to 0.

7. Create a second menu item at the same level of indentation as the first. Set the **Name** of the second element to the same name as the first element and set its **Index** to 1.

8. Repeat steps 5–8 for subsequent elements of the array.

Note Elements of a menu control array must be contiguous in the menu control list box and must be at the same level of indentation. When you're creating menu control arrays, be sure to include any separator bars that you want appearing on the menu.

When you create an item such as mnuFile(0), you actually create a separator bar that is invisible at run time. The first time a user saves a file at run time, the separator bar becomes visible, and the first filename is added to the menu. Each time you save a file at run time, additional menu items are loaded into the array, making the menu grow.

To hide menu items created at run time, use the Hide method or set the control's Visible property to False. To remove an item in a control array from memory, use the Unload statement. You can also determine the number of items in the array by using a control array's Ubound property. The following code demonstrates adding items to a menu control array and using the Ubound property to determine the next available index. Figure 2.21 illustrates the result of the following code.

```
Dim i As Integer
'Add 5 new items to the mnuFile menu
For i = 1 To 5
    'Use the Ubound property to find the next available index number
    Load mnuFile(mnuFile.UBound + 1)
    'Give the new menu item a caption
    mnuFile(mnuFile.UBound).Caption = "This is new item " & _
        mnuFile.UBound
Next i
```

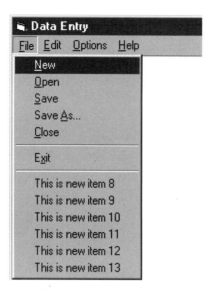

Figure 2.21 Dynamically adding new items to a menu

Lesson Summary

You can easily create a Visual Basic menu with the Menu Editor. Features to consider in designing menus include separator bars, access keys, and shortcut keys.

Pop-up menus are useful in contextual command situations.

Other characteristics of menus that you may wish to use in your application are enabling and disabling menu commands, displaying check marks on menu items, and making menu controls invisible. You can also add menu controls at run time by using a control array.

Summary

User Interface Design Principles

- Interface design is important to facilitate the programming and usability of an application.
- Design principles to consider in designing an application include composition and layout, color, images and icons, fonts, and the use of menus.

Managing Forms

- Forms are the basic element of the user interface in a Visual Basic application.
- Form events provide the functionality of an application. They are triggered in response to user actions such as a mouse click or a key press. Form events are generally triggered in this order:
  - Initialize
  - Load
  - Activate
  - Deactivate
  - Query Unload
  - Unload
  - Terminate

- Form methods perform an action on an object. Methods affect how efficiently an application utilizes computer resources such as memory and processing speed. There are four methods:
  - Show
  - Hide
  - Load
  - Unload

Using Controls

- Standard controls are included in the Visual Basic toolbox. Custom controls have an .ocx extension and must be added to the toolbox before you can use them.

- Setting control properties at design time sets default values. Setting control properties at run time sets them as the application is running.

- A control array is a group of controls that share the same name, type, and event procedures, but retain individual properties. They provide more efficient use of system resources by allowing you to add controls to an application at run time.

- Some of the most useful custom controls are:
  - ListView
  - ImageList
  - ToolBar
  - StatusBar

Using Menus

- The Menu Editor is helpful in creating menus.
- Menu options to consider include:
  - Separator bars
  - Access keys
  - Shortcut keys
- Pop-up menus are useful when contextual commands are appropriate.
- Options for designing menus include:
  - Enabling and disabling menu commands.
  - Displaying check marks on menu items.
  - Making menus and menu items invisible.

Lab: Creating the Chateau St. Mark User Interface

In this lab, you will create the Chateau St. Mark hotel reservation application in Visual Basic. You will add controls and work with control arrays. In subsequent labs, you will continue to add to the hotel reservation application and explore each of the tasks you try here in more detail. The completed form will look like Figure 2.22.

To see a demonstration of the solution, run the Lab02.exe animation located in the Animations folder on the Supplemental Course Materials CD-ROM that accompanies this book.

Estimated lesson time: 55 minutes

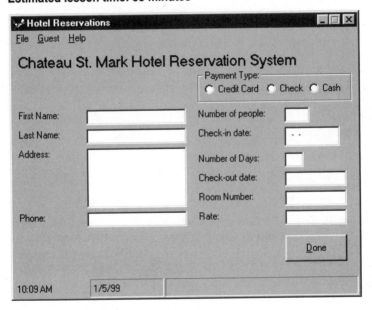

Figure 2.22 The Chateau St. Mark hotel reservation form

Exercise 1: Creating the User Interface

In this exercise, you will create the user interface by adding controls to the Chateau St. Mark reservations form. Some of these controls will be implemented as control arrays.

➤ **To create a new Visual Basic project**

1. Open a new **Standard EXE** project. Define the following project and form properties:

Object	Property	Value
Project1	Name	HotelReservation
Form1	Name	frmReservations
	BorderStyle	1 - Fixed Single
	Caption	Chateau St. Mark Hotel
	MinButton	True

2. Add the following controls to the form:

Control	Control Type	Property	Value
Text1	TextBox	Name	txtFirstName
		Text	\<blank\>
Text2	TextBox	Name	txtLastName
		Text	\<blank\>
Text3	TextBox	Name	txtAddress
		Multiline	True
		Text	\<blank\>
Text4	TextBox	Name	txtPhone
		Text	\<blank\>
Text5	TextBox	Name	txtNumPeople
		Text	\<blank\>
Text6	TextBox	Name	txtNumDays
		Text	\<blank\>

Control	Control Type	Property	Value
Text7	TextBox	Name	txtCheckOut
		Text	<blank>
Text8	TextBox	Name	txtRoomNumber
		Text	<blank>
Text9	TextBox	Name	txtRate
		Text	<blank>
Frame1	Frame	Name	fraPmtType
		Caption	Payment Type
Command1	CommandButton	Name	cmdDone
		Caption	&Done

Note Use each control's TabIndex property to control the order in which the user will navigate through the form when pressing the Tab key.

▶ **To create control arrays**

1. On **frmReservation**, add the following three OptionButton controls to the Frame control by clicking **OptionButton** in the toolbox, and then drawing the controls inside of **fraPmtType**:

Control	Control Type	Property	Value
Option1	OptionButton	Name	grpPmtType
		Index	0
		Caption	Credit Card
Option2	OptionButton	Name	grpPmtType
		Index	1
		Caption	Check
Option3	OptionButton	Name	grpPmtType
		Index	2
		Caption	Cash

2. Add the appropriate labels for the textboxes on the hotel reservation form, as shown in Figure 2.22.

Exercise 2: Adding Custom Controls to the Form

In this exercise, you will add the Masked Edit and StatusBar Custom controls to the Chateau St. Mark reservation form. You will modify the properties of these controls at design time in the Properties Pages and programmatically at run time. The form with status bar is illustrated in Figure 2.23.

➤ **To add ActiveX controls to your project and form**

1. On the **Project** menu, click **Components**.

2. Select the **Microsoft Windows Common Controls 6.0** and the **Microsoft Masked Edit Control 6.0** check boxes.

3. Click **OK** to close the **Components** dialog box.

   The new controls appear in the toolbox.

4. Add the following controls to the form and set their properties:

Control	Control Type	Property	Value
MaskEdBox1	MaskedEdBox	Name	mskCheckIn
		Mask	##-##-####
StatusBar1	StatusBar	Name	staAdditionalInfo

5. Add a Label control with the Caption property set to **Check-in Date**. Position the label to the left of the MaskEdBox control.

➤ **To modify an ActiveX control's properties**

1. Right-click on the status bar and click **Properties**.

   The control's Property Pages appear.

2. Click the **Panels** tab in the **StatusBar Property Pages** dialog box and set the following properties for Index 1:

Index 1 Property	Value
ToolTip Text	The current time
Key	Time
Style	5 – sbrTime
Bevel	0 – sbrNoBevel

3. On the **Panels** tab, click the **Insert Panel** button.

4. Change the Index property to **2** by clicking the arrow to the right of the **Index** text box and setting the following properties:

Index 2 Property	Value
ToolTip Text	The current date
Key	Date
Style	6 – sbrDate
Bevel	2 – sbrRaised

5. On the **Panels** tab, click **Insert Panel**.

6. Change the Index property to **3** by clicking the arrow to the right of the **Index** text box and setting the following properties:

Index 3 Property	Value
ToolTip Text	Additional information
Key	addinfo
Style	0 - sbrText
Bevel	1 - sbrInset
AutoSize	1 – sbrSpring

7. Click **OK**.

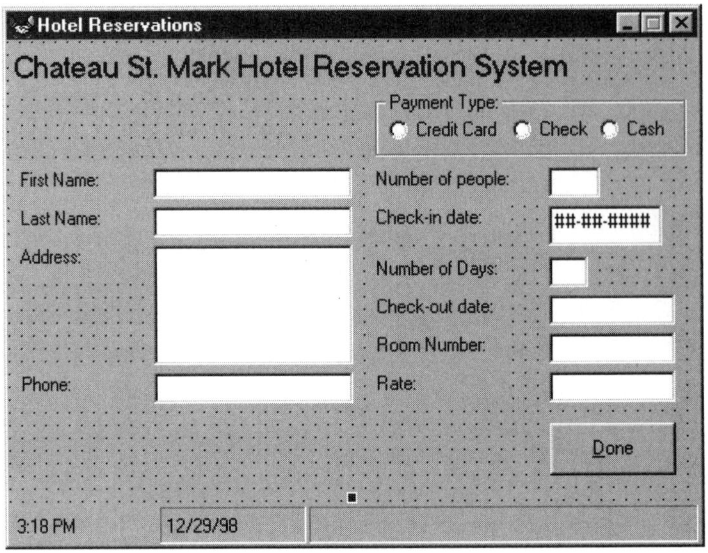

Figure 2.23 Form layout with StatusBar

➤ **To add text to the StatusBar panel**

1. Double-click one of the option buttons in the **Payment Type** frame.

   The following procedure appears:

   ```
   Private Sub grpPmtType_Click(Index As Integer)

   End Sub
   ```

2. Add the following code to the **grpPmtType_Click** event procedure:

   ```
   Private Sub grpPmtType_Click(Index As Integer)
       Select Case Index
           Case 0  'Credit card
               staAdditionalInfo.Panels("addinfo").Text = _
                   "Visa, Master Card or American Express accepted."
           Case 1  'Check
               staAdditionalInfo.Panels("addinfo").Text = _
                   "Picture ID and check guarantee card required."
           Case 2  'Cash
               staAdditionalInfo.Panels("addinfo").Text = _
                   "Hotel's do not carry a lot of extra change."
       End Select
   End Sub
   ```

3. Save your application to the \Labs\Lab02\Partial folder. Save the project as Hotelres.vbp. Save the form as Frmrsvn.frm.

4. Run and test the application.

Exercise 3: Adding a Menu Bar

In this exercise, you will use the Menu Editor to create a menu bar for the Chateau St. Mark hotel reservation form. You will add code to the Click event of the Exit menu item.

➤ **To add a menu to the project**

1. Click the **frmReservation** form.

2. On the **Tools** menu, click **Menu Editor**, or click the **Menu Editor** button on the toolbar.

3. In the **Caption** text box, enter **&File**.

   The ampersand (&) provides an access key to the menu.

4. In the **Name** text box, enter **mnuFile.** This is the name that you will use to refer to the menu control in code. Figure 2.24 illustrates the menu in the Menu

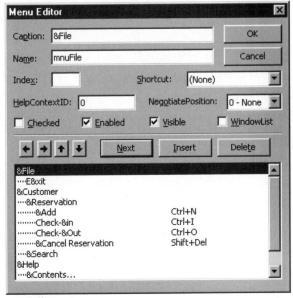

Editor.

Figure 2.24 Menu Editor showing reservation application menu

5. Repeat steps 3 and 4 to create the following menu structure:

Menu Item	Property	Value
File	Caption	&File
	Name	MnuFile
Exit	Caption	E&xit
	Name	mnuFileExit
Guest	Caption	&Guest
	Name	mnuGuest
Reservation	Caption	&Reservation
	Name	mnuGuestReservation
Add	Caption	&Add
	Name	mnuGuestReservationAdd
Check-In	Caption	Check-&In
	Name	mnuGuestReservationCheckIn
Check-Out	Caption	Check-&Out
	Name	mnuGuestReservationCheckOut
Cancel Reservation	Caption	&Cancel Reservation
	Name	mnuGuestReservationCancel
Search	Caption	&Search
	Name	mnuGuestSearch
Help	Caption	&Help
	Name	mnuHelp
Contents	Caption	&Contents...
	Name	mnuHelpContents
About	Caption	&About
	Name	MnuHelpAbout

6. Click **Ok** to close the Menu Editor.

➤ **To add code to menu items**

1. On the **Forms** menu, click **File**, and then click **Exit**.

   The **mnuFileExit_Click** event appears.

2. Add the Unload method to the **mnuFileExit_Click** event. For example:

```
Private Sub mnuFileExit_Click()
    Unload Me
End Sub
```

3. Save and test the application.

Review

The following questions are intended to reinforce key information presented in this chapter. If you are unable to answer a question, review the appropriate lesson and then try the question again. Answers to the questions can be found in the Appendix, "Questions and Answers," located at the back of this book.

1. Your boss told you to follow the "look" of Microsoft Word in designing the user interface of your new insurance form.

   What specific elements will you look at?

   Why did he want you to do this?

2. When would you have to set a startup form?

3. What causes form events to fire?

4. What is the difference between standard controls and custom controls, and where do you get them?

5. Why would you set control properties at design time?

   Why would you set them at run time?

6. What is a control array?

    When do you need a control array?

C H A P T E R 3

Validating and Processing User Input

About This Chapter

In this chapter, you will learn to respond to user input. The technique you choose will be based on the type of interaction you want to provide. You can validate data at the form level, which is a centralized style of validation. The alternative is field-level validation, which validates data based on each data element within a user interface.

Before You Begin

To complete the lessons in this chapter, you must have:

■ Read Chapter 2.

Lesson 1: Overview of Validation

Whether you're writing a simple calculator application or a complex database front end, you'll need to validate information entered by a user. This lesson examines several ways to validate input, ranging from trapping individual keystrokes to validating all fields on a form simultaneously.

After this lesson you will be able to:

■ Describe the purpose of data validation.

■ Explain the two data validation techniques.

Estimated lesson time: 10 minutes

The Importance of Validation

In most applications, a user enters information for the application to process. Data validation ensures that every data value entered into your application is accurate and of a valid data type. You can use several different approaches to implement data validation in your application: user interface code, database constraints, or business rules. In this chapter, you will focus on data validation in user interface code.

Verifying the data type is one of the most common tasks in data validation. Data type validation answers simple questions, such as "Is the string alphabetic?" and "Is the number numeric?" Usually you can handle such simple validations with your application's user interface.

A well-designed application can prevent most data-entry errors. For example, when you require a numeric value, create a field that only accepts numbers; the user will be unable to enter non-numeric values. You could create an application that calculates the cost of goods sold based on income and expense values entered by a user; a field for inventory cost would require a numeric value. You would want to prevent users from entering alphabetic characters in this case. Setting up your application to accept the proper information from the user can prevent logic errors in calculations, and can even prevent run-time errors such as type mismatch (Visual Basic run-time error number 13).

Types of Validation

In Visual Basic, you can choose two different methods to handle data validation:

■ Form-level validation

Form-level validation verifies data after all fields on a form have been completely filled in by a user. For example, a customer entry form requires a user to fill in a name, an address, a phone number, a city, a state, and a zip code. The user must fill in all fields and then click an OK button before validation verifies the data in each field.

■ Field-level validation

Field-level validation verifies the data in each field one at a time, as each field is filled in. For example, a user types in a value for a zip code field on a customer entry form. The moment the user types in the information or before the user moves to another field on the form, validation of the zip code field takes place. In in this example, you could use the Change event for the TextBox control to verify that the zip code value was numeric.

Providing User Feedback

When users type invalid data into fields on your form, give them an audio and/or visual cue to notify them of the invalid entry. How you handle this depends on the validation technique you choose to implement. If you use form-level validation, you can display a custom form that lists any data entry errors. For example, if a user enters an invalid zip code and forgets to type a value for a city field on a customer entry form, you could display a separate form that lists the two data entry errors.

With field-level validation, you can use audio cues to communicate errors. For example, if a user enters alpha characters into a zip code field that requires a numeric value, you can use the Visual Basic Beep statement as an audio cue. In addition, you can display a message box or use a StatusBar control to display the error description, as shown in the following example:

```
If Not IsNumeric(txtZipCode.Text) Then
    'Audio cue
    Beep
    'Visual cue
    StatusBar1.Panels("ErrorDescription").Text = _
        "Zip code must be numeric."
End If
```

Using the SetFocus Method

Focus is an object's ability to receive user input through a mouse or keyboard. In Microsoft Windows, although several applications can be running simultaneously, only one application has focus; it has an active title bar and can receive user input. On a Visual Basic form with several text boxes, only the text box with focus can receive input through the keyboard. When you set focus to a control, the GotFocus event for that control fires, and the LostFocus event fires for the control that previously had focus. Forms and most controls support these events.

Note Some controls, such as the Frame, Line, Image, and Label controls, cannot receive focus. Additionally, controls that are invisible at run time, such as the Timer control, cannot receive focus.

With both form-level and field-level validation, always set focus back to the field that contains invalid data. For example, if a user types an invalid zip code into a TextBox, use the SetFocus method to place the cursor on the TextBox to allow the user to make corrections, as in the following example:

```
If Not IsNumeric(txtZipCode.Text) Then
    Beep
    StatusBar1.Panels("ErrorDescription").Text = _
        "Zip code must be numeric."

    'Set the focus back to the zip code field
    txtZipCode.SetFocus
End If
```

If more than one field contains invalid data, set focus to the field that was entered incorrectly first. For example, suppose a form is to be filled out by a user in this order:

1. Name

2. Phone number

3. City

4. State

5. Zip code

If both the phone number and zip code contain invalid data, focus should be set to the phone number first. This will allow the user to review all input in the appropriate order.

Using the LostFocus Event

The LostFocus event occurs when an object loses focus. Losing focus is a result of a user action, such as tabbing to another field or clicking another object. Furthermore, you can change focus between controls programmatically by using the SetFocus method. It is possible to use the LostFocus event procedure to validate the data in a field. However, this validation technique can result in an infinite loop where one or more controls are using the SetFocus method in the LostFocus event. The following code uses the LostFocus event to validate the data contained in the txtZipCode field.

```
Private Sub txtZipCode_LostFocus()
    If Not IsNumeric(txtZipCode.Text) Then
        'Audio cue
        Beep
        'Visual cue
        StatusBar1.Panels("ErrorDescription").Text = _
            "Zip code must be numeric."
        txtZipCode.SetFocus
    End If
End Sub
```

Lesson Summary

Data validation ensures that every value that the user enters into your application is accurate. Visual Basic provides two data validation methods:

- Form-level validation takes place after a user has filled in all fields on a form.
- Field-level validation takes place as each field on a form is filled in.

When a user types invalid data into fields on your form, you should provide an audio and/or visual notification of the invalid data entry. With either form-level or field-level validation, you should always set focus back to the field that contains invalid data. For example, if a user types an invalid zip code into a TextBox use the SetFocus method to place the cursor in the zip code TextBox to allow the user to make corrections.

Lesson 2: Implementing Form-Level Validation

Form-level validation is the process of validating data in all fields on a form simultaneously. After the user has filled in all fields, you validate data in all fields through a central procedure such as a button or menu Click event. You can also implement a form-level keyboard handler. In this case, form events fire before the control events fire. Form events include KeyPress, KeyDown, and KeyUp. By setting a form's KeyPreview property to True, the control that has focus will have its keyboard event triggered instead of its form event. Form-level validation is used to:

- Establish a form-level keyboard handler.
- Enable and disable controls based on user input.

After this lesson you will be able to:

- Define the use of the KeyPreview property.
- Create a form-level keyboard handler.

Estimated lesson time: 30 minutes

Overview of Form-Level Validation

When you use form-level validation, you verify the data in each field on a form in a single procedure. For example, you might have a customer entry form with fields for name, address, phone number, city, state, and zip code. Each of these fields can be implemented as a TextBox control. The user types values in each field, then clicks a CommandButton. In the CommandButton's Click event, you can include code to validate the data in each field based, for example, on the following rules:

- The name field must be at least one character.
- The address field must be from zero through 50 characters in length.
- The phone number field must be numeric.
- The city field must be greater than zero characters.
- The state field must be two characters in length.
- The zip code field must be numeric and five digits in length.

Implementing code to validate data in this manner is a simple example of form-level validation.

Form-Level Keyboard Handler

A keyboard handler is a more advanced technique of form-level validation. With a centralized keyboard handler, you can manage data input for all fields on a form. For example, if you want all command buttons to remain disabled until the correct values have been entered into each field, you can use keyboard events to validate data in each field. Within these keyboard events, you can write code to perform specific actions when keys are pressed.

When you implement form-level validation using a keyboard handler, you use three main events: KeyPress, KeyUp, and KeyDown.

Using the KeyPress Event

When a user presses a key that has a corresponding ASCII value, the KeyPress event occurs. These keys include any alphabetic and numeric characters (alphanumeric a-z, A-Z, and 0-9). In addition, a few special keyboard characters, such as those produced by the ENTER and BACKSPACE keys, are also recognized by the KeyPress event because they have an ASCII value (ENTER is 13 and BACKSPACE is 8). The KeyPress event does not trap special keyboard characters such as the function keys.

A KeyPress event procedure is useful for intercepting keystrokes entered in a TextBox or ComboBox control. The KeyPress event has a KeyASCII argument that contains the value corresponding to the ASCII value of the key that was pressed. If you want to make sure that the key pressed by the user is a numeric value, for example, you can evaluate the KeyASCII argument in the KeyPress event.

Using the KeyDown and KeyUp Events

Special keys, such as the arrow, function, editing, and navigation keys, do not trigger the KeyPress event because they are not standard ASCII characters. To trigger responses to these keys, use the KeyDown and KeyUp events. You can also use these events to trap combinations of keystrokes, such as CTRL+DEL or SHIFT+CTRL+D.

Using the KeyPreview property

If a form has no visible and enabled controls, it automatically receives all keyboard events. However, if the form has controls, the form's keystroke events will not fire unless the form's KeyPreview property is set to True. The KeyPreview property determines whether the form's keyboard events fire before the controls' keyboard events. For example, assume that there is a KeyDown event procedure for a form and a KeyDown event procedure for a TextBox control on that form. If the KeyPreview property for the form is set to True, the Form_KeyDown event procedure will execute first. The following example sets the KeyPreview to True and uses the KeyDown event to execute a statement when the Function keys are pressed:

```
Private Sub Form_Load ()
    'The form events will be fired before the control events
    KeyPreview = True
End Sub

Private Sub Form_KeyDown (KeyCode As Integer, Shift As Integer)
    Select Case KeyCode ' Indicates the physical key pressed
        Case vbKeyF1
            MsgBox "F1 key was pressed."
            '[statements]
        Case vbKeyF2
            MsgBox "F2 key was pressed."
            '[statements]
        Case vbKeyF3
            MsgBox "F3 key was pressed."
            '[statements]
    End Select
End Sub
```

Enabling and Disabling Controls Based on Input

When you implement form level validation, it is important to provide visual cues to your users to allow them to determine which tasks they need to perform. For example, a form may contain multiple fields, such as first name, last name, address, city, state, and zip code that need to be completely filled in before any further processing can take place. You can do this with a For Each statement in a keyboard event to loop through each control on a form and validate its data.

The following code loops through form controls each time a key is pressed. If the user does not enter the required values, the OK button remains disabled. When the user has typed all required information, you can set the command button's Enabled property to True. This lets the user know that the task is successfully completed. Figure 3.1 illustrates the appearance of the form.

```
Private Sub Form_KeyUp(KeyCode As Integer, Shift As Integer)
    'The KeyUp event is used to also check the Backspace key.
    Dim ctl As Control
    'Loop through the Controls collection and validate each control.
    For Each ctl In Controls
        'Check the type of the current control.
        If TypeOf ctl Is TextBox Then
            'Does the current textbox have the required value?
            If ctl.Text = "" Then
                cmdOK.Enabled = False
                Exit Sub
            End If
        End If
```

```
         Next ctl
         'If all required values are entered,
         'give the user access to the OK button.
         cmdOK.Enabled = True
End Sub
```

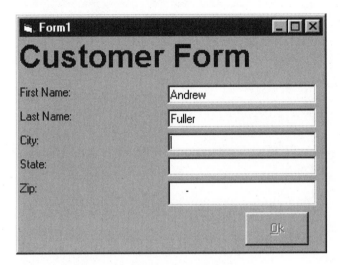

Figure 3.1 Disabling command buttons

Practice: Enabling and Disabling Controls

In this practice you will keep the OK button disabled until all required fields are filled in. Figure 3.2 illustrates the form layout.

➤ **To add control arrays to a form**

1. Open a new **Standard EXE** project.

2. Add three TextBox controls and one CommandButton control to **Form1**.

3. Set the properties for the CommandButton control as specified in the following table:

Control	Property	Value
Command1	Name	**cmdOk**
CmdOK	Caption	**&Ok**

4. Leave the default properties for the TextBox controls. Figure 3.2 illustrates the appearance of the form.

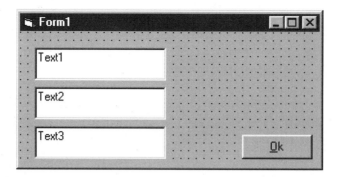

Figure 3.2 Practice form layout

➤ **To add code to the cmdOk_Click event**

1. Add the following code to the **cmdClick_Click** event.

```
Private Sub cmdOk_Click()
    Dim ctl As Control
    For Each ctl In Controls
        If TypeOf ctl Is TextBox Then
            If ctl.Text = "" Then
                Msgbox "All fields require data."
                Exit Sub
            End If
        End If
    Next ctl
    Unload Me
End Sub
```

2. Run your application. Leave at least one of the textboxes blank. Click the **OK** button.

   The form will not unload until all of the textboxes have data entered.

3. Save your project in the \Practice\Ch03 directory.

   Save the project files using the default names provided by Visual Basic.

Lesson Summary

Form-level validation is used to:

- Establish a form-level keyboard handler.
- Enable and disable controls based on user input.

Form-level validation lets you manage data input on a form. You can monitor these control values by:

- Enabling a command button to loop through the Controls collection and validate each control after all fields have valid data.
- Validating all the fields when the user tries to execute a command, such as an OK button's Click event.

Lesson 3: Implementing Field-Level Validation

You may want to validate data as it is entered into each field. Field-level validation provides immediate direction to the user and gives the developer control over user actions. In this lesson, you will learn how to validate data using field-level validation.

After this lesson you will be able to:

- Validate data with control properties.
- Establish a field-level keyboard handler using control events.
- Describe different functions you can use to validate information.
- Implement the MaskedEdit control.

Estimated lesson time: 45 minutes

Using the Textbox Control Properties

The TextBox control contains several design-time properties that restrict the type of values users can enter. Some of these properties, which are illustrated in Figure 3.3, include the following:

- MaxLength
- PasswordChar
- Locked

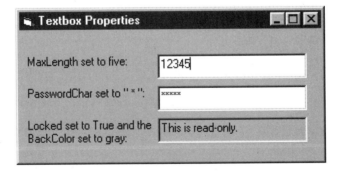

Figure 3.3 Textbox properties

Setting the MaxLength Property

You use the MaxLength property to set a maximum number of characters that the user can enter into a text box. The system beeps when the user tries to type more characters than specified in the MaxLength property.

Using the PasswordChar Property

The PasswordChar property lets you hide (or mask) characters that are entered into a text box. For example, if you set the PasswordChar property to an asterisk (*), the user will see only asterisk characters in the textbox. This technique is often used to hide passwords in logon dialog boxes.

Although any character can be used, most Windows-based applications use the asterisk (*) character. The PasswordChar property does not affect the Text property; the Text property contains exactly what the user types or what was set.

Setting the Locked Property

The Locked property setting determines whether a user can edit the text in a text box. If the Locked property is set to True, the user can view the text in the text box but cannot edit the text. The Locked property lets you set the text box as read-only for the user; you retain the capability to change the Text property programmatically.

Using Events for Field-Level Validation

Field-level keyboard events let you immediately test keystrokes. You can also check for validity and for the format of the characters as they are entered. Field-level events are specific to the control in which they occurred. The events used to perform validation at the field-level are KeyPress, KeyDown, and KeyUp. Controls such as a TextBox have additional events—for example, the Change event—that you can use to validate user input.

Formatting and Validating Characters

The KeyPress event recognizes uppercase and lowercase characters as different characters. For example, if the user types "A", the KeyAscii value passed to the event is 65, but if the user types "a", the KeyAscii value passed to the event is 97. You can also use the KeyPress event to convert these characters as they are entered into the control. The following example uses the KeyPress event to convert all of the characters entered into the text box to uppercase characters:

```
Sub txtSubdivision_KeyPress(KeyAscii As Integer)
    'Use the Chr function to return the character
    'associated with the specified character code
    'After the character is converted to upper case,
    'convert the uppercase character back into an ASCII value
    KeyAscii = Asc(UCase(Chr(KeyAscii)))
End Sub
```

The KeyUp and KeyDown events recognize the actual state of the keyboard. For example, when the user presses a key, the KeyDown event fires. When the user releases that key, the KeyUp event fires. You can also use these events to determine if any special keys (CTRL, ALT, SHIFT, etc.) were used. This allows you to track key combinations such as CTRL+C.

You can use the KeyCode argument to determine which special key was pressed to fire the KeyDown event. The Shift argument indicates whether SHIFT, CTRL, or ALT was pressed. Only by examining this argument can you determine whether an uppercase or a lowercase letter was typed in the KeyDown event. The following code shows how to use the Shift argument to determine whether special keys were used in the KeyDown event:

```
Private Sub Text1_KeyDown(KeyCode As Integer, Shift As Integer)
    Select Case Shift 'Key
        Case 1
            Print "You pressed the SHIFT key."
        Case 2
            Print "You pressed the CTRL key."
        Case 3
            Print "You pressed both SHIFT and CTRL."
        Case 4
            Print "You pressed the ALT key."
        Case 5
            Print "You pressed both SHIFT and ALT."
        Case 6
            Print "You pressed both CTRL and ALT."
        Case 7
            Print "You pressed SHIFT, CTRL, and ALT."
    End Select
End Sub
```

The following code checks both the KeyCode and the Shift arguments to determine whether a capital letter "A" was pressed:

```
Private Sub Text1_KeyDown(KeyCode As Integer, _
    Shift As Integer)
    If KeyCode = 65 And Shift = 1 Then 'or vbKeyA and vbShiftMask
        Print "The user pressed the capital 'A'."
    End If
End Sub
```

Validating Data in the Change Event

Several controls use the Change event, although how and when this event occurs varies with each control. The TextBox control fires the Change event each time the user enters a character into the text box. Figure 3.4 illustrates a form that disables an OK button until all values have been entered. The code that follows the figure shows the procedure EnableOK, which is called from each TextBox's Change event when data is entered.

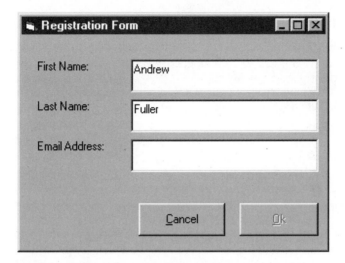

Figure 3.4 Using the TextBox Change event

```
Private Sub EnableOk()
    'Check the value of each control. If all have values,
    'enable the OK button
    If txtFirst.Text <> "" And txtLast.Text <> "" _
        And txtEmail.Text <> "" Then
        cmdOk.Enabled = True
    Else
        cmdOk.Enabled = False
    End If
End Sub

Private Sub txtEmail_Change()
    'Call the EnableOk procedure each time a character is typed
    Call EnableOk
End Sub

Private Sub txtFirst_Change()
    'Call the EnableOk procedure each time a character is typed
    Call EnableOk
End Sub

Private Sub txtLast_Change()
    'Call the EnableOk procedure each time a character is typed
    Call EnableOk
End Sub
```

Validation Functions

Visual Basic includes several functions that assist in the validation process. These functions are used to verify that correct types data are received. The most frequently used functions are:

- IsNumeric
- IsDate

The IsNumeric function returns a value of True if the argument is numeric: if the argument is not numeric, False is returned. The IsDate function returns a value of True if the argument is a valid date; if the argument is not a valid date, False is returned. These functions can also be used with the InputBox function.

The InputBox function displays a standard dialog box that prompts the user to enter a string value. The user can type an alphanumeric value into a text box and click OK or Cancel. When the user clicks OK or presses ENTER, the InputBox function returns a string value equal to the contents of the TextBox control within the InputBox dialog box. If the user clicks Cancel, the InputBox function returns an empty string ("").

The InputBox does not validate the type of data entered into the InputBox. Use the IsNumeric and IsDate functions for this task. In the following code, a value is received from the user and evaluated using the IsNumeric and IsDate functions:

```
Private Sub cmdValueInput_Click()
    Dim strValue As String
    strValue = InputBox("Enter the value.")
    If IsDate(strValue) Then
        Print "The value is a valid date."
    ElseIf IsNumeric(strValue) Then
        Print "The value is a valid number."
    Else
        Print "Not a correct value."
    End If
End Sub
```

Using the Masked Edit Control

The Masked Edit control is another method for restricting data input. This control supplies visual cues about the type of data being entered or displayed. When you create a Masked Edit control, you use special characters to require entry of only certain types of data, such as a number or character. For example, the area code for a phone number could be required when other data, such as a telephone extension, is optional. Figure 3.5 illustrates the appearance of a Masked Edit control.

Figure 3.5 MaskEdit control

Note The Masked Edit control can be added to Toolbox by selecting Microsoft Masked Edit Control 6.0 from the Components dialog box.

The Masked Edit control has several properties that assist in the validation of user input. Some of the frequently used properties are:

- Mask
- Format
- Text and ClipText
- AutoTab

Mask Property

To define the Masked Edit control, use the Mask property. The Mask property forces data to be entered into a predefined template. You can set this property at design time or at run time. Although you can use standard formats at design time, and the control will distinguish between numeric and alphabetic characters, you may want to write code to validate content such as the correct month or time of day. Each character position in the Masked Edit control corresponds to either a placeholder of a specified type or to a literal character.

The following code shows how to use the Mask property of the Masked Edit control to create an input mask for entering a United States telephone number, complete with placeholders for area code and local number:

```
mskPhone.Mask = "(###)###-####"
```

Figure 3.6 illustrates the appearance of the resulting mask.

```
(425)555-12__
```

Figure 3.6 MaskEdit control's Mask property

When the Mask property is an empty string (""), the control behaves like a standard TextBox control. When you define an input mask, underscores appear beneath every placeholder in the mask. You can replace a placeholder only with a character that is of the same type as the one specified in the input mask.

To clear the Text property when you have a mask defined, set the Text property to the default mask setting. For example:

```
mskPhoneNumber.Text = "(___)___-____"
```

Format Property

Use the Format property to define the format for displaying and printing the contents of a control, such as numbers, dates, times, and text. You use the same format expressions as defined by the Visual Basic Format function, except that you cannot use named formats such as "Currency".

Text and ClipText

The Text property returns the data that the user has typed, along with the mask. The ClipText property returns only the data the user has typed. This is particularly important when implementing a Masked Edit control with a database. Figure 3.7 illustrates the text entered into the Masked Edit control, and the code that follows shows the use of these properties.

```
(425)555-1212
```

Figure 3.7 The Text and ClipText properties

```
'The user entered 4255551212
Print "The user entered " & mskPhoneNumber.ClipText
'The control shows (425)555-1212
Print "The control shows " & mskPhoneNumber.Text
```

The ClipText property of the MaskEdit control shown in Figure 3.7 returns a value of 4255551212, and the Text property returns (425)555-1212.

AutoTab

When the AutoTab property is set to True, and the user enters the maximum number of characters specified by the Mask property for the control, the insertion point automatically moves to the control with the next TabIndex.

The Validate Event

Visual Basic 6.0 includes a Validate event for controls, which occurs before a control loses focus. This event occurs only when the CausesValidation property of the control that is about to receive the focus is set to True. Use both the Validate event and CausesValidation property for a control to evaluate input before allowing the user to move focus away from that control. The Validate event also includes a Cancel argument, which will cause the control to retain focus when set to True.

Using the Validate Event

The simplest way to validate data is to use the Validate event. The Validate event also provides you with control over when focus can be moved to other controls. In previous versions of Visual Basic, you had to use the LostFocus event to Validate data, and then use the SetFocus method to keep focus on the control being validated. Because the LostFocus event occurs after the focus has moved away from the control, it can potentially force your program into an infinite loop. By using the Validate event, you can prevent the focus from ever shifting to another control until all validation rules have been met. Possible uses for the Validate event include:

- A data entry application needs to perform more sophisticated validation than can be provided by the Masked Edit control.

- A form needs to prevent users from moving off a control, by pressing the TAB key or an accelerator key, until data has been entered in a field.

Setting the CausesValidation Property

The CausesValidation property works in tandem with the Validate event to limit when a control can lose focus. You can set the CausesValidation property to determine whether the Validate event will occur on a second control from which the focus is being shifted. If validation code is contained in the Validate event for a TextBox, and the user clicks on a CommandButton that has its CausesValidation property set to True, the Validate event for the text box will fire. However, if the CausesValidation property for the CommandButton is set to False, the Validate event will not fire. By default, the CausesValidation property is set to True for all controls.

➤ **To use the Validate event of a TextBox**

1. Add a TextBox to a form.

2. In the Code window, click the Validate event from the procedure list, as illustrated in Figure 3.8.

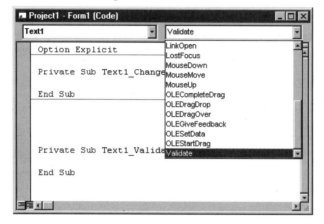

Figure 3.8 Selecting Validate from the procedure list

3. Type a validation code in the Validate event for the TextBox.

4. Set the CausesValidation property to **False** for any controls for which you do not want the Validate event to fire.

Practice: Using the Validate Event With the CausesValidation Property

In this practice, you will create a customer information entry form and use the Validate event to validate fields on the form. You will also use set the CausesValidation property of a Help button to avoid running any validation code when this command button is clicked.

To see a demonstration, run the Chap03.exe animation located in the Animations folder on the Supplemental Course Materials CD-ROM that accompanies this book.

➤ **To create a data entry form**

1. Start Visual Basic.

2. From the **New Project** dialog box, select **Standard EXE,** then click **OPEN**.

3. Add five TextBox controls, five Label controls, and two CommandButton controls to the form.

4. Arrange the controls on the form as illustrated in Figure 3.9.

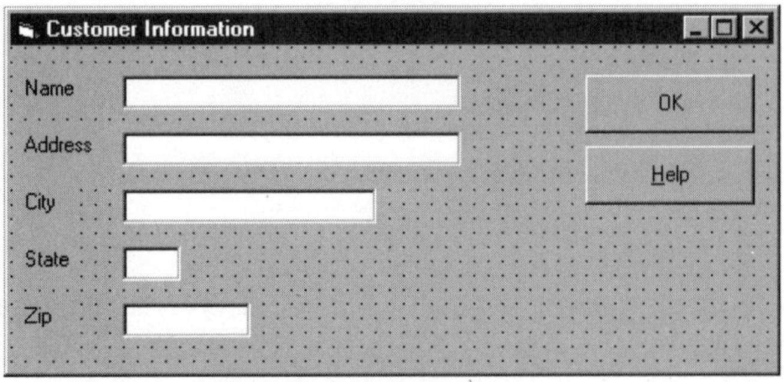

Figure 3.9 The Customer Information form

5. Change the default names of each TextBox to more meaningful names:
   txtName, txtAddress, txtCity, txtState, txtZipCode, cmdOK, and
   cmdHelp.

6. In the Validate event for **txtName**, type the following code:

```
If Len(txtName.Text) < 1 Then
    MsgBox "You must type a name."
    Cancel = True
End If
```

7. In the Validate event of txtAddress, type the following code:

```
If Len(txtAddress.Text) < 1 Then
    MsgBox "You must type an address."
    Cancel = True
End If
```

8. In the Validate event of txtCity, type the following code

```
If Len(txtCity.Text) < 1 Then
    MsgBox "You must type a city."
    Cancel = True
End If
```

9. In the Validate event of **txtState**, type the following code:

```
If Len(txtState.Text) <> 2 Then
    MsgBox "State must be two characters."
    Cancel = True
End If
```

10. In the Validate event of **txtZipCode**, type the following code:

```
If Not IsNumeric(txtZipCode.Text) Then
    MsgBox "Zip code must be numeric"
    Cancel = True
ElseIf Len(txtZipCode.Text) <> 5 Then
    MsgBox "zip code must be 5 digits."
    Cancel = True
End If
```

11. In the **Properties** window, set the CausesValidation property of the **cmdOK** control to **False**.

12. From the **Project** menu, click **Add Form**.

13. Select **About Dialog**, then click **Open**.

    A new pre-made form is added to your project.

14. In the Click event of **cmdHelp**, type the following code:

```
frmAbout.Show vbModal
```

15. From the **Run** menu, click **Start**.

16. Focus will be set to **txtName**, so press the **TAB** key to try to move to the address field.

    Notice that you receive a message box as you coded in the Validate event for **txtName**.

17. Click **OK** to close the message box.

18. Click the **Help** command button on the form.

    Notice that **frmAbout** is now loaded and visible because the Validate event did not fire for **txtName**. This is because you set the CausesValidation property of **cmdHelp** to **False**.

19. From the **Run** menu, click **End**.

20. Save your project as Validate.vbp, and save Form1 as frmMain.frm.

Lesson Summary

Field-level validation provides immediate direction to the user and gives the developer more control over user actions.

The TextBox control contains several design-time properties that restrict the type of values users can enter. Some of these properties are:

- MaxLength
- PasswordChar
- Locked

Field-level keyboard events let you immediately test keystrokes. Field-level events are specific to the control in which they occur. The field-level events include:

- KeyPress
- KeyDown
- KeyUp

Visual Basic includes several functions that assist in the validation process. You use these functions to verify that the correct types of data are received. Commonly used functions are:

- IsNumeric
- IsDate

Another method you can use to restrict data input is the Masked Edit control. This control supplies visual cues about the type of data entered or displayed. The MaskEdit control provides several methods, properties, and events that are useful tools for validating user input.

Visual Basic 6.0 includes a Validate event for controls, which occurs before a control loses focus. This event occurs only when the CausesValidation property of the control that is about to receive the focus is set to True. You use both the Validate event and CausesValidation property for a control to evaluate input before allowing the user to move focus away from that control. Possible uses for the Validate event include:

- A data entry application needs to perform more sophisticated data entry validation than can be provided by the MaskedEdit control.
- A form needs to prevent users from moving off a control by pressing the TAB key or an accelerator key until data has been entered in a field.

Summary

Overview of Validation

Data validation ensures the accuracy of data that the user enters in an application.

Visual Basic provides two data validation methods:

- Form-level validation takes place after all fields on a form have been filled in.
- Field-level validation takes place as each field on a form is filled in.

In designing data validation:

- Provide an audio and/or visual notification of invalid data entry.
- Set focus back to the field that contains invalid data.

Implementing Form-Level Validation

Use form-level validation to:

- Establish a form-level keyboard handler.
- Enable and disable controls based on user input.

Form-level validation lets you to manage data input on a form. Monitor these control values by:

- Enabling a command button to loop through the Controls collection and validate each control when all fields have valid data.
- Validating all the fields when the user tries to execute a command such as an OK button's Click event.

Implementing Field-Level Validation

Field-level validation provides immediate direction to the user and gives the developer more control over user actions.

A TextBox control contains several design-time properties that restrict the type of values users can enter. Some of these properties are:

- MaxLength
- PasswordChar
- Locked

Field-level keyboard events let you immediately test keystrokes. These events are specific to the control in which they occur. The field-level events include:

- KeyPress
- KeyDown
- KeyUp

Visual Basic includes several functions that assist in the validation process. You use them to verify that the correct types of data are received. Commonly used functions are:

- IsNumeric
- IsDate

The Masked Edit control also restricts data input and supplies visual cues about the type of data entered or displayed. It provides several methods, properties, and events that are useful for validating user input.

Controls in Visual Basic 6.0 have a Validate event. It occurs before a control loses focus, but only when the CausesValidation property of the control that is about to receive the focus is set to True. Use the Validate event and CausesValidation property together to evaluate input before allowing the user to move focus away from that control. Examples of the Validate event include:

- A data entry application must perform more sophisticated data entry validation than can be provided by the MaskedEdit control.
- A form must prevent users from moving off a control, by pressing the TAB key or an accelerator key, until data has been entered in a field.

Lab: Adding Field and Form Level Validation

In this lab, you will add form and field level validation to the Chateau St. Mark hotel reservation system. You will modify control properties and add code to control events to validate data entered into the form. In subsequent labs, you will continue to add to the application and explore each of the tasks you try here in more detail. You can continue to work with the files you created in Lab 2, or use the files provided in the \Labs\Lab03\Partial folder. The solution code is in the \Labs\Lab03\Solution folder.

To see a demonstration of the solution, run the Lab03.exe animation located in the Animations folder on the Supplemental Course Materials CD-ROM that accompanies this book.

Estimated lesson time: 45 minutes

Exercise 1: Controlling User Navigation

In this exercise, you will create two procedures that control user navigation by enabling and disabling the form's controls. These procedures will be called from form and control events.

➤ **To open the hotel reservation application project**

- Open either the reservation application project that you have been working on or the reservation application project located in the \Labs\Lab03\Partial folder.

➤ **To create sub procedures that enable and disable controls**

1. Open **frmReservation's** code module. On the Visual Basic **Tools** menu, click **Add Procedure....**

2. Using the **Add Procedure** dialog box, create two private Sub procedures named **DisableControls** and **EnableControls**.

   The following two procedures are displayed in the form's module:

   ```
   Private Sub DisableControls()

   End Sub

   Private Sub EnableControls()

   End Sub
   ```

3. The **DisableControls** procedures code will loop through the controls collection using the For Each... statement. It will disable all but the Menu and Label controls, and set the MaskEdBox and the Textbox controls' **BackColor** property to **grey**. Add the following code to the **DisableControls** procedure:

```
Private Sub DisableControls()
    Dim ctl As Control
    For Each ctl In Controls
        'Leave Labels and Menus enabled
        If TypeOf ctl Is Menu Or TypeOf ctl Is Label Then
            ctl.Enabled = True
        Else
            ctl.Enabled = False
        End If
        If TypeOf ctl Is TextBox Or _
            TypeOf ctl Is MaskEdBox Then _
            ctl.BackColor = "&H8000000F" 'Set the back color to grey
    Next ctl
End Sub
```

4. At the end of the **DisableControls** procedure, add code that will also disable the **Check-In**, **Check-Out** and the **Cancel Reservation** menu items. The finished code should look like the following:

```
Private Sub DisableControls()
    Dim ctl As Control 'holds the active control object
    For Each ctl In Controls
        If TypeOf ctl Is Menu Or TypeOf ctl Is Label Then
            'Leave Labels and Menus enabled
            ctl.Enabled = True
        Else
            ctl.Enabled = False
        End If
        If TypeOf ctl Is TextBox Or _
            TypeOf ctl Is MaskEdBox Then _
            ctl.BackColor = "&H8000000F" 'Set the back color to grey
    Next ctl

    'Disable the menu items
    mnuGuestReservationCheckIn.Enabled = False
    mnuGuestReservationCheckout.Enabled = False
    mnuGuestReservationCancel.Enabled = False
End Sub
```

5. The **EnableControls** procedure will enable all of the controls, including the menu items, and returns the TextBox and MaskEdBox controls' **BackColor** to **white**. The finished code should look like the following:

```
Private Sub EnableControls()
    Dim ctl As Control
    For Each ctl In Controls
        ctl.Enabled = True
        If TypeOf ctl Is TextBox Or TypeOf ctl Is MaskEdBox _
            Then ctl.BackColor = "&H80000005"
    Next ctl
    mnuGuestReservationCheckIn.Enabled = True
    mnuGuestReservationCheckout.Enabled = True
    mnuGuestReservationCancel.Enabled = True
End Sub
```

➤ **To call the DisableControls and EnableControls procedures**

1. Call the **DisableControls** procedure from the **Form_Load** event and the **cmdDone_Click** event.

2. From the **mnuGuestReservationAdd_Click** event, call the **EnableControls** procedure and set the focus to the **txtFirstName** TextBox control. The finished code should look like the following:

```
Private Sub mnuGuestReservationAdd_Click()
    EnableControls
    txtFirstName.SetFocus
End Sub
```

3. Save and test the application.

Exercise 2: Field-Level Validation

In this exercise, you will use the IsNumeric function and the KeyPress event to validate user input on the reservation form.

➤ **Validating data entry on the reservation form**

1. In the KeyPress event for the **First Name**, **Last Name** and **Address** text boxes, add code that converts the text to uppercase. For example:

```
Private Sub txtFirstName_KeyPress(KeyAscii As Integer)
    KeyAscii = Asc(UCase(Chr(KeyAscii)))
End Sub
```

2. Use the KeyPress event of the **Phone Number** text box to accept only numbers, parenthesis ( ), hyphens (-) and the Backspace characters. If incorrect values are entered, beep and then display a message to the **addinfo** panel of the StatusBar control. The finished code should look like the following:

```
Private Sub txtPhone_KeyPress(KeyAscii As Integer)
    'exit sub for allowable characters
    If Chr(KeyAscii) = vbBack _
        Or Chr(KeyAscii) = "-" _
        Or Chr(KeyAscii) = "(" _
        Or Chr(KeyAscii) = ")" Then Exit Sub
    'check for alpha characters
    If Not.IsNumeric(Chr(KeyAscii)) Then
        Beep
        KeyAscii = 0
        staAdditionalInfo.Panels("addinfo").Text = _
            "Phone number must be numeric."
    End If
End Sub
```

3. On the **txtNumPeople** and **txtNumDays** text boxes, set the MaxLength property to **3**.

   The MaxLength property specifies the maximum number of characters that can be entered. This value limits the users to a three digit number.

4. Using the KeyPress events of the **txtNumPeople**, **txtNumDays**, and **txtRate** text boxes, verify that a numeric value is typed. Be sure to allow the user to press the Backspace key. This example shows the completed **txtNumPeople_KeyPress** event.

```
Private Sub txtNumPeople_KeyPress(KeyAscii As Integer)
    'Allow for the use of the Backspace character
    If Chr(KeyAscii) = vbBack Then Exit Sub
    If Not IsNumeric(Chr(KeyAscii)) Then
        Beep
        KeyAscii = 0 ' Cancel the keystroke
        staAdditionalInfo.Panels("addinfo").Text = _
            "Values must be numeric."
    End If
End Sub
```

   Add similar code to the **txtNumDays_KeyPress** and **txtRate_KeyPress** events.

5. Save and test the application.

Exercise 3: Using the Validate and LostFocus Events

In this exercise, you will use the Validate and LostFocus events to validate the data entered into the reservation form.

➤ **To use the Validate and LostFocus events**

1. In the **mskCheckIn_Validate** event, add code to verify that a valid date has been entered into the control. For example:

```
Private Sub mskCheckIn_Validate(Cancel As Boolean)
    If Not IsDate(mskCheckIn.Text) Then
        staAdditionalInfo.Panels("addinfo").Text = _
            "Not a valid date format (ex. '07-23-2000')"
        Cancel = True
    End If
End Sub
```

2. In the **txtNumDays_LostFocus** event, add the following code to calculate and format the guest's check-out date:

```
Private Sub txtNumDays_LostFocus()
    If mskCheckIn.ClipText <> "" And txtNumDays.Text <> "" Then
        txtCheckOut.Text = Format(DateAdd("d", _
            Val(txtNumDays.Text), mskCheckIn.Text), "mm-dd-yyyy")
    End If
End Sub
```

3. Set the Locked property of the **Check-out date** text box to **True**.

4. Save and test the application.

Exercise 4: Form-Level Validation

In this exercise, you will check that the required values were entered into the form before letting the user continue.

➤ **To implement form level checking**

1. Add code to the **Done** button so that it loops through all of the controls and displays a message box if the required fields do not have values. The following is the completed code for the **cmdDone_Click** event:

```
Private Sub cmdDone_Click()
    Dim ctl As Control

    For Each ctl In Controls
        If TypeOf ctl Is TextBox Then
            If ctl.Text = "" Then
                MsgBox "All fields must be entered."
                Exit Sub
            End If
        ElseIf TypeOf ctl Is MaskEdBox Then
            If ctl.ClipText = "" Then
                MsgBox "All fields must be entered."
                Exit Sub
            End If
        ElseIf TypeOf ctl Is OptionButton Then
            If ctl.Value = "" Then
                MsgBox "Payment type is required."
                Exit Sub
            End If
        End If
    Next ctl
    DisableControls
End Sub
```

2. Save and test your application.

Review

The following questions are intended to reinforce key information presented in this chapter. If you are unable to answer a question, review the appropriate lesson and then try the question again. Answers to the questions can be found in the Appendix, "Questions and Answers," located at the back of this book.

1. What are the two main types of validation?

2. Why should you use the Validate event to validate data rather than using the LostFocus event?

3. There are two textboxes on a form, and the user types the letter "a" into one of the textboxes. If the form's KeyPreview property is set to True, will the TextBox control's KeyPress event fire?

4. What is the difference between the Text and ClipText properties of the Masked-Edit Control?

C H A P T E R   4

Using the Debugging Tools

About This Chapter

This chapter discusses the tools that help you find and resolve errors in your Visual Basic application. It begins with an explanation of the various ways to check your code to locate problems and then describes how you can test your application.

Before You Begin

To complete the lessons in this chapter, there are no prerequisites.

Lesson 1: Debugging Your Application

Because programs today are large and complex, a certain number of errors are inevitable. Even very careful programmers have errors once in a while. Program errors are referred to as bugs, and finding and removing these bugs is called debugging. In this lesson we discuss the kinds of errors that your program can have and ways to step through the lines of code to discover where these errors occur.

After this lesson you will be able to:

- Describe the types of errors that can occur in a Visual Basic application.
- Explain the three modes in which you work while developing a Visual Basic application.
- Explain the use of these tools from the **Debug** menu and toolbar:
  - Step Into
  - Step Over
  - Step Out
  - Set Next Statement
  - Show Next Statement

Estimated lesson time: 30 minutes

Types of Errors

In a Visual Basic program, three different types of errors can occur: syntax errors, run-time errors, and logic errors. When you encounter a syntax error or a run-time error, you can use the Visual Basic online Help resource to aid you in determining the cause. When a run-time error dialog box appears, you can click the button to bring up online Help. With a syntax error, simply place the insertion point on the statement, or keyword, that you need help with and press F1. Finding and fixing logic errors, however, can be much more complicated.

Syntax Errors

A syntax error occurs in code when a statement is constructed incorrectly. Examples of syntax errors include an incorrectly typed keyword, omission of required punctuation, or an incorrect construct (such as an If keyword on a line without a conditional operator).

The following example shows a syntax error in an If...Then statement:

```
Dim intCount As Integer
If intCount = 0 MsgBox "Bad number"
```

If is a valid word in the Visual Basic language, but without a then, it doesn't meet the syntax requirements.

Visual Basic includes an Auto Syntax Check option that can detect syntax errors as you type in a statement. With this option enabled, Visual Basic interprets your code as you enter it. When an expected part of the syntax is not found, Visual Basic highlights the incorrect statement and displays a message box explaining the error.

➤ **To set or clear the Auto Syntax Check option**

1. On the **Tools** menu, click **Options**.

2. On the **Options** dialog box, click the **Editor** tab.

3. Click **Auto Syntax Check**.

If you have selected the Auto Syntax Check option when you have a syntax error, Visual Basic displays an error message as soon as you move to a new line in the Code window, as shown in Figure 4.1.

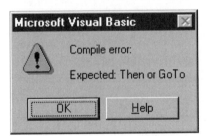

Figure 4.1 Compile error message box

Run-Time Errors

Another type of error is the run-time error. Run-time errors occur while the application is running and are detected by Visual Basic when the statement attempts an operation that is impossible to carry out. Run-time errors are especially important to plan for since they can be detected by the user.

An example of this is division by zero:

```
Dim sngYearlyWage As Single
Dim sngHourlyWage As Single
Dim sngHours As Single
sngYearlyWage = 55000
sngHours = 0
sngHourlyWage = sngYearlyWage / sngHours
```

The variable sngHours contains zero, making the division an invalid operation, even though the statement itself is syntactically correct. The application must run before it can detect this error.

You can include code in your application to trap and handle run-time errors when they occur. Chapter 5 discusses the methods available for trapping these types of errors.

Logic Errors

The third type of error is the logic error. Logic errors occur when your code does not perform the way that you intended. These errors can be especially difficult to find because an application can run without performing any invalid operations and still produce incorrect results. The way to verify that your application does not have logic errors is to run test data through the program and analyze the results. Logic errors, like run-time errors, can occur when the user is interacting with the application.

The Debug Menu (Toolbar)

Visual Basic has primarily three modes that you work in when developing an application: design mode, run mode, and break mode.

- Design mode lets you customize forms and write code. The program has not been compiled yet and is not running.
- Run mode lets you check the execution of your program's code, but no statements can be changed in this mode.
- Break mode halts the application, and gives you an opportunity to check the condition of your program at that moment. However, the program has not terminated. It is only suspended, allowing you to look around at the current "frozen" state of the application. Break mode is critical when debugging an application.

Using Break Mode

To aid you in identifying logical errors, Visual Basic allows you to execute your code one statement at a time. You can also view the value of one or more variables or control properties. To do this you must first enter into break mode to get to your code window.

Visual Basic switches to break mode under the following circumstances:

- You choose one of the Step options from the Debug menu or toolbar.
- Execution reaches a line that contains a breakpoint. You set a breakpoint by selecting the line where the break should occur and clicking the Toggle Breakpoint button.

- Execution reaches a Stop statement.
- A break expression defined in the Add Watch dialog box changes or becomes true.
- An untrapped run-time error occurs.

Once your program is placed in break mode, you can use the debugging tools to step through your code either one statement at a time or in blocks of code. The following table lists features of the Debug menu and toolbar:

Feature	Action	Shortcut key	Description
	Start	F5	Runs the application from the startup form (or Sub Main) specified on the General tab of the Project Properties dialog box. If in break mode, the Start button changes to Continue.
	Break	CTRL+BREAK	Stops execution of a program temporarily. Click the Continue button to resume running the program.
	End		Stops running the program and returns to design mode.
	Toggle Breakpoint	F9	Creates or removes a breakpoint. A breakpoint is a place in the code where Visual Basic automatically halts execution and enters break mode.
	Step Into	F8	Runs the next executable line of code, stopping at the next executable line of code that follows. If the next executable line of code calls another procedure, Step Into stops at the beginning of that procedure.
	Step Over	SHIFT+F8	Runs the next executable line of code, stopping at the next executable line of code that follows. If the next executable line of code calls another procedure, the procedure runs completely before stopping at the next executable line of code in the first procedure.

(continued)

Feature	Action	Shortcut key	Description
	Step Out	CTRL+SHIFT+F8	Executes the remainder of the current procedure and breaks at the next executable line of code in the calling procedure.
	Locals Window		Displays the Locals window.
	Immediate Window	CTRL+G	Displays the Immediate window.
	Watch Window		Displays the Watches window.
	Quick Watch	SHIFT+F9	Displays the Quick Watch dialog box with the current value of the selected expression.
	Call Stack	CTRL+L	Displays the Calls dialog box, which lists the currently active procedure calls—procedures in the application that have started but are not completed.
(Menu Item)	**Run to Cursor**	CTRL+F8	When your application is in break mode, use Run To Cursor to select a statement further down in your code where you want execution to stop. Your application will run from the current statement to the selected statement.
(Menu Item)	**Edit Watch**	CTRL+W	Displays the Edit Watch dialog box in which you can edit or delete a watch expression.
(Menu Item)	**Set Next Statement**	CTRL+F9	Sets the execution point to the line of code you choose (in the current procedure).
(Menu Item)	**Show Next Statement**		Highlights the next statement to be executed.

Using Step Into

You can use Step Into to execute code in your application one statement at a time. When you use Step Into to step through your code, Visual Basic temporarily switches to run time, executes the current statement, and advances to the next statement. Then it switches back to break mode. After you have stepped through a statement, you can see its effect by looking at your application's forms or the debugging windows.

➤ **To use Step Into**

- ■ Select one of the following methods:
  - On the **Debug** menu, click **Step Into**.
  - On the **Debug** toolbar, click **Step Into**.
  - Press **F8**.

Using Step Over

Step Over functions the same as Step Into except when the statement contains a call to another procedure. Step Into steps to the beginning of the called procedure, whereas Step Over executes the called procedure as a unit and then steps to the next statement in the present procedure. Use Step Over if you want to stay at the same level of code and don't need to analyze the called procedure.

Suppose, for example, that you are stepping through the statements in a procedure named PrintInvoice, and PrintInvoice contains a procedure call to GetPrinterList.

If you use Step Over, the Code window continues to display the PrintInvoice procedure. The code in the GetPrinterList procedure is executed, and the application is placed back in break mode on the statement immediately after the call to GetPrinterList.

➤ **To use Step Over**

- ■ Select one of the following methods:
  - On the **Debug** menu, click **Step Over.**
  - On the **Debug** toolbar, click **Step Over**.
  - Press **SHIFT+F8**.

Using Step Out

Step Out advances past the remainder of the code in the current procedure. If the procedure was called from another procedure, execution advances to the statement immediately following the statement that called the procedure.

➤ **To use Step Out**

- ■ Select one of the following methods:
  - On the **Debug** menu, click **Step Out**.
  - On the **Debug** toolbar, click **Step Out**.
  - Press **CTRL+SHIFT+F8**.

Using Run to Cursor

While your application is in break mode, you can place the insertion point on a statement further down in your code. Then use Run To Cursor to execute the statements preceding your cursor. This lets you "step over" uninteresting sections of code, such as large loops.

➤ **To use Run To Cursor**

1. Put your application in break mode.

2. Place the cursor where you want to stop.

3. Press **CTRL+F8**, or, on the **Debug** menu, click **Run To Cursor**.

Using Set Next Statement

While debugging your application, you can use Set Next Statement to skip over a section of your code. Unlike the way the Run To Cursor command handles code, the Set Next Statement command does not execute the code between the present break point and your cursor. With the Set Next Statement command, you can set a different line of code to execute next, provided it falls within the same procedure. This is helpful, for instance, when a section in your code contains a known bug. You can jump over that section of code and continue tracing other problems. Also, you may want to return to an earlier statement to test part of the application using different values for properties or variables.

➤ **To use Set Next Statement**

1. Put your application in break mode.

2. Place the cursor on the line of code that you want to execute next.

3. On the **Debug** menu, click **Set Next Statement**.

Using Show Next Statement

The Show Next Statement command is used to place the cursor on the line of code that will be executed next. This feature is convenient if you've been executing code in an error handler and aren't sure where execution will resume.

➤ **To use Show Next Statement**

1. Put your application in break mode.

2. On the **Debug** menu, click **Show Next Statement**.

Lesson Summary

Three types of errors may occur in a Visual Basic program:

- Syntax errors, which are due to incorrectly constructed statements.
- Run-time errors, which occur when a statement attempts an operation that is impossible to carry out. The user of your application can detect these errors.
- Logic errors, which occur when the code does not perform as you intended. The application will run, but will produce incorrect results.

While developing an application, you work in design mode, run mode, or break mode. Break mode halts the application so you can check your program at a particular moment; it is therefore critical in the debugging process.

There are several tools you can use to debug your application. They are accessed from the Debug menu or toolbar, or by a shortcut key. The most useful tools are:

- Step Into
- Step Over
- Step Out
- Set Next Statement
- Show Next Statement

Lesson 2: Testing Your Application

Visual Basic provides several tools to help diagnose problems. These tools help you examine your application's flow, as well as the variable and property changes.

After this lesson you will be able to:

- Explain the use of the Immediate window.
- Explain the Debug object and how you use its two methods.
- Explain the use of the Locals window.
- Explain how to use Watch expressions.

Estimated lesson time: 30 minutes

The Immediate Window

When you are debugging your application, there may be times when you want to evaluate expressions, change the value of variables, or execute different procedures. You can use the Immediate window (Figure 4.2) to accomplish all of these tasks.

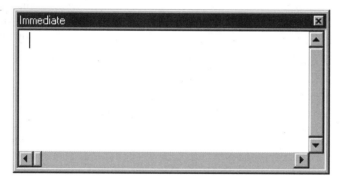

Figure 4.2 The Immediate window

Evaluating Variables and Expressions

The Immediate window can be used to evaluate any valid Visual Basic statement, but it does not accept data declarations. You can enter calls to Sub and Function procedures, which allows you to evaluate the effect of a procedure given a different set of arguments. While you are in break mode, enter a statement in the Immediate window as you would in the Code window. For example:

```
NaturalLog=log(35)
```

When you press the ENTER key, Visual Basic switches to run time to execute the statement, and then returns to break mode. At that point, you can see the results and test any possible effects on variables or property values.

Printing Information in the Immediate Window

When your application is in break mode, you can examine data by printing values directly in the Immediate window. Once you have focus on the Immediate window, you can use the Print method. A question mark (?) is used as shorthand for the Print method. The question mark means the same as Print, and can be used in any context where Print is used. The following example prints the current value of a variable in the Immediate window:

```
Print strCustomerName
```

You can use the ? command to accomplish the same thing, as in the following example:

```
? strCustomerName
```

Printing Values of Properties

Any valid expression that is within scope can be evaluated from the Immediate window. The currently active form or module determines the scope. If the code in which you entered break mode is attached to a form, you can view the properties of that form and the properties of any control on that form by using nonexplicit arguments, as in the following:

```
? Caption
? Text1.Text
```

Assuming that Text1 is a control on the currently active form, the first statement prints to the Immediate window the string value of the current form's caption. The second statement prints the text in the Text1 control.

If execution is suspended in a module or another form, you must explicitly specify the form name as follows:

```
? Form1.Caption
? Form1.Text1.Text
```

Note Referencing an unloaded form in the Immediate window loads that form.

Viewing and Testing Multiple Instances of Procedures

You can repeatedly run a procedure in the Immediate window to test the effect of different arguments. A separate instance of each call to a procedure is maintained in Visual Basic. This allows you to test variables and properties in each instance of a call to a procedure. To see an example of how this works, open a new project and enter the following code in the form module:

```
Private Sub Form_Click()
    FirstProcedure
End Sub
Sub FirstProcedure()
    Dim intFirst As Integer
    intFirst = 10
    SecondProcedure
End Sub
Sub SecondProcedure()
    Stop
End Sub
```

Run the application and click the form. The Stop statement puts Visual Basic into break mode and the Immediate window is displayed. In the Code window, change the value of intFirst to 15 in the procedure FirstProcedure, switch to the Immediate window, and type the following:

```
FirstProcedure
```

This calls the procedure and restarts the application. Open the Call Stack dialog box and you'll see a listing of each separate run of the program, separated by the [<Debug Window>] listing. You can use the Call Stack dialog box to select any instance of a procedure, and then print the values of variables from that procedure in the Immediate window.

For example, if you double-click the earliest instance of FirstProcedure (the one closest to the bottom) and use the Immediate window to print the value of intFirst, it will return 10. If you double-click the second instance of FirstProcedure, 15 will be returned as the value of intFirst.

Changing Values of Variables

Sometimes when testing your application, you need to evaluate the effects of particular data values. When in break mode, you can use statements in the Immediate window to set values:

```
VScroll1.Value = 250
intDenominator = 0
```

Once the values of one or more properties or variables are changed, you can resume execution to see the results.

Immediate Window Shortcuts

Here are some shortcuts you can use in the Immediate window:

- Once you enter a statement, you can execute it again by moving the cursor back to that statement and pressing ENTER.
- Before pressing ENTER, you can edit the current statement to alter its effects.

- You can use the mouse or the arrow keys to move around in the Immediate window. Don't press ENTER unless you are at a statement you want to execute.

- CTRL+HOME moves the cursor to the top of the Immediate window.

- CTRL+END moves the cursor to the bottom of the Immediate window.

- The HOME and END keys move to the beginning and end of the current line.

Using the Debug Object

The Debug object gives developers the option of debugging their applications at full speed. The Debug object has two methods that help with debugging your code during run time. The first is the Print method, which allows output from your code to the Immediate window. The second is the Assert method, which conditionally suspends execution at the line on which the method appears.

Debug.Print

The Debug object's Print method allows you to send output from your program to the Immediate window without entering break mode. This gives you the ability to track variable values at full execution speed while creating a history list of the values in the Immediate window. For example, the following statement prints the value of intCount to the Immediate window every time the statement is executed:

```
Debug.Print "Count = " & intCount
```

When your application is compiled into an executable file, all of the Debug.Print statements are removed. However, Visual Basic does not remove function calls that are arguments to the Debug.Print statement. Thus, any effects that those functions have on your program will continue to occur in a compiled executable, even though the function results are not printed. If your application uses only Debug.Print statements with strings or simple variable types as arguments, all the Debug.Print statements will be removed.

Debug.Assert

The Debug object's Assert method forces a run-time break when an expression evaluates to False. If the expression evaluates to True, the program operation continues. For example:

```
Function Division(x As Long, y As Long, z As Long) As Long
    Debug.Assert (y <> 0 And z <> 0)
    Division = x / y / z
End Function
```

If you call the Division function as:

```
q = Division (240, 2, 3)
```

the program will continue as normal. However, if you pass a zero as a denominator, then the Assert method forces a break. The following example would force a break at the Debug.Assert statement:

```
q = Division (240, 0, 3)
```

The preceding example allows you to debug your application for incorrect parameters that have been passed to the function. If a break occurs at the Debug.Assert statement, you can check the program variables to determine which value is inappropriate. This is especially useful when the argument values come from other functions, as in this example:

```
q = Division(calcX(), calcY(), calcZ())
```

The Assert method is used only for debugging your programs within the design environment. When you compile your application into an executable program, Visual Basic removes all of the Assert statements from the final code.

Using the Locals Window

The Locals window shows the value of all variables that are within the scope of the current procedure. As the execution of your program goes from procedure to procedure, the information shown on the Locals window changes to only the variables that are used in the current procedure. For example, you would use the Locals window to monitor how all your values change as the code runs. To access the Locals window, select Locals Window from the View menu or from the Debug toolbar. Figure 4.3 shows the Locals window.

When the Locals window is visible, it is automatically updated every time your program changes from run mode to break mode or when you navigate in the Call Stack dialog box.

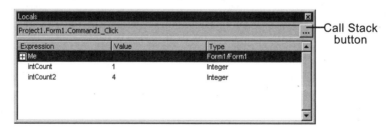

Figure 4.3 Locals window

Call Stack Button

The Call Stack button opens the Call Stack dialog box, which lists the procedures in the call stack.

Expression Column

The Expression column lists the name of the variables.

The first variable in the list <Me> is a special module variable and can be expanded to display all module level variables and properties of objects within the current scope. Global variables and variables in other projects are not accessible from the Locals window.

Value Column

The Value column lists the value of each of the variables and properties.

When you select an item and click on its value in the Value column, the cursor changes to an I-beam, allowing you to edit the value. Once you have changed a value, press the ENTER key or move to another field to validate the change. If you enter a value that is illegal, the Edit field remains active and the value you entered is highlighted. A message box describing the error also appears. You can cancel a change that you made by pressing the ESC key.

Within the Value column, all numeric variables must have a value listed. String variables can have an empty Value list.

Type Column

The Type column lists the variable type. You cannot edit the data in this column.

Setting Watch Expressions

As you work through debugging your application, a calculation may not produce the desired result, or problems may occur when a certain variable or property assumes a particular value. Not all debugging problems are immediately traceable to a statement, so sometimes you may need to observe the value of a variable or expression throughout a procedure. In this case, you define a watch expression, or expression whose value you want to monitor. Visual Basic can automatically monitor the watch expressions that you define. When your application enters break mode, these watch expressions appear in the Watches window, where you can observe their values.

You can also set watch expressions that put your application into break mode whenever the expression's value changes or equals a specified value. These are sometimes called break expressions. Break expressions are extremely helpful when you are debugging a section of your code that uses a large number of iterations. For example, instead of stepping through a loop in your program one statement at a time, you can set a watch expression to put your application into break mode when a counter variable reaches a certain value.

Adding a Watch Expression

Watch expressions can be added at design time or while your application is in break mode. In either case, the Add Watch dialog box, shown in Figure 4.4, is used to add watch expressions.

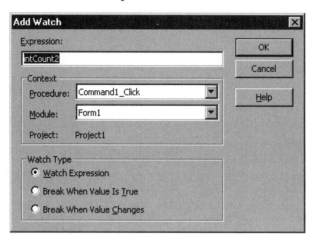

Figure 4.4 Add Watch dialog box

The first component of the Add Watch dialog box is the Expression box. This is where you enter the expression to be evaluated. The expression can be a variable, a property, a function call, or any other valid expression.

The second component is the Context option group. These options allow you to set the scope of variables watched in the expression. You should use the Context option if you have variables of the same name with different scope. This will then allow you to restrict the scope of variables in watch expressions to a specific procedure or to a specific form or module. You can also have it apply to the entire application by selecting All Procedures and All Modules.

The third component is the Watch Type option group. This sets how Visual Basic responds to the watch expression. The Watch Expression option displays the expression's value in the Watches window when the application enters break mode. The other two options have the application enter break mode automatically when the expression evaluates to a True (nonzero) statement or each time the value of the expression changes.

➤ **To add a watch expression**

1. On the **Debug** menu, click **Add Watch**.

2. Enter the expression that you want to evaluate in the **Expression** box.

3. Use the **Context** options if you need to set the scope of the variables to watch,.

4. Select an option in the **Watch Type** group to determine how you want Visual Basic to respond to the watch expression.

5. Click **OK**.

Note You can add an expression to the Watches window by dragging and dropping from the Code window.

Editing or Deleting a Watch Expression

The Edit Watch dialog box lists all of your current watch expressions. You can use this dialog box to edit and delete any watch listed in the Watches window.

➤ **To edit a watch expression**

1. In the **Watches** window, click the watch expression you want to edit.

2. Double-click the watch expression, or, on the **Debug** menu, click **Edit Watch**.

   The **Edit Watch** dialog box appears.

3. Make any changes to the expression, the scope for evaluating variables, or the watch type.

4. Click **OK**.

Identifying Watch Types

The icons on the left edge of each expression in the Watches window identify the type of that watch expression. There are three types of watch expressions:

- Watch expression
- Break when expression is true
- Break when expression has changed

Using Quick Watch

While in break mode, you can use Quick Watch to see the value of a property, variable, or expression. The Quick Watch dialog box shows the value of the expression you select in the Code window. You can then add this expression to the Watches window by clicking the Add button.

➤ **To display the Quick Watch dialog box**

1. Select a property, variable, or expression in the **Code** window.

2. Press **SHIFT+F9**, or, on the **Debug** toolbar, click **Quick Watch**.

3. Click **Add** if you want to add the expression to the **Watches** window.

The Call Stack Dialog Box

The Call Stack dialog box shows a list of all the procedure calls that are active in your program. Procedure calls are considered active when the procedure has been started but not completed.

The Call Stack dialog box, shown in Figure 4.5, lets you trace the flow of your application as it executes through nested procedures. For example, suppose a procedure in your application calls a second procedure. The calling procedure will not complete until the second procedure finishes. While the second procedure executes, both procedures are active and displayed in the Call Stack dialog box.

Figure 4.5 Call Stack dialog box

The Call Stack dialog box can be displayed only when your application is in break mode.

➤ **To display the Call Stack dialog box**

Select one of the following methods:

- On the **View** menu, click **Call Stack**.
- On the **Debug** toolbar click **Call Stack**.
- Press **CTRL+L**.
- In the **Locals** window, click the button next to the **Procedure** box.

Tracing Nested Procedures

The Call Stack dialog box lists all the active procedure calls in a series of nested calls. At the bottom of the Call Stack dialog box's list is the earliest active procedure. Each subsequent procedure call is placed on the top of the list. The information shown in the list begins with the module or form name, followed by the name of the called procedure.

The Call Stack dialog box can be used to display the call statement of that nested procedure.

➤ **To display the call statement from the Calls Stack dialog box**

1. In the **Call Stack** dialog box, select the procedure that has the call statement you want to display.

2. Click **Show**.

The cursor location in the Code window indicates the statement that calls the next procedure in the Call Stack dialog box. If you choose the last procedure in the Call Stack dialog box (the procedure at the top of the list), the cursor appears at the statement where your program entered into break mode.

Lesson Summary

Visual Basic includes several tools to help you debug your application.

- The Immediate window is used to evaluate any valid Visual Basic expression. It does not accept data declarations.

- The Debug object has two methods:

  - Print sends output from your program to the Immediate window without entering break mode. It creates a history list of the values in the Immediate window.

  - Assert forces a run-time break when the specified expression evaluates to False.

- The Locals window shows the value of all variables within the scope of the current procedure.

- Watch expressions are those expressions whose value you wish to monitor. Use the Watch window when a problem is not immediately traceable to a statement.

Summary

Debugging Your Application

Three types of errors may occur in a Visual Basic program:

- Syntax errors are due to incorrectly constructed statements. Visual Basic can help you fix these errors by alerting you to incorrect syntax as you enter code.

- Run-time errors occur when a statement attempts an operation that is impossible to carry out. Users can detect these errors and therefore, run-time errors should be carefully planned for using error handlers. Using error handlers will be discussed in the next chapter, "Implementing Error Handlers".

- Logic errors occur when the code does not perform as you intended. The application will run, but will produce incorrect results. These errors are generally the most difficult to resolve. Using the debugging tools included with Visual Basic can make this process easier.

Working in break mode halts the application so you can check the program at a specific moment; it is critical in the debugging process.

Helpful tools available from the Debug menu or toolbar are:

- Step Into
- Step Over
- Step Out
- Set Next Statement
- Show Next Statement

Each of these tools can be used to help fix logic errors that have been introduced into a project.

Testing Your Application

Visual Basic includes several tools to help you debug your program by testing various aspects of the application while it is running.

- The Immediate window lets you evaluate any valid Visual Basic expression. It does not accept data declarations, but will allow you to set the value of variables.

- The Debug object has two methods:
  - Print sends output from your program to the Immediate window without entering break mode. It creates a history list of the values in the Immediate window.
  - Assert forces a run-time break when the specified expression evaluates to False.
- The Locals window shows the value of all variables within the scope of the current procedure.
- Watch expressions are those expressions whose value you wish to monitor. Use the Watch window when a problem is not immediately traceable to a statement.

Lab: Debugging an Application

In this lab, you will be given a small application that contains syntax, run-time, and logic errors. Use the Visual Basic debugging tools to fix these problems. If you have difficulty implementing a solution for this lab, you can view the solution code provided in your \Labs\Lab04\Solution folder.

To see a demonstration of the solution, run the Lab04.exe animation located in the Animations folder on the Supplemental Course Materials CD-ROM that accompanies this book.

Estimated lesson time: 35 minutes

➤ **To open the Lab 4 project**

1. Start Visual Basic.

2. On the **New Project** dialog box, click the **Existing** tab.

3. Use the **Look in** drop-down list to browse to the prjDebug.vbp file located in the \Labs\Lab04\Partial folder, then click **Open**.

➤ **To debug the Click event for Add Values**

1. On the **Run** menu, click **Start**.

2. Type **10** for the first value, then type **10** for the second value, then click **Add Values**.

   Notice that a compile error occurs, as illustrated in Figure 4.6.

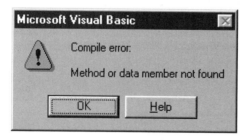

Figure 4.6 Visual Basic Compile error dialog box

3. Click **OK** to close the **Compile error** dialog box, then correct the line of code that caused the compile error.

   The compile error description reads, "Method or data member not found." This is because Text is an invalid property for a label.

4. Change the label's property value in your code to correct this error.

5. On the **Run** menu, click **Start** to run the application again.

6. Type **10** for the first value, then type **10** for the second value, then click **Add Values**.

   Notice that a Type mismatch run-time error occurs, as illustrated in Figure 4.7.

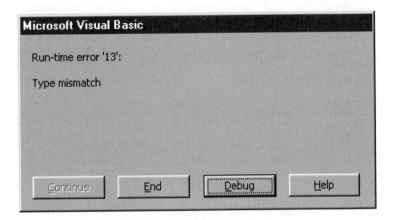

Figure 4.7 The Visual Basic Run-time error dialog box

7. On the **Run-time error** dialog box, click **Debug** to correct this error.

   Because we want to assign the value of the **Result** variable to the **Caption** property of **lblResult**, the highlighted line of code illustrated in Figure 4.8 contains a logic error.

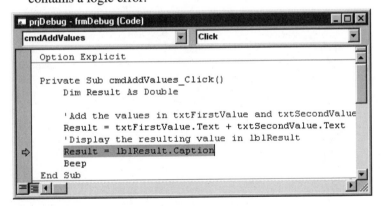

Figure 4.8 Code statement highlighted in the Code window

8. Correct this logic error.

9. After you have fixed the logic and syntax errors, press **F5** to continue running the application.

   Notice that the results display as 1010 instead of 20, as illustrated in Figure 4.9. This is due to a logic error in the Click event for **Add Values**.

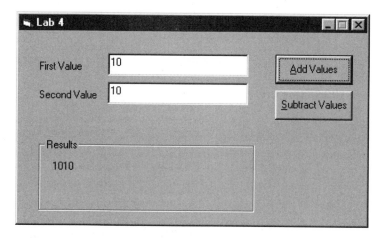

Figure 4.9 Invalid results displayed for Add Values

➤ **To use the Add Watch window**

1. Stop the application and, on the **Debug** menu, click **Add Watch.**

   The **Add Watch** window appears.

2. Create a watch expression that will cause the code to break when the value of the **Result** variable changes in the **cmdAddValues_Click** event. Set the properties shown in the **Add Watch** window illustrated in Figure 4.10.

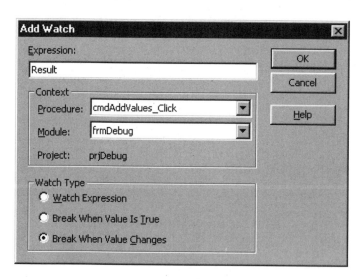

Figure 4.10 The Add Watch window

3. Run and test the application by typing **10** for the first value, then type **10** for the second value, then click **Add Values**.

   The code will break when the value of the **Result** variable changes.

4. When your code breaks, test the values of **txtFirstValue.Text**, **txtSecondValue.Text**, and **Result**.

   Test the text box values by holding your mouse over them or by using the **Immediate** window. Notice that the value of the text boxes are strings and the value of **Result** is numeric.

5. Stop the application and correct the logic error in the Click event for **Add Values**.

➤ **To debug the Subtract Values Click event**

1. On the **Run** menu, click **Start**.

2. Type **20** for the first value and **10** for the second value.

3. Click **Subtract Values** to test the Click event procedure.

   Notice that the result is displayed as 2010. This is the result of a logic error in the subroutine.

4. On the **Run** menu, click **End**.

5. To eliminate the logic error, change the code statement in the **Subtract Values** Click event procedure from an addition (+) to a subtraction (-).

6. After you have corrected the logic error, start the application, then type **20** for the first value and **hello** for the second value.

7. Click **Subtract Values** to test the Click event procedure.

   Notice that a type mismatch run-time error occurs.

8. Click **Debug** to correct the code statement that caused the run-time error.

9. After you correct the code statement that caused the run-time error, press **F5** to continue running the application.

   If you have corrected the code statement properly, your results will display as 20, as illustrated in Figure 4.11.

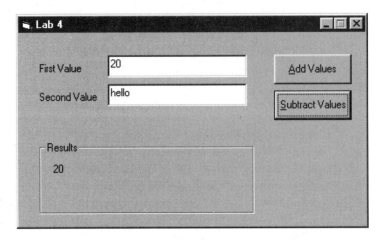

Figure 4.11 Results displayed after correcting Subtract Values

10. On the **Run** menu, click **End**.

11. Save and test your application.

The solution provided in the \Labs\Lab04\Solution folder shows some techniques that you can use to prevent errors in your application. In Lab 5, you will learn how to prevent run-time errors using error handling.

Review

The following questions are intended to reinforce key information presented in this chapter. If you are unable to answer a question, review the appropriate lesson and then try the question again. Answers to the questions can be found in the Appendix, "Questions and Answers," located at the back of this book.

1. What are the three types of errors that can occur in a Visual Basic program and when does each occur?

2. What is the purpose of break mode in the debugging process?

3. What is the difference between the Step Into, Step Over and Step Out debugging tools?

4. What tasks can you perform using the Immediate window?

5. Identify and explain the two methods of the Debug object.

6. Why do you use the Locals window?

7. What is a watch expression and when do you use it?

C H A P T E R 5

Implementing Error Handling

About This Chapter

In this chapter, you will learn how to implement error handling in a Visual Basic application. Three types of error-handling techniques will be introduced: normal error handlers, inline error handlers, and centralized error handlers. Depending on the needs of your application, you can implement any of these to add stability to your program.

Before You Begin

To complete the lessons in this chapter, you must have:

- Read Chapter 4.

Lesson 1: Creating an Error Handler

Sometimes it is impossible to create an error-free application. For example, suppose your program offers the user the ability to save data to a file on a floppy disk. Even though your code may work as expected, you cannot guarantee that the user has first inserted a floppy disk into the drive. In this case, a run-time error will occur even though the code itself is accurate. Visual Basic's error-handling capability provides a technique for dealing with problems like this. To implement error handling, you create special statements called *error handlers*. Error handlers are also useful to control mistakes that you may have made when writing the code. Error handlers execute only if a run-time error is encountered.

After this lesson you will be able to:

- Describe how Visual Basic manages run-time errors.
- Create an error handler in your application.
- Describe the errors-calling chain used by Visual Basic.

Estimated lesson time: 45 minutes

How Visual Basic Handles a Run-Time Error

When Visual Basic encounters a run-time error, it checks to see whether an error handler has been enabled. If it has not, Visual Basic automatically presents the user with a message box showing the error number and a brief description. Unfortunately, when the user clicks OK to this message, the Visual Basic program immediately terminates. Code in an Unload event that might have queried the user to first save their changes is ignored. For this reason, allowing Visual Basic to automatically handle run-time errors is not recommended.

Implementing a Local Error Handler

Error handlers are specific to individual procedures. This means that each event or general procedure you create should have its own error handler. There are three basic steps in creating an error handler:

1. Enable an error handler.
2. Add code to handle the possible errors.
3. Resume normal execution of the program.

Enabling an Error Handler

The first step in controlling run-time errors is to enable an error handler. Each procedure that contains code should include an error handler of some kind. To enable an error handler, use the On Error GoTo statement and provide the name of a label in your procedure. The label marks a point in code that you want Visual

Basic to jump to when a run-time error occurs. Labels follow the same naming rules as variables. However, you must add a colon to the end of the name.

The following example enables an error handler called OpenError:

```
Private Sub cmdOpen_Click()
    On Error GoTo OpenError
    '[code that opens a database]

    Exit Sub
OpenError:
    '[Code to handle an error goes here]
End Sub
```

Visual Basic does not stop executing when it reaches a label. If you do not tell Visual Basic to exit the procedure, the error handler code executes even when there is no run-time error. Use the Exit Sub or Exit Function statement before the start of an error handler to avoid this problem.

Handling Errors

The second step in creating an error handler is to add code under the label to manage the potential errors that could occur. Visual Basic's Err object can be used to determine the specific error. The Err object's Number property provides the Visual Basic error code. Use this property to have your application prompt the user to take corrective action, such as when a floppy disk is not present, or to proceed with an orderly shutdown when a critical error occurs. If you want the user to see a description of the error, use the Description property of the Err object.

The following example uses the Err object to determine what error occurred:

```
ErrorHandler:
Select Case Err.Number
    Case 53
        'File not found
        MsgBox Err.Description
        MsgBox "Please enter a valid filename."
    Case Else
        'An unplanned error occurred
        MsgBox "The following error occurred: " & Err.Description
End Select
```

Note When writing error handlers that use a Select Case, consider including the Case Else statement to handle errors that you did not plan for.

Resuming Execution

When the error has been handled, the final step is to resume execution of the application. There are three ways to return control:

- Retry the line of code that caused the initial error.
- Start from the line immediately following the one that caused the error.
- Terminate the application.

If the error handler prompted the user to correct the problem, such as asking the user to insert a floppy disk into the drive, you may want the application to retry the operation that initially failed. To cause Visual Basic to retry the line of code that failed, use the Resume keyword. To skip the line of code that caused the error and continue executing your program, use the Resume Next statement. The final option is to close the form and exit the program by calling Unload Me, which ensures an orderly shutdown.

Note Avoid using the End keyword. End will not run code associated with Unload or QueryUnload events and data could be lost.

In the following example, the error handler prompts the user to retry the operation, ignore the problem, or exit the application:

```
Dim Answer As Integer
ErrorHandler:
Answer = MsgBox("An error occurred.", vbAbortRetryIgnore)
Select Case Answer
    Case vbRetry
        Resume
    Case vbIgnore
        Resume Next
    Case vbAbort
        Unload Me
End Select
```

Practice: Creating an Error Handler

In this practice, you will create an error handler that runs when a file cannot be opened.

To see a demonstration, run the Chap05.exe animation located in the Animations folder on the Supplemental Course Materials CD-ROM that accompanies this book.

➤ **To create the file open procedure**

1. Start Visual Basic and open a new **Standard EXE** project.

2. Add a Command button to the form.

3. In the Click event for the Command button, add the following code:

```
Dim filename As String
Dim answer as integer
filename = InputBox("Please enter the file name to open:")
Open filename For Input As #1
Close #1
```

➤ **To create an error handler**

1. In the Click event for the Command button, add the following statement after the variable declarations:

```
On Error GoTo MyHandler
```

This enables the error handler.

2. In the same event, add the following code before the **End Sub** statement:

```
Exit Sub
MyHandler:
Select Case Err.Number
    Case 53
        'The file was not found
        Answer = MsgBox("The file was not found.", _
            vbAbortRetryIgnore)
        Select Case Answer
            Case vbRetry
                filename = InputBox("Please enter the filename" & _
                    " to open:")
                Resume
            Case vbIgnore
                Resume Next
            Case vbAbort
                Unload Me
        End Select
End Select
```

3. Save this application to the \Practice\Ch05 directory, then test your work. Be sure to try entering a valid filename and an invalid filename.

Errors-Calling Chain

If the procedure that generates a run-time error does not have an error trap, Visual Basic checks the calling procedure to see whether *it* has an error trap. If it does not, Visual Basic repeats the process until the first procedure is checked. If an error handler is not present in any of the procedures, the default message box is displayed to the user and the application terminates. This process is called the *errors-calling chain*.

Figure 5.1 illustrates an example of the errors-calling chain. The following sequence of steps occur:

Step 1: ProcedureA, which contains an error handler, calls ProcedureB.

Step 2: ProcedureB, which does not have an error handler, calls ProcedureC. An error occurs in ProcedureC and since there is no local error handler in ProcedureC, the errors-calling chain is invoked.

Step 3: Visual Basic halts execution of code in ProcedureC and checks ProcedureB, the calling procedure, for an error trap.

Step 4: Since no error trap is found in ProcedureB, Visual Basic checks with the originating procedure, ProcedureA. An error handler is found in ProcedureA and the code in this error handler is executed.

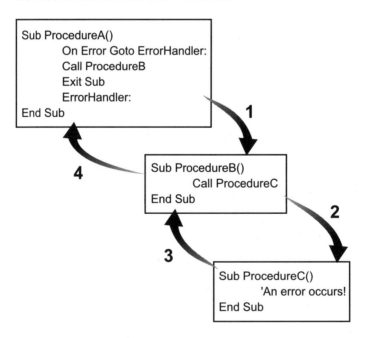

Figure 5.1 Example of an errors-calling chain

Resuming Execution from the Calling Chain

Visual Basic automatically uses the calling chain to resolve a run-time error, which does not require any additional coding on your part. However, resuming execution of the program is more complex and requires the developer to add specific code statements. The Resume and Resume Next statements are used to continue execution of your program and apply only to the line of code that called the procedure that caused the error, not the actual line of code where the error occurred. Figure 5.2 illustrates the Resume and Resume Next statements when used with a calling chain. Depending on which statement is used, the application may retry the entire procedure, or may skip the line and continue running the application on the next executable line of code. When creating an error handler, the developer will need to decide how the application needs to resume after an error has been encountered.

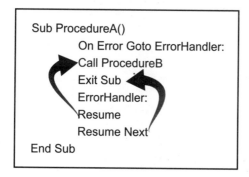

Figure 5.2 Resume and Resume Next in a calling chain

The recommended practice is to place local error-handling code in each procedure rather than relying on the calling chain for error handling.

Disabling an Error Handler

Depending on the needs of your application, you may have to disable an error handler from within your code. To do this, use the On Error GoTo 0 statement. This statement disables only a local error handler and has no effect on the errors-calling chain. The following example enables an error handler and then later disables it:

```
Private Sub cmdOpen_Click()
    Dim Answer As Integer

    'Enable the error handler
    On Error GoTo ErrorHandler

    '[code that opens a database]

    'Disable the error handler
    On Error GoTo 0

    Exit Sub

ErrorHandler:
    Answer = MsgBox("An error occurred.", vbAbortRetryIgnore)
    Select Case Answer
        Case vbAbort
            Unload Me
        Case vbRetry
            Resume
        Case vbIgnore
            Resume Next
    End Select
End Sub
```

Visual Basic Error Handling Options

When testing error handlers, you may want to control how Visual Basic manages errors at design time. There are three error trapping options:

- Break on All Errors

  Any error causes the project to enter break mode, whether or not an error handler is active and whether or not the code is in a class module. You will learn more about using class modules in Chapter 6, "Introduction to Class Modules."

- Break in Class Module

  Any unhandled error produced in a class module causes the project to enter break mode at the line of code in the class module that produced the error.

  When you debug an ActiveX component project by running an ActiveX client test program in another project, use this option. Set it in the ActiveX component project to break on errors in its class modules instead of always returning the error to the client test program. You will learn more about creating ActiveX components in Chapter 10, "Creating and Managing COM Components."

- Break on Unhandled Errors

  If an error handler is active, the error is trapped without entering break mode. If there is no active error handler, the error causes the project to enter break mode. An unhandled error in a class module, however, causes the project to enter break mode on the line of code that invoked the offending procedure of the class.

➤ **To access the Visual Basic options for error handling**

1. On the **Tools** menu, click **Options**.

2. Click the **General** tab.

3. Select the appropriate error-handling option.

Lesson Summary

You can not always plan for every possible error in an application. Visual Basic includes a default error handler that presents a message to the user, then terminates the application. However, this solution does not allow the user to save any work or properly close the application. Therefore, you should implement your own error handlers to resolve run-time errors. An error handler is associated with a specific procedure and should be added to every event or general procedure that you have included in your code.

Use these steps to create an error handler:

- Retry the line of code that caused the initial error.

- Start from the line immediately following the one that caused the error.

- Terminate the application.

Although it is best to add an error handler to each procedure, Visual Basic will automatically check the calling chain to find an error handler before it displays the default error message box. If an error handler is found in a parent procedure, that error-handler code will be used. This may allow the user to resolve the problem or at least save changes before the application terminates.

Visual Basic also provides various options for managing run-time errors at design time. Your application can enter break mode when any error occurs, when the error occurs in a class module, or when any unhandled error occurs.

Lesson 2: Using Inline Error Handling

Implementing inline error handling is an alternative to creating procedure-specific error handlers. An inline error handler checks code after each statement to see whether an error has occurred. If an error has occurred, code is immediately run to resolve the error. To create an inline error handler, you use many of the same code statements that you use in a normal error handler.

After this lesson you will be able to:

- Compare and contrast an inline error handler and a normal error handler.
- Create an inline error handler in your applications.

Estimated lesson time: 15 minutes

Creating an Inline Error Handler

To create an inline error handler, use the On Error Resume Next statement. If an error occurs, this statement prevents a run-time error from stopping the execution of your program. To see whether an error has occurred, use the Err object's Number property. If the Number property's value is greater than zero, an error has occurred.

The following example enables an inline error handler and opens a file:

```
On Error Resume Next
Open "c:\MyFile.dat" For Input As #1
Select Case Err.Number
    Case 0:
        'No error occurred
    Case 53:
        'File not Found
        'Prompt the user user for the correct filename
    Case 55:
        'File already open
        'Add code here to resolve this error
    Case Else
        'An unknown error occurred
        'Add code here to resolve this
End Select
```

Clearing the Err object

With a normal error handler, an error is cleared automatically, but when you use an inline error handler, you must manually clear the error from the Err object after it has been resolved. To manually clear the error from the Err object, use the Clear method. The following example clears the Err object:

```
'Reset Err.Number
Err.Clear
```

If you do not first clear the Err object, subsequent inline error handlers will report the same error. If a new error occurs, the previous error will be removed from the Err object.

Disabling an Inline Error Handler

To disable an inline error handler, use the On Error GoTo 0 statement. This is the same procedure that you use with a normal error handler. The following example disables an inline error handler:

```
On Error GoTo 0

'If an error occurs next, the default Visual Basic
'error handler will be used
Open "C:\AnotherFile.dat" For Input As #2
```

Lesson Summary

An inline error handler is an alternative to a normal error handler for trapping potential run-time errors. With an inline error handler, use the On Error Resume Next statement to disable the normal Visual Basic handler. Then add code after each executable line to check the Err object. The Number property notifies your application when a run-time error occurs.

When all run-time errors are resolved, call the Clear method to remove the error from the Err object. To disable an inline error handler, use the On Error GoTo 0 statement.

Lesson 3: Implementing Centralized Error Handling

Another technique for managing potential errors is to create centralized procedures that contain specific error-handling information. For example, your application may open a number of files from network drives. You can create the same error handler in each procedure that opens a file, or you can create a general function procedure that provides this capability. You then add a detailed error handler to this general procedure.

Consider using a centralized error handler when the same error-handling code is repeated throughout your application. For example, if your application contains a number of procedures that make a connection to a database, you need to create error handlers for each procedure. The code in these error handlers will probably be very similar since all of them trap for database connection errors.

After this lesson you will be able to:

- Describe when to use a centralized error handler.

- Create a centralized error handler in your applications.

Estimated lesson time: 15 minutes

Creating a Centralized Error Handler

A centralized error handling provides very detailed control over possible errors because you associate a procedure with a specific task. Before you create a centralized error handler, you must create a general function procedure that contains all the code necessary to perform the task, such as opening a database or reading data from a file. Then you add an error handler to the procedure that includes all the possible error numbers associated with the task. Depending on whether or not the procedure is successful, you can pass return data from the function.

The following example creates a centralized error handler using the OpenFile general procedure:

```
Private Sub cmdGetData_Click()
    Dim filename As String
    filename = InputBox("Please enter the file name to open:")
    If OpenFile(filename) = True Then
        MsgBox "The file was opened successfully."
    Else
        MsgBox "The file was not opened. Please check the file name."
    End If
End Sub
```

```
Function OpenFile(filename As String) As Boolean
    'Turn on the local error handler
    On Error GoTo OpenError:

    'Open the file
    Open filename For Input As #1

    'It worked, so pass back True
    OpenFile = True

    'Exit the function before running the
    'error handler code by mistake
    Exit Function

' A local error handler
OpenError:
    Select Case Err.Number
        Case 53
            'The file was not found
        Case 55
            'The file is already open
        Case Else
            'An unexpected error occurred.
    End Select
    'The operation failed, so send back False
    OpenFile = False
End Function
```

A centralized error handler is easier to maintain than a normal error handler. To change or update it, you update your code in only one place.

Lesson Summary

A centralized error handler is a more efficient solution for controlling potential run-time errors if:

- Your application performs the same general task in many different places.
- The code has to be changed; updating a single procedure can reduce the overall cost of maintaining the application.

Summary

Implementing Error Handling

- Visual Basic's default error handler presents a message to the user, then terminates the application without allowing the user to save changes or shut down properly.

- An error handler is specific to a procedure and should be created for every event or general procedure that you have included in your code.

- Visual Basic checks the calling chain. If an error handler is present, its code will be used.

- Visual Basic's environmental options for managing run-time errors at design time let your application enter break mode when:
  - any error occurs
  - the error occurs in a class module
  - any unhandled error occurs

Using Inline Error Handling

An inline error handler is an alternative to a normal error handler for trapping for potential run-time errors.

- Use the On Error Resume Next statement to disable the normal Visual Basic handler.

- Add code after each executable line to check the Err object. The Number property notifies your application if a run-time error occurs.

- Call the Clear method to remove the error from the Err object when all run-time errors have been resolved,

- Use the On Error GoTo 0 statement to disable an inline error handler.

Implementing Centralized Error Handling

A centralized error handler is a more efficient solution for controlling potential run-time errors if:

- Your application performs the same general task in many different places.

- The code has to be changed; updating a single procedure can reduce the overall cost of maintaining the application.

Lab: Implementing Error Handling

In this lab, you will implement procedural and inline error handling to avoid run-time errors that occur in an application provided with this course.

To see a demonstration of the solution, run the Lab05.exe animation located in the Animations folder on the Supplemental Course Materials CD-ROM that accompanies this book.

Estimated lesson time: 45 minutes

Exercise 1: Implementing Procedural Error Handling

➤ **To open the project**

1. Start Visual Basic.

2. Open the prjLab5.vbp file located in the \Labs\Lab05\Partial folder.

➤ **To test the project**

1. On the **Run** menu, click **Start**.

2. Click the **Import File Text** button.

   The common dialog box appears and prompts you to open a file.

3. Browse to the \Labs\Lab05\Partial folder, click the Lab5.txt file, then click **Open**.

   Notice that the text is imported from the text file without any run-time errors, as illustrated in Figure 5.3

Figure 5.3 Text imported from the Lab5.txt file

➤ **To implement error handling**

1. Click the **Import File Text** button, browse to the \Labs\Lab05\Partial folder, select the Lab5.bmp file, then click **Open**.

   Notice that a run-time error occurs, as illustrated in Figure 5.4. This is because the application is written only to handle text files for input.

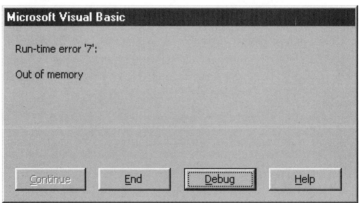

Figure 5.4 Visual Basic Out of memory run-time error

2. Click **End** to stop the application.

3. Using procedural error handling (On Error Goto...), implement an error-handling procedure to trap any "Out of memory" errors that could occur in the future.

Note Input validation is another efficient solution, but for illustration purposes implement procedural error handling for this exercise.

Exercise 2: Implementing Inline Error Handling

In this exercise you will add a button to the frmEditor to start an application using the Shell command. You will then implement inline error handling to prevent application run-time errors.

➤ **Add a command button to the frmEditor**

1. Add a command button to **frmEditor**. Set the Name property to **cmdOpenApp** and set the Caption property to **&Open Application**, as shown in Figure 5.5.

Figure 5.5 Form with new command button

2. Add the following code to the **cmdOpenApp_Click** event:

```
Private Sub cmdOpenApp_Click()
    Dim strFile As String
    strFile = InputBox("Enter file name and path to be opened.")
    Shell strFile, vbNormalFocus
End Sub
```

3. Save and run the application.

4. Test the **Open Application** button by entering **Calc.exe** into the input box.

   If Calc.exe is installed on your computer, the calculator appears. If it is not installed on you computer, you get a run-time error. You can install Calc.exe in the Windows Setup tab for Add/Remove Programs in Control Panel.

5. Test the **Open Application** button again by entering an invalid program name. For example, **xyz**.

   You receive a run-time error because xyz is not a valid application name.

6. Click the **End** button to terminate the application.

➤ **To implement inline error handling**

1. Use the **On Error Resume Next** statement to implement inline error handling.

2. In your code, evaluate the **Err.Number** property and display a message box to the users informing them when errors occur.

3. Save and test your application.

Review

The following questions are intended to reinforce key information presented in this chapter. If you are unable to answer a question, review the appropriate lesson and then try the question again. Answers to the questions can be found in the Appendix, "Questions and Answers," located at the back of this book.

1. If you do not implement an error handler and a run-time error occurs, what does Visual Basic do?

2. Why should you create your own error handlers instead of using the default Visual Basic handler?

3. What is the last step in implementing an inline error handler?

4. When should you consider using a centralized error handler instead of normal, procedure-based error handlers?

C H A P T E R   6

Introduction to Class Modules

About This Chapter

This chapter discusses using existing class modules in Visual Basic. You will also learn how to create new class modules for use in your Visual Basic projects. Eventually, you will create classes for use in other applications. This is made possible by COM technology, which is introduced in lesson 1. The Class Builder utility is also introduced to teach you how to visually create class modules and add properties, events, and methods.

Before You Begin

To complete the lessons in this chapter, you must have:

- Read Chapters 1-5.

Lesson 1: Introduction to COM

In an effort to create applications that can interact with one another, and to provide developers the ability to resuse code, Microsoft created the Component Object Model (COM). COM provides powerful capabilities to Visual Basic programmers. For example, if you want to use the Microsoft Word spell checker in a custom application, you can use Microsoft Word software components, called objects, to provide spell check functionality to your application. Users of your application do not have to do anything in order for the Microsoft Word spell checker to execute; this is done automatically through your Visual Basic code. This process is made possible by COM technology, which is used by Visual Basic internally. In other words, you do not use COM directly—Visual Basic uses COM in a way that is transparent to you.

In addition, COM allows you to create software components that can be reused by other Visual Basic applications. These software components provide "services" to client applications. In other words, your application (using Microsoft Word objects) acts as a client that requests services from a component (Microsoft Word). Any custom components that you create in Visual Basic can be used by applications written in other languages that support the COM standard, such as Visual C++.

Originally, COM was designed to work on a single computer. With the introduction of Distributed COM (DCOM) your applications can use objects that are on other computers on a network. For example, you could write code that connects to a remote database server and returns data to client computers across a network. By packaging this code into a COM component, it can be installed on a server and used by client applications. If an update needs to be made to the code, you only need to recompile and install the component on the server. The client computers do not need to be updated.

After this lesson you will be able to:

- Define the Component Object Model.
- Explain the difference between code and class modules.
- Describe object-oriented programming and component development.
- Describe how Visual Basic allows you to create COM components.

Estimated lesson time: 15 minutes

Component Object Model

Microsoft has defined an open, extensible standard for software interoperability. The Component Object Model (COM) makes it possible for software components that you create to work with other software components, including software you buy off-the-shelf.

COM allows software components, derived from any combination of pre-existing components you have developed and components from different software vendors, to connect to and communicate with each other.

Because COM enables interoperability among applications written in different languages, a word processor application written by one vendor can connect to a spreadsheet object written by another vendor. The word processor application could then be used to import data from the spreadsheet object. Additionally, the spreadsheet object could receive data through a COM object residing on a mainframe. The word processor, spreadsheet, and mainframe database do not have to know anything about each other's implementation. The word processor only needs to know how to connect to the spreadsheet; the spreadsheet only needs to know how to expose its services for other software components to connect.

Component Development and Object-Oriented Programming

Component-based software development reduces programming time by allowing developers to assemble applications from tested, standardized components. Visual Basic gives you the tools to rapidly create, debug, and deploy software components. It is the easiest way to create ActiveX components such as ActiveX controls, ActiveX documents, and code components (ActiveX DLLs and ActiveX EXEs).

ActiveX is technology based on COM. An ActiveX component is a unit of executable code, such as an .exe, .dll, or .ocx file that follows the ActiveX specification for creating reusable objects. ActiveX technology allows programmers to assemble these reusable software components into objects that provide services to clients.

Component software development using ActiveX technology should not be confused with object-oriented programming (OOP). OOP is a way to build object-based software components. ActiveX is a technology that allows you to combine object-based components created by different development tools or across different applications. To put it another way, an OOP language allows you to create reusable objects for a single development environment, while ActiveX and COM make objects work together in multiple environments.

How Component Development Promotes Reusability

You can use an OOP tool such as Microsoft Visual C++ to construct a set of objects. Other Visual C++ developers can use and further extend these objects. However, if you package your objects in an COM component, they can be used and further extended with any programming tool that supports COM technology, such as Visual Basic.

A client application or component object does not care what language a COM object was written in, only that it can communicate with the object. This allows application and component objects to communicate with each other regardless of the language or development tool in which they were created.

COM and Visual Basic

As you define the functionality required by your application, look for places where you can use pre-existing COM components instead of having to write the code to implement a given functionality yourself. For example, you could create a function procedure that logs a user into a server. In your corporation, you may be required to include this procedure in every application you create. Instead of adding this code to every program, you can implement this logon procedure in a COM component that can be easily reused from project to project.

There are many reasons to use COM components in an application, including:

- Reusability

  Once you create a COM component, other developers can use it. This enables easy access to your component's features in other applications without requiring developers to write extensive code.

- Reduced complexity

  You can create a COM component to hide programming complexity from other programmers. Other programmers need only know what information to provide to your component, and what information to retrieve.

- Easier updating

  Components make it easier for you to revise and update your applications. For example, you can create a COM component that encapsulates business rules. If the business rules change, you update just the component, not all the applications that use the component.

When you use COM components in a Visual Basic project, you do not have to understand all of the mechanics involved in making these components work together. It is more important to know how to use the component that adds the functionality you need to your application. You can find detailed information about COM at http://www.microsoft.com/com/default.asp.

Class Modules

Class modules (.cls files) are the foundation of object-oriented programming in Visual Basic. They are analogous to a blueprint for a house. Just as a house is built from a blueprint, new objects are created from class modules. These new objects include your own customized properties and methods.

A class module is similar to a standard code module (.bas file) because both contain functionality that can be used by other modules within the application. The difference is that a class module provides functionality in the form of an object:

- Data in a standard module has program scope, which means that it exists for the life of your program.

- Class module data exists for each object that is created from the class. Each object's data exists only for the lifetime of the object; it is created when the object is created, and destroyed when the object is destroyed.

- Variables declared as public in a standard module are visible from anywhere in your project. Variables declared as public in a class module can only be accessed by referencing a particular instance of a class or object.

Most commonly, class modules exist in code components. A code component can be thought of as a container for multiple classes. For example, you could create a "vehicles" code component that contains multiple classes; these classes can be used to create objects such as cars, trucks, and vans. A client application uses a code component by creating an object from one of the classes the component provides, and invoking the object's properties, methods, and events.

Creating COM Components With Visual Basic

The greatest benefit of COM is the ability to create COM components that can be easily implemented in many applications. A COM component is a unit of executable code, such as an .exe, .dll, or .ocx file that follows the COM specification for creating objects. These are created from class modules in Visual Basic. A COM component exposes objects that can be used by other applications. Visual Basic handles much of the complexity of creating COM .exe and .dll files. You can create three types of COM components with Visual Basic:

- ActiveX Controls

  ActiveX controls (formerly known as OLE controls) are standard user-interface elements that allow you to rapidly assemble reusable forms and dialog boxes.

- Active Documents

  Active documents are COM components that must be hosted and activated within a document container. Active document technology is an extension to OLE documents. It enables generic shell applications, such as Microsoft Internet Explorer, to host different types of documents.

- ActiveX Code components

  AcitveX Code components (COM executable programs and DLLs) are groups, called libraries, of classes. Client applications use COM objects by creating instances of classes provided by the COM .exe or .dll file. Client applications call the properties, methods, and events provided by each COM object. In Visual Basic, the project templates you use to create a COM components are referred to as ActiveX EXEs and ActiveX DLLs.

Lesson Summary

- You can create ActiveX components that contain class modules that are used to create objects in applications. ActiveX is a technology based on the Component Object Model (COM), which is Microsoft's standard for software interoperability.

- OOP is a way to build object-based software components; ActiveX is a technology that allows you to combine object-based components created by many different tools.

- Visual Basic class modules are the foundation of OOP.

- With Visual Basic you can create three types of COM components:

  - ActiveX controls
  - Active documents
  - ActiveX Code components

Lesson 2: Using Class Modules

Just like forms and standard modules, you can use class modules in one or more Visual Basic application. The class module can be contained within a compiled ActiveX EXE or ActiveX DLL. In this case, the class module would not be added to the project. Instead, a reference would be made to the ActiveX EXE or ActiveX DLL. After the reference has been set, you can create objects from classes in the component and write code using the object's properties, methods, and events. In this chapter, you will focus on creating class modules for use within a single Visual Basic project. For information about using class modules in COM components, see Chapter 8.

After this lesson you will be able to:

- Describe how create an instance of a class.

- Use an object's properties and methods.

- Write an event procedure to handle object events.

Estimated lesson time: 20 minutes

Adding A Class Module to a Project

Before you can use a class module, you must first manually add a new class to the project, or load an existing one.

➤ **To add an existing class module to a project**

1. On the **Project** menu, click **Add Class Module**.

   The **Add Class Module** dialog box appears.

2. Click the **Existing** tab.

3. Browse for the Class Module (.cls file) that you want to add to the project, then click **Open**.

After you add the class to your project, you must declare an object variable to store the object. You declare an object variable in the same way you declare other variables, with Dim, ReDim, Static, Private, or Public.

Declaring Object Variables

In most cases, you know at design time the type of object you want to create and use in your application. It is much more efficient, in these cases, to use specific object variables to point to the objects you create. A specific object variable refers to a particular object type and can only hold pointers to that type. If you try to store a different object type in that variable, an error will result.

For example, you can declare any type of Visual Basic object, such as a form or control and then assign values to these variables:

```
Dim frm As Form
Dim ctl As Control

Set frm = Form1
Set ctl = Command1
```

However, a run-time error will occur if you try to assign the wrong type of object to the object variables:

```
'These two lines of code will cause a run-time error
Set frm = Command1
Set ctl = Form1
```

Once you've added a class module to a project, you can create an object variable based on its type. In the following example, a House object variable is created based on the CHouse class:

```
Dim House as CHouse
```

Using External Objects

In some cases, you might want to declare object variables from external sources, such as Excel, Word, or Internet Explorer. Before you can use an object external to Visual Basic or your application, you must set a reference to that object's type library. A type library contains standard descriptions of exposed objects, properties, and methods that are available from a software component. The files that contain type libraries are called object library files, which have a .olb extension.

If a reference has been set to the object's type library, Visual Basic detects an object variable at design time when you write code for the client application. Visual Basic can display information about the available methods and properties, as well as check the syntax of each method or property call. Another advantage is that you can use the Visual Basic Object Browser to view information about the object's methods, properties, and events.

➤ **To set a reference to an object library in Visual Basic**

1. On the **Project** menu, click **References**.

2. Select the object library to reference, then click **OK**.

The following example declares a variable called "ie" in the General Declarations section that will hold a pointer to Microsoft Internet Explorer objects only:

```
Dim ie As InternetExplorer
```

Generic Object Variables

There are cases when you do not know at design time the specific type of object your application will use. In these situations, you can use generic object variables to hold pointers to any type of object. For example, you might want to write a function that acts on any one of several different classes of objects. In this case, you must declare the variable As Object.

The following example uses the Object data type to declare a generic object variable:

```
Dim objGeneric As Object
```

Since the specific object to be used will not be known until run time, you cannot set a reference to a library for the object in Visual Basic. You should only use generic variables when absolutely necessary since they have several disadvantages, which are discussed in Chapter 8: Connecting to COM Servers.

Creating Objects from Components

Once you have made the component available to your application and have declared an object variable to hold an instance of the component, you can create the object.

In Visual Basic there are three ways to create an object to access an component:

- Use the New keyword with a Set statement.
- Use the GetObject function.
- Use the CreateObject function.

You *instantiate*, or create, an object from a class using one of these statements or functions. Therefore, to use an object, you must declare the object variable, then create an instance of the object. An object variable is a pointer to a location in memory where an object will be stored. Once the object variable is instantiated, the memory location will contain a newly created object.

Note This chapter will focus on using the New keyword to create instances of a class. The CreateObject and GetObject functions will be covered in detail in Chapter 8.

Using the New Keyword with the Set Statement

Whenever you assign a value to an object variable in Visual Basic, you must use the Set statement. The Dim, Private, Public, ReDim, and Static statements only declare a variable that refers to an object. No actual object is referred to until you use the Set statement to assign a specific object.

Generally, when you use the Set statement to assign an object reference to a variable, a new object is not created for that variable. However, when you use the New keyword in the Set statement, you are actually creating an instance of the object. The following example shows how to use the New keyword with the Set statement to create an instance of the CHouse class:

```
Sub CreateHouseObject()
    Dim House As CHouse

    Set House = New CHouse
End Sub
```

You can also use the New keyword in a Dim statement to declare an object variable. If you use New when declaring the object variable, a new instance of the object is created on first reference to it, so you don't have to use the Set statement to assign the object reference. Avoid using variables declared using the New keyword because it can slow your application. Every time Visual Basic encounters a variable declared using the New keyword, it must test whether or not an object reference has already been assigned to the variable.

Lesson Summary

- Class modules give the capability to create reusable objects through ActiveX EXEs and DLLs.

- You can also use class modules to create objects within a single application.

- If the class module has been included in a compiled ActiveX EXE or DLL, you can set a reference to the component in the Visual Basic IDE. After the reference has been set, you can create objects from classes in the component and write code using to use the object.

Lesson 3: Creating Class Modules

At this point, you have written code to manipulate forms and controls in your Visual Basic projects. A form in Visual Basic is much like a class module that you can create. A form has properties, methods, and events that are used to manipulate form objects when your program executes. When you create your own custom classes, part of the class development includes creating the corresponding properties, methods, and events.

After this lesson you will be able to:

- Create properties for a class.
- Create methods for a class.
- Create events for a class.
- Describe how to handle object events.
- Create event procedures.

Estimated lesson time: 40 minutes

Creating Property Procedures

Properties are attributes or characteristics of an object. For example, a house object could have a color property. At any time, you can change the color of the house by assigning a value to the color property. In addition, you can assign the value of a property to a variable as shown in the following example:

```
Dim MyNewHouse As CHouse
Dim ColorPropertyValue As String

'Create an instance of the house object
Set MyNewHouse = New CHouse

'Get the color property value and display
'the value in a message box
ColorPropertyValue = MyNewHouse.Color
MsgBox "House color is: " & ColorPropertyValue

'Set the house color property to red
MyNewHouse.Color = "RED"
```

You implement properties for a class by creating *property procedures*. There are three types of property procedures:

1. Property Get

   Property Get procedures return the current property value. This is shown in the example above when the ColorPropertyValue variable is set to MyNewHouse.Color.

2. Property Let

   Property Let procedures assign a new value to a property. This is shown in the example above where MyNewHouse.Color is set to RED.

3. Property Set

   A Property Set procedure is used in lieu of a Property Let procedure when the property itself is an object. When you assign a value to an object, you must use the Visual Basic Set statement. An example of a property which is an object itself would be the Font property of the TextBox control.

```
'The Pen property may be set to different Pen implementations
Property Set Pen(P As Object)
    Set CurrentPen = P    ' Assign Pen to object.
End Property
```

Practice: Designing a Class Module

In the following procedures, you will create a new project, add a new class module, and add a property to the object.

To see a demonstration, run the Chap06.exe animation located in the Animations folder on the Supplemental Course Materials CD-ROM that accompanies this book.

➤ **To create a class module**

1. Start Visual Basic.

2. In the **New Project** dialog box, select **Standard EXE**, then click **OK**.

3. On the **Project** menu, click **Add Class Module**.

4. In the **Add Class Module** dialog box, select **Class Module,** then click **Open**.

5. In the **Properties** window, set the **Name** property for the class module to CHouse.

➤ **To create property procedures**

1. In the **Code** window, type the following:

```
'Contains the color property setting
Private mvarColor As String

Public Property Get Color() As String
    'Return the current color setting
    Color = mvarColor
End Property

Public Property Let Color(argColor As String)
    'Set the current color setting
    mvarColor = argColor
End Property
```

2. Place a command button on **Form1**.

3. In the **Click** event for the command button, type the following:

```
Dim MyNewHouse As CHouse
Dim HouseColorValue As String

Set MyNewHouse = New CHouse
MyNewHouse.Color = "RED"

HouseColorValue = MyNewHouse.Color
MsgBox "House color is: " & HouseColorValue
```

4. On the **Run** menu in Visual Basic, click **Start**.

5. When the program is running, click the **Command1** button.

   Notice that the property value has been set and then assigned to a variable which appears in a message box.

6. Click **OK** to close the message box.

7. On the **Run** menu in Visual Basic, click **Stop**.

Creating Methods

Methods represent the functionality your class provides. For example, a House class may have a method such as Build. To create a method for an object, you create Public Sub or Function procedures within a class module.

The following example creates a method that builds the House:

```
Public Function Build() As Boolean
    'Call procedures to build the house
    LayFoundation sngLength, sngWidth
    ..

    ..
    PlaceCarpetAndTile
    'If successful
    Build = True
End Function
```

Using the CHouse Class

Once you've created an instance of a class, you can use the methods and properties of the class. You can use the Object Browser in Visual Basic to view the properties, methods, and events that are defined for a class.

The following example creates an instance of the CHouse class, and sets and retrieves the Color property:

```
Dim MyHouse As CHouse

Set MyHouse = New CHouse
'Call Property Let procedure
MyHouse.Color = "WHITE"
'Call Property Get procedure
MsgBox MyHouse.Color
```

The following example creates an instance of the CHouse class and calls the Paint method:

```
Dim MyHouse As CHouse
Dim bHousePainted As Boolean

Set MyHouse = New CHouse
'Call the Paint Method
bHousePainted = MyHouse.Paint
If bHousePainted Then
    MsgBox "House painted successfully!"
End If
```

When you write code that uses objects, it is good practice to release the memory used by your objects when you are finished with them. Once you have finished using an object, use the Set statement to assign the value Nothing to the variable for the object. The following example releases the memory for the MyHouse object:

```
Set MyHouse = Nothing
```

Creating Events

An object provides notification that some action has occurred through the use of events. Properties and methods are *incoming interfaces* because they are invoked outside of the object. By contrast, events are *outgoing interfaces*, because they are initiated within the object and handled outside of the object. For example, when you change the Caption property of a form in Visual Basic, the form object contains the actual code that makes the change; you do not see this code. However, you create and develop event procedures yourself by writing code in Visual Basic.

Class modules have two built-in events: Initialize and Terminate.

- The Initialize event occurs when an instance of a class is created, but before any properties have been set. When you write a class module, you use the Initialize event to initialize any data used by the class. You can also use the Initialize event to load forms used by the class.

- The Terminate event occurs when the object variable goes out of scope or is set to the value Nothing. When you write a class module, you use the Terminate event to save information, unload forms, or perform tasks that should occur when the class terminates.

Declaring Custom Events

You can also declare custom events for your class. You define the event and then write code to cause the event to occur. When you work with an object that exposes an event, you can write code in an event handler to take action when the event occurs. For example, a command button in Visual Basic has a Click event; you can create a Click event procedure containing code to respond.to that event. Similarly, a Customer object could have an OverDue event that occurs when they have an unpaid invoice for more than 90 days. Events are declared in the General Declarations section of a class module using the Event keyword. The following example shows how to declare an event for a class:

```
Public Event Status(ByVal StatusText As String)
```

Using the RaiseEvent Keyword

When you want an event for a class to occur, use the RaiseEvent statement within the class module. The RaiseEvent statement is followed by the event name and any arguments for the event procedure. The following example code raises the Status event to provide status information during a method that takes a long time to process:

```
Public Sub Build()
    RaiseEvent Status("Laying foundation...")
    LayFoundation sngLength, sngWidth
    PlaceCarpetAndTile
    RaiseEvent Status("Installing carpet and tile...")
End Sub
```

Handling Events

In order to support an object's events, you must declare the object variable using the WithEvents keyword. For example, you can use the following code to handle the Build event of a House object:

```
Private WithEvents MyNewHouse As CHouse
```

The variable MyNewHouse must be a module-level variable, which is declared in the General Declarations section. After you declare the MyNewHouse object using the WithEvents keyword, MyNewHouse will appear in the code window as an object, along with its associated events, as shown in Figure 6.1.

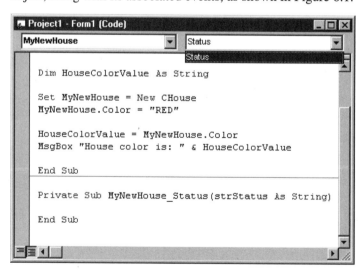

Figure 6.1 Object displayed in code window

The following example shows how to declare an event procedure for the MyHouse object:

```
Private Sub MyNewHouse_Status(strStatus As String)
    MsgBox "Current status: " & strStatus
End Sub
```

Limitations of the WithEvents Keyword

There are several limitations on the use of object variables declared using the WithEvents keyword:

- A variable declared using the WithEvents keyword cannot be a generic object variable. That is, you cannot declare it As Object — you must specify the class name when you declare the variable.

- You cannot use the WithEvents keyword in conjunction with the New keyword. For example, the following example is invalid:

  ```
  Private WithEvents MyHouse As New House
  ```

- You cannot declare variables using the WithEvents keyword in a standard module (.bas file). You can declare them only in class modules, form modules, and other modules that define classes.

- You cannot create arrays of variables using the WithEvents keyword.

Lesson Summary

- When you create class modules, you can write code to provide properties, methods, and events.

- Properties are characteristics of an object and can be thought of as *nouns*, such as color, size, or name.

- Methods are procedures that perform services for the object, such as the Show method of a form in Visual Basic.

- An event allows an object to send notifications, such as the Load or Unload event of a form in Visual Basic.

- Event procedures can be written to handle object events.
  - When you want to handle an object's events, you must use the WithEvents keyword when declaring the object.

Lesson 4: Using the Class Builder

You can create a class module and add methods, properties, and events manually, or you can use the Class Builder Add-In. The Class Builder automates the process of adding properties, methods, and events to a class.

After this lesson you will be able to:

- Explain how to add a new class using the Class Builder.
- Describe how to create an object model.

Estimated lesson time: 20 minutes

Loading the Class Builder

Before you can use the Class Builder, you must load it into the Visual Basic development environment.

➤ **To add the Class Builder Add-In**

1. On the **Add-Ins** menu, click **Add-In Manager**.
2. In the list of available add-ins, select VB 6 Class Builder Utility.
3. Under **Load Behavior**, select the **Loaded/Unloaded** check box, then click **OK**.

Creating a New Class

With the Class Builder, you can visually define a class and its interface, as shown in Figure 6.2.

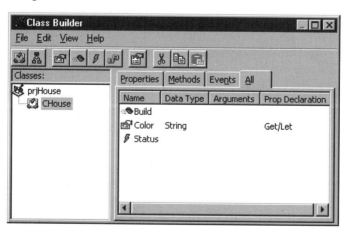

Figure 6.2 The class builder utility

➤ **To use the Class Builder to create a class**

1. On the **Add-Ins** menu, click **Class Builder Utility**.

2. In the Class Builder, on the **File** menu, point to **New**, then click **Class**.

3. In the **Class Module Builder** dialog box, enter a name for the class.

4. On the **Attributes** tab, enter a description for the class and a Help context ID if there is an associated Help file.

Creating the Class Interface

Once you've created a class, you need to define the properties, methods, and events of the class. Collectively, these are called the interface of the class.

➤ **To add a property to a class**

1. Select the class in the Class Builder.

2. On the **File** menu, point to **New**, then click **Property**.

3. Type a property name and select a data type.

4. The Declaration should be set to Public Property (Get, Set, Let). Click **OK** to close the dialog box.

Note You can also add descriptive text and associate a Help context ID number for each property, method, and event by selecting the Attributes tab and typing in the relevant information.

---

5. On the **File** menu, click **Update Project**, then exit the Class Builder.

Object Models

As you add more classes to your project, you'll probably discover that the objects you are using have clear relationships to each other. An object model defines a hierarchy of objects that gives structure to an object-based program. By defining the relationships between objects that are part of the program, an object model organizes the objects in a way that makes programming easier. Object models give structure to an object-based program. They define the relationships among the objects you use in your program; this organizes your objects in a way that makes programming easier.

Typically, an object model expresses the fact that some objects are bigger—or more important—than others are. These objects can be thought of as containing other objects, or as being made up of other objects. For example, you could create a SmallBusiness object as the core of your program. You might want the SmallBusiness object to have other types of objects associated with it, such as Employee, Customer and Products. An object model for this program is shown in Figure 6.3.

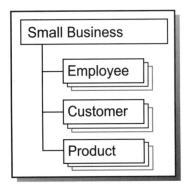

Figure 6.3 An object model

You can define four class modules, named SmallBusiness, Employee, Customer, and Product, and give them each appropriate properties and methods, and then make the connections between objects. You have two tools for this purpose: Object properties and the Collection object. The following code shows one way to implement the hierarchy in Figure 6.3:

```
'Code for the Declarations section of the
'SmallBusiness class module.

Public Name As String
Public Product As New Product
Public Employees As New Collection
Public Customers As New Collection
```

Object Relationships

Objects in a hierarchy are linked together by object properties, that is, properties that return references to objects. An object that contains other objects will have properties that return either references to the objects themselves, or references to collections of objects. Object properties work well when the relationship between objects is one-to-one. However, an object of one type frequently contains a number of objects of another type. In the SmallBusiness object model, the Employees property is implemented as a Collection object, so that the SmallBusiness object can contain multiple Employee objects.

You should use collections when the number of properties is unknown. For example, you have a bicycle object with two wheels, and there is a set of spokes for each wheel. You can easily define the wheels as: FrontWheel and BackWheel. However, Spokes would be better implemented as a collection. In other words, it would be much easier to reference a Spokes collection rather than: Spoke1, Spoke2, Spoke3, etc.

Note The Class Builder utility, included in the Professional and Enterprise editions of Visual Basic, can generate much of the code you need to implement an object model. Class Builder creates robust object properties and collection classes, and allows you to rearrange your model easily.

Lesson Summary

- An object model defines a hierarchy of objects that gives structure to an object-based program. By defining the relationships between objects that are part of the program, an object model organizes the objects in a way that makes programming easier.

- Objects in a hierarchy are linked together by object properties, that is, properties that return references to objects. An object that contains other objects will have properties that return either references to the objects themselves, or references to collections of objects. Although you can create single object properties, you should use collections when the number of properties is unknown.

Summary

Introduction to COM

The Component Object Model (COM) is Microsoft's standard for software interoperability. ActiveX technology is based on COM.

Object oriented programming (OOP) is a way to build object-based software components; ActiveX is a technology that allows you to combine object-based components created by many different tools. Class modules are the foundation of OOP.

The COM components that you can create with Visual Basic are:

- ActiveX controls
- Active documents
- ActiveX Code components.

Using Class Modules

Class modules let you:

- Create reusable objects through ActiveX EXEs and DLLs.
- Create objects within a single application.

If the class module has been included in a compiled ActiveX EXE or DLL, you can set a reference to the component in the Visual Basic IDE. After the reference has been set, you can create objects from classes in the component and write code using to use the object.

Creating Class Modules

When you create class modules, you can write code to provide properties, methods, and events.

- Properties are characteristics of an object such as color, size, or name.
- Methods are procedures that perform services for the object, such as the Show method of a form in Visual Basic.
- Events allow objects to send notifications, such as the Load or Unload event of a form in Visual Basic.
  - To handle an object's events, use the WithEvents keyword when declaring the object.

Using the Class Builder

An object model defines a hierarchy of objects that gives structure to an object-based program. This organizes the objects in a way that makes programming easier.

- Objects in a hierarchy are linked together by object properties.
- An object that contains other objects has properties that return either references to the objects themselves, or references to collections of objects.
  - Use object collections when the number of properties is unknown.

Lab: Creating Class Modules

In this lab, you will continue to develop the Chateau St. Mark hotel reservation system. You will use the Class Builder to create a Reservation class module. You can continue to work with the files you created in Lab 3, or you can use the files provided for you in the \Labs\Lab06\Partial folder. The solution code can be found in the \Labs\Lab06\Solution folder.

To see a demonstration of the solution, run the Lab06.exe animation located in the Animations folder on the Supplemental Course Materials CD-ROM that accompanies this book.

Estimated Lesson Time: 30 Minutes

Exercise 1: Creating Class Modules with the Class Builder

In this exercise, you will use the Class Builder to create the CReservation class module. You will add several methods and an event to this class module.

➤ **To load the Class Builder Utility add-in**

1. Open your application file or the Hotelres.vbp file located in the \Labs\Lab06\Partial folder.

2. On the **Add-Ins** menu, click **Add-In Manager...**

   The **Add-In Manager** dialog box appears.

3. In the **Add-In Manager** dialog box, click the **VB 6 Class Builder Utility** and select the **Loaded/Unloaded** check box.

4. Click **OK** to close the **Add-In Manager** dialog box.

➤ **To create the CReservation Class**

1. On the **Add-Ins** menu, click **Class Builder Utility...**

   The **Class Builder Utility** appears.

2. On the **Class Builder** toolbar, click **Add New Class**.

   The **Class Module Builder** dialog box appears.

3. Click the **Properties** tab, then enter **CReservation** for the Name property.

4. Click **OK**.

5. Add the following four methods to the **CReservation** class module: **AddReservation**, **CheckIn**, **CheckOut**, and **CancelReservation**.

   Each method will be a Public Function with a Boolean return type. Arguments for these methods will be added in later labs.

6. Add an event called **ResError**.

The event will have two arguments: **Number** and **Description**. **Number** will be a Long data type passed by value. **Description** will be a String value passed by value.

7. Add a MsgBox statement to each method in the class. Your code should look like to the following:

```
Option Explicit
'To fire this event, use RaiseEvent with the following syntax:
'RaiseEvent ResError[(arg1, arg2, ... , argn)]
Public Event ResError(ByVal Number As Long, _
    ByVal Description As String)

Public Function CancelReservation() As Boolean
    MsgBox "CancelReservation code will run here."
End Function

Public Function CheckOut() As Boolean
    MsgBox "CheckOut code will run here."
End Function

Public Function CheckIn() As Boolean
    MsgBox "CheckIn code will run here."
End Function

Public Function AddReservation() As Boolean
    MsgBox "AddReservation code will run here."
End Function
```

8. Declare the following private variable in the General Declarations section of **frmReservation**.

```
Private WithEvents Res As Creservation
```

Note The WithEvents keyword specifies that the variable Res will be used to handle an object's events. You specify the kind of object by supplying the name of the class (CReservation) from which the object will be created.

---

9. In Load event of **frmReservation**, create an instance of **CReservation** as follows:

```
Private Sub Form_Load()
    Set Res = New CReservation
    DisableControls
End Sub
```

➤ **To call the CReservation methods**

1. Above the DisableControls procedure in the **cmdDone_Click** event, call the **AddReservation** method of the Res object.

2. In the **mnuGuestReservationCheckIn_Click** event, call the **CheckIn** method of the Res object.

3. In the **mnuGuestReservationCheckout_Click** event, call the **CheckOut** method of the Res object.

4. In the **mnuGuestReservationCancel_Click** event, call the **CancelReservation** method of the Res object.

5. Save and test your application.

   Accept the default filename for the CReservation class module.

Review

The following questions are intended to reinforce key information presented in this chapter. If you are unable to answer a question, review the appropriate lesson and then try the question again. Answers to the questions can be found in the Appendix, "Questions and Answers," located at the back of this book.

1. What is COM?

2. What is the purpose of a class module in Visual Basic?

3. Why should you use specific object variables rather than generic object variables whenever possible?

4. What are three ways to create an object to access an external component?

5. If you were to create an object model based on a bicycle, how would you implement it?

C H A P T E R   7

Introduction to ActiveX Data Objects

About This Chapter

In this chapter, you will learn how to write code to use ActiveX Data Object (ADO) for several purposes.

Before You Begin

To complete the lessons in this chapter, you must have:

■ Read Chapter 6.

Lesson 1: How Visual Basic Accesses Data

Almost all applications require some form of data access. For stand-alone desktop applications, local data access is typically easy to implement with little or no programming effort. For enterprise applications, data access is considerably more complex, often involving remote databases with different data formats and storage mechanisms.

As a developer, you will have to decide which data access technology you should use to build an application. The data access technologies provided by Visual Basic typically reduce development time, simplify code, and yet still provide high performance while exposing many features.

After this lesson you will be able to:

■ Describe the three data access interfaces available in Visual Basic.

■ Explain the difference between using Jet and using ODBCDirect in DAO.

■ Explain why you should use ADO as your data access method.

Estimated lesson time: 25 minutes

Data Access Interfaces

A data access interface is an object model that represents various facets of accessing data. In Visual Basic, three data access interfaces are available to you: ActiveX Data Objects (ADO), Remote Data Objects (RDO), and Data Access Objects (DAO). Using Visual Basic, you can programmatically control connecting to the database, retrieving records, and changing the value of records.

While you may use any of the three data access technologies to interact with a database, ADO is the newest and most powerful. However, it is important to understand where DAO and RDO fit in the overall Visual Basic data access strategy. For example, you may be required to upgrade an existing RDO-based application to use ADO for data access. Likewise, many Visual Basic programs still use the original DAO technology. These applications will eventually need to migrate to ADO in order to provide more advanced functionality.

Data Access Objects

The first data access technology introduced in Visual Basic was DAO. DAO lets you access and manipulate data in local or remote databases and manage the structure of certain types of databases. DAO provides a hierarchical object model, which makes using DAO easy. DAO supports two basic ways to access data. You choose between these ways based on the type of database your application will connect to.

- Microsoft Joint Engine Technology (Jet) allows you to access data in desktop data sources, such as Microsoft Access, FoxPro, Paradox, or Lotus 1-2-3.

- ODBCDirect allows you to access remote database servers without using the Microsoft Jet database engine. This provides better performance and also requires less memory.

ODBCDirect is part of the DAO 3.5 object library, and is an extension to DAO, not a separate technology. ODBCDirect actually uses RDO to access remote databases. DAO 3.5 ships with Microsoft Access 97, Visual Basic 5.0 or later, Microsoft Office 97, and Visual C++ 5.0 or later.

The biggest limitation to DAO is the fact it was not designed to connect to remote databases, such as in a client/server environment. While ODBCDirect provides this functionality, it is not very efficient. In addition, DAO was only designed to work with databases, and cannot access other sources, such as an e-mail system.

Remote Data Objects

Unlike DAO, which is designed to access desktop databases, RDO provides an object model for accessing remote data. The RDO programming model is similar to the DAO model, except that it is designed to work with client/server databases rather than desktop databases. RDO takes advantage of intelligent database servers that use sophisticated query engines, such as SQL Server and Oracle. More emphasis is therefore placed on using compiled queries that are stored in the database and utilizing server functionality.

RDO was designed to give Visual Basic developers the ability to access remote data without having to code to the open database connectivity (ODBC) application programming interface (API).

The ODBC API is a component of Microsoft Windows implemented to provide a standard, open, vendor-neutral way of accessing data stored in a variety of proprietary personal computer, minicomputer, and mainframe computer databases. RDO is a programming interface to the ODBC API and provides most of the functionality of ODBC in the form of an object model. RDO ships with the Enterprise Editions of Visual Basic, Visual C++, and Microsoft Visual Studio.

RDO is limited in that it does not access desktop databases very efficiently and can access relational databases only through existing ODBC drivers. In addition, RDO does not meet the needs of Internet developers, who must access special types of data in addition to traditional relational sources, as ADO does.

ActiveX Data Objects

ADO is Microsoft's newest data access technology and is an interface to OLE DB. OLE DB is Microsoft's strategic low-level interface to all types of data. This concept is called Universal Data Access (UDA). For example, OLE DB and ADO provide developers the same interface to not only access data from relational and nonrelational databases, but also other data sources, such as e-mail, file systems, project management tools, spreadsheets, and custom business objects. OLE DB has been designed to build on the success of ODBC by providing an open standard for accessing all kinds of data. However, OLE DB does not use, nor require, ODBC. It effectively replaces the ODBC layer. Because of OLE DB, you can build solutions that span desktop, midrange, mainframe, and Internet technologies using a variety of data stores.

With the release of Visual Basic 6, and ADO version 2.0, Microsoft now recommends the use of ADO for all data access. If you are developing a new application, you should definitely use ADO. If you're considering migration to ADO, you have to decide if characteristics and benefits of ADO are enough to justify the cost of converting existing software. Older code written in RDO and DAO will not automatically convert to ADO code. However, whatever solutions you previously developed using other data access strategies, it can definitely be implemented using ADO. Eventually, you should convert to ADO because it features a simpler—yet more flexible—object model than either RDO or DAO. In addition, other development tools can use ADO. For example, if you want to build a Web-based front-end to a database using the Active Server Pages (ASP) technology, the same code you would use in a Visual Basic application can be used in ASP.

Relational Database Concepts

In this chapter, you will use ADO to work with a relational desktop database. In order to do this, you must have a basic understanding of a relational database model. The relational model is the standard for database design. The database stores and presents data as a collection of tables. A structure is defined by establishing relationships between tables; this links data in the database instead of modeling the relationships of the data according to the way it is physically stored. The relational database model offers the following benefits:

- Organizes data in a collection of tables making the design easy to understand.

- Provides a relationally complete language for data definition, retrieval, and update. It is nonprocedural and criteria-based.

- Provides data integrity rules that define consistent states of the database to improve data reliability.

A relational database management system (RDBMS) is software that allows you to represent your data according to the relational model. Relational databases support a standard language called Structured Query Language (SQL). SQL has evolved into a comprehensive language for controlling and interacting with a database management system (DBMS). SQL is a standard approved by the American National Standards Institute (ANSI). The Northwind database (Nwind.mdb) is a sample relational database that is included with Microsoft Access and Visual Basic.

Note Structured Query Language is discussed in detail in Lesson 3.

Tables

The relational database model presents data as a collection of tables. A table is a logical grouping of related information. For example, the Northwind database has a table that lists all of the employees and another table that lists all the customer orders. Tables are made up of rows and columns. Rows are often referred to as records and columns are referred to as fields. Figure 7.1 shows the Employees table from the Northwind database.

Employee ID	Last Name	First Name	Title
1	Davolio	Nancy	Sales Representative
2	Fuller	Andrew	Vice President, Sales
3	Leverling	Janet	Sales Representative
4	Peacock	Margaret	Sales Representative
5	Buchanan	Steven	Sales Manager
6	Suyama	Michael	Sales Representative
7	King	Robert	Sales Representative
8	Callahan	Laura	Inside Sales Coordinator
9	Dodsworth	Anne	Sales Representative

Figure 7.1 The Employees table from the Northwind database

Records

A record contains information about a single entry in a table. For example, a record in an Employees table would contain information on a particular employee.

Fields

A record is composed of multiple fields. Each field in a record contains a single piece of information about the record. For example, an Employee record has fields for Employee ID, Last Name, First Name, and so forth.

Keys

To uniquely identify a row, each table should have a primary key. The primary key is a field, or combination of fields, whose value is unique for each row, or record, in the table. For example, the Employee ID field is the primary key for the Employees table. No two employees can have the same ID.

A table can also contain fields that are foreign keys. A foreign key "points to" a primary key field in a related table. For example, in the Northwind database, the

Orders table contains a Customer ID field. Each Customer ID in the Orders table identifies which customer made the order.

The relationship between the Orders and Customers table is a one-to-many relationship—that is, each customer may have more than one order. Figure 7.2 illustrates how one customer can have many orders.

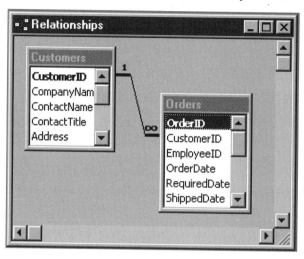

Figure 7.2 Relationship between an Orders and Customers table

Lesson Summary

As a developer, you will have to decide which data access technology you should use to build an application. The data access technologies provided by Visual Basic typically:

- Reduce development time
- Simplify code
- Provide high performance while exposing many features

A data access interface is an object model that represents various facets of accessing data. In Visual Basic, three data access interfaces are available to you:

- ActiveX Data Objects (ADO)
- Remote Data Objects (RDO)
- Data Access Objects (DAO)

Visual Basic uses a relational database model. The relational database model presents data as a collection of tables. A table is a logical grouping of related information.

- Each record in a table contains information about a single entry in the table. A record is composed of multiple fields.
- Each field in a record contains a single piece of information about the record.
- To uniquely identify a row, each table should have a primary key. The primary key is a field or combination of fields whose value is unique for each record in the table.
- A table can also contain fields that are foreign keys. A foreign key "points to" a primary key field in a related table.

Lesson 2: Introduction to OLE DB and ADO

You can use ADO in Visual Basic to access data in your applications. The ADO object model provides an easy-to-use set of objects, properties, and methods for creating applications that access and manipulate data.

Because ADO is an interface to OLE DB, Microsoft's newest and most powerful data access technology, ADO provides high-performance access to a variety of information sources (including relational data and nonrelational data). This includes mainframe ISAM (indexed sequential access method)/VSAM (virtual storage access method), hierarchical databases, desktop databases such as Microsoft Access, and remote databases such as Oracle and Microsoft SQL Server. In addition, ADO can access other data such as e-mail servers, file system stores, text files, graphical and geographical data, custom business objects, and more.

After this lesson you will be able to:

- Describe the benefit of OLE DB.
- Explain how OLE DB works with ADO.

Estimated lesson time: 15 minutes

What Is OLE DB?

OLE DB is a set of COM interfaces that provide applications with uniform access to data stored in diverse information sources, regardless of location or type. In general, OLE DB attempts to make it easy for applications to access data stored in diverse database management systems (DBMS) and other information sources. DBMS sources can include:

- Mainframe databases such as IMS and DB2
- Server databases such as Oracle and SQL Server
- Desktop databases such as Access, Paradox, and FoxPro

Other sources can include:

- Information stored in file systems for Windows NT or UNIX
- Indexed-sequential files
- E-mail systems such as Exchange
- Spreadsheets, project management tools, and many other sources

Components of OLE DB

Conceptually, OLE DB has three types of components: data consumers, service components, and data providers, as illustrated in Figure 7.3.

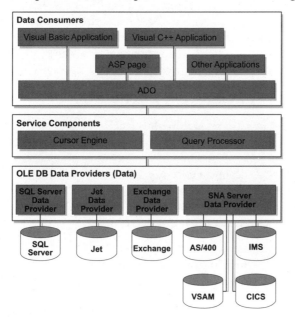

Figure 7.3 Components of OLE DB

Data Consumers

Data consumers are applications that use the data exposed by data providers. ADO is the programmatic interface for using OLE DB data. Examples of consumers include high-level data access models such as ADO, business applications written in development tools such as Visual Basic, C++, or Java, and development tools themselves. Any application that uses ADO is an OLE DB data consumer.

Service Components

Service components are elements that process and transport data and extend the functionality of data providers. For example, a cursor engine is a service component that can consume data from a sequential, forward-only data source to produce scrollable data. Service components are designed to integrate efficiently to help OLE DB component vendors develop high-quality OLE DB components.

Data Providers

Data providers are applications, such as Microsoft SQL Server or Exchange. This includes operating system components, such as a file system, indexed-sequential files, spreadsheets, document stores, and mail files that have data that other applications may need to access. These data providers expose OLE DB interfaces that service components or data consumers can access directly. There is also an OLE DB provider for ODBC. This provider makes any ODBC data available to OLE DB data consumers. However, OLE DB is not dependent on ODBC.

How OLE DB Relates To ADO

ADO provides consistent, high-performance access to data and supports a variety of development needs, including the creation of front-end database clients and middle-tier business objects that use applications, tools, languages, or Internet browsers. ADO is designed to be the one data interface needed for single and multi-tier client/server development, as well as Web-based data-driven solution development. The primary benefits of ADO are ease of use, high speed, low memory overhead, and a small disk footprint.

ADO provides an easy-to-use interface to OLE DB, which provides the underlying access to data. ADO is implemented with minimal network traffic in key scenarios, and a minimal number of layers between the front end and data source—all to provide a lightweight, high-performance interface. ADO is easy to use because it uses a familiar metaphor—the COM automation interface, available from all leading Rapid Application Development (RAD) tools, database tools, and languages, including Visual Basic, Java, VBScript, JScript, and C/C++.

Lesson Summary

- OLE DB is a set of COM interfaces that provide applications with uniform access to data stored in diverse information sources, regardless of location or type.
- Because ADO is an interface to OLE DB, Microsoft's newest and most powerful data access technology, ADO provides high-performance access to a variety of information sources (including relational data and nonrelational data).
- Conceptually, OLE DB has three types of components:
  - Data providers
  - Data consumers
  - Service components

Lesson 3: Overview of Structured Query Language

Structured Query Language (SQL) is a language used for querying, updating, and managing relational databases. SQL can be used to retrieve, sort, and filter specific data from the database. In addition, you can add, change, and delete data in a database using SQL statements.

It is important to have a fundamental understanding of the SQL language so your applications will communicate effectively with the database. By using SQL, an application can ask the database to perform tasks rather than requiring application code and processing cycles to achieve the same result. More importantly, effective use of SQL can minimize the amount of data that must be read from and written to a remote database server. Finally, effective use of SQL can minimize the amount of data sent across the network. Minimizing disk I/O and network I/O are the most important factors for improving application performance.

After this lesson you will be able to:

- Describe the purpose of SQL.
- Define the syntax of a simple SQL statement.
- Filter records in a query using a simple SQL statement.

Estimated lesson time: 20 minutes

The SQL Select Statement

The SQL **Select** statement returns information from the database as a set of records. The select statement is divided into three major sections:

- SELECT

  The Select section allows you to specify which fields will be returned from the query.

- FROM

  The From section allows you to specify which tables will be used to get the fields specified in the SELECT section of the SQL statement.

- WHERE (Optional)

  The Where section allows you to specify a criteria used to limit the selection of records. You can filter queries based on multiple fields.

The minimum syntax for a Select statement is:

SELECT *fields* FROM *tables*;

To perform this operation, the database engine searches the specified table or tables, extracts the chosen fields, selects rows that meet the criterion, and sorts or groups the resulting rows into the order specified. You can select all fields in a table by using the asterisk (*). For example, the following SQL statement will return all the fields of all the records from an Employees table:

```
SELECT *
FROM Employees;
```

However, it is not very efficient to always return all the data from a table. By adding a Where clause to the end of the statement, you can specify only certain records to be returned. The following example retrieves all fields from all records in the Employees table that have a last name equal to Davolio:

```
SELECT *
FROM Employees
WHERE LastName = 'Davolio';
```

Note the use of the apostrophes (') surrounding the word Davolio in the above example. Apostrophes are used when the value in a Where clause is a string. In this case, LastName is a string value in the database. When a numeric value is specified in a Where clause, apostrophes are not used, as shown in the following example.

```
SELECT *
FROM Employees
WHERE EmployeeID = 1;
```

The WHERE IN clause

Using the Where clause with the In operator, you can determine whether the value of an expression is equal to any of several values in a specified list. For example, you can use the Where In clause to return the last names and residing countries of all employees, as illustrated in the following example and in Figure 7.4.

```
SELECT LastName, Country
FROM Employees
WHERE Country IN ('UK', 'USA');
```

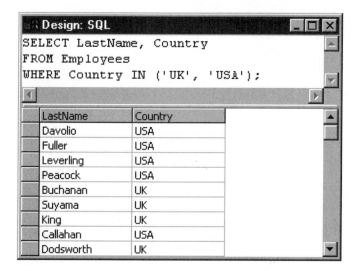

Figure 7.4 Using the In operator with a Where clause to filter records

The Where Between Clause

A selection of records between two criteria can also be returned. Note the use of the number signs (#) surrounding the dates in the following example:

```
SELECT OrderID
FROM Orders
WHERE OrderDate
BETWEEN #01/01/93# AND #01/31/93#;
```

Using the LIKE Operator

You can use the Like operator to find values in a field that match a pattern that you specify. You can specify the complete value, as in LIKE 'Smith', or you can use wildcard characters to find a range of values. For example, LIKE 'Sm%'. If you enter LIKE 'C%' in an SQL query, the query returns all field values beginning with the letter C. In the following example, all records where the last name starts with the letter D are returned. This is also illustrated in Figure 7.5.

```
Select LastName
FROM Employees
WHERE LastName LIKE 'D%';
```

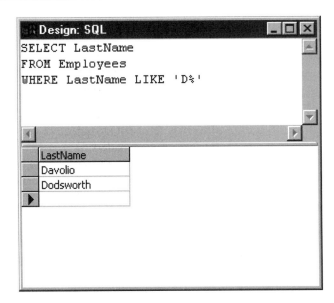

Figure 7.5 Syntax and results of a SQL statement using the Like operator

The ORDER BY Clause

By default, records are returned in the order they were entered in the database. The optional Order By clause can be used to sort a query's resulting records on a specified field, or fields, in ascending or descending order. The ASC option indicates ascending order, DESC indicates descending order. The default sort order is ascending (A to Z, 0 to 9). The following example selects all fields from the Employees table sorted descending by last name:

```
SELECT *
FROM Employees
ORDER BY LastName DESC;
```

Lesson Summary

Structured Query Language (SQL) is a language used in querying, updating, and managing relational databases. SQL can be used to retrieve, sort, and filter specific data to be extracted from the database. The SQL Select statement returns information from the database as a set of records. The Select statement is divided into three major sections: SELECT, FROM, and WHERE. In different environments, databases have different implementations of the same SQL functionality, both syntactically and semantically. You must be aware that each implementation of SQL has its own support for different data types, referential integrity, and compiled queries.

Lesson 4: The ADO Data Control

Although you can use ADO directly in your applications, the ADO Data control has the advantage of being a graphical control complete with record navigation buttons. It is also an easy-to-use interface that allows you to create database applications with a minimum of code.

The ADO Data control uses Microsoft ADO to quickly create connections between data-bound controls and data providers. Data-bound controls are any controls that feature a DataSource property, including the CheckBox, ComboBox, Image, Label, ListBox, PictureBox, and TextBox controls. Additionally, Visual Basic includes several data-bound ActiveX controls such as the DataGrid, DataCombo, Chart, and DataList controls. You can also create your own data-bound ActiveX controls, or purchase controls from other vendors. When you bind controls to an ADO Data control, each field is automatically displayed and updated when navigating through records. This is done internally by Visual Basic; you do not have to write any code.

Previous versions of Visual Basic included Data controls based on the DAO and RDO technologies. The older DAO Data control is presented in the Visual Basic toolbox by default. Both controls are still included with Visual Basic for backward compatibility. However, because of the flexibility of ADO, it's recommended that new database applications, that may require a data control, be created using the ADO Data control.

After this lesson you will be able to:

- Describe how to connect the ADO Data control to a data source.
- Add the ADO Data control to the Visual Basic toolbox.
- Use the ADO Data control in an application.

Estimated lesson time: 30 minutes

Using the ADO Data Control

The ADO Data control is similar to the intrinsic data control and the Remote Data control (RDC). The ADO Data control allows you to quickly create a connection to a database using ADO. The data control that appears in the Visual Basic toolbox by default is the older, DAO Data control. You must manually add the ADO Data control to the toolbox.

➤ **To add the ADO Data control to the toolbox**

1. On the **Project** menu, click **Components**.

2. On the **Components** dialog box, click the **Microsoft ADO Data control 6.0** (OLE DB), as illustrated in Figure 7.6.

3. Click **OK**.

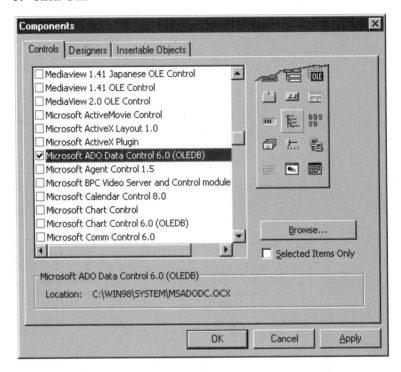

Figure 7.6 The Components dialog box

Connecting to a Data Source

At design time, you can create a connection to a data source by setting the ConnectionString property of the ADO Data control to a valid connection string. Then, set the RecordSource property to a table (or SQL statement) from which to retrieve records. Setting these properties is an easy process because Visual Basic provides Property Pages to set the values. When setting the ConnectionString property of the ADO Data control, you have three data source options.

■ Use Data Link File

This option specifies that you are using a custom connection string that connects to the data source. When this is selected, you can click Browse to access the Organize Data Sources dialog box, from which you can select your Data Link file.

■ Use ODBC Data Source Name

This option specifies that you are using a system-defined data source name (DSN) for the connection string. You can access a list of all system-defined DSNs through the combo box in the Property Page dialog box, as illustrated in Figure 7.7. When this option is selected, you can click New to access the

Create New Data Source Wizard dialog box to add to or modify DSNs on the system.

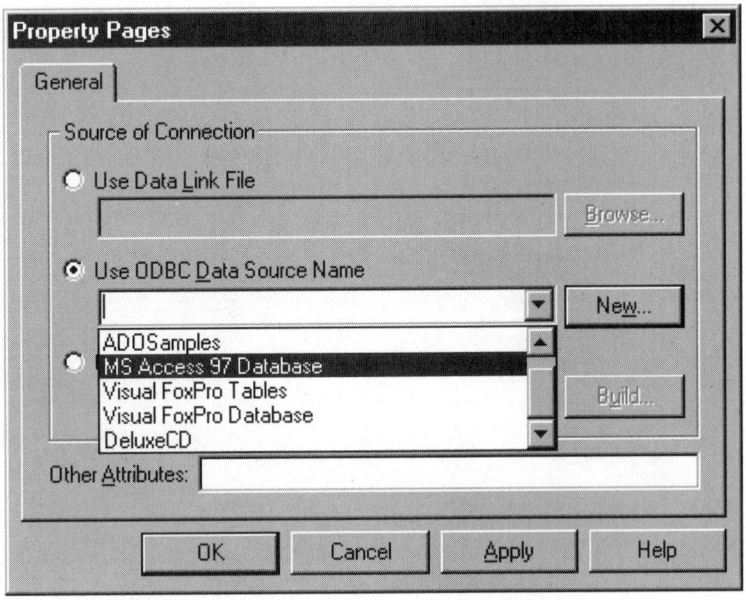

Figure 7.7 Using the ODBC data source name option

- Use Connection String

  This option specifies that you are using a connection string to access data. If the Use Connection String text box is empty, the wizard appears, or you can click Build to access the Data Link Properties dialog box. Use this dialog box to specify the connection, authentication, and advanced information required to access data using an OLE DB provider.

Setting a Connection String

In the following procedure, we will focus on using a connection string to connect to a data source. In this process, you will choose an OLE DB provider, specify a database name and location, and test the connection.

➤ **To set the ConnectionString property value**

1. Place an ADO Data control on a form.

2. On the **Properties** window, click the **ConnectionString** property, then click the ellipsis (**...**) to open the **Property Pages**.

3. Click on the ellipsis located on the right side of the ConnectionString property within the **Properties** window.

4. Click the **Use Connection String** option, then click **Build**.

5. Select the **Microsoft Jet 3.51 OLE DB Provider**, then click **Next**.

6. Click the ellipsis to the right of the **Select or enter database name** text box to browse the database name.

7. On the **Select Access Database** dialog box, click Nwind.mdb, then click **Open**.

8. Click **Test Connection** in the Data Link Properties window.

    A message box will appear notifying you whether or not the connection succeeded.

9. Click **OK** to close the message box, then click **OK** to close the Data Link Properties window.

    A string value will be automatically generated for the Use Connection String value as illustrated in Figure 7.8.

10. Click **OK** to close the ConnectionString Property Pages window.

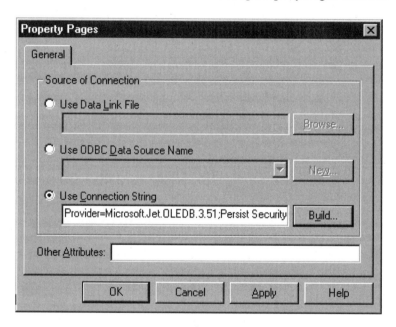

Figure 7.8 A ConnectionString value

Setting the RecordSource Property

After you set the ConnectionString property of the ADO Data control to connect to a database, you can set the RecordSource property to establish where the records will come from. The RecordSource property can be set to either a database table name, a stored query name, or a Structured Query Language (SQL) statement. To improve performance, avoid setting the RecordSource property to an entire table. Set the RecordSource to a n SQL string that retrieves only the necessary records. An SQL query must use syntax appropriate for the data source.

In other words, Microsoft Access and Microsoft SQL Server use different SQL syntax; therefore, you must use the appropriate syntax for the particular database.

The RecordSource property can be set at design time by using the Property Pages in Visual Basic as shown in Figure 7.9.

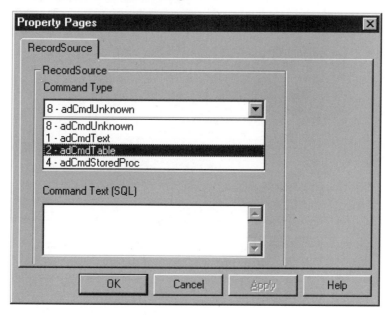

Figure 7.9 RecordSource property page

In the RecordSource property page dialog box, you set the command type parameter that tells ADO which type of command object to use. The following table explains the different command type options.

Value	Description
adCmdUnknown	The type of command in the CommandText property is not known. This is the default value.
adCmdText	Evaluates CommandText as a textual definition of a command or stored procedure call.
adCmdTable	Evaluates CommandText as a table name whose columns are all returned by an internally generated SQL query.
adCmdStoredProc	Evaluates CommandText as a stored procedure name. This can be a stored procedure in a SQL Server database or a query in an Access database.

If you select either adCmdTable or adCmdStoredProc, you set the table or stored procedure name in the Table or Stored Procedure Name drop-down list box below the command type drop-down list box, as illustrated in Figure 7.10.

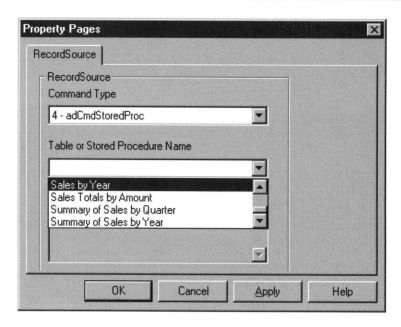

Figure 7.10 Selecting a stored procedure as a RecordSource

Practice: Connecting an ADO Data Control to a Data Source

In this practice you will add an ADO Data control to the Visual Basic toolbox, add the control to a form, and connect it to a data source. The data source will be the Northwind sample database (Nwind.mdb), included with Visual Basic.

To see a demonstration, run the Chap07.exe animation located in the Animations folder on the Supplemental Course Materials CD-ROM that accompanies this book.

➤ **To add an ADO Data control to your project**

1. Start Visual Basic, click Standard EXE in the **New Project** dialog box, then click **OK**.

2. On the **Project** menu, click **Components**.

3. In the **Controls** tab of the **Components** dialog box, click the Microsoft ADO Data control 6.0 (OLE DB), then click **OK**.

   The ADO Data control will be added to the Visual Basic toolbox.

➤ **To connect the ADO Data control to a data source**

1. Select the ADO Data control on the Visual Basic toolbox and add it to Form1.

2. Right-click on the ADO Data control and click **ADODC Properties**.

   The ADO Data control **Property Pages** dialog box appears. In the **General** tab, make sure the Use Connection String option is selected.

3. To set the connection string, click **Build**.

4. Highlight Microsoft Jet OLE DB Provider and click **Next**.

   You are using the Jet OLE DB provider because you will connect to a Microsoft Access database.

5. The **Connection** tab is used to select or type a database name. Click the ellipsis to the right of the **Select or enter database name** text box to browse the database name.

6. On the **Select Access Database** dialog box, click Nwind.mdb and click **Open**.

7. Click **Test Connection** in the Data Link Properties window.

   A message box appears notifying you whether or not the connection succeeded.

8. Click **OK** to close the **Data Link Properties** dialog box.

9. Now that the connection string value has been built, click the **RecordSource** tab on the **Property Pages** dialog box.

10. For the **Command Type**, click 1 – adCmdText.

11. For the **Command Text (SQL)** value, type the following SQL statement:

```
SELECT * FROM Customers;
```

   Your screen should look like Figure 7.11.

12. Click **OK** to close the ADO Data control's **Property Pages** dialog box.

   Your ADO Data control is bound to a data source. Now you can use it to retrieve information from the Customers table in the Nwind.mdb database.

13. On the **File** menu in Visual Basic, click **Save Project**.

   Save your project as prjADO.vbp in the \Practice\Ch07 folder. You will use this project in the Binding Controls to the ADO Data control practice in the next section.

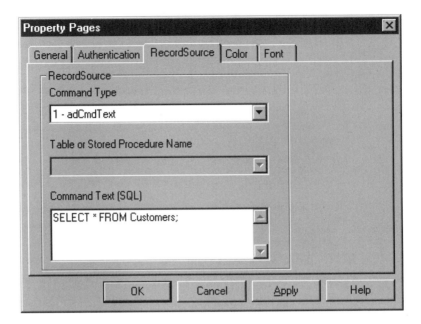

Figure 7.11 The Property Pages dialog box

Binding Controls

After you set the ConnectionString and RecordSource properties for the ADO Data control, you can add a bound control to display data on your form.

A bound control is one that is "data-aware." When an ADO Data control moves from one record to the next, either through code or when the user clicks the ADO Data control arrows, all bound controls connected to the ADO Data control change to display data from fields in the current record. In addition, if the user changes the data in the bound control, those changes are automatically posted to the database as the user moves to another record. The benefit of using bound controls is that it minimizes the amount of code you must write. Because the value of the bound control is automatically retrieved from and written to the database, there is little or no programming involved.

Setting the DataSource and DataField Properties

In order to bind a control to an ADO Data control, you must set the DataSource and DataField properties of the bound control. The DataSource property specifies the source through which the control is bound to the database (for example, an ADO Data control).

The DataField property specifies a valid field name in the Recordset object created by the data source. This value determines which field is displayed in the bound control. The DataSource and DataField properties can be set at design time in the Properties window, as illustrated in Figure 7.12.

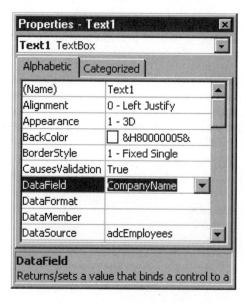

Figure 7.12 Setting the DataSource and DataField properties

You can also set the DataSource and DataField properties at run time. If you set the DataSource property at run time using code, you must use the Set keyword because the DataSource property is an object. The following example sets the DataSource and DataField properties:

```
Set txtCompanyName.DataSource = adcEmployees
txtFirstName.DataField = "CompanyName"
```

Practice: Binding Controls

In this practice, you will use the project you created in the Connecting an ADO Data control to a Data Source practice.

➤ **To bind controls to an ADO Data control**

1. Open the prjADO.vbp project you saved in the Connecting an ADO Data control to a Data Source practice located in the \Practice\Ch07 folder.

2. Add two textboxes to your form above the ADO Data control.

3. On the Properties window, set the DataSource property of Text1 to Adodc1.

4. Set the DataField property to CompanyName.

5. Set the DataSource property of Text2 to Adodc1.

6. Sey the DataField property of Text2 to Phone.

7. On the **Run** menu, click **Start**.

You can move through the records viewing company names and phone numbers by clicking the navigational arrows on the ADO Data control. Your program should look like the illustration in Figure 7.13.

8. On the **Run** menu, click **End**.

9. To save your project, click **Save Project** on the **File** menu.

Figure 7.13 Company name and phone numbers displayed in bound controls

Using the Data Form Wizard

Although you can bind controls to the ADO Data control manually, you can also use the Data Form Wizard to create forms containing bound controls. The Data Form Wizard is an add-in that you can use to create database viewer applications.

Using the Data Form Wizard, you can create a form that displays, adds, deletes, and edits data in a database. The wizard reduces the task of adding the controls and setting properties to a few easy steps. The Data Form Wizard:

■ Creates and adds a new form to the current project.

■ Adds an ADO Data control and sets the RecordSource property to your specification.

■ Automatically sets the ADO Data control's ConnectionString property.

■ Performs the following tasks for each field selected in a table:

   • Adds a label with the field name.

   • Adds a bound control. The type of control depends on the type of data stored in the field.

Data Type	Control
String, date, and numeric	TextBox
Boolean	CheckBox
Memo fields	Multi-line TextBox
Binary data	OLE Container

Picture   PictureBox

- Adds command buttons to perform various data-access functions, including Add, Delete, Refresh, Update, and Close.
- Adds code behind the command buttons and ADO Data control, including comments.

➤ To install the Data Form Wizard add-in

1. On the **Add-Ins** menu, click **Add-In Manager**.

2. On the **Add-In Manager** dialog box, click VB 6 Data Form Wizard, select the Loaded/Unloaded check box for the load behavior, then click **OK**.

Your screen should look similar to the illustration shown in Figure 7.14.

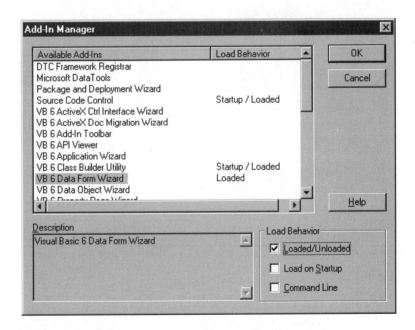

Figure 7.14 Adding the Data Form Wizard from the Add-In Manager dialog box

➤ To use the Data Form Wizard to connect to the Nwind.mdb database

1. On the **Add-Ins** menu, click **Data Form Wizard**.

2. Click **Next** to accept the default profile.

3. Click **Access** on the **Database Type** list, then click **Next**.

4. Click **Browse**, click the Nwind.mdb file, then click **Open**.

The Database Name should be set to C:\Program Files\Microsoft Visual Studio\VB98\Nwind.mdb. If you cannot find the Nwind.mdb file in

C:\Program Files\Microsoft Visual Studio\VB98, run Visual Basic setup to add this component.

5. Click **Next** to accept the database name.

6. Set the **Form Layout** to Single Record, set the **Binding Type** to ADO Data control, and then click **Next**.

7. Click **Customers** for the **Record Source**, click the fields of your choice, and then click **Next**.

8. Select from the **Add**, **Update**, **Delete**, **Refresh**, and **Close** check boxes, then click **Finish**.

   The form created for you by the Data Form Wizard should look like the illustration in Figure 7.15.

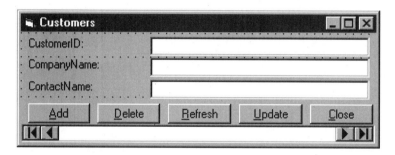

Figure 7.15 A form with bound control created by the Data Form Wizard

Lesson Summary

- The ADO Data control is a graphic control (with record navigation buttons) and an easy-to-use interface that allows you to create database applications with a minimum of code. To use the ADO Data control in Visual Basic 6.0, you must add it to the toolbox.

- At design time, you can create a connection to a data source by setting the ConnectionString property of the ADO Data control to a valid connection string. After you set the ConnectionString property of the ADO Data control to connect to a database, you can set the RecordSource property to establish where the records will come from.

- Once you have set the ConnectionString and RecordSource properties for the ADO Data control, you can add a bound control to display data on your form.

Lesson 5: Coding the ADO Data Control

So far you have learned how to set the ADO Data control's properties to connect to a database and bind controls to the ADO Data control. In this lesson, you will learn about manipulating data with the ADO Data control. The ADO Data control allows you to view and edit records without writing any code. However, to support more advanced features, you will need to write some code. Using the ADO Data control, and a bound control's properties, methods, and events, you can gain more control over how your application interacts with external data.

After this lesson you will be able to:

- Describe how a Recordset object relates to the ADO Data control.
- Add new records to a Recordset.
- Update existing records in a Recordset.
- Delete records from a Recordset.
- Find records within a Recordset.

Estimated lesson time: 45 minutes

Creating a Recordset

The ADO Data control has a property called a Recordset, which is a group of records. The Recordset property of the ADO Data control is an object itself, and has its own properties and methods. A Recordset object represents the records in a base table or the records that result from running a query. Recordset objects are constructed using records (rows) and fields (columns). You can use Recordset objects to manipulate the data in a database. At any time, the Recordset object refers to only a single record within the set as the *current record*.

To retrieve a set of records, you set the RecordSource property of the ADO Data control. The RecordSource property is a string value that can be a query or table name within a database from which to retrieve records.

You can also use the Filter property to selectively screen out records in a Recordset object. For example, you can set the recordset to contain only records where the CusomerID value is greater than ten.

```
adcCustomers.Recordset.Filter = "CustomerID > 10"
```

Checking the Recordset Position

After you have set the RecordSource property, you can check the Recordset object's BOF and EOF properties. These properties indicate if you are at the beginning or end of the Recordset. If there are no records in the Recordset, the value of both BOF and EOF is True.

Modifying Records in a Recordset

Although the ADO Data control can automatically modify and update records without you having to add any code, you can use the Update method to modify the data instead of using the arrows on the ADO Data control.

The ADO Data control automatically changes a record in the database when you:

1. Move to the record that you want to modify.
2. Change any of the information displayed in the bound controls.
3. Click any arrow on the ADO Data control to move to another record.

However, using a command button allows you to add code to the Click event to perform tasks, such as validating fields on the form before updating a record. To perform an update to the current record, use the Update method. For example, in the Click event for the Update button, you can add the following code:

```
adcCustomers.Recordset.Update
```

If you want to cancel any changes made to the current record, or to a new record prior to calling the Update method, you can use the CancelUpdate method. The syntax for the CancelUpdate method is shown in the following example:

```
adcEmployees.Recordset.CancelUpdate
```

Adding Records to a Recordset

New records can be added to a Recordset by calling the AddNew method. The AddNew method initializes the bound controls and the new record becomes the current record. If you call AddNew while editing another record, ADO automatically calls the Update method to save any changes and then creates the new record. The following example code will add a new record to the adcCustomers recordset:

```
adcCustomers.Recordset.AddNew
```

To save changes to the new record, you can either call the Update method of the Recordset object, or you can click any one of the navigation buttons on the ADO Data control. You can use the CancelUpdate method to cancel any changes made to a new record prior to navigating with the ADO Data control, or calling the Update method.

Deleting Records from a Recordset

Using the Delete method, you can delete the current record or a group of records in a recordset. The Delete method has an AffectRecords parameter that is used to set how many records the Delete method will affect.

AffectRecords value	Definition
adAffectCurrent	This option will delete only the current record and is the default option.
adAffectGroup	This option can be used to delete all records that satisfy the current Filter property setting. You must set the Filter property in order to use this option.

Retrieving field values from the deleted record generates an error. After deleting the current record, the deleted record remains current until you move to a different record. Once you move away from the deleted record, it is no longer accessible.

To invoke the Delete method, use the following syntax:

```
Recordset.Delete AffectRecords
```

You can check the EOF property to see if you have deleted the last record. If EOF is True, move to the last record in the Recordset, as shown in the following example code:

```
adcCustomers.Recordset.Delete
adcCustomers.Recordset.MoveNext
If adcCustomers.Recordset.EOF = True Then
    adcCustomers.Recordset.MoveLast
End If
```

Note The Northwind database has referential integrity rules defined that prevent you from deleting certain records from the Recordset. For example, you cannot delete a Customer if they have records in the Orders table.

Searching for Records

To add a search feature to your application, use the Find method for the ADO Data control's recordset. The Find method searches an existing recordset for the record that satisfies the specified criteria. If the criteria is met, the recordset is positioned on that record; otherwise, the position is set on the end of the recordset (EOF).

The Find method has one required parameter, Criteria, and three optional parameters: SkipRows, SearchDirection, and Start.

The Criteria parameter is a string containing a statement that specifies the column name, comparison operator, and value to use in the search. The comparison operator in criteria may be ">" (greater than), "<" (less than), "=" (equal), or "like" (pattern matching).

In the following example, the first customer that resides in the state of Washington will be returned:

```
adcCustomers.Find "State = 'WA'"
```

Note The Find method can be slow unless you have limited the total number of records in the recordset. Another method for finding records is to use a SQL statement when setting the RecordSource property of the ADO Data control. You can also set the ADO Data control's Filter property to limit the number of records in a recordset.

Verifying Find Results

When you search for records using the Find method, you can use the EOF or BOF properties of the Recordset object to determine whether a particular record was found. If the search fails to find the record, you should return to the record where the search began. The following example code shows how to use the EOF and BOF properties:

```
'If the record isn't found
If .EOF Or .BOF Then
    'Return to the starting record
    .Bookmark = varBookmark
    MsgBox "Record not found."
End If
```

Building Criteria with Partial Values

When you add searching capabilities to an application, offering the user the ability to search on a partial value is typically preferable than requiring a complete value. For example, a user may not know the exact name of a company and may only provide a portion of the company name. You can perform a search based on a partial name.

To search based on a partial string, you can use the **Like** keyword in SQL. Remember, when searching on a string, you must add single quotes around the string. If the comparison operator is LIKE, the string value may contain "%" (one or more occurrences of any character) or "_" (one occurrence of any character). The following example code shows the use of the **Like** keyword:

```
'Match states such as Maine and Massachusetts
adcStates.Find "State LIKE 'M%'"
```

The value in criteria may be a string, floating point number, or date. String values are delimited with single quotes (for example, state = 'WA').

There are three optional parameters for a recordset object's Find method:

- SkipRows

  SkipRows is an optional Long data type value, whose default value is zero. It is used to specify the offset from the current row or start bookmark to begin the search.

- SearchDirection

  SearchDirection specifies whether the search should begin on the current row or the next available row in the direction of the search. The search stops at the start or end of the recordset, depending on the value of searchDirection. It can be one of the following enumerated values:

  - adSearchForward (0)—search forward from the current record
  - adSearchBackward (1)—search backward from the current record.

- Start

  The Start parameter is a Variant bookmark to use as the starting position for the search. This argument is a Variant and can be either a bookmark or one of the following enumerated values:

  - adBookmarkCurrent (0)—the current record
  - adBookmarkFirst (1)—the first record or adBookmarkLast (2)—the last record.

The following example implements the Find method of a recordset object using all four parameters:

```
Dim varBookmark As Variant

With adcFood.Recordset
    'Mark the current record
    varBookmark = .Bookmark
    'Specify the search criteria, start and direction
    .Find "CategoryName = 'Condiments'", 0, adSearchForward, _
        adBookmarkCurrent
    'If the record isn't found
    If .EOF Or .BOF Then
        'Return to the starting record
        .Bookmark = varBookmark
        MsgBox "Record not found."
    End If
End With
```

Practice: Searching for Records in a Recordset

In this practice, you will continue to build on the project you created in the two practices earlier in this chapter. You will add functionality to your application to search for company names.

➤ **To add search functionality to your application**

1. Open the prjADO.vbp project you saved in the Binding Controls practice located in the \Practice\Ch07 folder.

2. Add a command button to your form between Text2 and Adodc1.

3. On the Properties window, set the Name property of Command1 to cmdSearch.

4. Set the Caption property of cmdSearch to &Search.

5. In the Click event of cmdSearch, type the following code:

```
Adodc1.Recordset.MoveFirst
Adodc1.Recordset.Find "CompanyName = 'Frankenversand'"
If Adodc1.Recordset.EOF Then MsgBox "Record not found."
```

6. On the **Run** menu, click **Start**.

7. Click the **Search** button on your form.

Notice that the record containing the company name Frankenversand is the current record. Your application should look like the illustration in Figure 7.16.

Figure 7.16 Using the Find method to search for the Frankenversand company name

8. On the **Run** menu, click **End**.

9. To save your project, click **Save Project** on the **File** menu.

Lesson Summary

The ADO Data control has a property called a Recordset, which is a group of records. The Recordset property of the ADO Data control is an object itself and has its own properties and methods. After you have set the RecordSource property, you can check the Recordset object's BOF and EOF properties. These properties indicate if you are at the beginning or end of the Recordset.

Although the ADO Data control can automatically modify and update records without you having to add any code, you can use the Update method instead of using the arrows on the ADO Data control. New records can be added to a Recordset by calling the AddNew method. Using the Delete method, you can delete the current record or a group of records in a recordset. You can check the EOF property to see if you have deleted the last record.

To add a search feature to your application, you use the Find method for the ADO Data control's recordset. The Find method searches an existing recordset for the record that satisfies the specified criteria. If the criteria is met, the recordset is positioned on that record; otherwise, the position is set on the end of the recordset (EOF).

Summary

How Visual Basic Accesses Data

- Visual Basic's data access technologies help to:
  - Reduce development time.
  - Simplify code.
  - Provide high performance while exposing many features.
- Visual Basic makes three data access interfaces available:
  - ActiveX Data Objects (ADO).
  - Remote Data Objects (RDO).
  - Data Access Objects (DAO).
- Visual Basic uses a relational database model. This model presents data as a collection of tables which are logical groupings of related information.

Introduction to OLE DB and ADO

- OLE DB is a set of COM interfaces that provide applications with uniform access to data stored in diverse information sources, regardless of location or type.
- Because ADO is an interface to OLE DB, Microsoft's newest and most powerful data access technology, ADO provides high-performance access to a variety of information sources (including relational data and nonrelational data).
- Conceptually, OLE DB has three types of components:
  - Data providers
  - Data consumers
  - Service components

Overview of Structured Query Language

- Structured Query Language (SQL) is used in querying, updating, and managing relational databases.
- SQL can be used to retrieve, sort, and filter specific data to be extracted from the database.

- The SQL Select statement returns information from the database as a set of records and is divided into three major sections: SELECT, FROM, and WHERE.

- In different environments, databases have different implementations of the same SQL functionality, both syntactically and semantically. Be aware that each implementation of SQL has its own support for different data types, referential integrity, and compiled queries.

The ADO Data Control

- The ADO Data control is a graphic control (with record navigation buttons) and an easy-to-use interface that allows you to create database applications with a minimum of code. To use the ADO Data control in Visual Basic 6.0, you must add it to the toolbox.

- At design time, you can create a connection to a data source by setting the ConnectionString property of the ADO Data control to a valid connection string. After you set the ConnectionString property of the ADO Data control to connect to a database, you can set the RecordSource property to establish where the records will come from.

- Once you have set the ConnectionString and RecordSource properties for the ADO Data control, you can add a bound control to display data on your form.

Coding the ADO Data Control

- The ADO Data control's Recordset property is an object itself and has its own properties and methods. After you set the RecordSource property, you can check the Recordset object's BOF and EOF properties to knoe if you are at the beginning or end of the Recordset.

- The ADO Data control can automatically modify and update records without additional code, You can use the Update method instead of using the arrows on the ADO Data control. New records can be added to a Recordset by calling the AddNew method. Using the Delete method, you can delete the current record or a group of records in a recordset. You can check the EOF property to see if you have deleted the last record.

- The Find method for the ADO Data control's recordset can add a search capability. It searches an existing recordset and if the criteria is met, the recordset is positioned on that record. Otherwise, the position is set on the end of the recordset (EOF).

Lab: Using the ADO Data Control

In this lab, you will add navigation capabilities to frmReservation. You will add the ADO Data control to frmReservation and connect to Microsoft Access' Reservation database. The database's Reservation table will be used as the data source for the ADO Data control. You will bind controls on the frmReservation to the ADO Data control at design time, and programmatically at run time. You can continue to work with the files you created in Lab 6, or use the files provided in the \Labs\Lab07\Partial folder. The solution code is in the \Labs\Lab07\Solution folder.

To see a demonstration of the solution, run the Lab07.exe animation located in the Animations folder on the Supplemental Course Materials CD-ROM that accompanies this book.

Estimated lesson time: 45 minutes

Exercise 1: Connecting to a data source

In this exercise, you will connect to a database using the ADO Data control's property pages.

➤ **To open the hotel reservation application project**

- Open either the reservation application project that you have been working on or the Hotelres.vbp project located in the \Labs\Lab07\Partial folder.

➤ **To add an ADO Data control to frmReservation**

1. Use the **Components** dialog box to add the **Microsoft ADO Data Control 6.0 (OLE DB)** component to the toolbox.

2. Place an ADO Data control on **frmReservation** as illustrated in Figure 7.17.

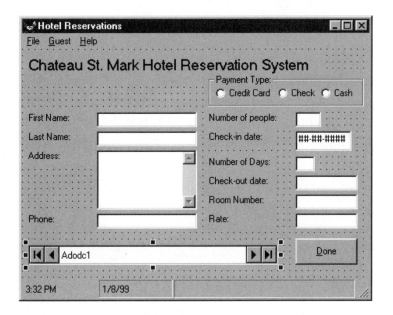

Figure 7.17 ADO Data control placed on frmReservation

➤ **To connect the ADO Data control to a data source**

1. Set the ADO Data control's Name property to **adcReservation**, and the Caption property to **Reservations**.

2. Use the ADO Data control's property pages to create a connection string using the **Microsoft Jet OLE DB** provider to connect to the Rsvn.mdb database located in the \Labs\Lab07 folder.

3. Set the RecordSource property of the ADO Data control to use a **Command Type** of **2- adCmdTable**, and use **Reservations** as the **Table or Stored Procedure Name**, as illustrated in Figure 7.18.

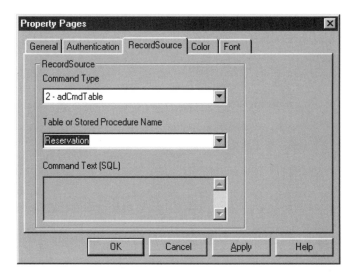

Figure 7.18 Setting RecordSource property of adcReservation

4. Set the **adcReservation** control's CursorType property to **3- adOpenStatic**.

   This will provide record browsing capability to users without allowing them to add, change, or delete records.

Exercise 2: Binding controls to the ADO Data control

In this exercise, you will bind controls on the frmReservation form to the adcReservation control. Some controls will be bound at design time, while others will be bound programmatically at run time.

➤ **To bind controls to adcReservation**

1. Using the **adcReservation** ADO Data control as the DataSource, set the DataField properties for all of the bound controls on **frmReservation**.

   Do not bind the **Payment Type** option buttons. They will be bound programmatically at run time.

2. Set the DataFormat property of **mskCheckIn** to **Date** as illustrated in Figure 7.19.

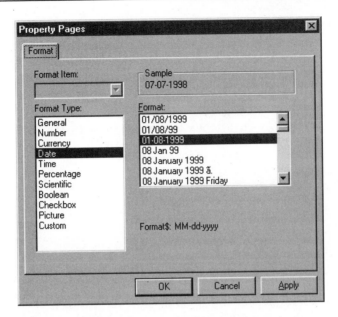

Figure 7.19 Formatting the mskCheckIn control

3. Type the following code statement before the End Sub statement in the **DisableControls** Sub procedure:

```
adcReservation.Enabled = True
```

The user will now be able to use the ADO Data control to navigate between records in the **Reservation** table.

4. To have the **Payment Type** option buttons programmatically display the correct type of payment (Credit Card, Check or Cash) from **adcReservation** recordset, add the following code to the **adcReservation_MoveComplete** event.

```
Dim strStatus As String
Dim dtCheckIn As Date
Dim intNumDays As Integer
'If no value has been entered into the recordset
'continue without stopping applicaiton
On Error Resume Next
'Check the payment type in the database and
'set the option buttons to correspond with the
'payment type value from the recordset
strStatus = adcReservation.Recordset![PaymentType]
Select Case strStatus
    Case "CREDIT CARD"
        grpPmtType(0).Value = True
    Case "CHECK"
        grpPmtType(1).Value = True
    Case "CASH"
        grpPmtType(2).Value = True
End Select

'Set the dtCheckIn and intNumDays variables
'to the values from the ADO Data control's recordset
dtCheckIn = adcReservation.Recordset![CheckInDate]
intNumDays = adcReservation.Recordset![NumberOfDays]
'Calculate the check out date and place it into
'the txtCheckOut control
txtCheckOut.Text = Format(DateAdd("d", intNumDays, dtCheckIn), _
    "mm-dd-yyyy")
```

5. Save and test your application.

Review

The following questions are intended to reinforce key information presented in this chapter. If you are unable to answer a question, review the appropriate lesson and then try the question again. Answers to the questions can be found in the Appendix, "Questions and Answers," located at the back of this book.

1. What are the three data access interfaces available in Visual Basic?

2. Why should you use ADO as a data access interface?

3. What is the difference between a primary key and a foreign key?

4. What are the three components of OLE DB?

5. What is Structured Query Language used for?

6. What operator do you use in SQL to find values based on a pattern (or partial expression?

7. What two properties do you set for an ADO Data control to connect to a database and source of data within the database?

8. What are two ways to update data in an ADO Data control's recordset?

C H A P T E R 8

Developing Solutions Using ADO

About This Chapter

In this chapter, you will learn how to create an advanced database application using the ActiveX Data Objects (ADO) object model. Unlike the ADO Data control, ADO objects give you greater control over how your application interacts with the data source. Various ways to return records will be covered as well as how to modify, add, and delete records in a data source. In addition, the new Data Environment will be discussed.

Before You Begin

To complete the lessons in this chapter, you must have:

- Read Chapter 6.
- Read Chapter 7 and completed the exercises.

Lesson 1: Introducing the ADO Object Model

In Chapter 7 you learned that there are two types of OLE DB applications: consumers and providers. An OLE DB consumer is any application that uses OLE DB, such as a Visual Basic application that connects to a database server. You can use the ADO object model to access OLE DB interfaces indirectly through the ADO objects.

The ADO object model provides an easy-to-use set of objects, properties, and methods for writing code to access data. ADO objects can be used in Microsoft Visual C++, Microsoft Visual Basic, Microsoft Visual Basic Scripting Edition, Java, and any platform that supports both COM and Automation. The ADO object model has fewer objects and is easier to use when compared to other data access objects such as Remote Data Objects (RDO) or Data Access Objects (DAO). The ADO object model is sometimes referred to as a "flat" object model.

You can use ADO objects to create more powerful and flexible applications than you can create with the ADO Data control. Although the ADO Data control gives you record navigation and update abilities, using ADO objects allows you to implement all of the data access and manipulation features needed by most applications.

After this lesson you will be able to:

- Describe the format of the ADO object model.
- Explain the three main components of the ADO object model.
- Explain the advantages of using ADO objects.

Estimated lesson time: 15 minutes

ADO Objects

The ADO object model is designed to present the most commonly used features of OLE DB. ADO objects provide you with fast and easy access to all types of data. As illustrated in Figure 8.1, the ADO object model has three main components: the Connection object, the Command object, and the Recordset object.

- The Connection object makes a connection between your application and an external data source, such as Microsoft SQL Server. The Connection object also provides a mechanism for initializing and establishing the connection, executing queries, and using transactions. It is the highest-level object in the ADO object model.

- The Command object is used to build queries, including user-specific parameters, to access records from a data source. Typically, these records are returned in a Recordset object. Command objects are created from a database table, stored query, or a Structured Query Language (SQL) query. You can also create relationships between Command objects to retrieve a set of related data in the form of a hierarchy.

- The Recordset object is used to access records returned from an SQL query. You use Recordset objects to present records to the user. A Recordset object can also be used to edit, add, or delete records in the data source.

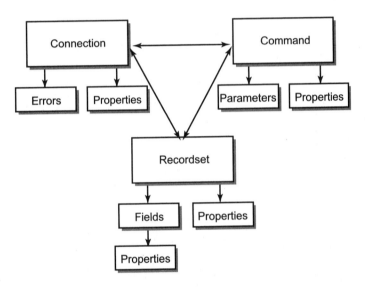

Figure 8.1 ADO object model

The ADO object model differs from the RDO and DAO object models in that many of the objects can be created independently of one another. ADO objects are stored in a hierarchical format, which is de-emphasized so that you create only the objects that you need for your solution. You can create a Recordset, Connection, or Command object directly without having to create parent objects. For example, you can create a Recordset object without first explicitly creating a Connection object. ADO implicitly creates the required Connection object for you.

ADO Collections

In addition to the three main objects, ADO supports three collections that can provide additional functionality to your applications:

- Errors collection

  Any operation involving ADO objects can generate one or more provider errors. As each error occurs, one or more Error objects are placed in the Errors collection of the Connection object. Each Error object represents a specific provider error, not an ADO error. In Visual Basic, the occurrence of an ADO-specific error will use the normal Visual Basic Err object.

- Parameters collection

  A Command object has a Parameters collection made up of Parameter objects. A Parameters collection contains all the Parameter objects of a Command object. You use it to pass specific data to a parameterized query in a Microsoft Access database. For example, if you want to call a stored query that returns all customers that live in a specified country, you would use a Parameter object to pass the name of the country to the stored query.

- Fields collection

  A Recordset object has a Fields collection made up of Field objects. Each Field object corresponds to a column in the Recordset. You use the Fields collection to access specific fields in an existing Recordset object.

Lesson Summary

The ADO object model provides you with a set of objects for writing code to access data. The ADO object model has three main components: the Connection object, the Command object, and the Recordset object.

- The Connection object lets you initialize and establish a connection to a data source, execute queries, and use transactions.

- The Command object lets you issue commands to a database using the Parameters collection.

- The Recordset object lets you manipulate result sets using various methods. Using a Recordset object, you can add, update, delete, and scroll through records. You can also retrieve and update each record using the Fields collection and the Field object. In addition, the ADO object model exposes the Error object that is used by data providers to return more detailed error information to a Visual Basic application.

Lesson 2: Connecting to a Data Source

In Chapter 7 you learned how to connect to a data source using the ConnectionString property of an ADO Data control. In this lesson, you will learn how to connect to a data source using an ADO Connection object. In Visual Basic, you can create a Connection object two ways: by declaring a Connection object in code or by using a Data Environment.

Like the ADO Data control's ConnectionString property, you can use the Connection object to establish a connection to a data source and pass client information, such as username and password, to the database for validation.

After this lesson you will be able to:

- Describe how to create an ADO Connection object in Visual Basic.

- Explain how to connect to a data source using code.

Estimated lesson time: 25 minutes

Using a Connection Object

A Connection object represents a physical connection to a data source. To create a Connection object, you supply the name of either an ODBC data source or an OLE DB provider.

Note To support as many data sources as possible, you can use ADO and ODBC to access a database. However, when using a data source that has an associated OLE DB provider—such as Microsoft Access, Microsoft SQL Server, or Oracle—it is recommended that you use this provider instead of the older, ODBC driver.

When you open the Connection object, you attempt to connect to the data source. A typical ADO-based application uses the following operations to access a data source:

1. Create the Connection object

   Specify the connection string with information such as data source name, user identification, and password.

2. Open the connection

   Open the ADO connection to the data source.

3. Execute an SQL statement

   Once the connection is open, you can run a query. You can run this query asynchronously, if you choose, which means that ADO will populate the recordset in the background; this lets your application perform other processes without waiting.

4. Use the records returned from the query

   The records are now available to your application to browse or update. Whether you can add, update, or delete data in the recordset depends on the *cursor type*. A cursor is a temporary table in memory that contains the results of a query.

5. Terminate the connection

   The connection to the data source is dropped.

Creating a Connection Object in Code

A Connection object represents an open connection to a data source. Using the Connection object, you can establish a connection to a data source and pass client information, such as username and password, to the database for validation. Using the collections, methods, and properties of a Connection object, you can do the following:

- Configure the connection using the ConnectionString, ConnectionTimeout, and Mode properties.

- Specify an OLE DB provider with the Provider property.

- Establish, and later close, the physical connection to the data source with the Open and Close methods.

- Execute a command, such as calling a stored procedure, with the Execute method.

- Manage transactions on open connections. You can also use nested transactions if the provider supports them. You manage transactions using the BeginTrans, CommitTrans, and RollbackTrans methods, as well as the Attributes property.

Note A transaction delimits the beginning and end of a series of data access operations that transpire across a connection. ADO ensures that changes to a data source using a transaction all occur successfully or not at all.

- Examine errors returned from the data source with the Errors collection.

Creating the Connection Object

Before you use ADO in your Visual Basic application, you must first set a reference to the Microsoft ActiveX Data Objects 2.0 Library.

➤ **To create a reference to the ADO Object Library**

1. On the **Project** menu, click **References**.

2. Click **Microsoft ActiveX Data Objects 2.0 Library**, then click **OK**.

Once you have made a reference to the ADO object library, you can declare a Connection object in your application. Once you have created a Connection object, you must specify an OLE DB data source provider. You do this by setting the Provider property.

Depending on the type of data source you are connecting to, you need to either specify an OLE DB provider or use an ODBC driver. The following table displays the provider parameter values for different OLE DB providers.

OLE DB provider	ConnectionString
Microsoft Jet	"Provider=Microsoft.Jet.OLEDB.3.51;"
Oracle	"Provider=MSDAORA;Data Source=ServerName;User ID=John;Password=password"
Microsoft ODBC Driver provider	Provider=MSDASQL.1;UID=admin;Extended Properties="DBQ=c:\Program Files\Microsoft Visual Studio\VB98\NWIND.MDB;FIL=MS Access;"
SQL Server	"Provider=SQLOLEDB;Data Source=sql65server;User ID=sa;Password='';Initial Catalog=pubs"

The final step before establishing a connection to a data source is to specify the connection information. You do this by setting the Connection object's ConnectionString property. Connection string arguments that are provider specific are passed directly to the provider, and are not processed by ADO.

When you are finished with the connection, use the Close method to disconnect from a data source. If you are connected to a remote database, any server-side resources that were in use under this active connection are released.

Note While not required, it is proper coding technique to explicitly close all open connections before the application is terminated.

Practice: Creating a Connection with Code

In this practice, you will write code to connect to a database using an OLE DB provider.

To see a demonstration, run the Chap08.exe animation located in the Animations folder on the Supplemental Course Materials CD-ROM that accompanies this book.

➤ **To connect to an OLE DB provider using code**

1. Start Visual Basic and create a new **Standard EXE** project.

2. On the **Project** Menu, click **References**.

3. Click **Microsoft ActiveX Data Objects 2.0 Library** and click **OK**.

4. Add a CommandButton to **Form1**, set the Name property to **cmdConnect**, and the Caption property to **&Connect**.

5. In the **cmdConnect_Click** event procedure, type the following code:

```
Dim CN As Connection

'Instanciate the connection
Set cnData = New Connection
cnData.ConnectionString = "Provider=Microsoft.Jet.OLEDB.3.51;" & _
    "Data Source=C:\Program Files\Microsoft Visual Studio\" & _
    "VB98\Nwind.mdb"
cnData.Open

If cnData.State = adStateOpen Then MsgBox "Connection successful."
'Close the connection and release the cnData object
cnData.Close
Set cnData = Nothing
```

Note The Data Source parameter of the ConnectionString must point to the Nwind.mdb file on your hard drive. If the location of Nwind.mdb is different on your computer, you have to adjust the path to the appropriate location.

The ConnectionString has a parameter value that uses the Microsoft Jet OLE DB provider. Each OLE DB provider will require a different value for the ConnectionString property.

6. On the **Run** menu, click **Start**.

7. Click the **Connection** button in your application.

If the connection was succesful, you will receive a message box notifying you.

8. On the **Run** menu, click **End**.

Connection Events

One advantage of using ADO objects in your code, instead of using the ADO Data control, is that it gives you the ability to write code to respond to ADO events. An event is a notification issued by certain operations before the operation starts or after it completes. An event is actually a call to an event handler routine that you define in your application. The Connection object supports a number of events that allow your application to execute custom code. These events are associated with connecting to a data source, executing SQL commands, and managing transactions at the connection level.

The following table describes the events associated with the Connection object.

Event	Description
AbortTransaction	Fires after the RollbackTrans method is called.
BeginTransaction	Fires after the BeginTrans method is called.
CommitTransaction	Fires after the CommitTrans method is called.
ConnectComplete	Fires when a connection attempt has completed successfully, failed, or timed out.
Disconnect	Fires when an active connection is closed.
ExecuteComplete	Fires after the Execute method is called.
InfoMessage	Fires when a message is returned from OLE DB or the data source.
WillConnect	Fires after the Open method is called, but before the connection is established.
WillExecute	Fires after the Execute method is called, but before the command is completed.

Enabling ADO Events

When you declare an ADO object, you must use the WithEvents keyword to expose the object's events to your application. If you declare a Connection object with its events exposed, the Connection object appears in the Visual Basic object box list, and all the available events for the object appear in the Procedures/Events box list. Figure 8.2 illustrates the cnCustomer connection object in the Visual Basic object list.

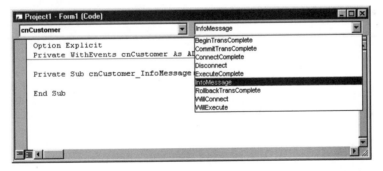

Figure 8.2 Connection object with events exposed

The following example code declares a Connection object and exposes its events:

```
Public WithEvents cnCustomers As Connection
```

After you declare the Connection object using the WithEvents keyword, use the connection as you normally would. The following example displays a message box to the user when a connection attempt has completed successfully:

```
Sub cnCustomers_ConnectComplete(ByVal pError As ADODB.Error, _
    adStatus As ADODB.EventStatusEnum, _
    ByVal pConnection As ADODB.Connection)

    If adStatus = adStatusOK Then
        MsgBox "The connection has been established."
    End If
End Sub
```

Lesson Summary

The first step in accessing data using ADO is to establish a connection to the data source. The ADO object model provides the Connection object for this purpose. Using the Connection object you can specify different data sources, such as Microsoft Access (using the Jet engine), Microsoft SQL Server, or an Oracle database.

When you declare the Connection object variable, you can optionally use the WithEvents keyword. When the Connection object's events are exposed, you can add code to respond to a variety of events, such as the completion of a connection request or transaction management. Once a connection has been established, your application can call stored queries or return records for processing.

Lesson 3: Retrieving Data

ADO lets you retrieve data from a data source and present the resulting records to the user. These records are called a recordset; they exist in the ADO recordset object. You can create a recordset by itself or by using a Command object. You typically return records from a Command object by calling a stored query or a stored procedure. Depending on the functionality that you provide, these records can then be updated by the user and saved back to the data source.

In addition to returning records, you can also use the Command object to run queries that modify or delete records. These queries are sometimes called action queries. An action query is different from a traditional query because they do not return records. An action query is usually saved in the database in the form of a stored query (Microsoft Access) or a stored procedure (Microsoft SQL Server). In this course, stored queries in Microsoft Access will be presented.

After this lesson you will be able to:

- Explain the purpose of a Recordset object.

- Retrieve records from a data source.

- Explain when to use the ADO Command object.

- Describe the relationship between a Command and a Connection object.

- Work with data in a recordset.

Estimated lesson time: 30 minutes

Retrieving Records with a Recordset Object

Once a connection has been established to the data source, you can return records using the Recordset object's Open method. To create a recordset, follow these steps:

1. Declare a recordset object variable.

2. Instantiate the object variable.

3. Use the Open method to request records from a data source.

The following syntax is used to access records in a data source:

recordset.Open *Source, ActiveConnection, CursorType, LockType, Options*

The following table describes the arguments used by the Open method:

Argument	Description
Source	*Optional*. A Variant that evaluates to an SQL statement or table name.
ActiveConnection	*Optional*. Either a Variant that evaluates to a valid Connection object variable name, or a String containing ConnectionString parameters.
CursorType	*Optional*. A CursorTypeEnum value that determines the type of cursor that the provider should use when opening the Recordset. Can be one of the following constants (see the CursorType property for definitions of these settings).
LockType	*Optional*. A LockTypeEnum value that determines what type of locking (concurrency) the provider should use when opening the Recordset. Can be one of the following constants (see the LockType property for more information).
Options	*Optional*. A Long value that indicates how the provider should evaluate the Source argument if it represents something other than a Command object, or that the Recordset should be restored from a file where it was previously saved.

Using an Explicit Connection Object

You can navigate through the records, or present them to the user, using the Recordset object. Depending on the options used when opening the recordset, you can also give the user the ability to edit, delete, or add new records. By default, a read-only recordset is created. In addition, the recordset only supports the MoveNext navigation method by default. This is called a forward-only recordset.

The following example opens a new recordset from an existing connection:

```
'Declare the recordset object variable
Dim rsStudents As Recordset

'Instantiate the object
Set rsStudents = New Recordset

'Retrieve records from the data source
rsStudents.Open "Select * from Students", cnSchool
```

Note Unless you use a Command object, you can only pass an SQL statement or a table name to the Open method.

Using an Implicit Connection Object

An alternative to using an existing Connection object is to open a new recordset using an implicit connection. One of the features of the ADO object model is the ability to call objects directly. When calling a recordset object directly, ADO automatically creates a Connection object in the background. The following example uses an implicit connection to return records from the Customer table:

```
'Declare the object variable
Dim rsCustomer As Recordset

'Instantiate the object
Set rsCustomer = New Recordset

'Open a new connection and return the appropriate records
rsCustomer.Open "Select * from Customers", _
    "Provider=Microsoft.Jet.OLEDB.3.51;" & _
        "Data Source=C:\temp\Nwind.mdb"
```

As you can see, using this technique reduces the amount of code that you have to write. However, for each recordset that uses an implicit connection, a new connection will be created on the data source. In most cases, these additional connections use valuable resources. It may be more efficient to create a single Connection object and open the required recordsets from that connection. You can create multiple recordsets from one connection without using additional connection resources.

Note Using implicit connections can cause scalability problems if you plan to move your Visual Basic application from Microsoft Access to Microsoft SQL Server. Consider using explicit Connection objects when accessing a data source.

Accessing Records in a Recordset

Once a recordset has been created, you can access the fields of each record in one of the following ways:

- Reference the name of the field

  If you know the name of the field you want to access, you can use the following syntax to access the current value of the field:

  RecordsetObject!FieldName

- Use the Fields collection

    If you do not know the name of the field, or you do not want to manually reference the field name, you can use the Recordset object's Fields collection. Use the following syntax to access the value of a field using the Fields collection:

    recordsetobject.Fields(0)

In the following examples, the CustomerName field is displayed in the Immediate window:

```
Debug.Print rsCustomer!CustomerName
```

 -or-

```
Debug.Print rsCustomer.Fields(0)
```

Note This assumes the CustomerName field is the first field in the collection.

Retrieving Records with a Command Object

In the previous example, records were returned based on an SQL string. Often, the records that will be returned result from a stored query in a Microsoft Access database. You must use a Command object to call a stored query. As with the Connection and Recordset objects, you must declare and then instantiate a Command object variable before using it in code.

Using the Command object's CommandText and CommandType properties, you can associate a stored query with the object variable. The CommandText property must be set to the name of the stored query. In the event the name contains spaces, you must enclose the entire name is square brackets. Stored queries in a Microsoft Access database are not the same as a stored procedure in a Microsoft SQL Server database. Therefore, the CommandType property must be set to the adCmdUnknown constant.

Note This course focuses on building desktop applications using a local Microsoft Access database.

In order to pass data to the query, you must use the Parameters collection. Each parameter needs to be added to the collection using the Append and CreateParameter methods. The Append method uses the following syntax:

CommandObject.Parameters.Append *object*

The object argument uses the CreateParameter method. The CreateParameter method uses the following syntax:

command.CreateParameter (*Name, Type, Direction, Size, Value*)

The following table describes the arguments used by the CreateParameter method:

Argument	Description
Name	A string representing the name of the Parameter object. You must use the same name as the parameter stored in the Microsoft Access database.
Type	A long value specifying the data type of the Parameter object. You must use the same data type as the parameter in the stored query.
Direction	A long value specifying the type of Parameter object. Parameters can send data to a query, or they can return data from a query. Microsoft Access stored queries only support input data.
Size	A long value specifying the maximum length for the parameter value in characters or bytes. This is required when using string parameters.
Value	A variant specifying the value for the Parameter object.

The following example creates an input parameter on the comStudent object:

```
comStudent.Parameters.Append comStudent.CreateParameter("StudentID", _
    adInteger, adParamInput)
```

When calling a Microsoft Access stored query, it is important that you use the same names and data types as the parameters in the database. If you use incorrect names or data types, a run-time error will occur.

The following example creates a Command object and passes two dates to the query:

```
Dim cnNorthwind As Connection
Dim comSalesByYear As Command
Dim rsSales As Recordset

'Instanciate the variables
Set cnUniversity = New Connection
Set comEnrollments = New Command
```

(continued)

```
'Open the database connection
cnUniversity.ConnectionString = "Provider=Microsoft.Jet.OLEDB.3.51;" & _
    "Data Source=C:\Databases\University.mdb"
cnNorthwind.Open

'Set up the Command object
comEnrollments.CommandType = adCmdUnknown
comEnrollments.CommandText = "[Student Enrollments]"

'Create the parameters
comEnrollments.Parameters.Append _
    comEnrollments.CreateParameter("BeginningDate", adDate, _
        adParamInput)
comEnrollments.Parameters.Append _
    comEnrollments.CreateParameter("EndingDate", adDate, adParamInput)

'Set the parameter values
comEnrollments.Parameters("BeginningDate").Value = "10/1/97"
comEnrollments.Parameters("EndingDate").Value = "12/1/97"

'Associate the object with an active connection
comEnrollments.ActiveConnection = cnUniversity

'Request the recordset
Set rsStudents = comEnrollments.Execute
```

Practice: Returning Records from a Database

In this practice, you will return records from the sample Northwind database that comes with Visual Basic. The following code assumes the nwind.mdb file resides in the C:\Program Files\Microsoft Visual Studio\VB98 folder. You may have to change this path if you installed Visual Basic to a different folder on your computer.

➤ **To connect to the Northwind database**

1. Start Visual Basic and create a new **Standard EXE** project.

2. Rename **Form1** to **frmMain**.

3. On the **Project** menu, click **References**.

4. Click **Microsoft ActiveX Data Objects 2.0 Librar**, then click **OK**.

5. Create two module-level variables in **frmMain**:

```
Dim cnNorthwind as Connection
Dim rsCustomer as Recordset
```

6. Add a command button called **cmdConnect** to **frmMain**.

7. In the Click event for **cmdConnect**, enter the following code to connect to the Northwind database and return all records in the **Customer** table:

```
Dim cnNorthwind As connection
Dim rsCustomer As Recordset
Set cnNorthwind = New connection
Set rsCustomer = New Recordset
cnNorthwind.ConnectionString = "Provider=Microsoft.Jet.OLEDB.3.51;" _
    "Data Source=" & _
    "C:\Program Files\Microsoft Visual Studio\Vb98\nwind.mdb", _
    "cnNorthwind.Open

rsCustomer.Open "Select * from customers", cnNorthwind

'Display the first customer ID to the debug window
Debug.Print rsCustomer!CustomerID
```

8. Save your application to the \Practice\Ch08 folder and test your work.

Lesson Summary

The ADO object model provides the Recordset object for returning and managing records in your application. You can create recordsets from an existing Connection object or as a stand-alone object. However, if you do not specify an active connection, the recordset creates an implicit connection for you. This can use unnecessary server resources and is not recommended.

In addition to the Recordset object, you can also use a Command object to interact with data. The Command object lets you access stored queries in a Microsoft Access database. When calling a stored query, you may have to pass user-supplied data to the query, such as returning all customers that live in a certain state. To pass this data to a query, you need to use the Parameters collection of the Command object.

Lesson 4: Navigating Records

When you open a recordset, the current record is positioned to the first record (if any) and the BOF and EOF properties are set to False. If there are no records, the BOF and EOF property settings are set to True.

You can use the Move, MoveFirst, MoveLast, MoveNext, and MovePrevious methods, as well as the AbsolutePosition, AbsolutePage, and Filter properties, to reposition the current record—assuming the provider supports the relevant functionality. Forward-only Recordset objects support only the MoveNext method. When you use the Move methods to visit each record (or enumerate the recordset), you can use the BOF and EOF properties to see if you've moved beyond the beginning or end of the recordset.

After this lesson you will be able to:

- Specify the cursor type used by a recordset.
- Bind controls to a **Recordset** object.
- Navigate records in a recordset.

Estimated lesson time: 30 minutes

Specifying a Cursor Type

A Recordset object uses a cursor type to determine how records can be navigated and updated. You set the CursorType property prior to opening the recordset, or pass a CursorType argument with the Open method. If you don't specify a cursor type, ADO opens a forward-only cursor by default.

There are four different cursor types defined in ADO:

- Dynamic cursor

  A dynamic cursor allows you to view additions, changes, and deletions by other users, and allows all types of movement through the recordset.

- Keyset cursor

  A keyset cursor behaves like a dynamic cursor, except that it prevents you from seeing records that other users add, and prevents access to records that other users delete. Data changes by other users will still be visible.

- Static cursor

  A static cursor provides a fixed copy of a set of records for you to use to find data or generate reports. It allows all types of movement through the recordset. Additions, changes, or deletions by other users are not visible.

■ Forward-only cursor

Forward-only recordsets only support the MoveNext navigation method. You cannot use any other navigation technique or a run-time error will occur. In addition, the RecordCount property will always return a value of -1.

Note Some OLE DB providers don't support all cursor types. Check the documentation for the provider.

In the following example, a new recordset is created using a Dynamic cursor:

```
rsCustomer.Open "Select * from Customers", cnNorthwind, adOpenDynamic
```

Using the Resync and Requery Methods

Both the Static and Forward-only cursors do not present updated record information to the user once the recordset has been built. Consider using the Recordset object's Resync method to update the values of the records in the current recordset. Resync does not return new records based on the original query. To do this you must use the Requery method. Requery uses additional resources because the query re-executed.

Presenting Data to the User

One of the benefits of the ADO Data control is the ability to bind controls. For example, when an ADO Data control is added to a form, a text box can be bound to the ADO Data control. Then, as records are navigated in the ADO Data control using the button on the control, the value in the text box automatically updates.

ADO Recordset objects also support the ability to bind controls. Now, when opening a recordset, you can easily present the resulting fields to the user without needing to write code to manually update the controls on a form. To bind a control to a recordset object, you need to specify the control's DataSource and DataField properties. Since the Recordset object is created at run time, you must bind the controls from within code. In the following example, two text boxes are bound to the rsCustomer recordset object:

```
'Bind the first text box
Set txtFirstName.DataSource = rsCustomer
txtFirstName.DataField = "FirstName"

'Bind the second text box
Set txtLastName.DataSource = rsCustomer
txtLastName.DataField = "LastName"
```

Binding controls to a Recordset object uses less code and is more efficient than manually populating controls each time the record changes. In addition, bound controls also support adding and editing records.

Navigating the Recordset

Once you create the recordset and presented the data to the user, you need to programmatically control how the user navigates the records. There are four primary methods for moving from one record to the next:

Method	Description
MoveNext	This method will move the user to the next record in the recordset. If they have moved to the end of the recordset, the EOF property is set to True. If the user attempts to move to the next record, past EOF, a run-time error will occur.
MovePrevious	This method will move the user to the previous record in the recordset. If they have moved to the beginning of the recordset, the BOF property is set to True. If the user attempts to move to the previous record, past BOF, a run-time error will occur.
MoveFirst	This method will move the user to the first record in the recordset.
MoveLast	This method will move the user to the last record in the recordset.

The Recordset EOF and BOF properties are used to monitor if the current record has moved outside the range of the recordset. If EOF or BOF are True, no record will be presented to the user. However, if the user attempts to navigate past this empty record, a run-time error will occur.

To implement any one of the above methods, use the following syntax:

object.method

The following example uses the MoveNext method to navigate to the next record:

```
Private Sub cmdMoveNext_Click()
    rsCustomer.MoveNext

    'Check if they moved past the last record
    If rsCustomer.EOF Then
        'The last record was passed
        rsCustomer.MoveLast
    End If
End Sub
```

Note Only one record can be the current record in a recordset at one time.

Additional Navigation Methods and Properties

You can also use any of the following methods and properties to navigate a recordset object that supports moving forward and backward:

Method/Property	Description
Move Method	Moves the position of the current record in a Recordset object.
AbsolutePage Property	Specifies in which page the current record resides.
AbsolutePosition Property	Specifies the ordinal position of a Recordset object's current record.
NextRecordset Method	Clears the current Recordset object and returns the next Recordset by advancing through a series of commands.

Note The NextRecordset method is issued when returning multiple recordsets. Multiple recordsets are outside the scope of this class.

Finding a Record in a Recordset

In addition to navigating a recordset, you may want to allow the user to search for a specific record. There are two general ways to provide this functionality: re-query the database using a specific WHERE clause, or use the Find method. Depending on the size of the recordset, network bandwidth, and server load, you may decide it is more efficient to locate the record in an existing recordset. To do this, use the Find method. Use the following syntax to call the Find method:

```
RecordsetObject.Find (criteria, SkipRows, searchDirection, start)
```

The following table describes the arguments used by the Find method:

Argument	Description
Criteria	A string containing a statement that specifies the column name, comparison operator, and value to use in the search.
SkipRows	An optional Long value, whose default value is zero, that specifies the offset from the current row or *start* bookmark to begin the search.
searchDirection	An optional value that specifies whether the search should begin on the current row or the next available row in the direction of the search. Its value can be adSearchForward or adSearchBackward. The search stops at the start or end of the recordset, depending on the value of *searchDirection*.
Start	An optional Variant bookmark to use as the starting position for the search.

When specifying a criteria, you can use the following comparison operators: ">" (greater than), "<" (less than), "=" (equal), or "like" (pattern matching).

The following example locates a customer record using the Find method:

```
rsCustomer.Find "LastName = 'Smith'"
```

Note When using a string value in a Find, you must surround the value with single quotes.

Once the first record has been located, you can use the FindNext method to locate additional records. When the last record in the search has been found, EOF will be set to True. If the search direction was set to adSearchForward, BOF will be True.

Note You cannot use the Find method with a forward-only recordset. The recordset you create must be scrollable.

Using the Filter Property

ADO also supports the ability to filter the current recordset. Unlike Find, which searches for the first specific record based on a criteria, Filter will allow you to reduce the recordset to just records based on the criteria. Once you have finished with the filter, you can turn it off. This returns the recordset to its original state. The greatest benefit to using the Filter property is you do not have to return to the database to rebuild the recordset; all the processing occurs on the client computer. Like the Find method, the recordset that you create must support a scrollable cursor type (Dynamic, Keyset, or Static). The recordset cannot be forward-only. The following example uses the Filter property to limit the available records:

```
'This turns the Filter on
rsCustomer.Filter = "LastName Like 'S*'"
```

Use the adFilterNone constant to turn off the filter. The following example returns the recordset to its original state:

```
'This turns the Filter off
rsCustomer.Filter = adFilterNone
```

The Filter property will accept the same operators as the Find method. In addition, you can build compound Filters which provides a higher level of control over the available records without needing to return to the data source.

Lesson Summary

By default, a Recordset object is set to forward-only. This means that your application can only use the MoveNext method of navigation. In order to use any of the other navigation methods supported by ADO, such as MovePrevious, you must specify a scrollable cursor type. The cursor type controls the level of features that your application can potentially support. Certain cursor types provide greater functionality, but use additional overhead. Therefore, the cursor type should be chosen based on the needs of your application.

In addition to the basic navigation methods, you can also use the ADO Find method to search for records in the current recordset. Using this technique can provide better performance than re-querying the database. However, depending on the size of the recordset and the server load, you may find that using a specific WHERE clause is more efficient.

Lesson 5: Modifying Data

When developing solutions that access a database, you usually need to include functionality to modify the records as well as present them to the user. When using ADO, you can programmatically control the Recordset object to edit, add, and delete records. However, to include this functionality in a multi-user environment, you need to implement a locking scheme.

After this lesson you will be able to:

- Implement locking when opening a recordset.
- Edit records in a recordset.
- Add a new record to a recordset.
- Delete the current record in a recordset.

Estimated lesson time: 15 minutes

Locking a Recordset

In order to allow the user to edit a record, you must implement locking when you first open the recordset. By default, all ADO recordsets are read-only. You must select a locking scheme before ADO will save user changes back to the data source. The following table lists the options for locking:

Locking Option	Description
adLockReadOnly	(Default) Read-only—you cannot alter the data.
adLockPessimistic	Pessimistic locking, record by record—the provider does what is necessary to ensure successful editing of the records, usually by locking records at the data source immediately upon editing.
adLockOptimistic	Optimistic locking, record by record—the provider uses optimistic locking, locking records only when you call the Update method.
adLockBatchOptimistic	Optimistic batch updates—required for batch update mode, as opposed to immediate update mode.

In the following example, a recordset is opened using Pessimistic locking:

```
rsCustomer.Open "Select * from Customers", cnNorthwind, adOpenDynamic, _
    adLockPessimistic
```

Editing a Record

If the recordset has been opened for editing, you can allow the user to make changes and save the results back to the data source. In order to edit and post changes to a record, follow these steps:

1. Navigate to the appropriate record.
2. Change the field values (either programmatically or using bound controls).
3. Use the Update method to post the changes.

Records in a recordset are always in an edit state. You do not need to call a method to start the edit process. The following example changes the current record and then saves it to the data source:

```
rsCustomer!State = "CA"
rsCustomer.Update
```

Canceling an Edit

If you want to allow the user to cancel changes before they are posted, use the CancelUpdate method. When you call the CancelUpdate method, all the fields of the current record are restored to their initial values (the values they had when the recordset was first opened).

Adding a New Record

If you open a recordset and use a locking scheme that allows records to be edited, you can also add new records to that recordset. In order to add a new record, you must first call the AddNew method. Unlike an edit, you must tell the Recordset object to start the add process. Once the appropriate data has been entered in each field, use the Update method to save the new record to the data source. Any new records that have been added to the current recordset will appear at the end of the recordset. Use the Refresh method to re-build the recordset to include the new records in the appropriate order.

The following example adds a new customer to the rsCustomer recordset and then saves it to the data source:

```
rsCustomer.AddNew
rsCustomer!Name = "Alpine Ski Center"
rsCustomer!State = "AZ"
rsCustomer.Update
```

Note To cancel the creation of a new record, use the CancelUpdate method.

Deleting a Record

When using a recordset to delete records, only one record can be deleted at a time. In addition, only the current record is affected when the Delete method is called. Consider using the SQL DELETE command to delete multiple records in a data source.

The following example deletes the current record in the rsCustomer recordset:

```
rsCustomer.Delete
```

Unlike editing or adding a new record, you do not have to use the Update method to save the results to the data source. Therefore, be sure to verify with the user before calling the Delete method.

Lesson Summary

Be default, a recordset object is set to read-only. Before your application can edit, add, or delete records, you must open the recordset using a different locking scheme. The choices for locking are:

- adLockReadOnly
- adLockPessimistic
- adLockOptimistic
- adLockBatchOptimistic

After you create a recordset that can be edited, you can use the AddNew, Update, or Delete methods to modify the records and save the changes to the data source.

Lesson 6: Using the Data Environment

An alternative technique for accessing data is to use the Data Environment, which is new in Visual Basic 6. The Data Environment provides a graphical way to connect to a data source. However, like the ADO Data control, you need to eventually write code to support all of the basic features that a database front-end application normally provides.

After this lesson you will be able to:

- Connect to a data source using a Data Environment.

- Return records using an SQL command.

- Use a Command object with a Data Environment.

Estimated lesson time: 15 minutes

Creating a Connection

Before you can use a Data Environment, you need to add one to your project. This is similar to adding a form or module. Once added, you use the Data Environment designer at design time. From within the designer, you first set property values for a Connection object. When you add a Data Environment to your Visual Basic project, the Data Environment designer automatically includes a new connection, called Connection1. At design time, the Data Environment opens the connection and obtains data from the connection, including database object names, table structures, and procedure parameters.

➤ **To create a database connection**

1. On the **Project** menu, point to **More ActiveX Designers**, and click **Data Environment**.

2. Right-click on **Connection1** and click **Properties**.

   The **Data Link Properties** dialog box appears to allow you to specify data source connection information, as illustrated in Figure 8.3.

   - Provider tab

     In the Provider tab, select an OLE DB provider.

   - Connection tab

     The Connection tab contains different settings depending on the OLE DB provider you have chosen. For ODBC data providers, the Connection tab lets you select or enter the ODBC data source name (DSN) that you want to access, enter or build an ODBC connection string rather than using an existing DSN, enter information to log on to the server, and test the connection. For the Jet provider, the Connection tab lets you enter a database name, a username and password, and test the connection.

- Advanced tab

   The Advanced tab lets you view and set other initialization properties for your data.

- All tab

   The All tab lets you view and edit all of the OLE DB initialization properties that are available for your OLE DB provider. Properties may vary, depending on the OLE DB provider that you are using.

3. After you have set connection properties, click **OK** to close the **Data Link Properties** dialog box.

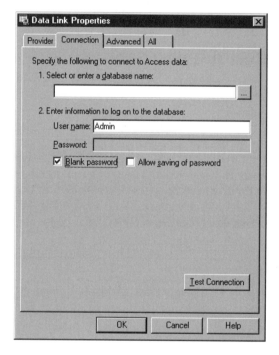

Figure 8.3 Setting Connection properties through the Data Link Properties dialog box

Presenting Records to the User

Once a connection has been designed, you can add Command objects to the connection. A Command object can reference a stored query or you can build it from a custom SQL string. Using an existing Command object, you can drag the Command object from the Data View window onto a form. All the fields associated with the object are automatically represented on the form.

➤ **To create a Command object**

1. Open the **Data Environment Designer** and select the appropriate connection.

2. Right-click the connection and click the **Add Command**.

   A new **Command1** appears under the selected connection.

3. Right-click **Command1** and select **Properties**.

4. In the **Command1 Properties** sheet, enter the appropriate information about the records that should be returned.

   When using a Microsoft Access database, you can choose a stored query by selecting **View** for the **Database Object**.

5. Click **OK** when finished.

➤ **To display records on a form**

1. From the **Data Environment Designer**, select the Command object that will be presented to the user.

2. Drag the Command object to the appropriate form.

   When you drop the command onto the form, all the fields associated with this command are added as text boxes to the form. In addition, labels are added automatically to describe the field to the user.

Note A new recordset object is created automatically. It will have the prefix "rs" added to the Command object name so that you can reference it from within your code.

In order to navigate the recordset or modify records, you need to add the appropriate code. However, all the text boxes that were created are automatically bound to the Data Environment's rsCommand1 object.

The following example calls the MoveNext method on the Recordset object created by the data environment:

```
DataEnvironment1.rsCommand1.MoveNext
```

Practice: Presenting Records Using a Data Environment

In this practice, you will connect to the Northwind database, present records using a Command object, and add navigation controls to the form.

➤ **To create a Data Environment**

1. Start Visual Basic and create a new **Standard EXE** project.

2. On the **Project** menu, point to **Move ActiveX Designers**, and click **Data Environment**.

3. Select the data environment in the **Project Explorer** window and rename it **deNorthwind**.

➤ **To connect to the Northwind database**

1. In the **Data Environment Designer**, rename **Connection1** to **conCustomers**.

2. Right-click **conCustomers** and click **Properties**.

3. Click **Microsoft Jet 3.51 OLE DB Provider** and click **Next**.

4. Enter the full path and filename of the nwind.mdb database.

   If you do not know the path, use the ellipses next to the text box to browse your hard drive. Nwind.mdb should be located in your C:\Program Files\Microsoft Visual Studio\Vb98 folder.

5. Click **Test Connection** to verify the data environment can access the Northwind database.

6. Click **OK** when finished.

➤ **To create a Command object**

1. In the **Data Environment Designer**, right-click **conCustomers** and click **Add Command**.

   A new **Command1** object is added to **conCustomers**.

2. Rename **Command1** to **comCustomerDetails**.

3. Right-click **comCustomerDetails** and click **Properties**.

4. Under **Database Object**, click **View**.

5. Under **Object Name**, click **Customers and Suppliers by City**.

6. Click **OK**.

➤ **To bind the Command object to a form**

1. Open **Form1**'s designer and resize and position it so both the form and data environment designers are in view.

2. From the **Data Environment Designer**, drag the **comCustomerDetails** object to **Form1**.

3. Resize the form and move the fields so all text boxes are in view.

4. Add two command buttons to the bottom of the form.

5. Name them **cmdPrevious** and **cmdNext**, respectively, and add the appropriate caption.

6. Add the following code to the Click event in **cmdPrevious**:

```
deNorthwind.rscomCustomerDetails.MovePrevious
If deNorthwind.rscomCustomerDetails.BOF Then
    deNorthwind.rscomCustomerDetails.MoveFirst
End If
```

7. Add the following code to the Click event in **cmdNext**:

```
deNorthwind.rscomCustomerDetails.MoveNext
If deNorthwind.rscomCustomerDetails.EOF Then
    deNorthwind.rscomCustomerDetails.MoveLast
End If
```

8. Save your application to the \Practice\Ch08 folder and test your work.

Lesson Summary

As an alternative to writing all the code to connect to a data source and retrieve records, Visual Basic 6 includes a tool called the Data Environment. Using a Data Environment, you can graphically set many of the Connection properties at design time and then automatically use them when the application runs. In addition, you can create Command objects and drag them to a form, creating a simple user interface. Another benefit of the Data Environment is that it requires less code to be written and lowers the chance of coding errors. However, the Data Environment relies heavily on binding and can reduce the overall efficiency of an application. Depending on you application needs, database support, and client computer, you will have to choose between using the Data Environment or manually writing all the necessary code.

Summary

Introducing the ADO Object Model

The ADO object model has three main components.

- The Connection object is used to:
  - Initialize/establish connection to a data source.
  - Execute queries.
  - Use transactions.
- The Command object is used to issue commands to a database using the Parameters collection.
- The Recordset object is used to:
  - Manipulate result sets.
  - Add, update, delete, scroll through records.

The ADO object model provides:

- A set of objects for writing code to access data.
- Detailed error data through the Error object.
- The Fields object allows retrieval and update of data.

Connecting to a Data Source

- The ADO object model's Connection object provides data access.
  - You can specify different souces such as Microsoft Access or an Oracle database.
- You can use the WithEvents keyword to respsond to events such as the completion of a connection request.
- The Visual Basic application can call stored queries or return records for processing after the connection is established.

Retrieving Data

- The Recordset object returns and manages records.
  - Create a Recordset from an existing connection or as a stand-alone object.
  - Specify an active connection; otherwise recordset creates an implied connection.
- The Command object can also provide interaction with data.
  - Use it to access stored queries in a Microsoft Access database.
  - You may have to use the Parameters collection to pass data to the query.

Navigating Records

- The Recordset object default is forward only so you must use the MoveNext method to navigate.
- Other navigation methods require specifying a scrollable cursor type which:
  - Provides greater functionality in some cases.
  - Uses additional overhead.
- The ADO Find method supports searching the current recordset.
- A specific Where clause may be more efficient in some cases.

Modifying Data

The recordset object is read-only by default. To edit, add, or delete records, the application must open the recordset with a locking scheme:

- adLockReadOnly
- adLockPessimistic
- adLockOptimistic
- adLockBatchOptimistic

An open recordset can use the AddNew, Update, and Delete methods to modify records and save changes to the data source.

Using the Data Environment

The Data Environment is a tool that lets you:

- Graphically set many Connection properties at design time, then automatically use them at run time.
- Create Command objects and drag them to a form to create a simple user interface.
- Write less code thus lessening the chance of coding errors.

The Data Environment relies heavily on binding. This may reduce the overall efficiency of an application.

Lab: Using ActiveX Data Objects

In this lab, you will write ADO code to create a Connection and Recordset object. The Recordset object will be created based on a SQL statement built from a Search form that you will create. You can continue to work with the files you created in Lab 7, or you can use the files provided for you in the \Labs\Lab08\Partial folder. The solution code is in the \Labs\Lab08\Solution folder.

To see a demonstration of the solution, run the Lab08.exe animation located in the Animations folder on the Supplemental Course Materials CD-ROM that accompanies this book.

Estimated lesson time: 20 minutes

Exercise 1: Creating ADO Objects

In this exercise, you will declare Recordset and Connection object variables. These variables will be used in Exercise 2. You will also create a custom search form to allow users to locate guest records.

➤ **To declare a Connection and Recordset object variable**

1. Open your application or the Visual Basic project located in the \Labs\Lab08\Partial folder.

2. Set a reference to the **Microsoft ActiveX Data Objects 2.0** object library.

3. In the General Declarations section of **frmReservation**, type the following code:

```
Private cnReservation As ADODB.Connection
Private rsReservation As ADODB.Recordset
```

➤ **To implement a custom Search form**

1. Create a new form and set the **Name** property to **frmSearch**.

2. Place three Label and TextBox controls, and one CommandButton on **frmSearch**, and set the following properties.

Control	Property	Value
Label1	Name	lblLastName
	Caption	Last Name
Text1	Name	txtLastName
	Text	<blank>
Label2	Name	lblFirstName
	Caption	First Name
Text2	Name	txtFirstName
	Text	<blank>
Label3	Name	lblPhone
	Caption	Phone
Text3	Name	txtPhone
	Text	<blank>
Command1	Name	cmdSearch
	Caption	&Search

Your form should look similar to Figure 8.4.

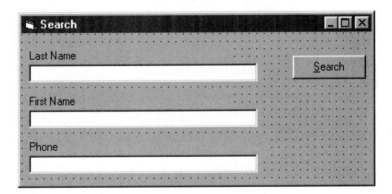

Figure 8.4 Position of controls on frmSearch

3. In the Click event of **cmdSearch**, type the following code:

```
'Hide the current form
Me.Hide
```

4. Save your work as **frmSearch.frm**.

Exercise 2: Writing ADO Code

In this exercise, you will write ADO code to query the Reservations table in the Rsvn.mdb database. The rsReservation Recordset object that you created in Exercise 1 will be based on information that the user enters into the fields on frmSearch.

➤ **To open the rsReservation recordset**

1. In the **mnuCustSearch_Click** event, type the following code:

```
Dim SQL As String
Dim msgRetVal As Integer

frmSearch.Show vbModal
'Create a SQL statement to search for a guest
SQL = "SELECT * FROM Reservation WHERE LastName LIKE '" & _
    frmSearch!txtLastName.Text & "%'" & _
    " AND FirstName LIKE '" & frmSearch!txtFirstName.Text & "%'" & _
    " AND Phone = '" & frmSearch.txtPhone.Text & "';"
Unload frmSearch
Set frmSearch = Nothing
'Create and open the connection
Set cnReservation = New ADODB.Connection
cnReservation.ConnectionString = _
    "Provider=Microsoft.Jet.OLEDB.3.51;" & _
    "Data Source=C:\Labs\Rsvn.mdb"
cnReservation.Open

Set rsReservation = New ADODB.Recordset
'Create and open the recordset
rsReservation.Open SQL, cnReservation, adOpenDynamic
```

2. Next, write the code necessary to bind fields from the recordset to the controls on frmReservation. Add the following code to the **mnuCustSearch_Click** event:

```
'If no records found, then display a message and exit the sub
If rsReservation.BOF And rsReservation.EOF Then
    MsgBox "Unable to locate guest."
    Exit Sub
End If

'Place each field from the record into the fields on frmReservation
txtFirstName.Text = rsReservation![FirstName]
txtLastName.Text = rsReservation![LastName]
txtAddress.Text = rsReservation![Address]
txtNumDays.Text = rsReservation![NumberOfDays]
txtNumPeople.Text = rsReservation![NumberOfPeople]
txtPhone.Text = rsReservation![Phone]
txtRate.Text = rsReservation![Rate]
```

```
txtRoomNumber.Text = rsReservation![RoomNumber]
mskCheckIn.Text = Format(rsReservation![CheckInDate], "mm-dd-yyyy")
txtCheckOut.Text = Format(DateAdd("d", _
    Val(txtNumDays.Text), mskCheckIn.Text), "mm-dd-yyyy")
Select Case rsReservation![PaymentType]
    Case "CREDIT CARD"
        grpPmtType(0).Value = True
    Case "CHECK"
        grpPmtType(1).Value = True
    Case "CASH"
        grpPmtType(2).Value = True
End Select
```

➤ **To test your application**

1. Start the application.

   The Reservation form appears.

2. On the **Guest** menu, click **Search**.

   The Search form appears.

3. Type **Fleming** for last name, **Brian** for first name, and **(206) 555-3412** (place a space after the close parenthesis) for phone number, as illustrated in Figure 8.5, and then click **Search**.

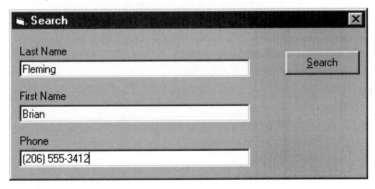

Figure 8.5 Entering search values

Visual Basic finds the record in the Reservation table. The recordset's field values appear in the controls on frmReservation, as illustrated in Figure 8.6.

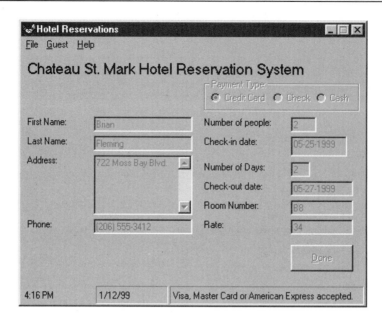

Figure 8.6 The frmReservation form containing the found record

4. On the **Run** menu, click **End**.

5. On the Visual Basic **File** menu, click **Save Project**.

Review

The following questions are intended to reinforce key information presented in this chapter. If you are unable to answer a question, review the appropriate lesson and then try the question again. Answers to the questions can be found in the Appendix, "Questions and Answers," located at the back of this book.

1. Which ADO objects can be used to establish the connection?

2. What is the ADO Parameters collection used for?

3. When would you use the Command object?

4. What method can be used to locate a specific record in an existing recordset without re-querying the database?

5. What new interface, other than the ADO Data control, is provided by Visual Basic 6 for graphically accessing a data source?

CHAPTER 9

Connecting to COM Servers

About This Chapter

In this chapter, you will learn how to expand the capabilities of your application by connecting to external Component Object Model (COM) servers. Using Microsoft Office programs, such as Microsoft Word, you can add existing functionality to your program without building similar features separately. In addition, you will learn how to extend your program by calling functions exposed in the Windows Application Programming Interface (API).

Before You Begin

To complete the lessons in this chapter, you must have:

- Read Chapter 6.

Lesson 1: Connecting to COM Components

In Chapter 6, "Introduction to Class Modules," you learned how to create class modules that are compiled inside an application and are available only to that project. In this chapter, you'll learn how to connect to external COM components to extend the functionality of your application.

After this lesson you will be able to:

- Describe the benefits of using a COM component.
- Explain how to register a COM component.
- Explain the benefits of using a type library.
- Describe how to set a reference to a type library.
- Describe type libraries.

Estimated lesson time: 15 minutes

Review of COM Components

COM is a standard, or model, for the interaction of objects. An important feature of COM is that objects are precompiled, so that the language in which they were created does not affect the client application that is making the connection. COM provides the standard model for integrating objects.

COM components are units of code that provide specific functionality. COM components can be either internal components, which are compiled into a project and are available only to that project, or external components, which are compiled into an executable (.exe) or dynamic-link library (.dll). Although COM components are typically libraries of classes, entire applications such as Microsoft Excel or Internet Explorer are also COM components. Client applications use a technique called automation to take advantage of the services that such components provide. Any client application can use an external component. Client applications use components in the same way, whether the component was compiled in a .dll or an .exe. In this lesson, you will learn how to create a Visual Basic client application that uses an external COM component.

Registering a Component

In Chapter 6, "Introduction to Class Modules," you added a COM component's class module, and its properties, methods, and events, to your project. You could then use the class module to create objects for use in a single application. However, you can also use external components in your application. External components, called servers, can be ActiveX DLLs or EXEs created in Visual Basic, or provided by third party developers. Before you can use an external server component, you must ensure that the actual component is available on your computer.

When you run the installation program for a component, it adds any required files and, typically, also registers the component. If you are using a component that does not have an installation program, use the Regsvr32 (Regsvr32.exe) utility to register the component yourself.

Note When you create your own ActiveX EXE program and run it from the Visual Basic IDE (Integrated Development Environment), it is automatically registered on your computer.

Using the Regsvr32 Utility

The Regsvr32 utility is located in the system directory (for example, C:\Windows\System). You can run Regsvr32 either from an MS-DOS prompt or from the Run command on the Windows Start menu. Because you cannot run a DLL by itself, you must use the Regsvr32 utility to register a DLL component. Regsvr32 has several options. For example, use the /u option to unregister a COM server; use the /s (silent) option to register a server without displaying subsequent dialog boxes. You can see a list of all Regsvr32 options by running Regsvr32.exe without specifying a DLL name, as shown in Figures 9.1 and 9.2.

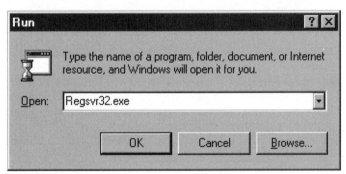

Figure 9.1 Running Regsvr32 without specifying a DLL name

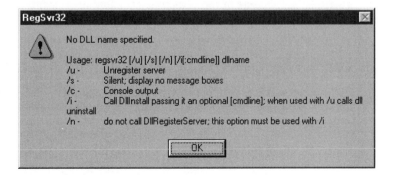

Figure 9.2 The RegSvr32 options dialog box

➤ **To register a DLL component**

1. Click the Windows **Start** button.

2. On the **Start** menu, click **Run**.

3. On the **Run** dialog box, type the following command:

   ```
   Regsvr32.exe <DLLPath>\<DLL name>.dll
   ```

   A dialog similar to that shown in Figure 9.3 appears.

4. Click **OK**.

Figure 9.3 RegSvr32 confirmation dialog box

You can register an ActiveX EXE simply by running it, or double-clicking the file in Windows Explorer. In addition, if you use the command-line options /regserver and /unregserver, you can register or unregister any ActiveX EXE without invoking the program's user interface.

Note You unregister a component to manually remove component references from the system registry. You can then delete the component's EXE or DLL file.

➤ **To register or unregister an EXE component**

■ Type the filename of the component (including the path) followed by /regserver or /unregserver.

   ```
   C:\MyProject\MyComponent.exe /regserver
   ```

Using Type Libraries

COM components, including Microsoft Excel and Microsoft Word, contain libraries of available properties, methods, and events. These libraries are called type libraries.

Type libraries also contain the specifications for one or more COM elements, such as the available properties and methods. A type library can be either an .olb or a .tlb file, or part of the .exe or .dll that the type library describes. These files are stored in a standard binary format. The type library viewers such as the Object Browser are used to review information about the COM elements in the library.

Viewing the type library provides you with the proper syntax for the classes, interfaces, methods, properties, and events of the COM object.

Setting References

There are many benefits to using type libraries. One benefit is that, at design time, you have immediate access to the component's Auto List Members. The Auto List Members is the drop-down list that appears as you enter code. This list contains the component's properties and methods. When a component does not have a type library, the properties, methods, and events are not validated until the application is run; in this case, you can not use the Auto List Members feature.

To make a library available to your application, you set a reference to the component's type library in Visual Basic.

To see a demonstration, run the Chap09.exe animation located in the Animations folder on the Supplemental Course Materials CD-ROM that accompanies this book.

➤ **To set a reference to a type library**

1. On the **Project** menu, click **References**.

   The **References** dialog box appears.

2. Click the reference to the type library you want to use, then click **OK**.

If a component is selected in the referenced library, but you are not using it, you should clear the check box in the References dialog box. By minimizing the number of object references your application uses, you reduce the size of your application and the time it takes for your project to compile. You cannot remove a reference for a component that is used in your project. You also cannot remove the "Visual Basic For Applications" and "Visual Basic objects and procedures" references, because they are necessary for running Visual Basic.

Lesson Summary

Component Object Model (COM) components are units of code that provide specific functionality. COM components are either internal components, which are compiled into a project and are available only to that project, or external components, which are compiled into an executable (.exe) or dynamic-link library (.dll).

Before you use an external component, make sure that it is available and registered on your computer. Use Regsvr32 to register both ActiveX DLLs and Active EXEs. There are several options available with Regsvr32. For example, use the /u option to unregister a server and the /s (silent) option to register a server without displaying a success dialog box.

A type library is a description of all objects, methods, events, and properties for a COM component. Set a reference to the component's type library to make it available to your application. Remove any components and library references which your application does not need to ensure more efficient compiling.

Lesson 2: Managing COM Components

COM is a component software architecture that allows applications to communicate with components supplied by different software vendors. This communication provides access to the functionality offered by different applications without exposing the user to different interfaces. For example, suppose a user enters a customer's order into a Visual Basic form. Visual Basic (the ActiveX client) then opens a line of communication with Microsoft Word (the ActiveX server). The customer's order is then sent to a Word document, where the application prints an invoice and an envelope.

After this lesson you will be able to:

- Describe how to create a reference to a component object.
- Explain how to control an ActiveX Server.
- Describe how to terminate a reference to a component.
- Describe how to use the Object Browser to access a component's properties and methods.

Estimated lesson time: 30 minutes

Overview of Automation

Automation is a feature that programs use to make their objects available to development tools, macro languages, and other programs. For example, a spreadsheet program may make a worksheet, chart, cell, or range of cells available, each as a different type of object. A word processor might make objects such as an application, a document, a paragraph, a sentence, a bookmark, or a selection available.

When a program supports Automation, you can use Visual Basic to access the objects it provides. You manipulate these objects in Visual Basic by invoking methods on the object or by getting and setting the object's properties.

An Automation operation has two components. One component, the server, contains the objects you want to use. The other component, the client, is the one you are currently working in, and from which you want to control the objects from the server. Many components, including Microsoft Access, Excel, Word, and PowerPoint, can act as either the client or server. Other components can act as one or the other, but not both.

Instantiation is the process of creating an instance of a class in memory. An object variable points to that location in memory after it is assigned a value with the Set statement. A component instantiated from within Visual Basic code is bound to the client until the client releases that instance of the object. After the server object has been instantiated and initialized, the client must call the server object's methods by using an object variable that references the ActiveX server.

The basic steps to successfully automate a COM object are:

1. Add a reference to the object library.
2. Declare a variable as the object type.
3. Assign the object returned by the CreateObject function, New statement, or GetObject function to the object variable you declared in step 2.
4. Use the properties and methods of the object variable to automate the component.

Declaring Object Variables

Before you create an instance of a component, you must declare an object variable that points to the COM object. You declare an object variable as either specific or generic, depending on how you plan to use the variable. In some cases, you do not know at design time the specific type of object your application will use. In these situations, you can use generic object variables to hold pointers to any type of object. For example, you might want to write a function that acts on any one of several different classes of objects. In this case, you must declare the variable as an Object. The following code uses the Object data type to declare a generic object variable:

```
Dim MyObj As Object
```

When you use this type of declaration, no information is known about the object at design time. Visual Basic must do additional work to access the object at run time. This causes a negative impact on the client application's performance. This type of variable declaration is called *late binding*; use it only if absolutely necessary.

If you know at design time the type of object you will be creating at run time, you should specifically declare the variable. The following code creates a variable that will hold pointers to Microsoft Excel objects only:

```
Public xlApp As Excel.Application
Private xlChart As Excel.Chart
Static xlSheet As Excel.Worksheet
```

The code which follows points to other registered objects, such as a Visual Basic project's Class module:

```
Static obj1 As Project1.Class1
```

Visual Basic checks the syntax of calls that use specific object variables. The compiler can produce more efficient code to access the object at run time. At design time, Visual Basic also provides the Auto List Members, which presents a drop-down list of available members (such as properties and methods). This type of object binding is referred to as *early binding*.

Instantiating an Object

When you declare an object variable, Visual Basic allocates sufficient memory to hold a pointer to an object. When an object is instantiated, Visual Basic creates the component in memory, and the object variable points to that instance of the component. As discussed in Lesson 1 of this chapter, you must properly register the component before you instantiate it; also, the component's object library must be referenced in the client application.

In Visual Basic, there are three ways to create an instance of a COM server object:

- Use the **GetObject** function.
- Use the **CreateObject** function.
- Use the **New** keyword with a **Set** statement.

Using the GetObject Function

Use the GetObject function if there is a current instance of the object or if you want to create the object with a file that already exists. The first argument of the GetObject function, pathname, specifies the full path and name of the file containing the object that you want to retrieve. If you omit the pathname, the second argument, class, is required. The class argument is a string value representing the class of the object. The class acts as the template from which an instance of an object is created at run time. The class defines the properties of the object and the methods used to control the object's behavior. Properties and methods also appear in the Auto List Members drop-down list.

The following example creates an instance of a Microsoft Word document object called MyDocument.doc and displays it in Print Preview mode:

```
Sub ShowDocument()
    'Creating a specific object variable
    Static wdDoc As Word.Document
    'Opens Microsoft Word and displays MyDocument.doc
    Set wdDoc = GetObject("C:\MyDocument.doc", "Word.Document")
    'By default new objects are not visible
    wdDoc.Parent.Visible = True
    wdDoc.PrintPreview
End Sub
```

The following code creates an instance of the application associated with the .xls extension and activates the object in the specified file:

```
Dim xl As Object
'Do not specify a class type
Set xl = GetObject("C:\MyFiles\Earnings.xls")
```

Using the CreateObject Function

If there is no current instance, and you don't want to open a file when the object is started, use the CreateObject function. In addition, if you must use a generic variable in your application because you do not know the specific object type until run time (late binding), use CreateObject to instantiate the class. If an object has registered itself as a single-instance object, Visual Basic will only create one instance of the object, no matter how many times you call CreateObject.

The following example uses the CreateObject function to create an instance of Microsoft Excel. It uses the reference to access the Visible property of Microsoft Excel, and then uses the Quit method to close the object. Finally, the reference itself is released by setting it equal to the Nothing keyword.

```
Dim xlApp As Object
Set xlApp = CreateObject("Excel.Application")

With xlApp
'Set Visible property to True to see the application
.Visible = True
'[statements]
'When you finish, use the Quit method to close the application
.Quit
End With
'Release the reference
Set xlApp = Nothing
```

Using the New Keyword with a Set Statement

If you have set a reference to the type library for the external component, and can use a specific object variable (early binding), then use the New keyword with the Set statement to create an instance of the class you want to use in your application.

The Dim, Private, Public, ReDim, and Static statements only declare a variable that refers to an object. No actual object is instantiated until you use the Set statement to assign a specific object. The following code uses the New keyword with the Set statement to create an instance of Microsoft Word:

```
Dim wd As Word.Application
Set wd = New Word.Application
With wd
    .Visible = True
    'Add a new document to the Word application
    .Documents.Add
    'Add text to the active document
    .Selection.TypeText Text:="This text was added"
    'Print the current document
    .ActiveDocument.PrintOut
End With
```

Practice: Automating Microsoft Excel

In this practice you will first create a reference to the Microsoft Excel 8.0 Object Library. The code displays Microsoft Excel by using the xlApp object variable to reference the Visible property. Then it opens a new workbook and programmatically enters values into a worksheet, printing and then closing the workbook. To close Excel, the code uses the Microsoft Excel Quit method and, finally, releases the Excel reference by using the Nothing keyword.

➤ **To create a new project**

1. Start Microsoft Visual Basic.

2. Open a new **Standard EXE** project.

➤ **To set a reference to the Microsoft Excel 8.0 Library**

1. On the **Project** menu, click **References**.

   The **References** dialog box appears.

2. Click the **Microsoft Excel 8.0 Object Library** reference, then click **OK**.

➤ **To add a control to the project and automate Microsoft Excel**

1. Add a command button to the form. Set the Name property to **cmdRunExcel** and the Caption property to **&Run Excel**. Figure 9.4 illustrates the form layout.

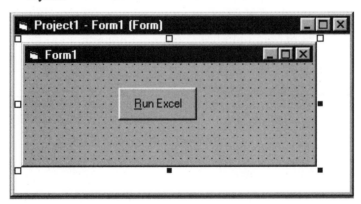

Figure 9.4 Practice form layout

2. Double-click the command button. In the **cmdRunExcel_Click** event, declare a variable to hold the pointer to Microsoft Excel by adding the following code:

```
Dim xlApp As Excel.Application
```

3. Create an instance of Microsoft Excel, and use Microsoft Excel's methods and properties, by adding the following code to the **cmdRunExcel_Click** event:

```
Set xlApp = New Excel.Application

With xlApp
    'Set Visible property to True to see the application
    .Visible = True
    'Add a new workbook
    .Workbooks.Add

    'Enter data into specific cells
    .Range("A1").Value = "Product"
    .Range("A2").Value = "Apples"
    .Range("A3").Value = "Oranges"
    .Range("A4").Value = "Bananas"

    'Print the active worksheet
    .ActiveSheet.PrintOut
    'Close the workbook without saving the changes
    'to the new worksheet
    .ActiveWorkbook.Close SaveChanges:=False

    'When you finish, use the Quit method to close the application
    .Quit
End With
'Release the reference
Set xlApp = Nothing
```

4. Save your project as XL.vbp, and save your form as frmXL.vbp in the \Practice\Ch09 folder, and then test your application.

Figure 9.5 shows the output from the practice.

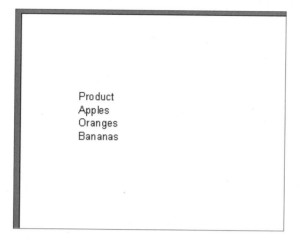

Figure 9.5 Practice output

Using the Object Browser

Use the Object Browser to display the classes, properties, methods, events, and constants available from various object libraries. You can use the Object Browser to find and use objects you create, as well as objects from other applications. Figure 9.6 illustrates the Object Browser window.

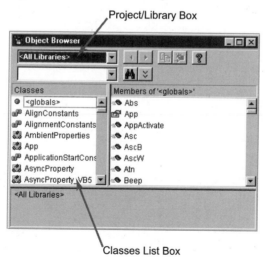

Figure 9.6 The Object Browser

➤ **To display a procedure in a project or library**

1. Click the **Object Browser** button on the **Standard** toolbar, or press **F2**. Figure 9.7 shows the **Object Browser** button.

Figure 9.7 The Object Browser button

2. In the **Project/Library** box, click the project or library containing the procedures you want to view.

3. In the **Classes** list box, click the class or module name that contains the desired procedure.

4. Click the procedure name in the **Members** list box, then click the **View Definition** button (Figure 9.8) on the **Object Browser** toolbar.

Figure 9.8 The View Definition button

Lesson Summary

The Component Object Model (COM) is a component software architecture that allows applications to communicate with components supplied by different software vendors. This communication, called Automation, provides access to the functionality offered by different applications.

When you perform an Automation operation, two components are involved:

- The ActiveX Client component is the application in which you are currently working and from which you want to control an external object.

- The ActiveX Server component contains the external object you want to use.

Before you create an instance of a component to use in a client application, you must declare an object variable to refer to the object. You declare an object variable as either specific or generic, depending on how you will use the variable.

In Visual Basic, there are three ways to create an object to access an external component:

- Use the GetObject function.

- Use the CreateObject function.

- Use the New keyword with a Set statement.

Use the Object Browser to display the classes, properties, methods, events, and constants available from the object libraries.

Lesson 3: Calling Win32 APIs

One advantage of using Visual Basic is that you can include functionality that is not directly provided by Visual Basic by accessing the Windows Application Programming Interface (Win32 API). The Win32 API consists of a group of special DLLs called *standard DLLs*. A standard DLL does not support a COM interface, so you cannot access the Windows API the same way you would Microsoft Word or Microsoft Excel. In this lesson, you will use standard DLLs to extend the functionality of your Visual Basic applications.

After this lesson you will be able to:

- Explain the differences between the COM and the Win32 API.
- Explain how to use the Win32 API.
- Describe how to use the API Text Viewer.
- Define and implement a Callback procedure.

Estimated lesson time: 20 minutes

COM Components and Win32 DLLs

When you use automation to execute methods and properties of an application such as Microsoft Word, you are using COM to call the procedures made available by Word. When using a standard DLL, such as the Win32 API, you are making direct function calls. There is no type library included with a standard DLL, and therefore features such as the Object Browser and Auto List Members are not supported. However, sometimes, you must use a standard DLL when a COM DLL is not available.

Using Win32 API

The Win32 API provides developers direct access to internal functions that are used by the Windows operating system. There are several advantages when using the Win32 API. You can:

- Accomplish tasks that are not possible in Visual Basic.

  Visual Basic is a comprehensive and powerful programming language. Even with its extensive capablilities, there may be requirements within your application that Visual Basic does not support.

- Obtain improved performance.

  The development tools used to create DLLs, in many cases, can produce faster, more efficient code. This code often out-performs code written in Visual Basic.

- Update independently of the application.

  Because a DLL is a separate file, you can update the DLL without recompiling the application that calls the DLL. This is true for both standard and COM DLLs.

Most applications use COM DLLs; Visual Basic DLLs are COM-based DLLs. You cannot create standard DLLs in Visual Basic. If you need standard DLLs, you can create them with third party development tool such as Microsoft Visual C++.

Although standard DLLs do not have type libraries, there are several tools that assist in the use of these APIs. These include:

- The documentation included with the API.
- Third party API reference manuals.
- The Visual Basic API Text Viewer.

Extending Applications with the Win32 API

You can call three primary Windows DLLs from Visual Basic. The Windows API is composed of these DLLs. They provide most of the Windows API functionality.

The 32-bit versions of the Windows operating system (Windows 95 and Windows NT) consist of the User32, GDI32, and Kernel32 DLLs.

- The User32 DLL manages Windows menus, controls, and dialog boxes.
- The GDI32 DLL provides graphical output, including drawing, fonts, and metafiles.
- The Kernel32 DLL handles operating system tasks such as memory management, resource management and other lower level operating functions.

In addition to these three DLLs, Windows 95 and Windows NT contain many other DLLs that provide extended functionality to Visual Basic. In this lesson, we will focus on using only the Win32 API DLLs.

Using Win32 API calls enhances the functionality and performance of your application. There are two steps when using these Win32 APIs in your Visual Basic code:

1. Declare the DLL function.
2. Call the DLL function.

Note Incorrect use or poorly designed DLLs can cause application or system failures. Always save your application before testing.

Declaring DLLs

Unlike COM DLLs, before using a standard DLL you must specify the location of the procedures; you also must identify the arguments with which they should be called. Use the Declare statement to provide this information. Typically, you use a standard module to make the appropriate declaration. DLLs declared in a standard module are public by default and can be called by code from anywhere in your Visual Basic application. To declare a DLL procedure in a form or class module, you must include the Private keyword in the declaration.

The DLL declare statement syntax is:

[**Public|Private**] **Declare Sub** *name* **Lib** "*libname*" [Alias "*aliasname*"] [(arglist)]

To declare a DLL, type the DLLs declaration statement into the Visual Basic module or use the API Text Viewer, which is provided with Visual Basic. The API Text Viewer allows you to copy and paste the declaration into a module. This reduces the chance that a DLL function is declared incorrectly. Figure 9.9 illustrates the API Text Viewer.

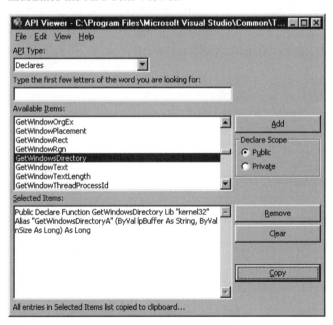

Figure 9.9 The API Text Viewer

➤ **To use the API Text Viewer to copy a declare statement.**

1. Click the Windows **Start** button. Then click the **Programs** menu and find the **Microsoft Visual Basic 6.0 Tools** menu in the **Microsoft Visual Basic 6.0** menu. On the **Microsoft Visual Basic 6.0 Tools** menu select **API Text Viewer**.

2. On the **File** menu, in the API Text Viewer, click **Load Text File...**

   The API Text Viewer gives you the choice of searching the API text file or converting the text file to a database file. When you are prompted to create a database, and you respond Yes, the API Text Viewer will create an .mdb database file. You can then load the .mdb file whenever you use the API Viewer.

3. On the **Select a Text API File** dialog box, click **Win32api.txt**.

4. On the **Available Items** list box, click the required procedure name. Then click the **Add** button to add the procedure to the **Selected Items** list box.

   The **Available Items** list box displays a list of the Win32 API. Change the way the API is declared by selecting **Declare Scope** under the **Add** button.

5. Click the **Copy** button to copy the added APIs to the Clipboard.

6. Paste the Declare statements into the appropriate module.

   The following is an example of the pasted GetWindowsDirectory function:

```
Private Declare Function GetWindowsDirectory Lib "kernel32" Alias _
    "GetWindowsDirectoryA" (ByVal lpBuffer As String, _
    ByVal nSize As Long) As Long
```

Calling DLLs

After you declare a DLL procedure, you can use it in your code just like a native Visual Basic procedure. In the following example, the function GetWindowsDirectory finds the current Windows directory on the user's computer:

```
Private Declare Function GetWindowsDirectory Lib "kernel32" Alias _
    "GetWindowsDirectoryA" (ByVal lpBuffer As String, _
    ByVal nSize As Long) As Long

Private Sub cmdFindWindows_Click()
    Dim strWinDir As String
    Dim lngLen As Long
    'Pass the DLL a string variable filled with null characters
    strWinDir = String(255, 0)
    'Call the function and pass the strWinDir variable
    'and the length of the variable
    lngLen = GetWindowsDirectory(strWinDir, Len(strWinDir))
    'Remove any remaining Null charactors
    'using the return value of the GetWindowsDirectory
    'and the Left function
    strWinDir = Left(strWinDir, lngLen)
    strWinDir = strWinDir & "\"
    MsgBox "Windows is in " & strWinDir
End Sub
```

When you call a DLL procedure, there are several issues to consider about how arguments are passed. For more information, search for "Passing Strings to a DLL Procedure" or "Passing Other Types of Information to a DLL Procedure" in MSDN Online Help.

Creating Callback Procedures

Some Windows API functions require a *function pointer* to be passed to them as an argument. A function pointer is a convention that enables you to pass the address of a user-defined, Visual Basic procedure as an argument to a Windows DLL. These Visual Basic procedures are referred to as *callback procedures*. A callback procedure is a procedure that will be called by the external DLL. The DLL can notify or give information to a client by using these procedures.

Using the AddressOf Operator

Visual Basic uses the AddressOf operator to pass a callback procedure to a DLL. The callback procedure must be located in a standard module, and it must have the correct syntax. Use the AddressOf operator to pass a pointer to the Window API. The pointer directs the API to the address of the callback procedure. Figure 9.10 illustrates how callback procedures work in Visual Basic. The CallTimer procedure calls SetTimer and uses the AddressOf operator to pass a pointer to the MyCallBack procedure. The timer then executes the MyCallBack procedure at the specified interval. The MyCallBack procedure then calls KillTimer, which stops the timer and frees the resource.

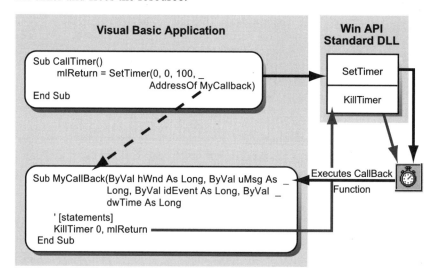

Figure 9.10 Callback procedures in Visual Basic

Another example of a Win32 API that requires a function pointer is EnumWindows. This function returns the handle of all windows that are owned by a particular task. The following is the declare statement of the EnumWindows function:

```
Declare Function EnumWindows lib "user32" _
    (ByVal lpEnumFunc as Long, ByVal lParam as Long ) As Long
```

EnumWindows is an enumeration function, which means that it can list the handle of every open window on your system. EnumWindows works by repeatedly calling the function you pass to its first argument (lpEnumFunc). Each time EnumWindows calls your function, EnumWindows passes the function the handle of an open window.

EnumWindows is called from your code; you must pass the user-defined callback function as the first argument to handle the stream of values. For example, you might write a function to add the values to a list box, convert the hWnd values to window names, or take whatever action you choose.

Practice: Creating a Callback Procedure

In this practice, you will first create a new Visual Basic project, then use the API Text Viewer to add the EnumChildWindows and GetWindowText procedures from the User32 DLL. You will then create and pass a callback procedure to the EnumChildWindows DLL. The application will display, in a list box, the names of all of the controls on the form.

➤ **To add controls to Form1**

1. Open a new **Standard EXE** project.

2. Add the following controls to **Form1**:

    - CommandButton
    - OptionButton
    - CheckBox
    - ListBox

3. Set the Name property of the command button to **cmdListWindows** and the Caption property to **&List Windows**.

    Your form should look like Figure 9.11.

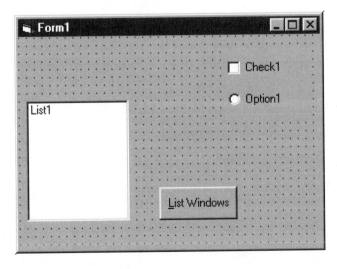

Figure 9.11 Practice form layout

➤ **To use the API Text Viewer to add Windows APIs**

1. On the **File** menu, in the **API Text Viewer**, click **Load Text File...**

    The **Select a Text API File** dialog box appears.

2. Click **Win32api.txt**.

    The **Available Items** list box appears.

3. Click **EnumChildWindows,** click **Private** for the **Declare Scope,** and then click **Add** to add the procedure to the **Selected Items** list box.

4. Click **GetWindowText,** click **Private** for the **Declare Scope,** and then click **Add**.

5. Click the **Copy** button.

    This copies the selected Declare statements to the Clipboard.

6. In Visual Basic, on the **Project** menu, click **Add Module,** click **Module**, then click the **Open** button.

7. In the **General Declarations** section of the new standard module, paste the copied declarations. To paste the declarations, use **CTRL+V** or, on the **Edit** menu, click **Paste**.

    The following declarations should appear in the General Declaration section:

```
Private Declare Function EnumChildWindows Lib "user32" _
    Alias "EnumChildWindows" (ByVal hWndParent As Long, _
    ByVal lpEnumFunc As Long, ByVal lParam As Long) As Long

Private Declare Function GetWindowText Lib "user32" _
    Alias "GetWindowTextA" (ByVal hwnd As Long, _
    ByVal lpString As String, ByVal cch As Long) As Long
```

➤ **To create the callback procedure**

1. While in the new standard code module, click **Add Procedure...** from the **Tools** menu.

2. Create a **Public** function called **EnumCallBack**, then click **Ok**. The procedure should look like the following:

```
Public Function EnumCallBack()

End Function
```

3. Add the following code to the **EnumCallBack** function:

```
Public Function EnumCallBack()
    Dim lngSize As Long
    Dim strPadString As String
    strPadString = String(255, 0)
    lngSize = GetWindowText(hWndChild, _
        strPadString, Len(strPadString))
    strPadString = Left$(strPadString, lngSize)
    Form1.List1.AddItem strPadString
    EnumCallBack = True
End Function
```

➤ **To call the Windows API**

1. Double-click the command button in **Form1**.

2. In the **cmdListWindows_Click** event, add the following code:

```
Private Sub cmdListWindows_Click()
    Dim blnRtn As Boolean
    blnRtn = EnumChildWindows(Form1.hwnd, AddressOf EnumCallBack, 0)
End Sub
```

3. Save your project as prjAPI.vbp in the \Practice\Ch09 folder, and then test your application.

Lesson Summary

The Windows Application Programming Interface (Win32 API) has standard DLLs. You can include functionality that is not directly provided by Visual Basic by accessing the Win32 API. Advantages to using the Win32 API include:

- Accomplishing tasks that are not possible in Visual Basic.
- Improving performance.
- Updating independently of the application.

Although most applications use COM DLLs, you can create standard DLLs with third party development tool such as Microsoft Visual C++.

The 32-bit versions of the Windows operating system (Windows 95 and Windows NT) consist of the User32, GDI32, and Kernel32 DLLs.

The two steps to using these Win32 APIs in your Visual Basic code are:

1. Declare the DLL function.
2. Call the DLL function.

Some Windows API functions require a function pointer to be passed to them as an argument. These Visual Basic procedures are referred to as callback procedures. A callback procedure is a procedure that will be called by the external DLL. Visual Basic uses the AddressOf operator to pass a callback procedure to a DLL.

Summary

Connecting to COM Components

Component Object Model (COM) components are units of code that provide specific functionality. They are either:

- Internal components, which are compiled into a project and are available only to that project.
- External components, which are compiled into an executable (.exe) or dynamic-link library (.dll).

An external component must be available and registered on your computer. Use Regsvr32 to register both ActiveX DLLs and Active EXEs.

A type library is a description of all objects, methods, events, and properties for a COM component. Set a reference to the component's type library to make it available to your application. To ensure more efficient compiling, remove any components and library references that your application does not need.

Managing COM Components

Automation supports accessing the functionality of different applications. The two components involved are:

- The ActiveX client—the application in which you are working, and from which you want to control an external object.
- The ActiveX server—the application that contains the external object you want to use.

Before creating an instance of a component in a client application, declare an object variable as either specific or generic.

To create an object to access an external component:

- Use the GetObject function.
- Use the CreateObject function.
- Use the New keyword with a Set statement.

Use the Object Browser to display the classes, properties, methods, events, and constants available from object libraries.

Calling Win32 APIs

You can include functionality that is not directly provided by Visual Basic by accessing the standard DLLs of the Windows Application Programming Interface (Win32 API). These DLLs let you:

- Accomplish tasks that are not possible in Visual Basic.
- Improve the performance of your application.
- Update independently of the application.

You can create standard DLLs with third party development tools such as Microsoft C++.

The 32-bit versions of the Windows operating system (Windows 95 and Windows NT) include the User32, GDI32, and Kernel32 DLLs.

To use these Win32 APIs in your Visual Basic code:

1. Declare the DLL function.
2. Call the DLL function.

Some Windows API functions require a function pointer to be passed to them as an argument. These Visual Basic procedures are referred to as callback procedures. A callback procedure is a procedure that will be called by the external DLL. Visual Basic uses the AddressOf operator to pass a callback procedure to a DLL.

Lab: Connecting to COM Components

In this lab, you will connect to Microsoft Word and Microsoft Excel and automate the process of creating a reminder letter and invoice for the guests. You will use the Reservations database, which is in the \Labs folder. You will also use the Chateau.dot file, which is in the \Labs folder. You can continue to work with the files you created in Lab 8, or you can use the files provided for you in the \Labs\Lab09\Partial folder. The solution code can be found in the \Labs\Lab09\Solution folder.

To see a demonstration of the solution, run the Lab09.exe animation located in the Animations folder on the Supplemental Course Materials CD-ROM that accompanies this book.

Estimated lesson time: 45 minutes

Exercise 1: Connecting to Microsoft Word

In this exercise you will add reporting features to the reservation application's existing menu. In the new Reports menu you will add Reminder and Invoice menu items. In the Reminder menu item you will create an instance of Microsoft Word, send frmReservation values to the Word template, and then show it in Print Preview.

➤ **Open the hotel reservation application project**

- Open the Chateau St. Mark hotel reservation system project.

➤ **To set a reference to the Microsoft Word type library**

1. On the **Project** menu, click **References**.

   The **References** dialog box appears.

2. Click the **Microsoft Word 8.0 Object Library**, then click **OK**.

➤ **To create the new Reports menu**

1. Add the following menu items using the Menu Editor. Position the new menu between the **Guest** and **Help** menus. The menu appearance is illustrated in Figure 9.12.

Menu Item	Property	Value
&Reports	Caption	&Reports
	Name	mnuReports
&Reminder	Caption	&Reminder
	Name	mnuReportsReminder
&Invoice	Caption	&Invoice
	Name	MnuReportsInvoice

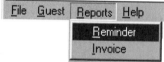

Figure 9.12 The Reports menu

➤ **To add code to automate Microsoft Word**

1. Add the following code to the **mnuReportsReminder_Click** event to create an instance of Microsoft Word:

```
Static wd As Word.Application
Static wdDoc As Word.Document
Dim strPmtType As String
'Create a new instance of word
Set wd = New Word.Application
```

2. Add the following code to the **mnuReportsReminder_Click** event to open the Chateau.dot template:

```
'Show the new instance of Word
wd.Visible = True
'Open the Chateau.dot Word template
Set wdDoc = wd.Documents.Add("C:\Labs\Chateau.dot")
```

3. Add the following code to the **mnuReportsReminder_Click** event to insert values into the template:

```
'Determine the payment type
If grpPmtType(0).Value = True Then
    strPmtType = "Credit Card"
ElseIf grpPmtType(1).Value Then
    strPmtType = "Check"
Else
    strPmtType = "Cash"
End If

'Fill the fields on the template with values from the form
With wdDoc
    .FormFields("wdFirstName").Range = txtFirstName.Text
    .FormFields("wdCheckIn").Range = mskCheckIn.Text
    .FormFields("wdNumOfDays").Range = txtNumDays.Text
    .FormFields("wdPmtType").Range = strPmtType
    .FormFields("wdCalcTotal").Range = _
        Format(CSng(txtNumDays.Text) * _
        CSng(txtRate.Text), "Currency")
    .FormFields("wdCheckOut").Range = txtCheckOut.Text
End With
```

4. Add the following code to the **mnuReportsReminder_Click** event to show the document in Print Preview:

```
'Send the new document to printprieview
wdDoc.PrintPreview
```

A new Word document based on the Chateau.dot template opens and the form fields are filled in with values from frmReservation. The document then displays in Print Preview.

▶ **To test the application**

1. Save and run the application.

2. On **frmReservation,** select **Search** on the **Guest** menu.

3. Enter the following values into the **Search** form:

Text box	Value
Last Name	Oberg
First Name	Bruce
Phone Number	(206) 555-9482

4. Click **Search**.

5. Select **Reminder** on the **Reports** menu.

   Word opens and the Reminder letter displays in Print Preview.

6. Close Word without saving the document.

Exercise 2: Connecting to Microsoft Excel

In this exercise you will create a Microsoft Excel invoice based on the current record in frmReservation.

Note You must have Microsoft Excel installed on your computer before you can use the automation code presented in this exercise.

➤ **To set a reference to the Microsoft Excel type library**

1. On the **Project** menu, click **References**.

2. Click the **Microsoft Excel 8.0 Object Library**, then click **OK**.

➤ **To add code to automate Microsoft Excel**

1. Add the following code to the **mnuReportsInvoice_Click** event to create an instance of Microsoft Excel:

```
Static xl As Excel.Application
Set xl = New Excel.Application
```

2. Add the following code to the **mnuReportsInvoice_Click** event to create a new Excel workbook, set font values, and insert values into the invoice spreadsheet:

```
With xl
    .Visible = True
    .Workbooks.Add
    'Define the properties the cell A1
    With .Range("A1")
        .Value = "Chateau St. Mark Invoice"
        .Font.Bold = True
        .Font.Name = "Times New Roman"
        .Font.Size = 26
    End With
    .Range("A4").Value = "Name:"
    .Range("B4").Value = txtFirstName.Text & " " & txtLastName.Text
    With .Range("A5")
        .Value = "Address"
        .VerticalAlignment = xlTop
    End With
    With .Range("B5")
        .Value = txtAddress.Text
```

```
        .ColumnWidth = 20
        .WrapText = True
    End With
    .Range("A6").Value = "Number of Days:"
    .Range("B6").Value = txtNumDays.Text
    .Range("A7").Value = "Rate:"
    .Range("B7").Value = txtRate.Text
    .Range("A8").Value = "Total Due:"
    'Calculate the total amount due
    .Range("B8").Value = _
        Format(CSng(txtNumDays.Text) * _
        CSng(txtRate.Text), "Currency")
End With
Columns("A:A").ColumnWidth = 25
```

3. Add the following code to the **mnuReportsInvoice_Click** event to show the invoice spreadsheet in Print Preview:

```
xl.ActiveWorkbook.PrintPreview
```

4. Save your work. In the next exercise, steps are provided to help you test creating an invoice using Microsoft Excel.

➤ **To test the application**

1. Save and run the application.

2. On **frmReservation**, select **Search** on the **Guest** menu.

3. Enter the following values into the **Search** form:

Text box	Value
Last Name	Oberg
First Name	Bruce
Phone Number	(206) 555-9482

4. Click **Search**.

5. Select **Invoice** on the **Reports** menu.

    Excel opens and the Invoice displays in Print Preview.

6. Close Excel without saving the document.

Review

The following questions are intended to reinforce key information presented in this chapter. If you are unable to answer a question, review the appropriate lesson and then try the question again. Answers to the questions can be found in the Appendix, "Questions and Answers," located at the back of this book.

1. If you are using a component that does not have an installation program, which utility would you use to register the component yourself?

2. What are the two most common additional options used with Regsvr32? When are these options used?

3. What benefits does the components type library provide?

4. What actions are performed in the following code?

```
Dim xl As Object
'Do not specify a class type
Set xl = GetObject("C:\MyFiles\Earnings.xls")
```

5. What are the two steps to implementing a Windows API?

6. What operator is used to pass a callback procedure to a DLL?

C H A P T E R   1 0

Creating and Managing COM Components

About This Chapter

In this chapter, you will learn to create Component Object Model (COM) components: ActiveX controls, ActiveX DLLs, ActiveX EXEs, and ActiveX documents.

Before You Begin

To complete the lessons in this chapter, you must have:

- Read Chapters 6, 7, and 8.

Lesson 1: Overview of Creating COM Components

A COM component is a unit of executable code, such as an .exe, a .dll, or an .ocx file, which provides specific functionality. In Chapter 9, you learned how to use a COM component to create objects in your applications; in this chapter, you will learn how to create custom COM components. Visual Basic lets you create three types of COM components: ActiveX controls, COM executable programs and DLLs, and ActiveX documents, and. ActiveX documents are most often used to create Internet applications; they are covered in Chapter 11, "Creating Internet Applications."

After this lesson you will be able to:

- Describe the characteristics of a COM component.
- Explain the types of COM components.

Estimated lesson time: 10 minutes

Designing COM Components

Visual Basic lets you create components ranging from code libraries to Automation-enabled applications. You can create and distribute ActiveX control packages, with full licensing capability, or Internet applications with ActiveX documents that can display themselves in Internet browsers. With the Enterprise Edition of Visual Basic, you can run code components—such as business rule servers—on remote computers.

A COM component is a library of code that has been compiled into either an executable program, a dynamic-link library (DLL), or an .ocx file for ActiveX controls. In Visual Basic, COM code components, such as ActiveX DLLs and ActiveX EXEs, are composed of one or more class modules in a Visual Basic project. ActiveX controls are COM components that provide a user interface.

COM components interact with application and other components through a client/server relationship. The client uses the features of a component, and the server is the component and its associated objects. There are two main types of servers: out-of-process and in-process.

To understand the significance of the two types of servers, you must understand the meaning of the word *process*. A process is a Windows application that is residing in an address space that the operating system has assigned to the application. A process has resources assigned to it, and one or more threads run in the context of the process. A process alone does not do anything; instead, threads are used to run an application.

A *thread* is the basic unit to which the operating system allocates processor time and is the smallest piece of code that can be scheduled for execution. It is the actual component of a process that is executing at one instant in time. A thread runs in the address space of the process and uses resources allocated to the process.

In-Process vs. Out-of-Process Components

Components can be run in any one of three places: in the same address space as the client (in-process), on the same computer (out-of-process), or on a remote computer (out-of-process).

In-process

An in-process component is implemented as a dynamic-link library (DLL) or as an ActiveX control. It runs in the same process space as its client application. This enables the most efficient communication between client and component, because you need call only the component function to obtain the required functionality. Each client application that uses the component starts a new instance of the component.

Out-of-process

An out-of-process component is implemented as an executable file, and runs in its own process space. Communication between the client and and an out-of-process component is slower than with an in-process component because parameters and return values must be marshaled across process boundaries from the client to the component, and back again. However, a single instance of an out-of-process component can service many clients, share global data, and insulate other client applications from problems that one client might encounter.

Components can also be stored on remote computers. Remote components are out-of-process components, but they are located on a separate computer from the client application. While communication time between a client and a remote component is much slower than with a local component, remote components allow processing to be done on a separate, and possibly more powerful, computer. The component can also be located closer to the work it is doing. For example, a component can be located close to a remote database with which it interacts.

When you work with out-of-process and remote components, you should ensure that the client minimizes the number of calls to objects created from the component. For example, a well-designed component should have a way to pass data in bulk with as few calls as possible.

The following table illustrates the server type of each component:

Component	Server Type
Application	Out-of-process
ActiveX EXE	Out-of-process
ActiveX DLL	In-process
ActiveX control	In-process

Component Project Templates

When you create a new project in Visual Basic, you choose from among a number of project templates. In the New Project dialog box, choose ActiveX EXE to create an out-of-process component or ActiveX DLL to create an in-process component. Selecting either type sets default values in your project that are important when creating components. You need to decide which type of component is best for a given situation. Each ActiveX component provides specific functionality:

- If you need an invisible component that provides a service, you'll want to build a code component: an ActiveX EXE or an ActiveX DLL.

- If you need a component that can run in the same process with your application, you'll want an ActiveX DLL. An example of this would be a component that performs complex calculations.

- If you need a component that can serve multiple applications and can run on a remote computer, you'll want an ActiveX EXE. For example, a business rules server that enforces tax rules would best be implemented as an ActiveX EXE.

- If you need a visible component that can be dropped into an application at design time, you'll want to build an ActiveX control. An example of this might be a phone number control that properly formats and validates phone numbers; such a control would undoubtedly be useful in many applications.

- If you need a visible component that can take over an application window at run time, choose an ActiveX document. ActiveX documents are covered in Chapter 11, "Creating Internet Applications."

Lesson Summary

An out-of-process component is an .exe file that runs in its own process, with its own thread of execution. Out-of-process servers can run either on a local computer or on a remote computer on a network. Communication between a client and an out-of-process component is called cross-process or out-of-process communication.

An in-process component, such as an ActiveX DLL or ActiveX control (.ocx file), runs in the same process as the client. It provides the fastest way of accessing objects, because property and method calls don't have to send and receive data across process boundaries.

In general, if an ActiveX component has been implemented as part of an executable file (.exe file), it is an out-of-process server and runs in its own process. If it has been implemented as a dynamic-link library, it is an in-process server and runs in the same process as the client application. Applications that use in-process servers usually run faster than those that use out-of-process servers because the application doesn't have to cross process boundaries to use an object's properties, methods, and events.

Lesson 2: Creating ActiveX Controls

ActiveX is based on COM technology. That makes it easy to create, integrate, and reuse software components (controls) in applications and over the Internet or intranets. With ActiveX, developers can create components in any programming language, integrate them with any scripting language, and run those components from any type of application.

An ActiveX control is a COM component with user interface elements, and is an extension to the Visual Basic toolbox. You use ActiveX controls just as you would any of the standard built-in controls, such as the TextBox control. ActiveX controls created in Visual Basic are used in many different container applications, such as other Visual Basic applications, Microsoft Office documents, and Web pages viewed with Microsoft Internet Explorer. Once you have created an ActiveX control, you can use it in your applications to assemble forms and dialog boxes.

After this lesson you will be able to:

- Explain how ActiveX relates to COM.
- Describe the Visual Basic files used in an ActiveX control project.
- Create and compile an ActiveX control.

Estimated lesson time: 60 minutes

What Is an ActiveX Control?

ActiveX controls, previously known as OLE controls or OCX controls, are COM components that provide visual elements (or user interface). An ActiveX control is a software component that can be integrated into Web pages, Microsoft Office, Microsoft Access, Visual Basic, or any host that supports ActiveX controls. Because ActiveX controls are implemented via COM, they have associated methods that can be called from other applications (EXEs), dynamic link libraries (DLLs), Web pages, or other controls. Visual Basic has built-in controls that are visible in the toolbox. It also comes with several ActiveX controls that you can add to the toolbox. For example, Figure 10.1 shows the ADO Data control—which packages some functionality of ADO into a simple, easy-to-use interface—added to the toolbox.

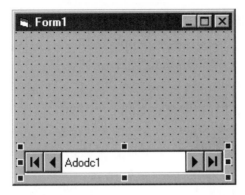

Figure 10.1 A form acting as a container for an ADO Data control

➤ **To add an ActiveX control to the Visual Basic toolbox**

1. On the **Project** menu, click **Components**.

   The **Components** dialog box appears. The items listed include all registered ActiveX controls, insertable objects, and ActiveX designers.

2. On the **Controls** tab, click the check box to the left of the control name(s) that you want to add.

3. Click **OK** to close the **Components** dialog box.

   The ActiveX controls that you selected now appear in the toolbox.

ActiveX controls are reusable objects that include visual elements and code that you can use to quickly create forms and dialog boxes. To use ActiveX controls, you must place them in some type of container, such as a form or an application.

Control Classes

In Visual Basic, an ActiveX control is always composed of a UserControl object, plus any controls—referred to as constituent controls—that you choose to place on the UserControl. Like Visual Basic forms, UserControl objects have code modules and visual designers, as illustrated in Figure 10.2. Place constituent controls on the UserControl object's designer, just as you would place controls on a form's designer.

> **Note** A *designer* is the visual design window in the Visual Basic development environment. The forms designer is included in all editions of Visual Basic. The Professional and Enterprise editions also have designers for ActiveX controls and documents.

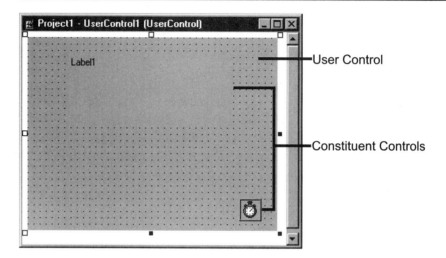

Figure 10.2 A UserControl containing two constituent controls

You can use any standard Visual Basic control on the UserControl object except the OLE container control. You add constituent controls to a UserControl object in the same way that you add controls to a standard Visual Basic form.

Files Associated with a UserControl

A control that you create in Visual Basic is known as a control class. A control class acts as a template for that control. When a control from the Visual Basic toolbox is placed on a form, Visual Basic creates an actual object from the control class—for example, Text1 or Label1. Like forms, Visual Basic stores user controls in text files that contain the source code and property values of the UserControl and its constituent controls. Visual Basic uses the extension .ctl for these source files.

If a UserControl or its constituent controls use graphical elements, such as bitmaps, Visual Basic cannot store them as plain text. Visual Basic stores those elements in a .ctx file with the same name you gave the .ctl file. This procedure is analogous to the .frx files used to store graphical elements used in forms. The .ctl and .ctx files completely define an ActiveX control's appearance and interface (properties, methods, and events).

You can include .ctl files in any of the project types. When you compile an ActiveX control project, Visual Basic compiles the control class into an .ocx file. A Visual Basic ActiveX control project can contain one or more .ctl files, each of which defines a separate control class. When you compile a control project, Visual Basic creates one .ocx file; it contains all of the controls in the project.

Your ActiveX control consists of a UserControl and its constituent controls; each instance actually contains those objects. Whenever you place an instance of your ActiveX control on a form, Visual Basic creates a UserControl object, along with instances of any constituent controls you placed on the UserControl designer. Visual Basic encapsulates these objects inside your control.

Practice: Creating an ActiveX Control

In this practice, you will create a control that displays the current date and time.

To see a demonstration, run the Chap10.exe animation located in the Animations folder on the Supplemental Course Materials CD-ROM that accompanies this book.

➤ **To create an ActiveX control**

1. Start Visual Basic.

2. On the **New Project** dialog box, click **ActiveX Control,** then click **OK**.

   A **UserControl** designer appears.

3. Add a Label control and a Timer control to **UserControl1**.

   These are the constituent controls.

4. Position the controls as illustrated in Figure 10.3.

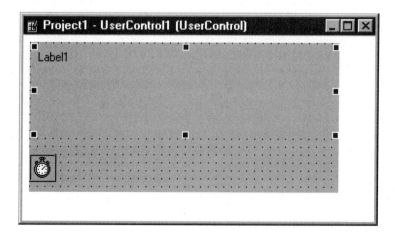

Figure 10.3 Positioning the constituent controls on the UserControl

5. On the **Project** menu, click **Project1 Properties**.

6. On the **General** tab, set the Project Name property to **MyTimer**.

7. Click **OK** to close the **Project Properties** dialog box.

8. Set the Name property of **UserControl1** to **ctlTimer**.

9. Change the Name property of the Label control to **lblDateAndTime**.

10. Set the Font property of **lblDateAndTime** to font style **Bold** and font size **18**.

11. Set the Alignment property of **lblDateAndTime** to **2 – Center**.

12. Set the Interval property of **Timer1** to **1000**.

13. In the Timer event for **Timer1**, type the following code:

```
lblDateAndTime.Caption = Now()
```

14. On the **File** menu, click **Save Project**.

Save the .ctl and .vbp files to the \Practice\Ch10 folder.

Implementing Your ActiveX Control

To use your new control in an application, place the control on a form. When you put a control on a form at design time, Visual Basic creates an actual instance of the control class. Although you might think of this control as a permanent fixture of the form, it is only a design-time instance of the control. If the form is closed for any reason—for example, its Close button is clicked, the project is closed, or F5 is pressed to place the project in Run mode—Visual Basic destroys the design-time instance.

When the project is placed in Run mode, Visual Basic creates a run-time instance of the control when the form is loaded. Visual Basic destroys this run-time instance when the form is unloaded.

Instances of controls are continually created and destroyed, so you must ensure that the property values are preserved. When you create a control, you must include code that saves and retrieves property values of the control. To store and retrieve information each time an object is created or destroyed, use the ReadProperty and WriteProperty methods of the PropertyBag object.

Creating a Property

When you create an ActiveX control in Visual Basic, you can add properties, methods, and events to the control. You can do this manually by writing code such as property procedures, or you can use the ActiveX Control Interface Wizard add-in shown in Figure 10.4.

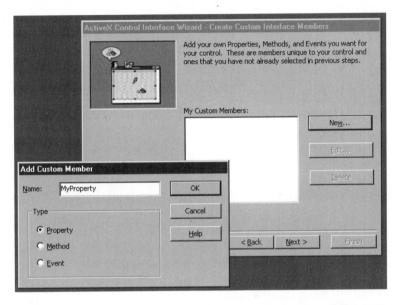

Figure 10.4 Adding a property using the ActiveX Control Interface Wizard

➤ **To run the ActiveX Control Interface Wizard**

1. On the **Add-Ins** menu, click **Add-In Manager**.

2. On the **Add-In Manager** dialog box, click **VB 6 ActiveX Ctrl Interface Wizard**.

3. Select the **Loaded/Unloaded** Load Behavior check box, then click **OK**.

4. On the **Add-Ins** menu, click **ActiveX Control Interface Wizard**.

Creating Property Pages

Property pages enable you to define a custom interface for setting properties of an ActiveX control—providing more flexibility than the Properties window. Property pages look a lot like forms, and designing them is somewhat similar to designing forms. The way property pages work, however, is quite different from the way forms work.

Visual Basic includes a Property Page Wizard that you can use to add a property page for your control:

■ Create the user interface for the property page.

■ Add code to synchronize the property page with the current state of the control.

■ Set up the appropriate property page relationships: associate properties with a property page, and associate a tabbed Property Page dialog box with your control.

➤ **To run the Property Page Wizard**

1. On the **Add-Ins** menu, click **Add-In Manager**.

2. On the **Add-In Manager** dialog box, click **VB 6 Property Page Wizard**.

3. Select the **Loaded/Unloaded** Load Behavior check box, then click **OK**.

4. On the **Add-Ins** menu, click **Property Page Wizard**.

5. Add a new property page for each grouping of properties in your control.

   If you have a property that is a standard data type (like color or font), the wizard will automatically add the standard property page to the list of property pages for your control.

6. Add the properties of your control to the property pages you've created.

7. Click **Finish**.

You must let Visual Basic know when a property value changes. To indicate that a property value has changed, you use the PropertyChanged method of the UserControl object within a property procedure. Calling the PropertyChanged method notifies Visual Basic that a property of your control has changed. This is important so that Visual Basic can mark your control as needing to be saved in the project where it is being used. Also, calling PropertyChanged notifies Visual Basic to update the property value in the Properties window and in any property pages for your control.

Saving Property Values

You save property values by calling the WriteProperty method in the WriteProperties event of the UserControl object. Visual Basic calls this event when the design-time control is destroyed.

The WriteProperty method takes three arguments: a string indicating the property to save, a value for the property, and a default value if the developer did not set an initial property. This method writes the data value to the property bag.

The PropertyBag object is a mechanism that allows you to store your control's properties that are set within the Visual Basic development environment. The PropertyBag object is used exclusively for creating ActiveX controls and Active documents. The PropertyBag object saves data to a .vbd, .obd, or some other kind of file, depending on the application.

The PropertyBag has two methods, the WriteProperty method, and the ReadProperty method. The PropertyBag object is exposed as part of the WriteProperties and ReadProperties event declaration.

The following example shows how to save current property values with the WriteProperty method of the PropertyBag object:

```
Private Sub UserControl_WriteProperties(PropBag As PropertyBag)
    PropBag.WriteProperty "UpperCase", mvarUpperCase, vbUpperCase
    PropBag.WriteProperty "Caption", Label1.Caption, "Username"
End Sub
```

For more information about the PropertyBag object, search for "Saving Properties to the PropertyBag" in MSDN Online Help.

Reading Property Values

You retrieve property values by calling the ReadProperty method in the ReadProperties event of the UserControl object. Visual Basic calls this event when either the design-time or run-time control is created. The ReadProperty method takes two arguments: a string designating the property name and a default value. If a property value has been saved, the ReadProperty method returns the value. If a property value has not been saved, the method returns the default value. The following example shows how to use the ReadProperty method to return the saved value of the Caption property:

```
Private Sub UserControl_ReadProperties(PropBag As PropertyBag)
    'Trap for invalid property values
    On Error Resume Next
    Label1.Caption = PropBag.ReadProperty("Caption", "Username")
End Sub
```

Default Property Values

When you read and write property values, it is important to provide default values. Visual Basic writes a line of code in the source file (.frm, .dob, .pag, or .ctl) of the control's container only if the property value differs from the default value that you provided. As a result of providing a default value, the file size is reduced and the application's performance is improved.

Initializing Property Values in the InitProperties Event

The first time you place an instance of a control on a container, the container receives the InitProperties event. Thereafter, only the ReadProperties event occurs. In the InitProperties event, you set the initial value for a property by using the same default value that you provide with the WriteProperty and ReadProperty methods when saving and retrieving the property value.

Since mapped properties are already initialized by the constituent control, you need to initialize only those properties that don't map to properties of constituent controls. The following code shows how to initialize the UpperCase property of an ActiveX control:

```
'Set up storage for the property
Dim mvarUpperCase As Boolean

'Use that default value in the InitProperties event
Private Sub UserControl_InitProperties()
    mvarUpperCase = vbUpperCase
End Sub
```

Figure 10.5 shows the evolution of the control and related files as it is created by a control developer, used by an application developer in a standard application, and then used by the user of the completed application.

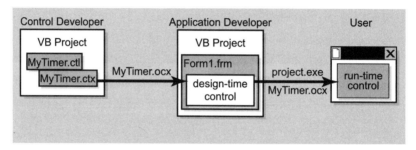

Figure 10.5 How an ActiveX control is implemented

In Visual Basic, you can add a Standard EXE project to your control project group to test the control. When you do this, Visual Basic automatically adds your ActiveX control to the toolbox. You can then add your ActiveX control to a form in your Standard EXE project. However, if the UserControl designer window is open, the control is disabled in the toolbox. When you close the UserControl window, the ActiveX control reappears in the Visual Basic toolbox, which allows you to implement the control on a form, as illustrated in Figure 10.6.

Figure 10.6 A UserControl available in the Visual Basic toolbox

Practice: Testing Your ActiveX Control

In this practice, you will use the ActiveX control that you created in the last practice and implement it in another project. You will see a design-time and a run-time instance of the control.

➤ **To create a design-time instance of your control**

1. Start Visual Basic and create a new Standard EXE project.

2. On the **File** menu, click **Add Project**.

3. On the **Add Project** dialog box, click the **Recent** tab, select the **MyTimer** control project you created in the last practice, then click **Open**.

   Notice that in the Project Explorer you have two projects, as illustrated in Figure 10.7. You will use the Standard EXE project as a container for your custom ActiveX control.

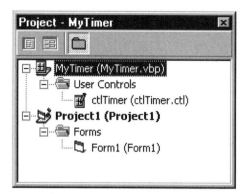

Figure 10.7 Adding a project to test an ActiveX control

4. Add the **ctlTimer** control from the Visual Basic toolbox to **Form1**.

   Notice that the time is updated in the ActiveX control every second—even though the Standard EXE project is not running. This is an example of creating a design-time instance of a control.

➤ **To create a run-time instance of the control**

1. On the **File** menu, click **Save Project Group**.

   Save the files to the \Practice\Ch10 folder.

2. On the **Run** menu, click **Start**.

   A new, run-time instance of the control is created. (If the MyTimer Project Properties dialog box appears, make sure the Start Component option is selected with the ctlTimer component, then click OK.)

3. On the **Run** menu, click **End**.

➤ **To compile your ActiveX control**

1. Click the **MyTimer** project in the **Project** window.

2. On the **File** menu, click **Make MyTimer.ocx**.

3. On the **Make Project** dialog box, set the directory to \Practice\Ch10 folder.

4. Click **OK** to compile the control into an .ocx file.

➤ **To use your compiled .ocx file**

1. On the **File** menu, click **New Project**.

2. On the **New Project** dialog box, click **Standard EXE,** then click **OK**.

3. Right-click on the Visual Basic toolbox, then click **Components**.

4. On the Components dialog box, click the **Controls** tab.

5. Click the check box to the left of the **MyTimer** control, as illustrated in Figure 10.8, then click **OK**.

Your ActiveX control is added to the Visual Basic toolbox.

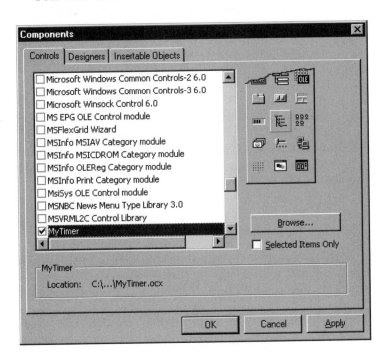

Figure 10.8 Adding MyTimer.ocx to your project

6. Place a **MyTimer** control on **Form1**.

Visual Basic creates a design-time instance of your control on the form.

Making Your ActiveX Control a Data Source

With Visual Basic, you can create an ActiveX control that provides data to other controls, in much the same was as the ADO Data control does. Although you can use the ADO Data control for simple data access, you can create more advanced functionality in your own ActiveX control. For example, you could create a control that is a data source for a computer's file system or for data stored in a proprietary data format. Your custom data source control can then be reused, and data-bound controls can bind to it.

➤ **To create an ActiveX control that is a data source**

1. Set the DataSourceBehavior property of your control to **vbDataSource**.

This creates an event procedure called **GetDataMember** that occurs when a data consumer requests a new data source

2. In the Initialize event procedure of your control, establish the data your source will provide.

This process involves creating a Connection object and a Recordset object, setting the connection parameters, and opening the recordset.

3. Write code in the **GetDataMember** event procedure to return a data object.

The GetDataMember event procedure has two parameters: DataMember and Data. The DataMember parameter is an optional parameter that specifies the name of the data member used if your control provides multiple data members. The Data parameter is the data object that the procedure returns to the data consumer. The following example returns data from a recordset called rsEmployees:

```
Private Sub UserControl_GetDataMember _
    (DataMember As String, Data As Object)
    'Return the data to the consumer
    Set Data = rsEmployees
End Sub
```

4. Add any additional functionality you want your data source control to contain.

For example, you may want to include features to navigate through records or display the current record.

Once you have created your data source control, you can place it on a form and add controls that bind to it. The GetDataMember event is invoked when a data consumer requests a new data source. Your control then uses the DataMember parameter, if appropriate, to identify the specific data member the consumer requires and returns data back to the consumer in the form of a Recordset object.

Practice: Creating a Data Source Control

In this practice, you will create an ActiveX control that can be used to bind to data bound controls.

➤ **To create an ActiveX control**

1. Start Visual Basic and open a new ActiveX control project.

2. Click on the UserControl, and set its DataSourceBehavior property to **1 – vbDataSource**.

3. Set the UserControl's Name property to **ctlSource**.

4. On the **Project** menu, click **References**.

5. On the **References** dialog box, click the **Microsoft ActiveX Data Objects 2.0 Library** check box, then click **OK**.

6. In the General Declarations section of the UserControl, type the following code:

```
Private CN As Connection
Private RS As Recordset
```

7. In the UserControl_Initialize event procedure, type the following code:

```
Dim SQL As String

Set CN = New Connection
Set RS = New Recordset

CN.ConnectionString = "Provider=Microsoft.Jet.OLEDB.3.51;" & _
     "Data Source=C:\Program Files\Microsoft Visual
Studio\VB98\Nwind.mdb"
CN.Open

SQL = "SELECT * FROM Customers"
RS.Open SQL, CN, adOpenStatic
```

8. In the UserControl_GetDataMember event procedure, type the following code:

```
Set Data = RS
```

9. Add a CommandButton to the UserControl, and set the following properties:

Property	Value
Name	CmdMoveNext
Caption	Move &Next

10. Add another CommandButton to the UserControl, and set the following properties:

Property	Value
Name	cmdMovePrevious
Caption	Move &Previous

Your control should look like the one shown in Figure 10.9.

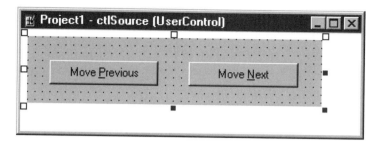

Figure 10.9 Form with two command buttons

11. In the cmdMovePrevious_Click event procedure, type the following code:

```
RS.MovePrevious
If RS.BOF Then RS.MoveLast
```

12. In the cmdMoveNext_Click event procedure, type the following code:

```
RS.MoveNext
If RS.EOF Then RS.MoveFirst
```

➤ **To test your ActiveX control**

1. On the **File** menu, click **Add Project**.

2. Click **Standard EXE**, then click **Open**.

3. In order to make your ActiveX control available on the toolbox, you must close the **Project 1 - ctlSource** (UserControl) design window.

4. Click your ActiveX control on the toolbox and add it to **Form1**.

➤ **To bind controls to your ActiveX control**

1. Put a Label control on **Form1**, and set the following properties:

Property	Value
Name	LblCustomerID
Caption	<blank>
DataSource	CtlSource1
DataField	CustomerID

2. Put another Label control on **Form1** and set the following properties:

Property	Value
Name	LblCompanyName
Caption	<blank>
DataSource	CtlSource1
DataField	CompanyName

3. Set the Caption property of **Form1** to **Customer Information**.

4. On the **File** menu, click **Save Project Group**.

   Save your project files to the \Practice\Ch10 folder.

5. Right-click on the **Standard EXE** project icon in Project Explorer, then click **Set as Start Up**.

6. On the **Run** menu, click **Start**.

7. Click **Move Next**, then click **Move Previous** on the Customer Information form.

   As you click the navigation buttons on your ActiveX control, notice that the labels are bound to the ActiveX control and the fields from the recordset are updated. Your form should look similar to the illustration in Figure 10.10.

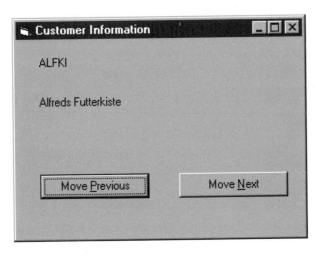

Figure 10.10 Your ActiveX control bound to Label controls

8. On the **Run** menu, click **End**.

Lesson Summary

Creating the user interface for an ActiveX control is similar to creating a standard Visual Basic form. You draw controls and then provide the code that defines the behavior of those controls.

When you design a control, you take advantage of the functionality of existing controls, while also adding your own functionality. As the control developer, you can choose which pieces of functionality from existing controls you wish to make available to the user of your custom control.

When you add an ActiveX control to a program, it becomes part of the development and run-time environment, and provides new functionality for your application.

To use the control in an application, you place the control on a form; this creates a design-time instance of that control. When a user runs the application containing the control, Visual Basic creates a run-time instance of the control.

Lesson 3: Creating ActiveX Code Components

COM executable programs and DLLs are libraries of classes. Client applications use COM objects by creating instances of classes provided by the COM .exe or .dll file. Clients call the properties, methods, and events provided by each COM object. In Visual Basic, you refer to the project templates that you use to create a COM executable program or COM DLL as ActiveX EXE and ActiveX DLL, respectively. In this lesson, you will learn how to create ActiveX DLLs.

After this lesson you will be able to:

- Describe the different types of code components.

- Create an in-process code component.

- Create an out-of-process component.

- Test and debug code components.

Estimated lesson time: 90 minutes

Understanding Code Components

Unlike ActiveX controls, which support user interaction, code components typically have no user interface. Instead, code components are like libraries of objects. A client application uses a code component by creating an object from one of the classes the component provides, and invoking the object's properties, methods, and events. For example, you can create a code component that encapsulates business rules your organization uses, so that all applications process the same data consistently.

Note Although you do not typically use ActiveX code components to interact directly with a user, you can use code components to provide standard libraries of modal and modeless dialogs.

Code components provide reusable code in the form of objects. A client is an application that uses a component's code by creating objects and calling their properties and methods. With Visual Basic, you can build code components to run in-process, which allows faster access to the objects of the properties and methods, or out-of-process, which gives the objects separate threads of execution from their clients. Visual Basic provides project templates for each type of component: ActiveX DLLs and ActiveX EXEs.

Note In earlier documentation, code components were referred to as OLE Automation servers.

Creating an ActiveX Code Component

An in-process code component, or ActiveX DLL, runs in another application's process. The client may be the application itself or another in-process component that the application is using, as illustrated in Figure 10.11.

An out-of-process code component, or ActiveX EXE, runs in its own address space. The client is usually an application running in another process, as illustrated in Figure 10.12. Because an out-of-process component runs in its own process, a client can tell it to perform a task, then go about its business while the component does the work. The component can tell the client when the task is done using an asynchronous notification, as explained in "Creating Call-Back Procedures" in Chapter 9, "Connecting to COM Servers."

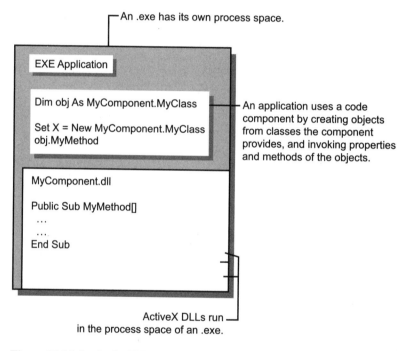

Figure 10.11 An ActiveX DLL running in the same process as a standard EXE

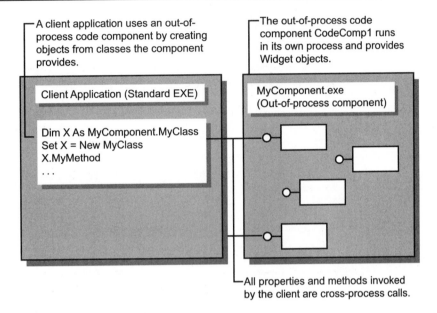

A client application uses an out-of-process code component by creating objects from classes the component provides.

The out-of-process code component CodeComp1 runs in its own process and provides Widget objects.

Client Application (Standard EXE)

MyComponent.exe
(Out-of-process component)

```
Dim X As MyComponent.MyClass
Set X = New MyClass
X.MyMethod
. . .
```

All properties and methods invoked by the client are cross-process calls.

Figure 10.12 An ActiveX EXE running in its own process space

Practice: Creating an ActiveX DLL

In this practice, you will create an ActiveX DLL that has a property and a method that can be used by a client application. You will add a Standard EXE project to your ActiveX DLL project, creating a project group, to test your ActiveX DLL.

➤ **To create a DLL in Visual Basic**

1. Create a new **ActiveX DLL** project in Visual Basic.

2. Name the project **SampleDLL**.

3. In the General Declarations section of the **Class1** module, type the following code:

```
Private UserName As String
Private strMessage As String
Public Sub SayHello()
    MsgBox "Hello " & UserName & "!"
End Sub
Public Property Let Name(Name As String)
    UserName = Name
End Property
Public Property Get Message()
    strMessage = "Hello from DLL."
    Message = strMessage
End Property
```

Note Normally you would need to register the DLL before calling it. Leaving it running in Visual Basic allows us to test the DLL because it is currently loaded in memory.

> ➤ **To create a test project**
>
> 1. On the **File** menu, click **Add Project**.
>
> 2. On the **Add Project** dialog box, double-click **Standard EXE**.
>
> 3. Click the **Standard EXE** project in the Project Explorer.
>
> 4. On the **Project** menu, click **References**.
>
> 5. Click the check box next to SampleDLL, then click **OK**.
>
> 6. Add a CommandButton to **Form1**.
>
> 7. In the Click event procedure for the CommandButton, type the following code:
>
> ```
> Dim obj As SampleDLL.Class1
> Dim strMessage As String
>
> Set obj = New Class1
> obj.Name = "John"
> obj.SayHello
>
> strMessage = obj.Message
> MsgBox strMessage, , "Message from DLL"
> ```
>
> 8. Right-click on the **Standard EXE** project in the Project Explorer, then click **Set as Start Up** on the drop-down menu.
>
> 9. On the **File** menu, click **Save Project Group**.
>
>   Save the files to the \Practice\Ch10 folder.

10. On the **Run** menu, click **Start**.

You will see two message boxes. The first message box is displayed from the ShowMessage method of your ActiveX DLL. The second message box displays the value of the Message property of the object you declared in the **Command1_Click** event.

11. Click **OK** to close each message box that appears.

12. On the **Run** menu, click **End**.

The Instancing Property

The Instancing property of a class determines whether or not the class is private. If it is not private, the class is available for other applications to use. Private means that other applications are not allowed access to type library information about the class and cannot create instances of it. Private objects are only for use within your component.

The Instancing property also determines how other applications create instances of the class. The property value can be set to one of the following:

- PublicNotCreatable

  PublicNotCreatable lets other applications use objects of the class only if your component creates the objects first. Other applications cannot use the CreateObject function or the New operator to create objects from the class.

- MultiUse

  MultiUse lets other applications create objects from the class. One instance of your component can provide any number of objects created in this fashion. An out-of-process component can supply multiple objects to multiple clients; an in-process component can supply multiple objects to the client and to any other components in its process.

- GlobalMultiUse

  GlobalMultiUse is like MultiUse, with one addition: properties and methods of the class can be invoked as if they were simply global functions. When you choose the value GlobalMultiUse for the Instancing property of a class, and then make the project, you can subsequently use the properties and methods of the class without having to explicitly create an instance of the class. Properties and methods of a GlobalMultiUse object (or global object) are added to the global name space of any project that uses the object. That is, in another project, you can set a reference to the component, and the names of the global object's properties and methods are recognized globally, just as if they were part of Visual Basic.

- SingleUse

  SingleUse lets other applications create objects from the class, but every object of this class that a client creates starts a new instance of your component. You cannot set the Instancing property to SingleUse in ActiveX DLL projects because that requires another instance of the server to load, and DLLs can only be loaded once.

- GlobalSingleUse

  GlobalSingleUse is used for out-of-process components only. If you set the Instancing property to GlobalSingleUse for a component, a separate instance of your component will be loaded into memory for each client. This requires a lot more memory than providing GlobalMultiUse objects. GlobalSingleUse is not allowed in ActiveX DLL projects because multiple instances of a DLL cannot be loaded into a client's process space.

The value of the Instancing property is restricted in certain project types. Possible values are shown in the following table:

Instancing Value	ActiveX EXE	ActiveX DLL
Private	Yes	Yes
PublicNotCreatable	Yes	Yes
MultiUse	Yes	Yes
SingleUse	Yes	No
GlobalSingleUse	Yes	No

Dependent Objects (PublicNotCreatable)

The value of the Instancing property determines the role than an object plays in your component's object model, as discussed in Chapter 6, "Introduction to Class Modules." If the Instancing property of a class is PublicNotCreatable, objects of that class are called dependent objects. Dependent objects are typically parts of more complex objects. For example, you might allow a client application to create multiple Wheel objects, but you might want Spoke objects to exist only as parts of a Wheel. You can make the Spoke class PublicNotCreatable; let the user add new spokes to a Wheel object by giving the Wheel class a Spokes collection with an Add method that creates new spokes only within the collection.

Your component can support as many dependent objects as necessary. You can write code in the Add method of a collection class to limit the number of objects in the collection, or you can allow the number to be limited by available memory.

For more information about creating an object model, search for "Organizing Objects: The Object Model" in MSDN Online Help.

Externally Creatable Objects

All values of the Instancing property besides PublicNotCreatable and Private define externally creatable objects. Externally creatable objects can be created by clients using the New operator or the CreateObject function, as discussed in Chapter 9, "Connecting to COM Servers."

MultiUse vs. SingleUse

In ActiveX DLLs, Instancing for an externally creatable class is commonly MultiUse. This setting allows an in-process component to supply any number of instances of the class to the client executable, and to any other in-process component.

For ActiveX EXEs, the Instancing values SingleUse and MultiUse define very different behaviors for a class. MultiUse makes the most efficient use of memory, because it allows one instance of your component to provide multiple objects to multiple client applications without duplication of resources or global data. For example, suppose your component provides a Widget class, and the Instancing property of the class is set to MultiUse. If one client application creates two Widget objects, or if two client applications each create a Widget object, all the Widgets will be supplied from one instance of your component. If the Instancing property of the Widget class is set to SingleUse, the result of both scenarios above is that a separate copy of your component will be loaded into memory for each Widget created.

MultiUse and Multithreading

You can mark your ActiveX EXE component for unattended execution, which allows you to create components that can run without operator intervention on network servers. Selecting the Unattended Execution option suppresses all forms of user interaction, including message boxes and system error dialogs.

➤ **To mark your ActiveX DLL or EXE project for unattended execution**

1. On the **Project** menu, click **<project> Properties** to open the **Project Properties** dialog box.

2. On the **General** tab, check the **Unattended Execution** check box, then click **OK**.

If your component is an ActiveX EXE marked for unattended execution, and the Instancing property of the Widget class is set to MultiUse, both scenarios above result in two Widget objects created in the same copy of your component, each on its own thread of execution. Visual Basic uses Apartment Model threading, meaning that each thread is like an apartment, and objects in different apartments are unaware of each other's existence. This is accomplished by giving each Widget its own copy of your component's global data.

Note Designing multithreaded components is a very complex task and the concepts involved are outside the scope of this class. Because you will be creating components and object models in the labs, key points were discussed in this lesson. If you want to learn more about creating multithreaded components, search for "Scalability and Multithreading" in MSDN Online Help.

Testing and Debugging

Active X code components are often difficult to debug since they are used within client applications and do not run stand-alone. Visual Basic provides two different component debugging scenarios:

- For in-process components, you can load a test project (Standard EXE or ActiveX EXE) and one or more component projects into the development environment as a project group. You can run all the projects in the group together, and step directly from test project code into in-process component code.

- For out-of-process components, you can use two instances of the development environment. One instance of Visual Basic runs the test project, while the second runs the component project. You can step directly from test project code into component code, and each instance of Visual Basic has its own set of breakpoints and watches.

When an ActiveX EXE project is in run mode, the client application can create objects and access their properties and methods. Each out-of-process component that a client uses must be in its own instance of the development environment. The client application and all of its in-process components can run together in a single instance of the development environment.

Creating a Test Application

To test a component, you need to create a client application. Components exist to provide objects for clients, which makes it hard to test them by themselves. When you test your component, you should utilize all of its features. Be sure to:

- Invoke all the properties, methods, and events of each object provided by your component, testing both valid and invalid values of all arguments. For example, rather than simply making one call to a method of an object, make a series of calls that use valid and invalid values for all arguments.

- Evaluate the highest and lowest valid values for arguments; these boundary conditions are a frequent source of problems for developers.

■ Test for both functionality and error cases. Make sure your component behaves well in case of errors, such as unexpected input. It's especially important to make sure you've covered all error conditions in event procedures of in-process components, because such errors can be fatal to client applications that use the component.

Using Break on Error in Components

You can change the way Visual Basic enters break mode when an error occurs in your component by setting the Error Trapping option in your component project.

➤ **To set the error trapping state**

1. In your component project, click **Options** on the **Tools** menu.
2. On the **Options** dialog box, click the **General** tab.

Suppose you have a component that provides a Rocket object that has a Launch method. There are three options in the Default Error Trapping State box, as described below. The following descriptions assume that the test application has called the Launch method of the Rocket object, and that an error has occurred in the Launch method's code.

■ Break on All Errors

Visual Basic activates the component project, gives the Launch method's code window the focus, and highlights the line of code that caused the error. Visual Basic always enters break mode on such an error, even if error handling is enabled in the Launch method.

■ Break in Class Module

If error handling is not enabled in the Launch method, or if you are deliberately raising an error for the client by calling the Raise method of the Err object in the Launch method's error handler, Visual Basic activates the component project, gives the Launch method's code window the focus, and highlights the line of code that caused the error. If error handling is enabled in Launch, then the error handler is invoked. As long as you don't raise an error in the error handler, Visual Basic does not enter break mode.

Note   You can press ALT+F8 or ALT+F5 to step or run past the error when setting either Break on All Errors or Break in Class Module.

■ Break on Unhandled Errors

Visual Basic never enters break mode in properties or methods of the component. If error handling is not enabled in the client procedure that called the Launch method, execution stops on the line of code that made the call.

To understand the behavior of Break on Unhandled Errors in a component project, remember that the component's properties and methods are always called from outside of the component. You can always handle an error in a property or a method by passing it up the calling chain into the client procedure that called the property or the method.

Using Start With Full Compile

You may find it more convenient to start the project group by pressing CTRL+F5, or by clicking Start With Full Compile on the Run menu, so that all compilation errors are resolved before your component begins supplying objects to your test application.

The default in Visual Basic is to compile code on demand. This means that there may be code in your component that is not compiled until the client calls it. Some compile errors cannot be fixed without returning to design mode, which requires returning the whole project group to design mode.

➤ **To disable demand compilation**

1. Click **Options** on the **Tools** menu.
2. Click the **General** tab of the **Options** dialog box, then clear the **Compile On Demand** check box.

Shutting Down an In-Process Component

In-process components will not unload while running in the development environment, even if all references to objects are released by the test project, and all other component shutdown conditions are met. The only way to test DLL unloading behavior is with the compiled component.

Checking Your Component in the Object Browser

With the test project (Standard EXE) selected in the Project window, you can use the Object Browser to verify that the public classes, methods, and properties of your component are available. You can also use the Object Browser to examine and add description strings, and to verify that Help topics are correctly linked.

The view you get in the Object Browser differs depending on which project is currently active, or selected, in the Project window. When your component project is active, the Object Browser shows both public members and Friend functions. When the test project is active, only the public members are visible.

Lesson Summary

COM executable programs and DLLs are libraries of classes. Client applications use COM objects by creating instances of classes provided by the COM .exe or .dll file.

With Visual Basic, you can build code components to run in-process, allowing faster access to their objects, or out-of-process, so that they have separate threads of execution from their clients. Visual Basic provides project templates for each type of these components: ActiveX DLLs and ActiveX EXEs.

An in-process component, or ActiveX DLL, runs in another application's process. The client may be the application itself, or another in-process component that the application is using. An out-of-process component, or ActiveX EXE, runs in its own address space.

The value of the Instancing property of a class determines whether it is private or available for other applications to use. The values can be:

- PublicNotCreatable
- MultiUse
- GlobalMultiUse
- SingleUse
- GlobalSingleUse

To test a component, you need to create a client application. Components exist to provide objects for clients, which makes it hard to test them by themselves. When you are testing your component, you should utilize all of its features.

You can also use the Object Browser to examine and add description strings, and to verify that Help topics are correctly linked.

Lesson 4: Using the Visual Component Manager

Component-based software development is a popular methodology used to build complex business applications. Instead of having to re-develop similar code routines for every application, developers of component-based applications can simply utilize existing components that contain the needed functionality. If a component does not already exist, it can be written once and then cataloged for future reuse and sharing with other applications.

With Visual Component Manager you can publish components to a repository-based catalog, where they can easily be located, inspected, retrieved, and reused. In this lesson you will learn the basic features of the Visual Component Manager.

After this lesson you will be able to:

- Explain the purpose the Visual Component Manager.
- Describe how to add a component from the Visual Component Manager into your Visual Basic Project.

Estimated lesson time: 45 minutes

Overview of Visual Component Manager

The biggest challenge of component-based development is managing all the separate components. Within a single application you may have hundreds or even thousands of separate components. Furthermore, you can use each of these components in various places in the program. You can also reuse many components in other applications. Locating the right component when you need it can save enormous development time and effort.

Visual Component Manager addresses the three main requirements for storing and organizing components: publishing, finding, and reusing them. It provides a single source to organize, find, and insert components into your project. It can also be the centralized location for approved project programming conventions, functional specifications, and architectural models and diagrams.

Visual Component Manager provides a single location for anything that can be added to a project. It allows you to catalog components, find them easily using flexible search criteria, and insert them into your project with point-and-click ease.

For example, you might create a template for a standard form used in all the accounting applications at the company, or a standard tax-calculation object that can be used in many applications. Cataloging these components on a shared repository database provides an easy way for all of the organization's developers to find and use the components. It also provides a convenient method of documenting information about components.

In addition to single components, Visual Component Manager can also store component libraries, templates, models, and complete application frameworks. For example, a tool developer might create a set of forms and basic modules that are the starting point for new forms and modules of the same type. By creating a template and storing it in Visual Component Manager, any developer can get a copy of the forms or modules, then add to them or change them without affecting the original.

Programmers often create modules that contain "utility" functions, which are used frequently. Storing such modules in Visual Component Manager provides an easy way to find and reuse such modules.

You can also associate additional files with components. A particular component may require the presence of additional support files such as .dll files, Help files, or documentation. With Visual Component Manager, you can associate multiple files with any component. This association becomes a part of the component item's properties in Visual Component Manager, and the associated files can be loaded along with the item.

When you use it in this way, Visual Component Manager can also be the central location for approved project programming conventions, functional specifications, architectural models, and diagrams.

Visual Component Manager provides a simple user interface to navigate through its contents, as well as a toolbar to quickly select the most common Visual Component Manager tasks. By default, it presents the three panes (the explorer, and the contents and properties panes) as illustrated in Figure 10.13.

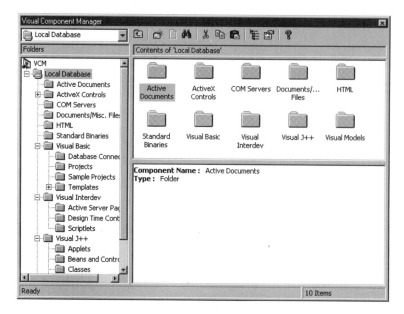

Figure 10.13 The three panes of the Visual Component Manager Explorer

The Explorer Pane

The explorer pane shows a hierarchical view of the repository databases currently loaded into Visual Component Manager, along with the folders and subfolders within each. Clicking on the small plus (+) sign to the left of any repository or folders expands the view to show the folders it contains.

You can hide the explorer and properties panes by clicking the toolbar buttons. The contents pane is always visible.

The Contents Pane

The contents pane displays the folders and items contained within the database or folder that is currently selected in the explorer pane. At the lowest level, the items displayed are components that have been published to Visual Component Manager.

The Properties Pane

The properties pane displays a list of all the properties and values assigned to the folder or item currently selected in the contents pane. At the component level, these properties include the component name, description, search keywords, and other identifying information about the component. The properties pane also doubles as a browse pane to display object hierarchies for COM objects when you click Browse Details on the shortcut menu.

Installing and Starting Visual Component Manager

Visual Component Manager is automatically installed when you install Microsoft Visual Basic. However, you must first add Visual Component Manager to the toolbar to access it.

➤ **To add Visual Component Manager to the Visual Basic toolbar**

1. On the Visual Basic **Add-ins** menu, click **Add-in Manager**.

2. In the add-ins list, scroll down and click **Visual Component Manager**.

3. Under **Load Behavior**, click the **Load on Startup** check box.

4. Click **OK** to add Visual Component Manager to the Visual Basic toolbar.

➤ **To start Visual Component Manager from Visual Basic**

■ On the Visual Basic toolbar, click the **Visual Component Manager** icon, as illustrated in Figure 10.14.

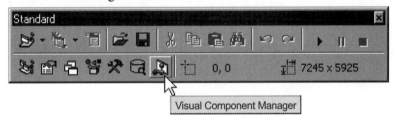

Figure 10.14 Accessing Visual Component Manager from the Visual Basic toolbar

– or –

■ On the **View** menu, click **Visual Component Manager**.

Publishing Components

Publishing a component means storing it in a Visual Component Manager repository database, along with attributes and search keywords that will make it easy for others to find and reuse it.

When you publish a component, you add it to a Microsoft Repository database. This can be a local (Microsoft Access) database on your own workstation, or it can be a shared Microsoft SQL Server database on a network server. A shared database gives everyone who has access to that server the ability to find and reuse your component.

To optimize Visual Component Manager's search capability, use careful thought and consideration when you publish a component. Enter the keywords most likely to describe the component to someone looking for it, such as describing its functionality.

The keyword scheme also lets you group and categorize components hierarchically. For example, Accounting components might be further subdivided with keywords such as Accounts Receivable, Payroll, etc. If you define keywords to match both the larger category and the subcategories, a user can find either all items with the Accounting keyword, or just a subset—with the Payroll keyword, for example.

To provide good examples of well-indexed component entries, Visual Component Manager allows you to install entries for all controls, templates, forms, and other components supplied by Microsoft Visual Basic. You have this option when you first run Visual Component Manager from within Visual Basic. Useful descriptions and keywords already exist, letting you find the component or tool you are looking for; you can then launch it or add it to your project with a click of the mouse.

Visual Component Manager provides three ways to publish items to the repository database:

- Select a component in the Windows Explorer and drag it to a folder in the Visual Component Manager.
- Select a project in your development environment and click Publish on the project's shortcut menu.
- Click New on the Visual Component Manager shortcut menu.

Each of these methods opens the Visual Component Manager Publish Wizard, which takes you step by step through the process of publishing a component for reuse. By filling in the requested information, you tell Visual Component Manager where and how to store the component. In addition, you tell Visual Component Manager how to manage its interaction with the Visual Studio and other development environments, and how to identify it with keywords and search attributes so it can be easily located by other developers who wish to reuse it.

When you use the Visual Component Manager Publish Wizard to publish your components, you enter the following information:

- Component Name

  Type the name that will appear in the contents pane to identify the component.
- Primary File Name

  Type the name of the primary component file. For example, if you are publishing an ActiveX control, the primary filename will be the .ocx file that encapsulates the control.

- Type

  Select the type of component you are publishing. This determines the handler assigned to the component for purposes of interacting with the tools environment and operating system, as well as providing a useful search criterion.

- Author

  Type the name of the person who wrote the component being published.

- The component includes

  Select the check box next to each kind of additional support file you want to publish along with the component. The options include:

  - Sample code

  - Source code

  - Documentation

  - Help file

- More Properties

  Type a verbal description and search keywords for the component you are publishing. A clear description and well-chosen keywords makes it easier for others to find your component and thus use your component.

  - Description

    Type a textual description of the component. The more detail you enter here, the better. A description of the component's suggested use, interfaces, inputs and outputs, and similar information make it easier for other developers to reuse the component.

  - Keywords

    Type the keywords or click Add to insert keywords from a list of keywords that have previously been used in your database. To insert new keywords, click on the plus (+) sign in the Add a Keyword dialog box.

- Select Additional File(s)

  Type the names of all the files that will be published as a part of the component, in addition to the primary file already listed. If the Publish Wizard has been launched from a project, the project files will be automatically included in the list, and you may add other files as well.

- COM Registration

  Specify which files, if any, Visual Component Manager must register for COM on the user's computer when this component is reused.

When you click Finish, the wizard publishes the component to Visual Component Manager.

Finding Components

Visual Component Manager's flexible keyword and search mechanism helps organize and cross-reference components. You can search for components by the component name, type, description, keywords, and annotations. With full text search capability, you can find components even if you don't know the exact component name.

➤ **To find an item in Visual Component Manager**

1. Click the **Find** button on the **Visual Component Manager** toolbar.

2. In the **Find Items** in **Visual Component Manager** dialog box, click the **Description** tab.

3. In the **Named** box, type the name of the component you want to find.

   You can also use the * wildcard character to represent any string. For example, ACCT* will find all components with names that begin with ACCT.

4. In the **Containing** text box, type one or more keywords or search strings.

   If you enter more than one word, Visual Component Manager finds all components containing one or more of the keywords. You can also place quotation marks around one or more words to use the entire string as a search criterion. You can use the wildcard character * to represent any character string.

5. In the **Of Type** list, specify the type of item you wish to search for.

6. Click the appropriate check box to select the areas to search for the specified text: **Keywords**, **Description**, and/or **Annotations**.

7. Click the **History** tab to narrow the search by specifying the author or person who last updated the component, publication dates, and history.

8. Click the **Related Files** tab to specify components that include sample code, source code, documentation, or Help files, as well as items with a specific name.

9. Click **Find Now** to begin the search.

   All items in the repository database that meet the search criteria are listed in the dialog box's **Results** pane as illustrated in Figure 10.15. See the **Description** tab (**Find Items** in the **Visual Component Manager** dialog box) for detailed information about each of the search options.

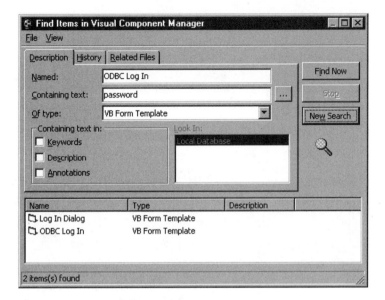

Figure 10.15 The Find dialog box's Results pane

Reusing Components

The Visual Component Manager provides several ways to reuse files and components in your Visual Basic projects. You can also reuse components, documents, specifications, and other items, although you will not directly interact with these tools. In these cases, the components are copied from the Visual Component Manager database to your local hard disk, and COM components are registered in your system registry.

When you locate a component you need, reusing it in your current project is usually as simple as clicking Add to project on the component's shortcut menu. When you select components that must be registered, Visual Component Manager automatically registers the component for you when adding it to your project.

➤ **To add a Visual Component Manger item to your Visual Basic project**

1. With Visual Basic running, locate and select the desired component item in the Visual Component Manager explorer or contents pane.

2. Right-click on the component, then click **Add to Project Group** as illustrated in Figure 10.16

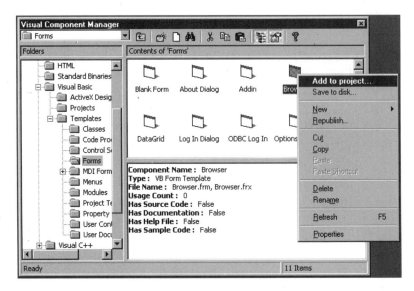

Figure 10.16 Adding a component to a project using the Visual Component Manager

Lesson Summary

You can reuse many components in other applications. You can save significant development time and effort if you can locate the right component when you need it. With Visual Component Manager, you can publish components to a repository-based catalog, where they can easily be located, inspected, retrieved, and reused. Visual Component Manager addresses the three main requirements for storing and organizing components: publishing, finding, and reusing them. It provides a single source to organize, find, and insert components into your project. It can also be the centralized location for approved project programming conventions, functional specifications, and architectural models and diagrams.

The Visual Component Manager Publish Wizard takes you step by step through the process of publishing a component for reuse. By filling in the requested information, you let Visual Component Manager know where and how to store the component. In addition, you let Visual Component Manager know how to manage its interaction with the Visual Studio and other development environments, and how to identify it with keywords and search attributes so it can be easily located by other developers who wish to reuse it.

Summary

Overview of Creating COM Components

An out-of-process component is an .exe file that runs in its own process, with its own thread of execution. Out-of-process servers can run either on a local computer or on a remote computer on a network.

An in-process component, such as an ActiveX DLL or an ActiveX control (.ocx file), runs in the same process as the client. It provides the fastest way of accessing objects, because property and method calls don't have to send and receive data across process boundaries.

In general, an ActiveX component that has been implemented as part of an executable file (.exe file) is an out-of-process server and runs in its own process.

An ActiveX component that has been implemented as part of a dynamic-link library is an in-process server and runs in the same process as the client application.

Creating ActiveX Controls

Creating the user interface for an ActiveX control is similar to creating a standard Visual Basic form. You draw controls and then provide the code that defines the behavior of those controls.

When you design a control, you take advantage of the functionality of existing controls and also add your own functionality. You choose which pieces of functionality from existing controls you wish to make available to the user of your custom control.

When you add an ActiveX control to a program, it becomes part of the development and run-time environment, and provides new functionality for your application.

To use the control in an application, place the control on a form; this creates a design-time instance of that control. When a user runs the application containing the control, Visual Basic creates a run-time instance of the control.

Creating ActiveX Code Components

COM executable programs and DLLs are libraries of classes. Client applications use COM objects by creating instances of classes provided by the COM .exe or .dll file.

With Visual Basic, you can build code components to run in-process, which allows faster access to their objects, or out-of-process, so that they have separate threads of execution from their clients. Visual Basic provides project templates for each type of components: ActiveX DLLs and ActiveX EXEs.

The value of the Instancing property of a class determines whether it is private or available for other applications to use. The values can be:

- PublicNotCreatable
- MultiUse
- GlobalMultiUse
- SingleUse
- GlobalSingleUse

Because components exist to provide objects for clients, it is hard to test them by themselves. You must create a client application. When you test your component, be sure to utilize all of its features.

You can also use the Object Browser to examine and add description strings, and to verify that Help topics are correctly linked.

Using the Visual Component Manager

Visual Component Manager addresses the three main requirements for storing and organizing components: publishing, finding, and reusing them. It provides a single source to organize, find, and insert components into your project. It can also be the centralized location for approved project programming conventions, functional specifications, and architectural models and diagrams.

The Visual Component Manager Publish Wizard simplifies publishing a component for reuse. You provide information that tells Visual Component Manager:

- Where and how to store the component.
- How to manage the component's interaction with the Visual Studio and other development environments.
- How to identify the component with keywords and search attributes, so that other developers who wish to reuse it can locate it easily.

Lab: Creating a Data-Aware Class

In this lab, you will convert the CReservation class to a data source that can be used to bind controls on frmReservation. You will write the code to add, check-in, check-out, and cancel guest reservations. In addition, you will create navigation buttons on frmReservation similar to those found on the ADO Data control. You can continue to work with the files you created in Lab 9, or you can use the files provided for you in the \Labs\Lab10\Partial folder. The solution code can be found in the \Labs\Lab10\Solution folder.

To see a demonstration of the solution, run the Lab10.exe animation located in the Animations folder on the Supplemental Course Materials CD-ROM that accompanies this book.

Estimated lesson time: 20 minutes

Lesson 1: Making the CReservation Class a Data Source

In this lesson, you will modify the CReservation class module that you created in Lab 6 to become a data source to which controls can be bound.

➤ **To make CReservation a data source**

1. Open your application or the **Hotelres.vbp** project in \Labs\Lab10\Partial folder.

2. Set the DataSourceBehavior property of **CReservation** to **vbDataSource**.

3. Cut the following two lines of code from the General Declarations section of **frmReservation**, and paste them into the General Declarations section of **CReservation**.

```
Private cnReservation As ADODB.Connection
Private rsReservation As ADODB.Recordset
```

From this point on, you will use the **CReservation** class module as the source of all guest and reservation data functionality.

4. Modify the declaration of the **rsReservation** variable so that it is declared as Public. For example:

```
Public rsReservation As ADODB.Recordset
```

5. In the **Class_GetDataMember** sub procedure, set the Data argument to the **rsReservation** object variable. Your code should look similar to the following:

```
Private Sub Class_GetDataMember(DataMember As String, Data As Object)
    Set Data = rsReservation
End Sub
```

6. In the **Class_Initialize** event, type the following code:

```
Dim SQL As String

SQL = "SELECT * FROM Reservation;"

'Create and open the connection
Set cnReservation = New ADODB.Connection
cnReservation.ConnectionString = _
    "Provider=Microsoft.Jet.OLEDB.3.51;" & _
    "Data Source=C:\Labs\Rsvn.mdb"
cnReservation.Open

Set rsReservation = New ADODB.Recordset
'Create and open the recordset
rsReservation.Open SQL, cnReservation, _
    adOpenDynamic, adLockPessimistic
```

7. Because you will be using the **CReservation** class to perform search functionality, delete the code contained in the **mnuCustSearch_Click** event procedure. Your **mnuCustSearch_Click** event procedure code should look like the following:

```
Private Sub mnuCustSearch_Click()
End Sub
```

Exercise 2: Binding Controls to the CReservation Class

In this exercise, you will bind controls on the frmReservation form to the CReservation class. Controls will be bound and updated programmatically at run time within the Form_Load event. In addition to binding controls to the CReservation class, you will also add recordset navigation buttons to frmReservation to browse the Reservation table.

➤ **To bind controls to CReservation**

1. In the **Form_Load** event procedure for **frmReservation**, type the following code:

```
Set txtFirstName.DataSource = Res
txtFirstName.DataField = "FirstName"
Set txtLastName.DataSource = Res
txtLastName.DataField = "LastName"
Set txtAddress.DataSource = Res
txtAddress.DataField = "Address"
Set txtPhone.DataSource = Res
txtPhone.DataField = "Phone"
Set txtNumPeople.DataSource = Res
txtNumPeople.DataField = "NumberOfPeople"
```

```
Set txtNumDays.DataSource = Res
txtNumDays.DataField = "NumberOfDays"
Set txtRoomNumber.DataSource = Res
txtRoomNumber.DataField = "RoomNumber"
Set txtRate.DataSource = Res
```

2. Create a private sub procedure called FillControls in **frmReservation**.

3. In the FillControls sub procedure, type the following code:

```
Private Sub FillControls()
    'Use the Recordset object to fill the advanced fields with data
    mskCheckIn.Text = Format(Res.rsReservation![CheckInDate], _
        "mm-dd-yyyy")
    txtCheckOut.Text = Format(DateAdd("d", Val(txtNumDays.Text), _
        mskCheckIn.Text), "mm-dd-yyyy")
    Select Case Res.rsReservation![PaymentType]
        Case "CREDIT CARD"
            grpPmtType(0).Value = True
        Case "CHECK"
            grpPmtType(1).Value = True
        Case "CASH"
            grpPmtType(2).Value = True
    End Select
End Sub
```

4. In the **Form_Load** event of **frmReservation**, call the FillControls sub procedure.

Exercise 3: Creating Recordset Navigation Controls

In this exercise, you will use the rsReservation Recordset object variable to browse records in the Reservation table.

➤ **To implement recordset navigation controls**

1. Add four CommandButtons to **frmReservation** and set the following properties.

Control	Property	Value
cmdMoveFirst	Caption	<<
cmdMovePrevious	Caption	<
cmdMoveNext	Caption	>
cmdMoveLast	Caption	>>

Your form should look similar to Figure 10.17.

Figure 10.17 frmReservation after adding navigation buttons

2. In the **cmdMoveFirst_Click** event procedure, type the following code:

```
Res.rsReservation.MoveFirst
FillControls
```

3. In the **cmdMovePrevious_Click** event, type the following code:

```
With Res.rsReservation
    .MovePrevious
    'Avoid a run-time error in case of BOF status
    If .BOF Then
        .MoveLast
    End If
End With
FillControls
```

4. In the **cmdMoveNext_Click** event procedure, type the following code:

```
With Res.rsReservation
    .MoveNext
    'avoid a run-time error in case of EOF status
    If .EOF Then
        .MoveFirst
    End If
End With
FillControls
```

5. In the **cmdMoveLast_Click** event procedure, type the following code:

```
Res.rsReservation.MoveLast
FillControls
```

6. In the DisableControls sub procedure, set the Enabled property to true for **cmdMoveFirst**, **cmdMovePrevious**, **cmdMoveNext**, and **cmdMoveLast**.

7. Save your work and run the hotel reservation application.

8. Test your navigation controls by clicking on each one.

   Notice that the controls on the form are updated with fields from each new record as you navigate.

Exercise 4: Implementing Reservation Processing Functionality

In this exercise, you will write code that enables users of the hotel reservation system to add, check-in, check-out, and cancel reservations. You will also implement record editing and search features to the application.

➤ **To implement reservation processing features**

1. In the General Declarations section of **frmReservation**, declare a private String variable named **strOperationStatus**.

2. In the **mnuGuestReservationAdd_Click** event procedure, type the following code to initialize controls on **frmReservation**:

```
Dim ctl As Control

Res.AddReservation
EnableControls
'Clear field values
For Each ctl In frmReservation.Controls
    If TypeOf ctl Is TextBox Then
        ctl.Text = ""
    ElseIf TypeOf ctl Is MaskEdBox Then
        ctl.Text = "__-__-____"
    ElseIf TypeOf ctl Is OptionButton Then
        ctl.Value = False
    End If
Next
txtFirstName.SetFocus
staAdditionalInfo.Panels("addinfo").Text = _
    "Click Done to update the Reservation table."
```

3. After the statement used to call DisableControls in the **cmdDone_Click** event, type the following code to update the recordset with the check-in date and payment type values:

```
If grpPmtType(0).Value Then
    Res.rsReservation![PaymentType] = "CREDIT CARD"
ElseIf grpPmtType(1).Value Then
    Res.rsReservation![PaymentType] = "CHECK"
ElseIf grpPmtType(2).Value Then
    Res.rsReservation![PaymentType] = "CASH"
End If
Res.rsReservation![CheckInDate] = mskCheckIn.Text
Res.rsReservation.Update
```

4. In the AddReservation function procedure in the **CReservation** class, type the following code to add a new record to the **rsReservation** recordset:

```
rsReservation.AddNew
rsReservation![Status] = "PENDING"
AddReservation = True
```

5. Type the following code for the CheckIn method of **Creservation** to update the status and check-in date information:

```
'Check the status to make sure it is pending
If rsReservation![Status] = "PENDING" Then
    rsReservation![Status] = "ACTIVE"
    rsReservation![CheckInDate] = Format(Date, "mm-dd-yyyy")
    rsReservation.Update
    CheckIn = True
Else
    CheckIn = False
End If
```

6. In the **mnuGuestReservationCheckIn_Click** event procedure, call the CheckIn method of the Res object and evaluate the return value. Your code should look like the following:

```
Dim blnCheckInResult As Boolean

blnCheckInResult = Res.CheckIn()
If blnCheckInResult Then
    MsgBox "Guest checked-in successfully."
Else
    MsgBox "Could not check-in guest. Status is " & _
        Res.rsReservation![Status]
End If
```

7. In the **CReservation** class, create a private function called MoveToArchive. This function will move the current record from the **rsReservation** recordset to the **ReservationArchive** table in the database. Your code should look like the following:

```
Private Function MoveToArchive() As Boolean
    Dim rsArchive As ADODB.Recordset
    Set rsArchive = New ADODB.Recordset

    On Error GoTo HandleError
    rsArchive.Open "ReservationArchive", cnReservation, _
        adOpenDynamic, adLockPessimistic
    rsArchive.AddNew
    With rsArchive
        ![FirstName] = rsReservation![FirstName]
        ![Lastname] = rsReservation![Lastname]
        ![Address] = rsReservation![Address]
        ![Phone] = rsReservation![Phone]
        ![PaymentType] = rsReservation![PaymentType]
        ![NumberOfPeople] = rsReservation![NumberOfPeople]
        ![Status] = rsReservation![Status]
        ![RoomNumber] = rsReservation![RoomNumber]
        ![Rate] = rsReservation![Rate]
        ![NumberOfDays] = rsReservation![NumberOfDays]
        ![CheckInDate] = rsReservation![CheckInDate]
        .Update
    End With
    rsReservation.Delete adAffectCurrent
    MoveToArchive = True
    Exit Function
HandleError:
    MoveToArchive = False
End Function
```

8. In the CheckOut method of the **CReservation** class, type the following code:

```
'Check the status to make sure the guest is checked in
If rsReservation![Status] = "ACTIVE" Then
    rsReservation![Status] = "INACTIVE"
    If MoveToArchive Then
        CheckOut = True
        rsReservation.MoveFirst
    End If
Else
    MsgBox "Could not check-out INACTIVE guest."
    CheckOut = False
End If
```

9. In the CancelReservation method of the **CReservation** class, type the following code:

```
rsReservation![Status] = "CANCELED"
If MoveToArchive Then
    CancelReservation = True
    rsReservation.MoveFirst
Else
    CancelReservation = False
End If
```

10. In the **mnuCustSearch_Click** event procedure, type the following code:

```
Dim strCriteria As String

frmSearch.Show vbModal
'Search based on any of the three fields
If Trim(frmSearch!txtLastName.Text) <> "" Then
    strCriteria = "[LastName] LIKE '" & _
        frmSearch!txtLastName.Text & "%'"
ElseIf Trim(frmSearch!txtPhone.Text) <> "" Then
    strCriteria = "[Phone] LIKE '" & frmSearch!txtPhone.Text & "%'"
ElseIf Trim(frmSearch!txtFirstName.Text) <> "" Then
    strCriteria = "[FirstName] LIKE '" & _
        frmSearch!txtFirstName.Text & "%'"
End If
With Res.rsReservation
    'Search for last name
    .Find strCriteria
    'If last name not found
    If .EOF Then
        MsgBox "Last name " & _
            frmSearch!txtLastName.Text & " not found."
    End If
End With
Unload frmSearch
```

11. Use the menu editor to add a new menu item under the **Guest** menu. Set the Caption to **Edit Record**, and set the Name to **mnuGuestEdit**, as illustrated in Figure 10.18.

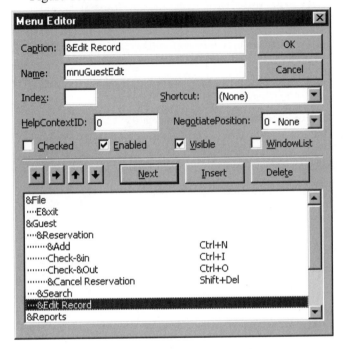

Figure 10.18 Creating the mnuGuestEdit menu item

12. In the **mnuGuestEdit_Click** event procedure, type the following code:

```
'Enable controls for record editing
'and check-in, check-out, and cancel
EnableControls
```

Now the user can browse through the records using the navigation buttons you created, edit the current record and check-in, check-out, and cancel reservations by clicking Edit Record on the **Guest** menu.

13. Save your application.

➤ **To test your application**

1. Start the hotel reservation application.

2. Add a new reservation using the Guest menu. Be sure to click **Done** when finished entering all the required data.

   Notice that the user interaction has remained the same even though we've added code that now uses a data bound class.

3. Search for this new reservation record using the code you have added to the **mnuCustSearch_click** event.

   As with the "add guest" functionality, searching for a guest has not changed the user experience. The same interactions are presented, but now our project is easier to manage and includes a class modeule that can be re-used in other applications.

Review

The following questions are intended to reinforce key information presented in this chapter. If you are unable to answer a question, review the appropriate lesson and then try the question again. Answers to the questions can be found in the Appendix, "Questions and Answers," located at the back of this book.

1. What is an out-of-process COM component?

   What are the advantages of implementing an out-of-process component?

   What are the disadvantages?

2. When creating an ActiveX control that will be used as a data source, what property of the UserControl must you set at design time?

3. Which type of ActiveX code component can have its Instancing property set to SingleUse?

4. What is the purpose of the Start With Full Compile option?

5. What are the three ways to publish items to the Visual Component Manager repository database?

CHAPTER 11

Creating Internet Applications

About This Chapter

In this chapter, you will learn to create Internet-based applications with Visual Basic. Visual Basic offers several ways to move your applications onto the Internet or a corporate intranet. This includes developing and deploying:

- Dynamic Hypertext Markup Language (DHTML) applications

  Every Hypertext Markup Language (HTML) document consists of a combination of HTML tags and their attributes. These elements define the structure of the document and determine how the content is presented. With DHTML, you can write scripts for any element on a Web page just as you do for an object on a Visual Basic form.

- ActiveX documents

  Also known as active documents, ActiveX documents are more than simple documents. They provide the functionality of an application with the ability to persist and distribute "copies" of the data intrinsic to the application.

- Internet Information Server (IIS) applications.

  IIS applications live on a Web server and respond to requests from a browser. The user interface is HTML. Compiled Visual Basic code processes the requests and responds to events.

Before You Begin

To complete the lessons in this chapter, you must have:

- A basic understanding of HTML and the Internet.
- Installed Internet Information Server or Personal Web Server (to create IIS applications).
- Installed Internet Explorer 4.x (in order to complete practices in Lesson 3).
- Read Chapter 1.

Lesson 1: Creating DHTML Applications

Visual Basic 6.0 supports Internet programming. You can add active content to Web pages with little effort. Visual Basic Internet applications link Visual Basic code to one or more HTML pages and handle events raised in those pages by interacting with programs on either a client or a server. You can create two types of Internet applications in Visual Basic: client-based DHTML applications and server-based IIS applications. In this lesson, you will learn how to create client-based DHTML applications.

After this lesson you will be able to:

- Describe Internet client and server relationships.
- Describe how to use Dynamic HTML.
- Create a Dynamic HTML application using the DHTML Page designer.

Estimated lesson time: 25 minutes

Review of the Internet and HTML

The Internet is a global, distributed network of computers operating on the TCP/IP protocol. An intranet is also a network of computers operating on the TCP/IP protocol, but it is not global. Generally, an intranet is restricted to a particular set of users and cannot be accessed by the outside world. A corporation may run an intranet to provide information to employees only, and run a separate Internet site for external users. Users within the company can access both, but users outside the company can access only the company's Internet site.

Corporate intranets facilitate distributing information, such as customer order information, sales data, performance figures, or training materials, to employees while preventing outside access to the data. Properly used, an intranet can be a very cost-effective tool.

Note In this chapter, we will use the term Internet to include both the global network of computers and intranet networks.

HTML is the language that displays .htm files in a Web browser on the Internet. An .htm file is a text document that contains a series of tags that tell the browser how to display the file. These HTML tags supply information about the page's structure, appearance, and content.

Visual Basic and Internet Development

A common way to think about Internet development is in terms of client/server relationships. The client is the browser on a desktop PC, and the server is the Web server. Most Internet interactions can be thought of in terms of requests and responses. The browser makes a request to the Web server (usually to display a page that the user wants to see) and the Web server returns a response (usually an HTML page, an element such as a file, or an image) to the browser.

Web designers usually create HTML pages, but you can also choose to create them in conjunction with developing your Visual Basic application. When you create an Internet application in Visual Basic, the user interface is typically an HTML page rather than a form. In many ways, an .htm file is analogous to a Visual Basic .frm file.

Introduction to DHTML Applications

DHTML is a technology extension of Internet Explorer 4.*x* that allows developers and users to interact with Web pages in diverse ways. A major benefit of DHTML is that much of the processing can be done on the client without having to transfer processing to the server.

A DHTML application is a Visual Basic application that uses a combination of DHTML and compiled Visual Basic code in an interactive, browser-based application. DHTML applications must be run on Internet Explorer 4.*x* .

In its simplest form, a DHTML application can be a single HTML page that uses Visual Basic code and the Dynamic HTML object model to instantly respond to actions that occur on the page. This might involve:

- Responding to user-initiated actions such as mouse movements or clicks.
- Responding to an action that the browser itself performs, such as opening a page or loading a picture.

In a more complex DHTML application, you might:

- Retrieve data from the page and use it to query a database.
- Update the page's appearance and behavior.
- Create HTML elements and insert them onto a page in response to user requests.

DHTML applications use Visual Basic code to perform much of the same processing you could accomplish with other methods of Internet application development, such as JavaScript or CGI. You write Visual Basic code to handle events that occur when a page is viewed in the browser. You can respond to events that occur on any element on the page—clicking a button, loading an image, passing the mouse over a certain part of the page, etc. While most of the processing associated with a DHTML application occurs on the client computer, the application can also make calls to the server.

Advantages of DHTML Applications

A major advantage of these applications is that they combine the power and capabilities of DHTML and Visual Basic's controls and codes. Another advantage is the conservation of server resources since much of the processing takes place on the client. This also provides a faster refresh or response to the user. In addition, you can use DHTML applications offline through the browser's cache. Security of your application is also an advantage. Although code embedded in an HTML page is accessible, a DHTML application is not since it is compiled on the client.

Using the DHTML Page Designer

To create a DHTML application, you use Visual Basic's DHTML Page designer (see Figure 11.1) to create the Web pages that act as the user interface of your application. You can write Visual Basic code and attach it to a Web page or import an existing Web page into the designer and modify it. The designer's Treeview window on the left displays a hierarchical representation of all of the elements within an HTML page. The Detail pane on the right presents a drawing surface on which you can create the new page or edit the contents of an existing page.

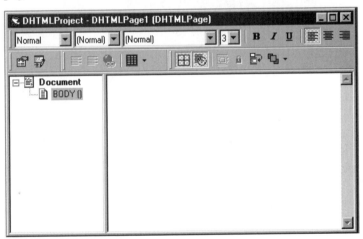

Figure 11.1 The DHTML Page designer

Note   There is a one-to-one relationship between DHTML Page designers and HTML pages. If you want to use more than one HTML page in your application, you can add more DHTML Page designers to your project by clicking Add DHTML Page on the Project menu.

Here is the basic process for creating a DHTML application in Visual Basic:

1. Create a new project in Visual Basic using the DHTML Application template.

   Your project contains a DHTML Page designer and a code module by default.

2. Create an HTML page or use an existing HTML page as the user interface for your application.

3. Assign an ID property to uniquely identify each element, such as a TextField or Button on the HTML page that you want to access programmatically.

4. Write code to add functionality to your application.

5. Test and debug your application as you would any other Visual Basic application.

   When you start your DHTML application from Visual Basic, it runs in Internet Explorer, but you will still debug your code in the Visual Basic IDE.

6. Compile your application, and use the Package and Deployment Wizard to package the DLLs and supporting files for distribution.

Modifying HTML with DHTML

In HTML, tags provide the formatting instructions. For example, a third-level heading is written <H3>My Heading</H3>. The H3 tags determine the size of the text that is displayed by the browser.

In DHTML, you can include additional information in these HTML tags to control and modify the appearance of the page. ID is a DHTML attribute that assigns a unique identifier to the heading and makes it programmable. This example shows the ID attribute added to the HTML tag:

```
<H3 ID=Subhead1>My Heading</H3>
```

In a Visual Basic application, you might replace text to customize the user's HTML page or change the appearance or format of the text on the HTML page. In a DHTML application, you handle text replacements differently. In a DHTML application, you can dynamically make changes to text, as well as to HTML tags, at run time.

You must specify whether you are replacing the current HTML text with straight text or text that includes additional HTML tags. Additionally, you must indicate whether the original tags for the element should be affected by the replacement. You do this with two sets of properties: innerText and outerText, and innerHTML and outerHTML.

To change text within HTML tags, use the innerText or innerHTML properties. InnerText provides changes that the system inserts as straight text, without performing any parsing. InnerHTML provides text replacements and additional

HTML tags that must be parsed and inserted between the original tags. For example:

Using innerText	Code
The original HTML	`<H3 ID=Subhead1>My Heading</H3>`
Using the innerText property	`Subhead1.innerText = "Heading One"`
Resulting HTML	`<H3 ID=Subhead1>Heading One</H3>`

Using innerHTML	Code
The original HTML	`<H3 ID=Subhead1>My Heading</H3>`
Using the innerHTML property	`Subhead1.innerHTML="<I>Heading One</I>"`
Resulting HTML	`<H3 Subhead1><I>Heading One</I></H3>`

To change both the text and the original tags around an element, use two properties called outerText and outerHTML. Both properties replace the text enclosed in the HTML for a specific element and the element tags themselves.

Practice: Creating a DHTML Application

In this practice, you will create a simple DHTML application using the DHTML Page Designer.

➤ **To create a DHTML project**

1. Create a new project in Visual Basic using the **DHTML Application** project template.

   The **Project Explorer** window appears.

2. Double-click the **Designers** folder, then double-click **DHTMLPage1.**

   The **DHTML Page designer** appears.

3. Click in the **Detail** pane, type **Mortgage Payment Calculator**, then press **Enter**.

4. Type the text shown in Figure 11.2.

   Note Do not press **Enter** after the last line.
   ---

5. With the cursor after **Total:**, press **F4** and set the ID property to **TotalPayment.**

6. Press the **Enter** key three times to add blank lines after **Total**.

7. From the HTML toolbox (see Figure 11.3), add three TextField controls and one Button control to the **Detail** pane.

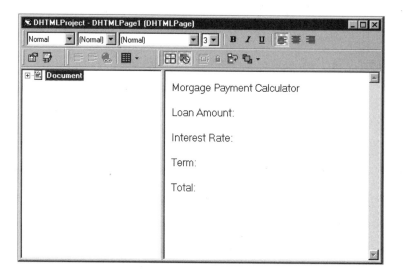

Figure 11.2 Practice text layout

Figure 11.3 The HTML toolbox

8. Set the following properties for the new controls. Figure 11.4 illustrates the layout of the controls.

Control	Properties	Value
TextField1	ID	LoanAmt
	Value	<blank>
	Title	Loan Amount
TextField2	ID	Interest
	Value	<blank>
	Title	Interest Rate
TextField3	ID	Term
	Value	<blank>
	Title	Term
Button1	ID	Calculate
	Value	Calculate

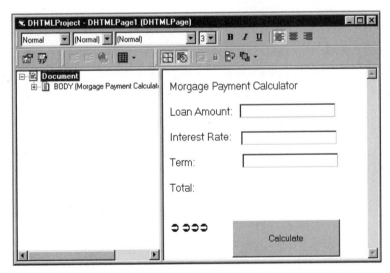

Figure 11.4 Practice control layout

9. Double-click the **Calculate** button and add the following code:

```
Dim MonthPmt As Double
MonthPmt = Pmt(Val((Interest.Value) / 100) / 12, _
    Val(Term.Value), Val(LoanAmt.Value))
TotalPayment.innerText = "Your monthly payment is: " & _
    Format(MonthPmt, "currency")
```

10. Save the application with the default filenames to the \Practice\Ch11 folder.

11. Test the application by pressing **F5**. In the **Project Properties** dialog box, select **DHTMLPage1** as the **Startup Component**, then click **OK**.

12. Enter the following values in the Web page, then click **Calculate**.

Field	Value
Loan Amount:	150000
Interest Rate:	7
Term:	360

The resulting value is $997.95.

Lesson Summary

HTML (Hypertext Markup Language) allows you to display documents in a Web browser. Tags, the foundation of HTML, are formatting instructions embedded in the text. When you create an Internet application in Visual Basic, your user interface is usually made up of HTML pages rather than forms.

A DHTML application is a Visual Basic application that uses a combination of Dynamic HTML and compiled Visual Basic code in an interactive, browser-based application. A DHTML application lets you:

- Retrieve data from the page and use it to query a database.
- Update the page's appearance and behavior.
- Create HTML elements and insert them onto a page in response to user requests.

A DHTML application resides on the browser (client), where it interprets and responds to actions the user performs in the browser.

Use the Visual Basic DHTML Page designer to create Web pages that act as the user interface of your application.

Two sets of properties let you manipulate text and/or the surrounding tags: innerText and outerText, and innerHTML and outerHTML.

Lesson 2: Creating ActiveX Documents

With Visual Basic, you can use ActiveX technology to create ActiveX documents. These are components that you can use on HTML pages or as alternatives to HTML pages. You can use other ActiveX components to create Internet solutions, including code components (.exe and .dll files) that run on the client or controls (.ocx files). All of these components help you create Internet solutions that meet your business needs. ActiveX documents allow you to create solutions that are available to users through an Internet browser.

After this lesson you will be able to:

- Describe the purpose of ActiveX documents.
- Identify the events used in ActiveX documents.
- Create an ActiveX document.
- List the files associated with ActiveX documents.

Estimated lesson time: 30 minutes

Overview of ActiveX Documents

ActiveX documents integrate tightly with the other elements of your Internet or intranet site. You can use ActiveX documents in conjunction with DHTML applications, IIS applications, or HTML pages that are not associated with a Visual Basic Internet application. You can deploy these components so that users can navigate transparently between ActiveX documents and other pages in your application or Web site.

Use ActiveX documents within your Internet applications when you want to:

- Use the Visual Basic programming model rather than the programming model used in DHTML or IIS applications.
- Gain control over the whole frame of the browser window rather than just a part of it.
  - When you display a Web page in the browser, HTML lets you specify the appearance of only the page itself. You cannot write HTML to control the menu, the scroll bar, or any other part of the browser window.
  - When you use an ActiveX document, you can control additional pieces of the window, such as menus, toolbars, scroll bars, and other items. For example, if you want one page of your DHTML application to contain a custom menu, you might use an ActiveX document.

Some objects in Visual Basic are *containers*; that is, they contain other Visual Basic objects. A form usually is a container; it contains one or more controls. Certain Visual Basic objects must be contained by another object. Still others can be either containers or contained, or both. ActiveX documents are not stand-alone applications—they can exist only in a container such as Internet Explorer. But they can also contain objects. Containers vary so you can't always predict the capabilities and limitations of your ActiveX document environment. Your application might work properly in Internet Explorer 4.*x* , but not in an earlier version.

Before you use an ActiveX document, you must place it within a container. Connecting an ActiveX document to its container is known as *siting*. Siting plays a key role in determining ActiveX document event behavior. It enables an ActiveX document to implement its functionality.

Advantages of ActiveX Documents

Several features help you provide installation, navigation, and persistence with your ActiveX documents. The advantages of ActiveX documents are:

- Automatic downloading of components over the Internet

    You can create a link to your ActiveX document that causes the browser to automatically find and download all components that are needed to run the component. You can also make an ActiveX document upgrade automatically if the version on the server is more recent.

- Hyperlinking of objects

    In a hyperlink-aware container, you can use the properties and methods of Visual Basic's Hyperlink object to jump to a given URL or navigate through the history list.

- Merging of menus

    As with documents that are made available through Microsoft Word or Microsoft Excel, the menus of Visual Basic ActiveX documents can be merged with the browser's menus. As the document is loaded in Internet Explorer, for instance, the browser's menu items will be merged with those you created to accompany your ActiveX document.

- Storing of data

    When you deploy an ActiveX document in Internet Explorer, you can store data through the PropertyBag object.

The UserDocument Object

When you create an ActiveX document, you are creating an ActiveX component that can be either in-process (ActiveX document DLL) or out-of-process (ActiveX document EXE). The base object of an ActiveX document—the UserDocument object—resembles a standard Visual Basic Form object, with some exceptions.

Several differences exist between a Visual Basic form object and the UserDocument object. The UserDocument object has most, but not all, of the events that are found on a Form object. The following lists show the events available exclusively for forms, and the events available only for UserControls.

Form Events	UserControl Events
Activate	AsyncReadComplete
Deactivate	EnterFocus
LinkClose	ExitFocus
LinkError	Hide
LinkExecute	InitProperties
LinkOpen	ReadProperties
Load	Scroll
QueryUnload	Show
Unload	WriteProperties

Another difference is that you cannot place embedded objects (such as an Excel or Word document) or an OLE Container control on a UserDocument, while you can place these on a Visual Basic form.

UserDocument Events

During the lifetime of a UserDocument object, the events that occur and the order in which they occur depend on a number of factors, including which container you use, whether the document has been sited, and what actions the user takes within the container.

The following are examples of events that can occur during the lifetime of an ActiveX document:

- Initialize

  The Initialize event occurs each time you create or recreate an instance of an ActiveX document. It is always the first event that occurs during the lifetime of an ActiveX document.

- InitProperties

  The InitProperties event occurs when an ActiveX document is sited in the document's container, but none of the ActiveX document's property values have been saved. Once a property value is saved, the InitProperties event is replaced by the ReadProperties event.

- ReadProperties

  The ReadProperties event occurs when you save a property with the PropertyBag object.

- Terminate

  The Terminate event occurs just before you destroy the ActiveX document. To remove any object references, set all global object references to Nothing with the Terminate event.

- Show

  The Show event occurs in one of the following two situations: when a user opens an ActiveX document that has been sited in its container, and when a user clicks the Back or Forward button to return to an ActiveX document in the History list of Internet Explorer.

- Hide

  The Hide event occurs in one of the following two situations: when a user navigates away from a document (immediately before the Terminate event), or when a user closes Internet Explorer while the document is open.

Note The functionality of the Show and Hide events depends on the container.

UserDocument Files

UserDocuments have two types of files that define the appearance and interface of an ActiveX document, including its properties, events, and methods:

- .dob files

  Visual Basic stores user documents in text files with a .dob extension. These files contain the source code, property values, and controls of the UserDocument object. A .dob file is analogous to a Standard EXE project's .frm file.

- .dox files

  Visual Basic stores any graphical elements in files with a .dox extension. These files are used for the controls of a UserDocument object, such as bitmaps. A .dox file is analogous to a Standard EXE project's .frx file.

When you compile the ActiveX document project, an .exe or a .dll file is created in addition to a Visual Basic document (.vbd). To open the ActiveX document in a browser such as Internet Explorer, users must be able to navigate to the .vbd file.

Creating an ActiveX Document

As with any Visual Basic project, when you create an ActiveX document, first consider the principles of design that were discussed in Chapter 2, "Creating the User Interface." Design the features and appearance of your document, and determine the properties, methods, and events it will provide.

➤ **To create an ActiveX document in Visual Basic**

1. Create a new Visual Basic project using either the **ActiveX Document DLL** or the **ActiveX Document EXE** project template.

   Create a .dll file if you want to create an in-process component.
   Create an .exe file if you want to create an out-of-process component.

2. Add controls and code to the UserDocument object to implement the user interface of your document, and write code to implement its properties, methods, and events.

3. Compile your document to create a .vbd file, then test it with all potential container applications.

Converting an Existing Standard EXE Project

You can convert existing Standard EXE projects to ActiveX document projects with Visual Basic's ActiveX Document Migration Wizard add-in. When you run the wizard, it converts the selected project forms to ActiveX documents, and changes the project type to either ActiveX EXE or ActiveX DLL.

You can use the ActiveX Document Migration Wizard to convert project forms other than Standard EXE projects to an ActiveX document project, but the option to convert the project type will be unavailable.

➤ **To load the ActiveX Document Migration Wizard add-in**

1. On the **Add-Ins** menu, click **Add-In Manager…**

   The **Available Add-Ins** list appears.

2. Double-click the **VB ActiveX Document Migration Wizard**.

   The word "Loaded" appears in the **Load Behavior** column, next to the VB ActiveX Document Migration Wizard.

3. Click **OK** to close the **Add-In Manager**.

➤ **To convert an existing project to an ActiveX project**

1. On the **Add-Ins** menu, click **ActiveX Document Migration Wizard**.

2. If you want to skip the introduction screen when you use this wizard in the future, click **Skip this screen in the future**, then click **Next**.

3. On the **Form Selection** screen, select the form that you want to convert, then click **Next**.

4. On the **Options** screen, select **Comment out invalid code, Remove original forms after conversion**, and **Convert to an ActiveX EXE or DLL**, then click **Next**.

5. On the **Finished** screen, click **Summary Report** to view the migration summary, then click **Finish**.

Practice: Creating an ActiveX Document

In this practice, you will create an ActiveX document application in Visual Basic.

➤ **To create an ActiveX document**

1. In Visual Basic, start a new **ActiveX Document EXE** project.

   Visual Basic automatically adds a **UserDocument** designer to the project. If the designer is not immediately visible, right-click its default name, **UserDocument1,** in the **Project Explorer** window, then click **View Object**. When the designer appears, its default name is visible in the title bar.

2. Change the name of **Project1** to **ActXDoc**.

3. Change the name of **UserDocument1** to **FirstDoc**.

4. Open the **FirstDoc** designer, then add a command button and a text box.

5. Set the following properties:

Object	Property	Value
Command button	Name	CmdNavigateTo
	Caption	Navigate To
Text box	Name	TxtURL
	Text	http://www.microsoft.com

6. Add the following code to the **cmdNavigateTo_click** event:

```
'Use the Hyperlink object method NavigateTo
'to go to the URL in txtURL.
Hyperlink.NavigateTo txtURL.Text
```

7. Save the project to the \Practice\Ch11 folder. Name the user document **FirstDoc.dob** and name the Project **ActXDoc.vbp**. Do not add the project to Visual SourceSafe.

8. Start the new application and leave it running in the background.

9. On the **Debugging** tab of the **Project Properties** dialog box, click **Wait for components to be created** and clear the **Use existing browser** check box, as illustrated in Figure 11.5.

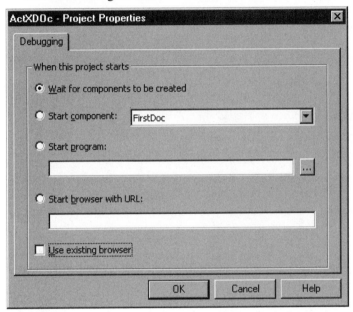

Figure 11.5 Selecting debug options for your ActiveX document

10. Start Internet Explorer, then browse to the following local file address:

```
C:\Program Files\Microsoft Visual Studio\VB98\FirstDoc.vbd
```

11. If you are prompted to select which application to open the ActiveX document with, select **iexplore**, as illustrated in Figure 11.6.

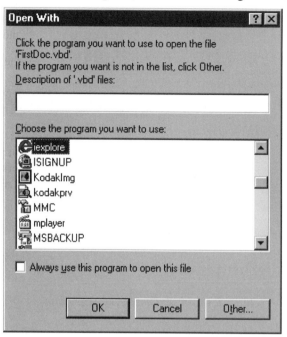

Figure 11.6 Selecting iexplore in the Open With dialog box

12. Your ActiveX document appears, as illustrated in Figure 11.7.

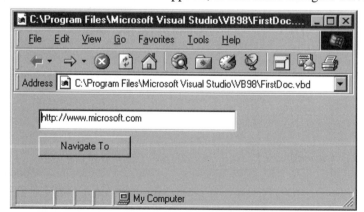

Figure 11.7 Your ActiveX document running within Internet Explorer

13. Click **Navigate To** to navigate to the specified URL.

Running and Debugging an ActiveX Document Project

Debugging an ActiveX document is similar to debugging other ActiveX components. You can use all the tools available in Visual Basic: setting breakpoints, watching variables, using Debug statements, and so on.

It's also important to remember that the container hosting the ActiveX document is its client, and uses objects the ActiveX document provides. If you stop the project while the host container is accessing the ActiveX document, an error will occur in the host container. To avoid this, quit Internet Explorer at the end of each of these procedures to release the reference.

If you run a project and view it in Internet Explorer, you can put it into break mode by pressing CTRL+BREAK without causing any errors in the host application (Internet Explorer). However, you should avoid modifying any code that causes Visual Basic to reset the project.

Lesson Summary

ActiveX documents are components you use to create solutions through a browser. You can use them on Web pages or as alternatives to Web pages. Use them when you want to:

- Use the Visual Basic programming model rather than the programming model used in DHTML or IIS applications.
- Gain control over the whole frame of the browser window, rather than just a part of it.

An ActiveX document must be sited, or placed within a container such as Internet Explorer 4.*x* .

Important features of ActiveX documents include:

- Automatic downloading and/or upgrading of components over the Internet.
- Hyperlinking of objects.
- Merging of menus.
- Storing of data.

The UserDocument object, the base object of an ActiveX document, is similar to a Visual Basic form object. The two have some of the same events, but each also has unique events. You cannot place embedded objects or an OLE Contrainer control on a UserDocument.

A UserDocument has .dob files and .dox files that are analogous to .frm and.frx files, respectively.

With the ActiveX Document Migration Wizard add-in, you can convert an existing Standard EXE project to an ActiveX document project as either an ActiveX EXE or ActiveX DLL. While you can also convert other types of projects, you cannot choose the ActiveX type.

Debugging an ActiveX document project is similar to debugging other ActiveX components. Be careful, however, not to stop the project while its host container is accessing the ActiveX document.

Lesson 3: Creating IIS Applications Using WebClasses

An IIS application is a server-side Web application created in Visual Basic. It utilizes one of the new features in Microsoft Visual Basic 6.0: the capability to include WebClasses in projects. A WebClass represents code that can run on an Internet server, and gives you the ability to put code behind URLs. WebClasses provide a way for you to create server-side applications that are hosted by IIS and can be viewed on client Web browsers.

Because Web development emphasizes separating the components of an application into logic, presentation style, navigational structure, and content or state, you can use WebClasses to separate application logic from the presentation (user interface) of the application. This helps you create multitier, distributed applications by including Web components to deliver part of functionality through Web browsers.

After this lesson you will be able to:

- Describe the structure of an IIS application.
- Describe how to use WebClasses to create Web-based applications.
- Explain the difference between form-based and Web-based applications.
- Create WebClasses using the WebClass Designer.

Estimated lesson time: 40 minutes

Overview of IIS Applications

An IIS application lives on a Web server and responds to requests from the browser. The application uses HTML to present its user interface and compiled Visual Basic code to process requests and respond to events in the browser.

A user sees an IIS application as a series of HTML pages. A developer sees it as a WebClass that is made up of WebItems. A WebClass is a Visual Basic component that resides on a Web server and responds to input from the browser. A WebItem is an element that can be returned to the browser as part of a response to an HTTP request. A WebItem is usually an HTML page, but it could also be a MIME-type file, such as an image, a .wav file, etc.

In an IIS application, you do not use Visual Basic to create the HTML pages that make up the application's user interface. A Web designer or a developer creates the pages using an HTML editor, a word processing package, or a text editor, and you link the finished pages into your WebClass.

The following table summarizes the differences between forms-based applications and Web-based applications:

Element	Forms-based application	Web-based application
User Interface	Visual Basic forms	HTML pages
User Interface Elements	Controls	Elements
File Format	.frm files	.htm files
Creator	Developer	Web designer and/or Visual Basic developer
Run Time	Visual Basic IDE, Windows	Web browser

Structure of IIS Applications

IIS applications are structured differently from standard, forms-based Visual Basic applications. The user interface consists of a series of HTML pages rather than traditional Visual Basic forms. An HTML page is like a Visual Basic form in that it contains all the visual elements that make up your application's user interface. You can place some of the same items onto a page as you do a form, including text, buttons, check boxes, and option buttons.

An IIS application consists of several pieces. Many of these are generated automatically when you build your project. The pieces include:

- One or more WebClasses, which are generated automatically when you create a WebClass project.

- One or more HTML templates and their events.

- One or more custom WebItems and their events.

- An .asp (Active Server Pages) file that hosts the WebClass in IIS. The .asp is generated automatically when you create a WebClass project; Visual Basic gives it the name you specify in the NameInURL property.

- A WebClass run-time component, Mswcrun.dll, which helps process requests.

- A project DLL (generated automatically on compile) that contains your Visual Basic code and is accessed by the run-time component.

Note A WebClass may contain a mixture of templates and custom WebItems, only templates, or only custom WebItems. You do not necessarily have to have both templates and custom WebItems in your WebClasses.

Note To use the IIS Application project template, you must have Internet Information Server or Personal Web Server installed on your computer. You can obtain either of these services by installing the NT Option Pack that is included on the Visual Basic CD.

Figure 11.8 shows how the server portions of an IIS application work together.

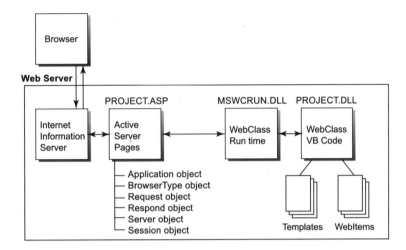

Figure 11.8 Structure of an IIS application

Like other Visual Basic applications, an IIS application has code modules and a visual designer. IIS application objects are stored in plain text files that contain the source code of the WebClass, events, property settings, and the WebItems for the WebClass. Visual Basic uses the .dsr extension for these files. In addition to the .dsr file, Visual Basic generates a .dsx file that contains a binary version of the application.

Using a WebClass to Respond to Client Requests

A WebClass is a Visual Basic COM component that sends information to a Web browser from an Internet server. It is the central unit of the application, processing data from the browser and sending information to the users. You define a series of procedures that determine how the WebClass responds to these requests. A WebClass typically contains WebItems that it uses to provide content to the browser in response to a request, and to expose events. A WebItem can be one of two things:

- An HTML template file

   An HTML template file is an HTML page that you associate with your WebClass. When the WebClass receives a request, it can send the HTML page to the browser for display. Templates differ from regular HTML pages only in that they often contain replacement areas that the WebClass can process before sending the page to the browser. This allows you to customize your response.

- A custom WebItem

   A custom WebItem does not have an associated HTML page it can return to the user. Instead, a custom WebItem is a programmatic resource that consists of one or more event handlers that are logically grouped together to help organize your Web application. These event handlers are called from the browser, either when the page loads or when a user selects an HTML element.

The event handlers can generate a response to the browser or pass processing to another of the WebClass's WebItems.

Writing Code to Respond to Events

Both templates and custom WebItems make the events available that the WebClass processes when certain actions occur in the browser. You can write event procedures for these events using standard Visual Basic code, thus linking the actions that occur on a Web page to Visual Basic processing.

Each WebClass can contain multiple templates and WebItems. In most applications, you only need one WebClass. You might, however, want to use multiple WebClasses if you want to break up your application into parts that can be reused in other applications.

WebClasses and .asp Files

Each WebClass in an IIS application has an associated .asp file that Visual Basic generates automatically during the compile or debug process. The .asp file hosts the WebClass on the Web server. In addition, it generates the WebClass' run-time component when the application is first started, and launches the first event in the WebClass' life cycle.

A WebClass is associated with only one client for its entire life cycle. Visual Basic creates a logical instance of the WebClass for each client that accesses it. For each client, however, the WebClass is capable of maintaining state between requests. Figure 11.9 shows the relationship between .asp files, WebClasses, and WebClass contents.

For more information about storing state information for an IIS application, search on "Storing State in Objects" in the MSDN Online Help.

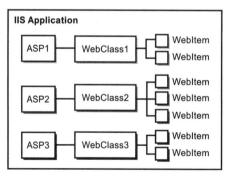

Figure 11.9 How a WebClass relates to ASP and WebItems

Using the WebClass Designer

The WebClass designer is a design-time tool in Visual Basic that lets you quickly create and modify the WebItems that represent the pages in your application. You use the designer to:

- Define the contents of the WebClass. A WebClass contains WebItems, which are the HTML pages and other items that the WebClass can send to the browser in response to a user request.
- Add events to the WebItems in the WebClass.
- Write code for each event in the WebClass.

The WebClass designer contains two panels. The Treeview panel on the left displays the WebItems that make up the WebClass. The WebItems represent the pages on your IIS server. These pages are entry points into the server's *namespace*. The server's namespace is a collection of symbols, such as filenames, folder names, or database keys, stored in a hierarchical structure. The Details panel on the right displays information about the currently selected item in the Treeview panel. Figure 11.10 illustrates WebItems within a WebClass.

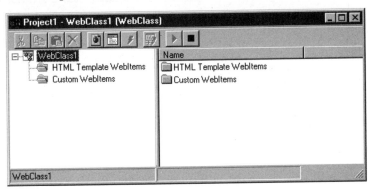

Figure 11.10 The WebClass designer

➤ **To create an IIS application in Visual Basic**

1. Create a new project in Visual Basic using the **IIS Application** project template.

   The project contains a WebClass designer and a code module by default. A reference is automatically set to the Microsoft Active Server Page Object Library.

2. Create custom WebItems to represent each page in your application, or import existing HTML pages as WebItems.

3. Define the functionality of your application by adding code to the WebItems and the Start event of your WebClass.

4. Test and debug your application as you would any other Visual Basic application.

   When you start your IIS application from Visual Basic, it will run in Internet Explorer, but you will still debug your code in the Visual Basic IDE.

5. Compile your application, and use the **Package and Deployment Wizard** to package the .dll and supporting files for distribution.

➤ **To create a custom WebItem**

1. On the **WebClass** toolbar, click **Add Custom WebItem**, as illustrated in Figure 11.11.

   A new WebItem appears at the end of the list of custom WebItems in the Treeview panel of the WebClass designer.

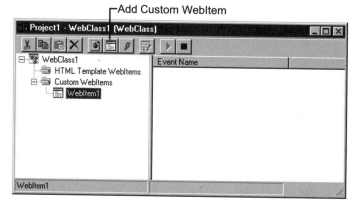

Figure 11.11 The Add Custom WebItem toolbar button

2. Type the name of the new WebItem.

➤ **To import an existing HTML page as a WebItem**

1. On the **WebClass** toolbar, click **Add HTML Template WebItem**.

   The **Add HTML Template** dialog box appears.

2. Select the HTML page you want to add as a WebItem, then click **Open**.

   A new WebItem appears at the end of the list of HTML template WebItems in the Treeview panel of the WebClass designer. In the Details panel, the tags in the HTML page are listed as objects you can use in your code.

3. Type the name for the new WebItem.

Writing Code for a WebClass

Since a WebClass is a COM component, you use the built-in events of the WebClass and the Active Server Pages object model to respond to Web browser requests. WebItems in your WebClass also have events, properties, and methods that you can use to define the functionality of your application. You can also add custom events to WebItems. You use the Active Server Page object model in your COM component to communicate with the Web browser. When the WebClass processes a request from the browser, it must send the browser a response. Generally, that response is a stream of HTML that the browser displays to the user. You can return HTML to the browser in two ways:

- Send the contents of an HTML template file directly to the browser using the WriteTemplate method.
- Produce the HTML stream with Visual Basic code.

In custom WebItems, you use the Write method of the Response object to write string information to the Web browser. The following example writes a heading to the Web browser:

```
Response.Write "<H1>Welcome to My Web Site!</H1>"
```

In HTML template WebItems, you use the WriteTemplate method of the WebItem to write the entire contents of the WebItem to the Web browser. The WriteTemplate method is the simplest way to send HTML to the browser in response to a user action. When the WebClass launches an event procedure for a template event that contains this method, it sends the template's HTML back to the browser. The resulting page displays to the user. The following example writes the contents of the WebItem named Welcome to the Web browser:

```
Welcome.WriteTemplate
```

Debugging and Deploying Your IIS Application

Just as with DHTML documents and ActiveX documents, you debug your IIS application using the standard Visual Basic debugging tools. When you run your application from the Visual Basic environment, the HTML pages that act as the user interface are opened in Internet Explorer. However, you will still debug your code using the Visual Basic Integrated Development Environment (IDE).

When you compile your application, Visual Basic generates a .dll file and a simple .asp file that instantiates your COM component on the Internet server. You can use the Package and Deployment Wizard to package your application for distribution. The wizard compresses the COM component and any supporting files into a .cab file, and provides you the opportunity to mark the component as safe. You can use the same wizard to deploy your .cab file and .asp file to a server on a network or to a folder. When you mark a control safe for scripting, you guarantee that no script can cause the control to damage the users' computers or data. Controls marked safe for scripting should not be able to obtain unauthorized information from the users' computers nor corrupt their systems.

Integration Between Visual Basic and Other Web Tools

You have learned how Visual Basic can be used to create middle tier components through WebClasses. Now let's review Web programming and how your component fits in.

Web programming has two parts. One is programming the HTML or DHTML that the browser displays. The other is programming the server. You can use Visual Basic 6.0 along with Microsoft FrontPage or Microsoft Visual InterDev to create Web pages. You can then import the Web pages directly into the WebClass designer in Visual Basic, and write code in the Web pages that access the server. You can use DHTML as a front-end to WebClasses. DHTML uses HTTP as its mechanism for communicating with the Web server.

Tools like FrontPage and Visual InterDev are very good at managing and building an entire site, while Visual Basic is better suited for building applications that can include Web client access as part of their functionality. Visual Basic adds value in Web development because it lets you create database applications and access COM components and services such as Microsoft Message Queue Server.

Using Web Classes to Create Distributed Applications

The middle tier in a three-tiered model is the component tier, where application logic is stored, as explained in Chapter 1, "Planning the Design of an Application." WebClasses populate the middle tier with application logic that can be accessed via HTTP, Microsoft Message Queue Server (MSMQ), or Distributed Component Object Model (DCOM). In addition, WebClasses can use ADO to connect to OLE DB data sources, including both structured sources of data such as SQL Server and unstructured sources of data such as Microsoft Index Server.

With Visual Basic 6.0, you can build very scalable applications, such as Web sites with more than one machine on the back end as servers and thousands of clients communicating with them on the front end through Web browsers.

Visual Basic 6.0 supports creating objects on remote computers via DCOM, communicating with servers via HTTP through WebClasses, and supports communication between computers using low-level protocols such as Winsock. In addition, Visual Basic can use MSMQ for communication between computers. With MSMQ, you can take class modules created in Visual Basic 6.0 and persist them directly onto a queue for delivery now or later to another computer.

Lesson Summary

An IIS application is a server-side Web application in Visual Basic that utilizes WebClasses, a new feature in Visual Basic 6.0. An IIS application has several components:

- One or more WebClasses, which are components that represent code that can run on an Internet server. They are generated automatically when you create a WebClass project.
- One or more HTML templates and their events.
- One or more custom WebItems and their events.
- An .asp (Active Server Pages) file that hosts the WebClass in IIS. It is generated automatically when you create a WebClass project.
- A WebClass run-time component.
- A project DLL that contains your Visual Basic code and is accessed by the run-time component. It is generated automatically on compile.

The WebClass designer enables you to quickly create and/or modify the WebItems that represent the pages in your application.

You use the standard Visual Basic debugging tools to debug IIS applications.

Summary

Creating DHTML Applications

HTML (Hypertext Markup Language) allows you to display documents in a Web browser. Tags are formatting instructions embedded in the text. When you create an Internet application in Visual Basic, your user interface is usually made up of HTML pages rather than forms.

The Internet is a global, distributed network of computers operating on the TCP/IP protocol. An intranet is also a network of computers operating on the TCP/IP protocol, but it is not global.

A dynamic HTML (DHTML) application is a Visual Basic application that uses a combination of Dynamic HTML and compiled Visual Basic code in an interactive, browser-based application. A DHTML application lets you:

- Retrieve data from the page and use it to query a database.
- Update the page's appearance and behavior.
- Create HTML elements and insert them onto a page in response to user requests.

A DHTML application resides on the browser (client), where it interprets and responds to actions the user performs in the browser.

Use the Visual Basic DHTML Page designer to create Web pages that act as the user interface of your application.

Two sets of properties let you manipulate text and/or the surrounding tags: innerText and outerText, and innerHTML and outerHTML.

Creating ActiveX Documents

ActiveX documents are forms that can appear in ActiveX document containers. An ActiveX document differs from a traditional document in that it offers not only the full functionality of an application, but also the ability to store and distribute copies of the data intrinsic to the application.

Some of the features you can include in your ActiveX documents are:

- Hyperlink objects
- Merge menus
- The **PropertyBag** object
- The ability to automatically download components over the Internet

Creating IIS Applications Using Web Classes

An IIS application is a server-side Web application in Visual Basic that utilizes WebClasses, a new feature in Visual Basic 6.0. An IIS application has several components:

- One or more WebClasses, which are components that represent code that can run on an Internet server. They are generated automatically when you create a WebClass project.
- One or more HTML templates and their events.
- One or more custom WebItems and their events.
- An .asp (Active Server Pages) file that hosts the WebClass in IIS. It is generated automatically when you create a WebClass project.
- A WebClass run-time component.
- A project DLL that contains your Visual Basic code and is accessed by the run-time component. It is generated automatically on compile.

The WebClass designer enables you to quickly create and/or modify the WebItems that represent the pages in your application.

You use the standard Visual Basic debugging tools to debug IIS applications.

Lab: Creating ActiveX Documents

In this lab, you will convert the existing forms in the hotel reservation project into ActiveX Documents. You will then run the application from Internet Explorer. You can continue to work with the files you created in Lab 10, or you can use the files provided for you in the \Labs\Lab11\Partial folder. The solution code can be found in the \Labs\Lab11\Solution folder.

To see a demonstration of the solution, run the Lab11.exe animation located in the Animations folder on the Supplemental Course Materials CD-ROM that accompanies this book.

Estimated lesson time: 20 minutes

Exercise 1: Converting Forms to ActiveX Documents

In this exercise, you will use the ActiveX Document Migration Wizard to convert forms in your application to ActiveX Documents.

➤ **To open the hotel reservation application project**

- Open either the reservation application project that you have been working on or the **Hotelres.vbp** project located in the \Labs\Lab11\Partial folder.

➤ **To convert forms to ActiveX documents**

1. Load the **VB 6 ActiveX Doc Migration Wizard** item using the Add-In Manager.

2. On the **Add-Ins** menu, click **ActiveX Document Migration Wizard...**

    The **ActiveX Document Migration Wizard** opens.

3. Click **frmReservation** in the **Form Selection** dialog box.

4. Click **Next**.

    The **Options** dialog box appears.

5. Select the **Comment out invalid code?**, **Remove original forms after conversion?**, and **Convert to ActiveX EXE?** check boxes.

6. Click **Next**.

    The **Finished!** dialog box appears.

7. Verify the request for a summary report is set to **Yes**.

8. Click **Finish** to convert **frmReservation** into an ActiveX Document.

    A dialog box notifies you that comments have been added to flag invalid code for frmReservation, as illustrated in Figure 11.12.

Figure 11.12 Notification of invalid code that was commented

9. Click **OK** to the Migration Wizard message box.

10. Review the summary report provided by Visual Basic and click **OK**.

➤ **To test your ActiveX Document**

1. On the Visual Basic **Run** menu, click **Start**.

    A **Project Properties** dialog box appears allowing you to set debugging options.

2. Click **OK** to accept the default debugging values.

    Your application opens in Internet Explorer, as illustrated in Figure 11.13.

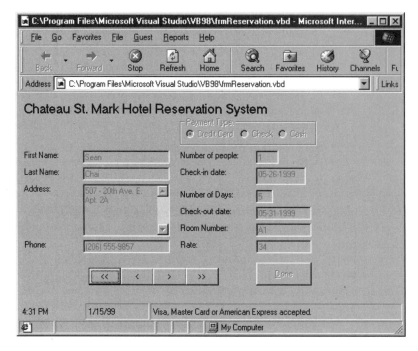

Figure 11.13 The Chateau St. Mark hotel reservation application in Internet Explorer

3. Navigate through the reservation records.

4. Close your application and save your project files.

Review

The following questions are intended to reinforce key information presented in this chapter. If you are unable to answer a question, review the appropriate lesson and then try the question again. Answers to the questions can be found in the Appendix, "Questions and Answers," located at the back of this book.

1. Explain some differences between working with an ActiveX document and a Standard EXE project.

2. Where does a DHTML application run?

3. What is a WebClass designer used for?

4. How do .dob and .dox files relate to ActiveX documents?

5. What files are created when you compile an ActiveX document project?

C H A P T E R   1 2

Packaging and Deploying an Application

About This Chapter

In this chapter, you will learn to plan and implement the distribution of an application, which includes using the Packaging and Deployment Wizard.

Before You Begin

To complete the lessons in this chapter, you must have:

- The Package and Deployment Wizard installed on your machine.

Lesson 1: Implementing Online Help

At some point, most users are going to have questions about how to use your application. The best way to handle users' questions is to provide a Help file for your application.

Visual Basic 6.0 supports the traditional Windows Help system (WinHelp) and the newer HTML Help. This lesson covers the steps necessary to call Help topics from either of these Help systems. It does not cover is how to create a Help file. There are authoring tools that can help you create Help files, including the new Microsoft HTML Help Workshop.

After this lesson you will be able to:

- Describe what you can do within Visual Basic to provide Help.
- Explain the purpose of these properties:
  - HelpFile
  - HelpContextID
  - WhatsThisHelp

Estimated lesson time: 30 minutes

Properties of Help Files

You set certain properties to provide links to the topics in your Help file. First, set the HelpFile property for your project to point to the correct Help file. Second, set the HelpContextID property of controls in your application to provide contextual Help for your users. The process of linking Help to your application is the same for both WinHelp and HTML Help systems.

HelpFile

There are two ways to set the HelpFile property. Using the App object, you can programmatically set the HelpFile property to specify the Help file name and location for your application. You can also define a valid help file for your application using the Project Properties dialog box. Setting the HelpFile property requires a written and compiled WinHelp (.hlp) or HTML Help (.chm) file.

➤ **To set the HelpFile property using Project Properties**

1. On the **Project** menu, click **Project Properties**.

2. On **Project Properties** dialog box, click the **General** tab.

3. Type the path and file name for your application's Help file (.hlp or .chm) in the **Help File Name** field.

To set the HelpFile property for your application during run time, use the App object in your program's code. The following example sets the location of the Help file as the application's directory, and states the name of the HTML Help file.

```
Private Sub Form_Load()
    App.HelpFile = App.Path & "\help.chm"
End Sub
```

You can specify a different Help file for the error messages in your application. By setting the HelpFile property of the ErrObject object, you can point your error messages to a different Help file. This is useful because you can use one Help file for the error messages of several different applications. Rather than compiling a new Help file with the same error messages, you compile one error message's Help file and call it by using the Err.HelpFile property in each application.

HelpContextID

To link your program's controls, forms, and menus to a topic in the Help file, you set the HelpContextID property of that component. The HelpContextID is a Long number that matches the Context ID of the topic in your WinHelp or HTML Help File.

For example, you set 103450 as the HelpContextID property of an OptionButton. When a user selects that OptionButton in your program and presses F1, Visual Basic searches for a topic with a Context ID of 103450 in the Help file specified in the application's HelpFile property. If the Context ID is not found in the Help file, an error occurs and the Help file's default topic is displayed.

If you leave a control's HelpContextID property at the default value (0), then Visual Basic searches for a valid HelpContextID for the control's container. If the container has a valid HelpContextID value and the user presses the F1 key, the topic for the container will be displayed.

➤ **To set the HelpContextID for a control**

1. Select the control for which you want to enter a HelpContextID.

2. On the **Properties** window, double-click **HelpContextID**.

3. Enter a valid Long integer.

Note For the CommonDialog control, the name of this property is HelpContext instead of HelpContextID.

➤ **To set the HelpContextID for a menu**

1. On the **Tools** menu, click **Menu Editor**.

2. Choose the menu item for which you want to enter a HelpContextID.

3. Enter a valid Long value in the **HelpContextID** box.

You can also set the HelpContextID property within your program's code. The following example sets the Help topic for a control, form, and the Err object.

```
Private Sub Form_Load()
    Text1.HelpContextID = 13124
    Form1.HelpContextID = 34234
    Err.HelpContext = 78798
End Sub
```

Note For the Err object, the name of this property is HelpContext instead of HelpContextID.

What's This Help

What's This Help gives the user quick access to Help text in a popup window without opening the Help viewer. You typically use it to provide simple assistance for user interface elements, such as data entry fields. Both WinHelp and HTML Help file formats support What's This Help topics.

To enable What's This Help on a form, you set the WhatsThisHelp property of that form to True. Next, select each control for which you want to provide Help and assign a unique value to the WhatsThisHelpID property of the control.

Add the What's This button to your form to allow users to click on a control to get help. To add a What's This button to a form's title bar, set the WhatsThisButton property to True. The form cannot have the Minimize and Maximize buttons.

➤ **To display the What's This button in the title bar of a form**

1. Select the form to which you want to add a What's This button.

2. On the **Properties** window, double-click the **WhatsThisHelp** property and set it to **True**.

3. Set the following properties:

Property	Value
Border Style	1 – Fixed or
	2 - Sizable
MaxButton	False
MinButton	False
Whats This Button	True
Or	
BorderStyle	3 – Fixed Dialog
Whats This Button	True

Other methods you can use are the WhatsThisMode method of a form and the ShowWhatsThis method of a control. After you have set the form's WhatsThisHelp property to True and defined the value for a control's WhatsThisHelpID, you can invoke the WhatsThisMode method within your code.

```
Private Sub mnuWhatsThis_Click()
    Form1.WhatsThisMode
End Sub
```

Implementing ToolTips

You use ToolTips to display information to users as they navigate your user interface. As shown in Figure 12.1, a ToolTip is a small label that is displayed when the mouse pointer is held over a control for a set length of time. The ToolTip should contain a description of the control's function. Normally, ToolTips are used with toolbars, but they also work well for most parts of an interface.

Figure 12.1 A ToolTip for the Visual Basic toolbar

At design time, you can add ToolTips to any button on a toolbar using the control's Property Page.

➤ **To add a ToolTip to a toolbar button**

1. Right-click on the toolbar control that contains the button for which you want to set the ToolTipText property.

2. Click **Properties**.

3. Click the **Buttons** tab.

4. Scroll the **Index** to the button for which you want to add the ToolTip.

5. Enter the help text in the **ToolTipText** property box.

At run time, you can change the ToolTip value by setting the ToolTipText property for the Button object. The following code sets the first button's ToolTipText property on Toolbar1 to Display Text:

```
Toolbar1.Buttons(1).ToolTipText = "Display Text"
```

Most of the controls in Visual Basic contain the property ToolTipText for displaying immediate help to the user. You can enter your ToolTip into the Properties window, or set the value from within your code. The following code implements a ToolTip for a TextBox:

```
txtAmount.ToolTipText = "Amount in dollars."
```

Lesson Summary

Visual Basic supports calling Help files, but it does not support creating Help files. Use a separate authoring tool such as Microsoft HTML Help Workshop to create Help files.

To set links, you must create the Help file separately, then use these properties:

- HelpFile specifies the Help file name and location.

- HelpContextID links a program's forms, controls, and menus to a Help file.

What's This Help provides Help in a popup window instead of a Help viewer. It is a form-level property.

Lesson 2: Creating an Executable

With Visual Basic, you can compile your code into one of two types of executable files: p-code (pseudo code) or native. Both of these types of executable files have advantages and disadvantages; you compile a project into p-code or native code or depending on the tasks that your application performs.

P-code instructions are translated or interpreted by a run-time dynamic-link library (DLL) before executing on the processor chip. Compiling to native code means that the resulting executable file will contain instructions that are native to the processor chip. When you compile to native code, you can use compiler switches (or options) to optimize your application when it runs. In this lesson, you will learn about the various compiler options and their purpose. In addition, you will learn how to implement conditional compilation, which is used to specify what code will be compiled based on a given condition.

After this lesson you will be able to:

- Explain the advantage of compiling with the native code option.

- Explain the options for compiling with the native code option.

- Describe when you would use conditional compilation.

Estimated lesson time: 40 minutes

Compiler Options

With the Professional or Enterprise edition of Visual Basic, you can compile your code either in standard Visual Basic pseudo code (p-code) or in native code. In the Standard edition of Visual Basic, you can compile programs only in p-code. Compiling your programs in native code provides several options for optimizing and debugging that are not available with p-code.

Visual Basic p-code is an intermediate step between the high-level instructions in your Basic program and the low-level native code that your computer's processor executes. Visual Basic translates p-code into native code during run time, and then executes the program. By compiling directly to native code format, you eliminate the intermediate p-code step.

When you compile your project with the native code option, your code is compiled to the native instructions of the processor chip, and not compiled in p-code. This speeds up the execution of loops and mathematical calculations, and also speeds up calls to external services.

You can debug programs compiled in native code using standard debugging tools, such as the debugging environment provided by Visual C++. You can also use options for optimizing native code. For example, you can optimize code for speed or for size. Figure 12.2 shows the Compile tab on the Project Properties dialog box.

➤ **To set the compile option to native code**

1. On the **Project** window, click the project you want to compile.
2. On the **Project** menu, click **Project Properties**.

   The **Project Properties** dialog box appears.
3. Click the **Compile** tab.
4. Click **Compile to Native Code**.
5. For advanced optimization options, click the **Advanced Optimizations** button.
6. Select the options you want, then click **OK**.

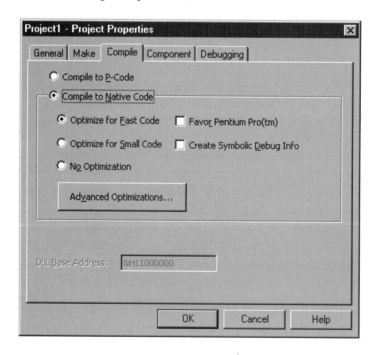

Figure 12.2 The Compile tab in the Project Properties dialog box

When compiling in native code, Visual Basic enables several options for customizing and optimizing the executable file.

When the compiler translates Visual Basic statements into machine code, often many different sequences of machine code can correctly represent a given statement or construct. Sometimes these differences offer trade-offs of size versus speed.

Optimize for Fast Code

Use the Optimize for Fast Code option to maximize the speed of compiled executable files. This option instructs the compiler to favor speed over size.

Selecting the Optimize for Fast Code option ensures that when the compiler recognizes such alternatives, it will always generate the fastest code sequence possible, even when that may increase the size of the compiled program.

Optimize for Small Code

Use the Optimize for Small Code option to minimize the size of compiled executable files. This option instructs the compiler to favor size over speed.

Selecting this option ensures that when the compiler recognizes such alternatives it will always generate the smallest code sequence possible, even when that may decrease the execution speed of the compiled program.

No Optimizations

Use the No Optimizations option to turn off all optimizations.

With this option selected, the compiler generates code that is significantly slower and larger than when optimization for fast or small code is selected.

Favor Pentium Pro

Use the Favor Pentium Pro option to optimize code generation in favor of the Pentium Pro (P6) processor. Code generated with this option will still run on earlier processors, but less efficiently.

The Pentium Pro microprocessor architecture allows certain code generation strategies that can substantially improve efficiency. However, code created using these Pentium Pro strategies does not perform as well on 80386-based and 80486-based computers or on Pentium computers. You should use this option only if all or most of the machines your program will run on use the Pentium Pro.

Create Symbolic Debug Info

Use the Create Symbolic Debug Info option to generate symbolic debug information in the compiled executable file.

Programs compiled to native code using this option can be debugged using Visual C++ (5.0 or later) or another compatible debugger. Setting this option will generate a .pdb file with the required symbol information for use with compatible symbolic debuggers.

Assume No Aliasing

Use the Assume No Aliasing option to tell the compiler that your program does not use aliasing.

An alias is a name that refers to a memory location that is already referred to by a different name. This occurs when you use ByRef arguments that refer to the same variable in two ways. For example:

```
Sub MyProcedure(x as integer, y as integer)
    x = 5    'Code is referring to the same variable
    '(the local z in Main)
    y = 6    'via two different names, x and y.
End Sub

Sub Main
    Dim z as integer
    MyProcedure z,z
End Sub
```

Using the Assume No Aliasing option allows the compiler to apply optimizations it couldn't otherwise use, such as storing variables in registers and performing loop optimizations. However, you should be careful not to check this option if your program passes ByRef arguments, because the optimizations could cause the program to execute incorrectly.

Remove Array Bounds Checks

Use the Remove Array Bounds Checks option to turn off error checking for valid array indexes and the correct number of dimensions of the array.

By default, Visual Basic checks every access to an array to determine whether the index is within the range of the array. If the index is outside the bounds of the array, an error is returned. Selecting the Remove Array Bounds Checks option turns off this error checking, which can speed up array manipulation significantly. However, if your program accesses an array with an index that is out of bounds, the program may access invalid memory locations without warning. This can cause unexpected behavior or program crashes.

Remove Integer-Overflow Checks

Use the Remove Integer-Overflow Checks option to turn off error checking to ensure that numeric values assigned to integer variables are within the correct range for the data types.

By default, Visual Basic checks every calculation of a variable with an integer-style data type (Byte, Integer, Long, and Currency) to be sure that the resulting value is within range of that data type. Selecting the Remove Integer-Overflow Checks option turns off this error checking, which can speed up integer calculations. If a value is out of range for the data type, however, no error is returned and incorrect results may occur.

Remove Floating-Point Error Checks

Use the Remove Floating-Point Error Checks option to turn off error checking to ensure that numeric values assigned to floating-point variables are within the correct range for the data types, and that division by zero or other invalid operations do not occur.

By default, Visual Basic checks every calculation of a variable with a floating point data type (Single and Double) to be sure that the resulting value is within range of that data type. Error checking is also performed to determine if division by zero or other invalid operations are attempted. Selecting this option turns off this error checking, which can speed up floating point calculations. If data type capacities overflow, however, no error is returned and incorrect results may occur.

Remove Safe Pentium FDIV Checks

Use the Remove Safe Pentium FDIV Checks option to turn off the generation of special code to make floating point division safe on Pentium processors with the floating-point division (FDIV) bug.

The native code compiler automatically adds extra code for floating-point operations to make these operations safe when run on Pentium processors that have the FDIV bug. Selecting the Remove Safe Pentium FDIV Checks option produces code that is smaller and faster, but in rare cases, this option might produce slightly incorrect results on Pentium processors with the FDIV bug.

Allow Unrounded Floating-Point Operations

Use the Allow Unrounded Floating-Point Operations option to tell the compiler to compare the results of floating-point expressions without first rounding those results to the correct precision.

Floating-point calculations are normally rounded off to the correct degree of precision (Single or Double) before comparisons are made. Selecting the Allow Unrounded Floating-Point Operations option lets the compiler perform floating-point comparisons before rounding. This is more efficient than comparing after rounding and it also improves the speed of some floating-point operations. A disadvantage of enabling this option is that calculations might be maintained to a higher precision than expected. In addition, two floating-point values that might be expected to compare as equal might not actually do so.

In general, this option should not be used if you perform equality comparisons directly on the results of floating-point computations. For example:

```
Dim Q As Single
    Q = <floating-point computation>
    If Q = <floating-point computation> then
End If
```

If the Allow Unrounded Floating-Point Operations option is set, the comparison of Q will be made with the result of the floating-point expression. It will likely have higher precision than that of a Single, so the comparison may fail. If the option is not set, the result of the floating-point expression will be rounded to the appropriate precision (Single) before the comparison, then the comparison will succeed.

Using Conditional Compilation

Conditional compilation lets you compile only selected parts of the program. You can include specific features of your program in different versions. For example, you can design an application to run on different platforms or change the date and currency display filters for an application distributed in several different languages.

To conditionally compile a part of your code, enclose it between #If...Then and #EndIf statements, using a Boolean constant as the branching test. To include this code segment in compiled code, set the value of the constant to –1 (True).

For example, to create French language and German language versions of the same application from the same source code, embed platform-specific code segments in #If...Then statements using the predefined constants conFrenchVersion and conGermanVersion:

```
#If conFrenchVersion Then
    '<code specific to the French language version>.
#ElseIf conGermanVersion then
    '<code specific to the German language version>.
#Else
    '<code specific to other versions>.
#End If
```

If the value of the conFrenchVersion constant is set to True at compile time, the conditional code for the French language version will be compiled. If the value of the conGermanVersion constant is set to True, the compiler uses the German language version.

Declaring Conditional Compilation Constants

You can set the conditional compilation constants in your project in three ways: in the Project Properties dialog box, in a command line argument, or in your code. The way you set a conditional compilation constant depends on the scope you want the constant to have.

Using the Project Properties dialog box or command line to set your conditional compilation constants makes the constants Public to all modules in the project. By using the #Const statement in your code, the constants are Private to the module in which they are declared.

➤ **To set the conditional compilation constants in the Project Properties dialog box**

1. On the **Project** menu, click the **Project Properties**.

2. Click the **Make** tab.

3. Type an argument, such as **conFrenchVersion = –1**, in the **Conditional Compilation Arguments** field.

If you have a complex #If...Then statement, containing one or more #ElseIf statements, you will need to set additional constants. You can set multiple constants by separating them with colons, as in the following example:

```
conFrenchVersion=-1:conANSI=0
```

If you want to start compilation from a command line, use the /d switch to enter conditional compilation constants, as shown here:

```
vb6.exe /make MyProj.vbp /d conFrenchVersion=-1:conANSI=0
```

Command-line declarations override declarations entered on the Project Properties dialog box. Arguments set on the Project Properties dialog box remain in effect for subsequent compilations.

Lesson Summary

You can compile a Visual Basic application as:

- Pseudo code (p-code), which is translated by a run-time DLL before execution.
- Native code, which provides several optimization options:
  - Optimize for Fast Code
  - Optimize for Small Code
  - No Optimizations
  - Favor Pentium Pro
  - Create Symbolic Debug Info
  - Assume No Aliasing
  - Remove Array Bounds Checks
  - Remove Integer-Overflow Checks
  - Remove Floating-Point Error Checks
  - Remove Safe Pentium FDIV Checks
  - Allow Unrounded Floating-Point Operations

Conditional compilation lets you include specific features of your application for in different versions, such as foreign language versions.

Lesson 3: Using the Package and Deployment Wizard

When you have finished writing, debugging, and testing your application, you're ready to distribute it to your users. The Visual Basic Package and Deployment Wizard helps you determine which files need to be distributed; it also compresses the files into a Cabinet file (.cab file) and creates a Setup program. After creating your installation files, you can distribute your application on disk, on CDs, across networks, or over an Internet or intranet site.

In most cases, you will package your applications using the Package and Deployment Wizard, which is provided with Visual Basic. It provides valuable shortcuts and automates some of the tasks you would otherwise have to perform yourself.

After this lesson you will be able to:

- Describe the components of an installation package.

- Name the two kinds of installation packages.

- Explain the three options of the Package and Deployment Wizard.

Estimated lesson time: 30 minutes

Installing a Desktop Application

Application packaging means creating a package that installs your application onto the user's computer. A package consists of the .cab file or files that contain your compressed project files, and any other files that the user needs to install and run your application. These files may include setup programs, secondary .cab files, or other needed files. The additional files vary based on the type of package you create.

You can create two kinds of packages: standard packages or Internet packages. If you plan to distribute on CD, floppy disk, or via a network share, you should create a standard package for your application. If you plan to distribute via an Internet or intranet site, you should create an Internet package.

The Package and Deployment Wizard and the Setup Toolkit are the two Visual Basic tools that you can use to package and distribute your applications. The Package and Deployment Wizard automates many of the steps by presenting you with choices about how to configure your Cabinet files. The Setup Toolkit, on the other hand, lets you customize what happens during the main installation process.

The Package and Deployment Wizard

The Visual Basic Package and Deployment Wizard, shown in Figure 12.3, helps you gather all the files needed for your installation by creating one or more Cabinet files. The Wizard automates the creation and deployment of these files.

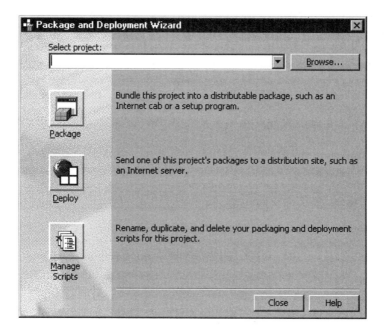

Figure 12.3 Package and Deployment Wizard

The Package and Deployment Wizard opening window has three options:

- Package

    The Package option packages your files into a Cabinet file that can be deployed, and creates a setup program that installs the Cabinet files. The wizard determines the files you need and walks you through choices to create the installation package for your project.

- Deploy

    The Deploy option helps you deliver your packaged applications to the appropriate distribution media, such as floppies, a network share, or a Web site.

- Manage Scripts

    The Manage Scripts option lets you view and manipulate the scripts you have saved from previous packaging and deployment sessions in the wizard. Each time you use the wizard, you save a script that contains all the choices you made. You can reuse these scripts again for a different application if you want to use similar settings and choices.

► **To start the Package and Deployment Wizard**

1. Click the **Start** menu.

2. Click **Programs**.

3. Click **Microsoft Visual Basic 6.0**.

4. Click **Microsoft Visual Basic 6.0 Tools**.

5. Click **Package & Deployment Wizard**.

You can also add the wizard to the Add-Ins menu. If you start the Package and Deployment Wizard from the Add-Ins menu, it uses the active project.

► **To add the Package and Deployment Wizard to the Add-Ins menu**

1. On the **Add-Ins** menu, click **Add-In Manager**.

2. In the list of available add-ins, click **Package and Deployment Wizard**.

3. Under **Load Behavior**, select the **Loaded/Unloaded** check box.

4. Click **OK**.

Deploying to the Web

You can deploy any installation package, whether it is a standard or Internet package, to the Web. When you choose Web Publishing as your deployment method, the wizard uses the project folder to determine how the files and directories should be copied to the Web site; files and directories that are within the project folder are deployed to the Web server with the same directory structure.

► **To deploy your installation package to a Web server.**

1. Start the **Package and Deployment Wizard**.

2. Click the **Deploy** button.

3. If you have previously saved deployment scripts, you can choose one, or you can choose **None** in the **Deployment script** drop-down list. Click **Next**.

4. Click the package that you want to deploy, then click **Next**.

5. Click **Web Publishing** in the **Deployment method** list box, then click **Next**.

6. Clear the check boxes next to the files and folders that you do not want to include with your deployment, then click **Next**.

7. Select the check boxes next to the files and folders that you want to include with your deployment, then click **Next**.

8. Type the destination URL and choose the appropriate protocol in the Web publishing protocol drop-down list, then click **Next**.

9. Type a name for this deployment script, then click **Finish**.

Note By default, the wizard does not deploy source files from within the project directory or the \Support subdirectory. The packaging portion of the wizard creates the \Support directory and places files in it that you can use to recreate your .cab files.

The Setup Toolkit

The Setup Toolkit is a project called Setup1.vbp that is installed with Visual Basic. It contains the forms and code that your application's setup program uses to install files onto the user's computer. This project creates the two setup programs that are used in the installation process:

- Setup.exe, which performs pre-installation processing on the user's computer, including installing the setup1.exe program and any other files needed for the main installation program to run.

- Setup1.exe, which is an application's main installation file; it can be customized through the Setup Toolkit. The Package and Deployment Wizard uses the setup1.exe file to create the setup programs.

You use the Setup Toolkit by loading the Setup1.vbp file into Visual Basic and making modifications to the appearance or functionality of the project. You can use the Setup Toolkit to modify the screens seen in the installation process, or to create a setup program directly. You might create a custom setup program if you need to add additional functionality not supported by the wizard to your installation sequence.

The Setup Toolkit project is located in the \Microsoft Visual Studio\vb98\Wizards\PDWizard\Setup1 directory.

Note Do not modify the Setup Toolkit files without making a backup copy in another directory first. If you modify setup1.exe, subsequent setup programs created by the Package and Deployment Wizard will use the modified version.

Allowing for Uninstall

When the user installs your application, the setup program copies the removal utility St6unst.exe to the \Windows or \Winnt directory. Each time you use the Visual Basic setup program to install an application, Visual Basic generates a removal log file (St6unst.log) in the application's installation directory. The .log file contains the following information:

- Directories created during installation.
- Files installed and their locations.

    This list contains all of the files in the setup program, even if some files were not installed on the user's machine because a newer version of the same file already existed. The log file indicates whether the file was a shared file and, if so, whether it replaced the existing file.

- Registry entries created or modified.
- Links and Start menu entries created with Windows.

In Windows, the setup program adds the application removal utility to the list of registered applications displayed in the Add/Remove Programs section of Control Panel. Users should use Add/Remove Programs to uninstall the application.

It is important to set the options correctly for any files that should be shared, either by adding the files to the Shared Files screen in the Package and Deployment Wizard, or by indicating the installation location for the file as a shared file directory. If you accidentally install a file that should be shared that does not the correct settings, users will be able to remove it when they uninstall your application. This may cause problems for other applications on the users' systems.

In the event of a failed or canceled installation, the application-removal utility automatically removes all of the directories, files, and registration entries that the setup program created in the installation attempt.

With Windows, shared files are *reference-counted* in the registry. For example, a shared file that is used by three applications will have a reference count of three. When you remove an application that uses a shared file, the reference count for the shared file decreases by one. When the count for the file reaches zero, the user will be prompted for final removal of that item.

Lesson Summary

An installation package includes the Cabinet (.cab) file(s) with your compressed project files, plus any other files needed to install and run your application.

You create a standard installation package to distribute the application by a CD, a floppy disk, or a network. Create an Internet installation package for Internet/intranet delivery.

The Package and Deployment Wizard automates the creation and deployment of installation files. It has three options:

- Package
- Deploy
- Manage Scripts

The Setup Toolkit contains the forms and codes that your application's setup program uses to install files on the user's computer.

Uninstall options must be carefully selected to ensure that files used by another application are not removed.

Summary

Implementing Online Help

Visual Basic supports calling Help files. It does not support creating Help files.

To set links, you must create the Help file separately, then use these properties:

- HelpFile specifies the Help file name and location.
- HelpContextID links a program's forms, controls, and menus to a Help file.

What's This Help provides Help in a popup window instead of a Help viewer. It is a form-level property.

Creating an Executable

You can compile a Visual Basic application as:

- Pseudo code (p-code), which is translated by a run-time DLL before execution.
- Native code, which provides several optimization options such as Optimize for Fast Code, Optimize for Small Code, and Favor Pentium Pro.

Conditional compilation lets you include specific features of your application for different versions such as foreign language versions.

Using the Packaging and Deployment Wizard

An installation package includes the Cabinet (.cab) file(s) with your compressed project files, plus any other files needed to install and run your application.

Create a standard installation package to distribute the application by a CD, a floppy disk, or a network. Create an Internet installation package for Internet/intranet delivery.

The Package and Deployment Wizard automates the creation and deployment of installation files. It has three options:

- Package
- Deploy
- Manage Scripts

The Setup Toolkit contains the forms and codes that your application's setup program uses to install files on the user's computer.

Uninstall options must be carefully selected to ensure that files used by another application are not removed.

Lab: Using Help Files and the Package and Deployment Wizard

In this lab, you will implement such help features as context-sensitive help, ToolTips, and What's This Help? You will also compile the Chateau St. Mark hotel application and use the Package and Deployment Wizard to create setup files. You can continue to work with the files you created in Lab 11, or you can use the files provided for you in the \Labs\Lab12\Partial folder. The solution code can be found in the \Labs\Lab12\Solution folder.

To see a demonstration of the solution, run the Lab12.exe animation located in the Animations folder on the Supplemental Course Materials CD-ROM that accompanies this book.

Estimated lesson time: 60 minutes

Exercise 1: Applying Help Files

In this exercise you will add help features to the Chateau St. Mark hotel reservation system. These help features include context-sensitive help, ToolTips, and What's This Help?

➤ **To open the hotel reservation application project**

- Open the Chateau St. Mark hotel reservation system project.

➤ **To add context-sensitive help**

1. In the Project's Properties, set the Help File Name property to \Labs\Lab12\Helpfile.hlp.

2. The following table contains the entire list of context IDs for the help file you added to the Reservation project. Do not set all of the following HelpContextIDs on **frmReservation**. Set only the HelpContextIDs for the user-input controls (TextBoxes, OptionButtons, CommandButtons, and MaskEdBox). Not all of the controls have been given a context ID. For example, **txtFirstName**'s HelpContextID property would be set to **21**.

Topic	HelpContextID
About the Buttons	2
About the guest Menu	7
About the Status bar	4
About the Text Entries	3
Add Reservation	20
Address	23
Cancel Reservation	18
Cash	14

Topic	HelpContextID
Check	13
Check-In	16
Check-in Date	26
Check-out Date	28
Credit Card	12
Done Button	10
First Name	21
Guest Menu	11
Last Name	22
Number of Days	27
Number of People	25
Payment Type	9
Phone	24
Rate	30
Room Number	29

3. Save and run the application.

➤ To test the context-sensitive help

1. Run the application.

2. On the **Guest** menu, select **Reservation**, then click **Add**.

3. Click in the **First Name** text box, then press **F1** to open the context-sensitive help.

   The **Help** dialog box that describes the text box appears.

4. Close the application.

➤ To create a ToolTip in Visual Basic

1. In the **frmReservation_Load** event, type the following code:

```
txtFirstName.ToolTipText = "Enter the guest's first name."
txtLastName.ToolTipText = "Enter the guest's last name."
```

   Add any additional ToolTips to the load event or the control's ToolTip properties that you want displayed.

2. Run the application.

3. From the **Guest** menu, select **Reservation**, then click **Add**.

4. Position your mouse pointer over **txtFirstName** on the **frmReservation** form.

   A ToolTip displays a message describing the functionality of the textbox.

5. Close the application.

Exercise 2: Setting Compile Options in your Application

In this exercise you will create an executable file for the Chateau St. Mark hotel reservation system application.

➤ **To set compile properties**

1. On the **Project** menu, click **HotelReservation Properties**.

   The **Project Properties** dialog box appears.

2. Click the **Compile** tab.

3. Click **Compile to Native Code**.

4. Click **Ok**.

➤ **To add final touches to the application**

1. On the **Project** menu, click **Components**, and remove all unused controls from the project.

   Note Visual Basic will not allow you to remove a control or reference that is being used by the project.

   ---

2. On the **Project** menu, click **References**, and remove all unused references from the project.

3. Define the application title and create an executable file.

   The application title is the default text displayed in the title bar of message boxes and input boxes when a specific string is not supplied.

   a. On the **File** menu, click **Make HotelRes.exe**.

   b. Click **Options** and set the Application Title to **Chateau St. Mark**.

   c. Click **OK** to create the .exe file.

4. Save your project and exit Visual Basic.

5. Test your compiled application by running the .exe file.

Exercise 3: Using the Package and Deployment Wizard

In this exercise, you will use the Package and Deployment Wizard to create a setup program for distributing your application.

➤ **To create a setup application**

1. On the **Start** menu, click **Microsoft Visual Basic 6.0**, then click **Microsoft Visual Basic 6.0 Tools**, and then click **Package & Deployment Wizard**.

2. In the **Package & Deployment Wizard**, click **Browse**, open the Hotel Reservation project provided in the \Labs\Lab12 folder, then click **Package**.

   Because you saved the project files after compiling the executable, the Package & Deployment Wizard detects a difference and prompts you to recompile. Click **No** to use the executable you created in the previous procedure.

   Note If you have previously run the Package & Deployment Wizard, the Packaging Script screen appears. This screen lists previously saved scripts for the current project and (None) if you do not want to use an existing script. The default is the last script that was run for the current project.

   ---

3. On the **Package Type** screen, select **Standard Setup Package** as the Package Type, then click **Next**.

4. On the **Package Folder** screen, select the \Labs\Lab12\Setup folder for the location of the distribution files, then click **Next**.

5. On the **Included Files** screen, browse through the list of included files, then click **Add**.

6. Locate the file Readme.txt in the \Labs\Lab12 folder, click **Open**, then click **Next**.

   Note If there are any files that Visual Basic did not include, use the Find utility on the Start menu to locate the files. There should only be one control dependency, Mscomctl.ocx. If there are any other file dependencies, clear their check boxes.

   ---

7. On the **Cab Options** screen, select **Single Cab** from the **Cab** options, then click **Next**.

8. On the **Installation Title** screen, leave the default title, then click **Next**.

9. On the **Start Menu Items** screen, note the default menu location, then click **Next**.

10. On the **Install Locations** screen, notice that you can modify the install location for each of the files listed. Without making changes, click **Next**.

11. On the **Shared Files** screen, click **Next**.

12. In the **Finished!** dialog box, name the script **Lab 12 Setup Package 1**, then click **Finish**.

13. The Setup Wizard creates the setup program for your application. Click **Close** in the **Report** dialog box.

14. When the Package & Deployment Wizard is finished, click **Close**.

➤ **To run the setup program**

1. Start Windows Explorer.

2. Open the setup folder (\Labs\Lab12\Setup).

3. Run the **Setup.exe** program by double-clicking it.

➤ **To run your application**

■ After setup is complete, run your application from the Programs group on the **Start** menu.

➤ **To uninstall your application**

1. On the **Start** menu, point to **Settings**, then click **Control Panel**.

2. Run the **Add/Remove Programs** application, then click the **Install/Uninstall** tab.

3. Select the application you installed in the previous exercise, then click **Add/Remove**.

4. If prompted to remove shared files, choose not to remove them.

➤ **To run your application**

1. Check the Programs group on the **Start** menu. Has your application been removed?

2. Look for the folder that was created by the Setup program. Has it been removed?

Review

The following questions are intended to reinforce key information presented in this chapter. If you are unable to answer a question, review the appropriate lesson and then try the question again. Answers to the questions can be found in the Appendix, "Questions and Answers," located at the back of this book.

1. What object and what property do you set to programmatically specify the Help file name and location for your application?

2. What properties must be set on both the form and the controls to enable What's This Help?

3. Which compiler option would you set to allow your compiled application to be debugged using Visual C++?

4. Which conditional statements do you code to use conditional compilation to selectively compile certain parts of the program?

5. What can you do to modify the screens seen in the installation process that you create with the Package and Deployment Wizard?

APPENDIX

Questions and Answers

Chapter 1

Lab Questions

Page 24

1. What are the benefits of implementing MSF?

    MSF helps organizations merge business and technology objectives, reduce the life cycle costs of using new technology, and successfully deploy Microsoft technologies to streamline business processes. MSF exposes critical risks, important planning assumptions, and key interdependencies that are required to successfully plan, build, and manage a technology infrastructure or a business solution.

    MFS helps to speed up development cycles, lower the cost of owning technology, improve execution of planned events, improve reaction to unplanned events, create scalable, reliable technology solutions, and improve core information technology competencies.

2. What are the models implemented in MSF? What are their purposes?

    Team Model—defines a team of peers working in interdependent and cooperating roles.

    Process Model—helps your team establish guidelines for planning and controlling results-oriented projects based on project scope, the resources available, and the schedule.

    Application Model—helps your team design distributed applications that take optimum advantage of component reuse.

    Enterprise Architecture Model—supports decisions relating to the information, applications, and technology needed to support a business. It is the key to successful long-term use of new technologies.

    Solutions Design Model—shows how applications must be designed from a user and business perspective (as opposed to the ideal streamlined development proposed in the Application Model).

(continued)

Infrastructure Model—establishes MSF principles for managing the people, processes, and technology that support networks in a large enterprise.

Total Cost of Ownership Model—supports the process of assessing, improving, and managing information technology costs and maximizing value.

3. What are the three design phases of the solution design model? What tasks are accomplished in these phases?

Conceptual involves business sponsors, users, managers, and constituencies. The goal of conceptual design is to understand what the users do and to identify business needs. Much of conceptual design is an analysis activity that leads to determining which processes and activities will go into the new system, how the needs of those processes and activities will be met, and what the user's experience will be of those activities.

Logical design activities are integrated directly with the resulting scenarios from conceptual design, and provide the basis for Physical design. Logical design describes the organization of the elements that make up the solution and how they interact. You assemble the elements for optimum efficiency, performance, and reuse.

Physical design describes a solution in a way that allows developers to construct the solution. Physical design communicates the necessary details of the solution, including organization, structure, technology, and relationships between elements that you will use to create the solution.

Review Questions

Page 27

1. What is the Microsoft Solutions Framework?

Microsoft Solutions Framework (MSF) is a suite of models, principles, and guides for building and deploying software. MSF is a collection of best practices used by the Microsoft product groups and Microsoft Consulting Services.

2. Which MSF Model directly focuses on software development?

The Solution Design Model provides a step-by-step strategy for designing business-oriented solutions driven by a specific business need. This model ties together the Application, Team, and Process Models, and makes it possible for the information system staff to focus resources where they can produce the most value. Because software development is a creative and complex process, you can apply MSF's Solution Design Model to software development.

3. What is an example of a single-tier application?

   An example of a single-tier application is Microsoft Excel, where the user interface and business rules are combined in the application. The business rules include calculating totals, spell check, and other mathematical functions. In addition, the routines that access and save the Excel application files (.xls) are part of the same application layer as the user interface and business rules.

4. When is a two-tier application most effective?

   Two-tier applications work well in departmental-scale applications with modest numbers of users (under 100); a single database; and secure, fast networking.

5. What are three ways to install Visual SourceSafe?

   Both the Visual SourceSafe Explorer and the Visual SourceSafe Database can be installed on the user's machine.

   The Visual SourceSafe Explorer and the Visual SourceSafe Database can both be installed on the server.

   The Visual SourceSafe Explorer will be installed on the user's machine and the Visual SourceSafe Database will be installed on a server.

6. What are some of the commands used in Visual SourceSafe to reuse files and how are they used?

   Sharing: To share a file, you create a shared link between two projects.

   Branching: Branching a file breaks the shared link, while retaining a copy of the file.

   Merging: The process of combining differences in two or more changed copies of a file into a new version of the file.

Chapter 2

Review Questions

Page 90

1. Your boss told you to follow the "look" of Microsoft Word in designing the user interface of your new insurance form.

   What specific elements will you look at?

   Why did he want you to do this?

   Look at the layout and colors. This includes: where various buttons, such as OK, are located; icons on toolbars; menu commands and their access keys; the order of the menus in Word (File is first, Edit is next, and so on.)

   The people in our company use Microsoft Word regularly, and they will more easily learn a new application that has an interface that looks familiar. Reducing their learning curve saves training time and expense.

2. When would you have to set a startup form?

   When the application has more than one form, you have to designate which will be the first one the user sees. By default, Visual Basic will use the first form in a project as the defaulkt startup form. As your applications become more complex, you will need to add additional forms. You may find that a form added later in the project should be used as the intial form.

3. What causes form events to fire?

   A user action such as a mouse click or a key press fires a form event. The system can also cause form events to fire, such as Windows shutting down.

4. What is the difference between standard controls and custom controls, and where do you get them?

   Standard controls are included in Visual Basic and are automatically available in the toolbox. Custom controls are additional controls that can be added to the toolbox if you want to use them in a project. Some come with Visual Basic. Additional controls come in the Professional and Enterprise editions of Visual Basic. Custom controls are also available from third-party developers.

5. Why would you set control properties at design time?

   Why would you set them at run time?

   You set properties at design time when you want to set defaults for the application. You set properties at run time when you want to control actions as the application runs.

6. What is a control array?

When do you need a control array?

A control array is a group of controls that share the same name, type, and event procedures. But each control has its own properties.

You use control arrays to save system resources and to add controls at run time.

Chapter 3

Review Questions

Page 124

1. What are the two main types of validation?

   Form-level validation is when you perform data validation after all fields on a form have been completely filled in by a user. For example, a customer entry form could require a user to fill in a name, an address, a phone number, a city, a state, and a zip code. After the user fills in these fields and clicks an OK button, validation takes place to verify the data in each field.

   Field-level validation is when each field is validated as it is filled in—in other words, fields are validated one at a time. For example, a user could type in a value for a zip code field on a customer entry form, and validation of the zip code field would occur either as the user types in the value or before the user moves to another field on the form. In Visual Basic, you can use the Change event for a TextBox control to verify that the zip code value is numeric.

2. Why should you use the Validate event to validate data rather than using the LostFocus event?

   It is possible to use the LostFocus event procedure to validate the data in a field, however this validation technique can result in an infinite loop where one or more controls are using the SetFocus method in the LostFocus event. The Validate event eliminates the problem and makes it easier to manage field-level validation.

3. There are two textboxes on a form, and the user types the letter "a" into one of the textboxes. If the form's KeyPreview property is set to True, will the TextBox control's KeyPress event fire?

   Yes, the KeyPreview property value will cause the form's KeyPress event to fire first, and the TextBox control's KeyPress event will fire next. By default, the form's KeyPreview property is False, causing the TextBox's KeyPress event to fire first.

   Using the form's KeyPreview property, you can implement form-level validation. This is particularly useful if you need to monitor user input regardless of which control on the form has focus.

4. What is the difference between the Text and ClipText properties of the Masked-Edit Control?

    The Text property returns the data that the user has typed, along with the mask. For example, if the Mask property is set for a stanadrd US phone number, the Text property would return:

    (111) 555-1234

    The ClipText property returns only the data the user has typed. Using the same example, the ClipText would return:

    1115551234

Chapter 4

Review Questions

Page 151

1. What are the three types of errors that can occur in a Visual Basic program and when does each occur?

   The types of errors include syntax, run-time, and logic errors.

   Syntax errors occur when code in a statement is constructed incorrectly.

   Run-time errors occur while the application is running and a statement attempts an operation that is impossible to carry out.

   Logic errors occur when code does not perform as you intended.

2. What is the purpose of break mode in the debugging process?

   Break mode stops the application and lets you check your code one statement at a time. In addition, usiong the various Visual Basic debugging tools, you can also wlak through your code in large blocks, such as by procedure or run to the point where you have placed the insertion point. This can be useful when you wish to "step over" many lines of code that you already know run correctly.

3. What is the difference between the Step Into, Step Over and Step Out debugging tools?

   Step Into runs the code one statement at a time, advances to the next statement and enters break mode.

   Step Over executes a called procedure while Step Into enters break mode after calling the procedure.

   Step Out moves past the remainder of the code in the current procedure.

4. What tasks can you perform using the Immediate window?

   The Immediate window lets you evaluate expressions, change the value of variables, and execute different procedures. You use the Immediate window when in break mode and manually interact with the application to test for logic errors.

5. Identify and explain the two methods of the Debug object.

   The Debug object's Print method lets you send output from the program to the Immediate window without entering break mode. It lets you track variable values at full execution speed and creates a history list of the values in the Immediate window.

   The Debug object's Assert method forces a run-time break when an expression evaluates to False. You only use this method in the Design environment.

6. Why do you use the Locals window?

You use the Locals window to monitor how your variables change as the code runs.

7. What is a watch expression and when do you use it?

A watch expression is an expression whose value you want to "watch" or monitor as the code runs. You define them and Visual Basic automatically monitors them. You use a watch expression when you can't trace a problem to a specific statement.

Chapter 5

Review Questions

Page 171

1. If you do not implement an error handler and a run-time error occurs, what does Visual Basic do?

   Provides the error number and description to the user and then terminates the application.

2. Why should you create your own error handlers instead of using the default Visual Basic handler?

   The Visual Basic default error handler does not give the user an opportunity to correct the error. In addition, the default handler does not run code associated with cleaning up the application, such as allowing the user to save changes. Only a custom error handler provides this capability.

3. What is the last step in implementing an inline error handler?

   Manually clear the Err object.

4. When should you consider using a centralized error handler instead of normal, procedure-based error handlers?

   If your application performs the same task in a number of different procedures, a centralized function that includes specific error-handling code can be more efficient and easier to maintain.

Chapter 6

Review Questions

Page 199

1. What is COM?

    The Component Object Model (COM) allows you to create software components that can be reused by other Visual Basic applications. These software components provide "services" to client applications. In other words, your application (using Microsoft Word objects) acts as a client that requests services from a component (Microsoft Word). Any custom components that you create in Visual Basic can be used by applications written in other languages that support the COM standard, such as Visual C++.

2. What is the purpose of a class module in Visual Basic?

    Class modules (.cls files) are the foundation of object-oriented programming in Visual Basic. They are analogous to a blueprint for a house. Just as a house is built from a blueprint, new objects are created from class modules. These new objects include your own customized properties and methods.

3. Why should you use specific object variables rather than generic object variables whenever possible?

    In most cases, you know at design time the type of object you want to create and use in your application. It is much more efficient, in these cases, to use specific object variables to point to the objects you create. A specific object variable refers to a particular object type and can only hold pointers to that type. If you try to store a different object type in that variable, an error will result.

4. What are three ways to create an object to access an external component?

    Dim ObjectVariable As New Class

    Set ObjectVariable = New Class

    Set ObjectVariable = CreateObject("Component.Class")

5. If you were to create an object model based on a bicycle, how would you implement it?

    You could create a Bicycle class that contains FrontWheel and BackWheel properties (implemented as objects). The FrontWheel and BackWheel objects could contain a Spokes collection.

Chapter 7

Review Questions

Page 241

1. What are the three data access interfaces available in Visual Basic?

   In Visual Basic, three data access interfaces are available to you: ActiveX Data Objects (ADO), Remote Data Objects (RDO), and Data Access Objects (DAO).

2. Why should you use ADO as a data access interface?

   ActiveX Data Objects (ADO) is Microsoft's newest data access technology and is an interface to OLE DB. OLE DB is Microsoft's strategic low-level interface to all types of data. This allows you to retrieve database and other data.

3. What is the difference between a primary key and a foreign key?

   A primary key is a field, or combination of fields, whose value is unique for each row, or record, in the table. For example, the Employee ID field is the primary key for the Employees table. No two employees can have the same ID.

   A foreign key "points to" a primary key field in a related table. For example, in the Northwind database, the Orders table contains a Customer ID field. Each Customer ID in the Orders table identifies which customer made the order.

4. What are the three components of OLE DB?

   Conceptually, OLE DB has three types of components: data consumers, service components, and data providers. Data consumers are applications that use the data exposed by data providers. Service components are elements that process and transport data and extend the functionality of data providers. Data providers are applications, such as Microsoft SQL Server or Exchange.

5. What is Structured Query Language used for?

   Structured Query Language (SQL) is a language used for querying, updating, and managing relational databases. SQL can be used to retrieve, sort, and filter specific data from the database. In addition, you can add, change, and delete data in a database using SQL statements.

6. What operator do you use in SQL to find values based on a pattern (or partial expression)?

   You can use the LIKE operator to find values in a field that match the pattern you specify.

7. What two properties do you set for an ADO Data control to connect to a database and source of data within the database?

You can create a connection to a data source by setting the ConnectionString property of the ADO Data control. Then, you can set the RecordSource property to a table (or SQL statement) from which to retrieve records.

8. What are two ways to update data in an ADO Data control's recordset?

The ADO Data control can automatically modify and update records without having to add any code. This is done when you modify a field or fields, then click on one of the navigational buttons on the ADO Data control. You can also use the Update method of the Recordset object to modify the data instead of using the arrows on the ADO Data control.

Chapter 8

Review Questions

Page 281

1. Which ADO objects can be used to establish the connection?

   The Connection object or Recordset object can be used to establish a connection to the data source. When used directly, a Recordset creates an implicit Connection object for you.

2. What is the ADO Parameters collection used for?

   When passing arguments into a stored query, you must first create a parameter for each value.

3. When would you use the Command object?

   The ADO Command object is used to reference stored queries in a Microsoft Access database. A recordset can then be created from this Command object if records are returned from the query.

4. What method can be used to locate a specific record in an existing recordset without re-querying the database?

   The ADO Find method.

5. What new interface, other than the ADO Data control, is provided by Visual Basic 6 for graphically accessing a data source?

   The Data Environment.

Chapter 9

Review Questions

Page 315

1. If you are using a component that does not have an installation program, which utility will you use to register the component yourself?

   Regsvr32 (Regsvr32.exe)

2. What are the two most common additional options used with Regsvr32? When are these options used?

   The /u option is used to unregister a COM server.

   The /s option is used to register a server without displaying subsequent dialog boxes.

3. What benefits does the components type library provide?

   Viewing the type library provides you with the proper syntax for the classes, interfaces, methods, properties, and events of the COM object.

4. What actions are performed in the following code?

   ```
   Dim xl As Object
   'Do not specify a class type
   Set xl = GetObject("C:\MyFiles\Earnings.xls")
   ```

   When the code is executed, the application associated with the specified extension starts, and the object in the specified file is activated without being displayed.

5. What are the two steps to implementing a Windows API?

   Declare the DLL function.

   Call the DLL function.

6. What operator is used to pass a callback procedure to a DLL?

   The AddressOf operator is used to pass a pointer to the Window API. The pointer directs the API to the address of the callback procedure.

Chapter 10

Review Questions

Page 371

1. What is an out-of-process COM component?

   What are the advantages of implementing an out-of-process component?

   What are the disadvantages?

   An out-of-process component is implemented as an executable file and runs in its own process space. The advantage of an out-of-process component is that a single instance of it can service many clients, share global data, and insulate other client applications from problems that one client might encounter. The disadvantage is that communication between the client and component is slower because data is sent across process boundaries from the client to the component and back again.

2. When creating an ActiveX control that will be used as a data source, what property of the UserControl must you set at design time?

   Set the DataSourceBehavior property of your control to vbDataSource when you want your control to act as a source of data for other objects. The DataSourceBehavior property must be set at design time.

3. Which type of ActiveX code component can have its Instancing property set to SingleUse?

   You can create multiple instances of ActiveX EXEs by setting the Instancing property to SingleUse. You cannot set the Instancing property to SingleUse in ActiveX DLL projects because that requires another instance of the server to load, and DLLs can be loaded only once.

4. What is the purpose of the Start With Full Compile option?

   The Start With Full Compile on the Run menu resolves compilation errors before your component begins supplying objects to your test application. The default in Visual Basic is to compile code on demand. This means that there may be code in your component that is not compiled until the client calls it. Some compile errors cannot be fixed without returning to design mode, which means returning the whole project group to design mode.

5. What are the three ways to publish items to the Visual Component Manager repository database?

    Select a component in the Windows Explorer and drag it to a folder in the Visual Component Manager.

    Select a project in your development environment and click Publish on the project's shortcut menu.

    Click New on the Visual Component Manager shortcut menu.

Chapter 11

Review Questions

Page 407

1. Explain some differences between working with an ActiveX document and a Standard EXE project.

   When working with a Visual Basic form, you can use any type of control or object to create an interface. However, you cannot place embedded objects (such as an Excel or a Word document) or an OLE Container control on a UserDocument.

   Before you can use an ActiveX document, you must place it within a container. A form does not require a container to be displayed.

2. Where does a DHTML application run?

   A DHTML application resides on the browser (client) computer, where it interprets and responds to actions the user performs in the browser. Most of the processing associated with a DHTML application occurs on the client computer, but the application can make calls to the server.

3. What is a WebClass designer used for?

   The WebClass designer is a design-time tool in Visual Basic that enables you to quickly create and modify the WebItems that represent the pages in your application. With the WebClass designer, you can define the contents of the WebClass, add events to the WebItems in the WebClass, and write code for each event in the WebClass.

4. How do .dob and .dox files relate to ActiveX documents?

   The .dob and .dox files define the appearance and interface of an ActiveX document, including its properties, events, and methods. These two files are analogous to the Standard EXE project files .frm and .frx files, respectively.

5. What files are created when you compile an ActiveX document project?

   When you compile an ActiveX document project, an .exe or a .dll file is created in addition to a Visual Basic document (.vbd). To open the ActiveX document in a browser such as Internet Explorer, users must be able to navigate to the .vbd file.

Chapter 12

Review Questions

Page 435

1. What object and what property do you set to programmatically specify the Help file name and location for your application?

   The HelpFile property of the App object.

2. What properties must be set on both the form and the controls to enable What'sThisHelp?

   To enable What'sThisHelp on a form, you set the WhatsThisHelp property of that form to True. You then select each control for which you want to provide Help and assign a unique value to the WhatsThisHelpID property of the control.

3. Which compiler option would you set to allow your compiled application to be debugged using Visual C++?

   Use the Create Symbolic Debug Info option to generate symbolic debug information in the compiled executable file. Programs compiled to native code using this option can be debugged using Visual C++ (5.0 or later) or another compatible debugger.

4. Which conditional statements do you code to use conditional compilation to selectively compile certain parts of the program?

   To conditionally compile a part of your code, enclose it between #If...Then and #EndIf statements, using a Boolean constant as the branching test.

5. What can you do to modify the screens seen in the installation process that you create with the Package and Deployment Wizard?

   You can use the Setup Toolkit to modify the screens seen in the installation process. The Setup Toolkit is a project called Setup1.vbp that is installed with Visual Basic. The Package and Deployment Wizard uses the Setup1 project when creating the setup programs.

Glossary

A

Abstract class A class that cannot be instantiated but is used as a base from which other classes can be derived.

Active window The window in which the user is currently working. An active window is typically at the top of the window order and is distinguished by the color of its title bar.

ActiveX A COM-based technology that provides the fundamental building blocks used in most Windows applications. ActiveX can be used to create controls, documents and components that run on desktops or the Internet. ActiveX components can be developed in many programming languages, including all of the Microsoft application development products.

ActiveX Component An object that conforms to the COM standard. Clients deal with a component object only through a pointer to an interface.

ActiveX Control The new name for programmable elements formerly known as OLE Controls, OCXs, or OLE Custom Controls. Controls previously built with the MFC Control Developer's Kit meet the ActiveX control specification.

ActiveX Document A document that contains ActiveX controls, Java applets, or ActiveX document objects. Also called active object or active script.

Add-in A customized tool that adds capabilities to the Visual Basic development environment. You select available add-ins by using the Add-In Manager dialog box, which is accessible from the Add-Ins menu.

Address Space The range of addresses an application can access. Each application can access up to 4 gigabytes of virtual memory.

ADO (ActiveX Data Objects) The single data interface for 1- to n-tier client/server and Web-based, data-driven solution development. ADO provides consistent, high-performance access to data, whether for a front-end database client or middle-tier business object using an application, tool, language, or even an Internet browser.

API *See* application programming interface.

Application Programming Interface
A set of DLL or EXE files containing reusable functions that can be used in multiple applications.

Applet Software components, similar to ActiveX controls, that are written in Java. They provide dynamic features on a Web page. A software vendor might choose to create a product as a Java applet because its interpreted nature lets it run on several different hardware platforms.

Application A computer program used for a particular kind of work, such as word processing. This term is often used interchangeably with "program."

Array A variable that contains a finite number of elements that have a common name and data type. Each element of an array is identified by a unique index number. Changes made to one element of an array do not affect the other elements.

ASCII file   American Standard Code for Information Interchange, a universally-recognized text file format. Also called a text file, text-only file, or flat file, an ASCII file contains characters, spaces, punctuation, carriage returns, and sometimes tabs and an end-of-file marker, but it contains no formatting information. This generic format is useful for transferring files between programs that could not otherwise understand each other's documents. *See* also text file.

ASP (Active Server Pages)   A server-side scripting environment used to create dynamic Web pages or build powerful Web applications. ASP is not a scripting language; rather, ASP provides an environment that processes scripts that incorporated into HTML pages.

Associate   To identify a file name extension as "belonging" to a certain application so that when you open any file with that extension, the application starts automatically.

Automation   The way a Windows Object exposes a set of commands and functions that other applications may use. These commands are typically referred to as programmable objects.

B

Back end   In a client/server program, the part of the program executing on the server.

Binary   A base-2 number system in which values are expressed as combinations of two digits, 0 and 1.

Browse   To look through lists of directories, files, user accounts, groups, domains, or computers.

Business Services   The units of application logic that control the enforcement and sequence of business rules, and the transactional integrity of the operations performed.

By reference   A way of passing the address of an argument to a procedure instead of passing the value. This allows the procedure to access the actual variable. As a result, the variable's actual value can be changed by the procedure to which it is passed. Unless otherwise specified, arguments are passed by reference.

By value   A way of passing the value, rather than the address, of an argument to a procedure. This allows the procedure to access a copy of the variable. As a result, the variable's actual value can't be changed by the procedure to which it is passed.

C

Character Code   The characters represented by a range of character codes. Under the ASCII and OEM character sets, the character codes 128 to 255 correspond to the extended ASCII character set, which includes line drawing characters, graphics characters, and special symbols.

Check box   A small, square box in a dialog box that can be selected or cleared, representing an option that you can turn on or off. When a check box is selected, an X appears in the box.

Class   A data structure and functions that manipulate that data. Objects are instances of a class; that is, an object must be a member of a given class.

Client   A computer that accesses shared network resources provided by a server. *See* also workstation.

Client Object   An object issuing a request for a

service. A given object may be a client for some requests and a server for other requests. *See* also server object.

Client/server A network in which specific computers take on the role of a server, with other computers on the network sharing the resources.

Clipboard A temporary storage area in memory, used to transfer information. You can cut or copy information onto the Clipboard and then paste it into another document or program.

Close Remove a window or dialog box, or quit a program

CLSID (Class ID) A universally unique identifier (UUID) that identifies a type of COM object. Each type of COM object (item) has its CLSID in the registry so that it can be loaded and programmed by other applications. For example, a spreadsheet may create worksheet items, chart items, and macrosheet items. Each of these item types has its own CLSID that uniquely identifies it to the system.

Code component The new name for programmable elements formerly known variously as OLE Servers. Code components do not supply a user interface.

Collection In object-oriented programming, a class that can hold and process groups of class objects or groups of standard types. A collection class is characterized by its "shape" (the way the objects are organized and stored) and by the types of its elements.

COM (Component Object Model) An object model and a set of programming requirements that enable COM objects (also called Components or objects) to interact with other objects. These objects can be within a single process, in other processes, or even

on remote machines. They can have been written in other languages, and may be structurally quite dissimilar. That is why COM is referred to as a binary standard - it is a standard that applies after a program has been translated to binary machine code.

Command button A button in a dialog box that completes or cancels the selected action. Common command buttons include OK and Cancel. If you click a command button that contains an ellipsis (for example, Browse...), another dialog box appears.

Component An object that conforms to the COM standard. Clients deal with a component object only through a pointer to an interface.

Compound document A document within a container application that contains data of different formats, such as sound clips, spreadsheets, text, and bitmaps. Each piece of integrated data (or "compound-document object") can exist within the compound document as a linked item or an embedded item.

Conceptual design In the Microsoft Solution Framework, what needs to be included in a product. While it should be non-technical, it should be detailed regarding the new functionality in the proposed solution, how the existing technology infrastructure will react to the introduction of this functionality, how the solution will interact with the user, and what is included in the performance criteria.

Container An application that can incorporate embedded or linked items into its own documents. It allows users to insert new items or edit existing items. *See* also server application.

Context menu A menu that is displayed at the location of a selected object (sometimes called a pop-up menu or shortcut menu). The menu contains commands that are contextual to the selection.

Context-sensitive help   Used to display help for a particular topic. In a help file, a number used to identify a Windows Help topic.

Control   A file in a Visual Basic project with an .ocx file name extension that is associated with a visible interface. Grid and CommonDialog are examples of controls.

Control array   A group of controls that share a common name, type, and event procedures. Each control in an array has a unique index number that can be used to determine which control recognizes an event.

Create an instance   Allocate and initialize an object's data structures in memory.

Cookie   A unique identifier that is opaque (not aliased to anything else). The cookie may be an index, a hash value, or a pointer to some object in memory, but only the subsystem knows this. To the subsystem user, the cookie is just the name of a resource.

Cursor   In database technology, a piece of software that returns rows of data to the requesting application. A cursor keeps track of the position in the result set, and multiple operations can be performed row by row against a result set with or without returning to the original table.

D

Data control   A built-in Visual Basic control used to connect a Visual Basic application with a selected data source. Bound controls require use of the Data control as a source of data.

DAO (Data Access Objects)   A high-level set of objects that insulates developers from the physical details of reading and writing records. In a database application, for example, these objects include databases, table definitions, query definitions, fields, indexes, etc.

Data services   Units of application logic. They provide the lowest visible level of abstraction for the manipulation of data

Data source   The data the user wants to access and its associated operating system, database management system (DBMS), and network platform (if any).

Data Source Name (DSN)   The logical name used by open database connectivity (ODBC) to refer to the drive and other information required to access data. The name is used by Internet Information Server for a connection to an ODBC data source, such as a SQL Server database. To set this name, use ODBC in the Control Panel.

Data type   In programming, a set of data that specifies the possible range of values of the set, the operations that can be performed on the values, and the way in which the values are stored in memory.

Data-aware   An application or control that can connect to a database.

Database   A data management system that stores information in tables-rows and columns of data and conducts searches by using data in specified columns of one table to find additional data in another table.

DBMS (Database Management System)   A layer of software between the physical database and the user. The DBMS manages all requests for database action (for example, queries or updates)

from the user. Thus, the user is spared the necessity of keeping track of the physical details of file locations and formats, indexing schemes, and so on. In addition, a DBMS may permit centralized control of security and data-integrity requirements.

DCOM   *See* Distributed Component Object Model.

Default   An operation or value that the system assumes, unless the user makes an explicit choice.

Delimiter   A special character that sets off, or separates, individual items in a program or in a set of data. Programming languages typically delimit such variable-length elements as comments, strings, and program blocks. Databases use two forms of delimiters: field delimiters and record delimiters. Characters used as delimiters include commas, semicolons, tabs, carriage returns, and colons.

Dialog box   In Windows, a child window used to retrieve user input. A dialog box usually contains one or more controls, such as buttons, list boxes, combo boxes, and edit boxes, with which the user enters text, chooses options, or directs the action of the command.

Distributed Component Object Model (DCOM)
A tool used to integrate client/server applications across multiple computers. DCOM can also be used to integrate robust Web browser applications.

DLL   *See* Dynamic-Link Library.

Dynamic-Link Library (DLL)   An application programming interface (API) routine that user-mode applications access through ordinary procedure calls. The code for the API routine is not included in the user's executable image. Instead, the operating system automatically modifies the executable image to point to DLL procedures at run time.

E

Early binding   Checking references to COM objects in Microsoft Visual Basic for Applications code once, during design time, rather than during runtime (late binding). Early binding is much faster than late binding and is the preferred method. Every automation application supports late binding, while only some applications support early binding.

Embedded object   A type of compound-document item in which all the information needed to manage the item is stored in the container document, but which is created and edited by a server application. Embedded items can be edited or activated in-place.

Error statement   A keyword used in Error Function, Error Statement, On Error Statement. Error is also a Variant subtype indicating a variable is an error value.

Error trapping   An action recognized by an object, such as clicking the mouse or pressing a key, for which you can write code to provide a response. Events can occur as a result of a user action or program code, or they can be triggered by the system.

Error-handling routine   User-written code that deals with some kinds of errors at run time.

Encapsulation   In object-oriented programming, the process of hiding the internal workings of a class to support or enforce abstraction. A class's interface, which is public, describes what a class can do, while the implementation, which is private or protected, describes how it works.

Event A notification message sent from one object to another (e.g., from a control to its container) in response to a state change or a user action. More generally, any action or occurrence, often generated by the user, to which a program might respond. Typical events include keystrokes, mouse movements, and button clicks.

Event-driven An application that responds to actions initiated by the user or program code, or that are triggered by the system.

Event procedure A procedure automatically invoked in response to an event initiated by the user, program code, or system. Event procedures are private by default.

Extension The type of file or directory, or the type of program associated with a file. In MS-DOS, this includes a period and up to three characters at the end of a file name. Windows NT supports long file names, up to the file name limit of 255 characters.

F

File-based database The Microsoft Jet and FoxPro engines are file-server based. The data and indexes reside either on the user's local machine or on a network file server. In either case, most processing is performed locally on the client machines.

Flat file *See* ASCII file.

Focus The area of a dialog box which receives input. To find the focus, look for highlighted text (for example, in a list box) or a button enclosed in dotted lines.

Folder A type of container of objects (typically files).

Font A set of attributes for characters.

Front end In a client/server program, the part of the program executing on the client.

Function A block of code, consisting of a return type, function name, optional parameters, and statements, that performs one or more specific tasks within the source program and returns a value to the caller. The purpose of or the action carried out by a program, routine, or other object.

G

General procedure A procedure that must be explicitly called by another procedure. In contrast, an event procedure is invoked automatically in response to a user or system action.

GIF (Graphic Interchange Format) An image file format.

GUI (Graphical User Interface) Refers to a Windows interface versus the standard text-based interface used in MS-DOS.

GUID (Globally Unique Identifier) Identifies a particular object class and interface. This identifier is a 128-bit value.

H

Hexadecimal A base-16 number system that consists of the digits 0 through 9 and the uppercase and lowercase letters A (equivalent to decimal 10) through F (equivalent to decimal 15).

Home page The initial page of information for a collection of pages. The starting point for a Web site or section of a Web site is often referred to as the home page. Individuals also post pages that are called home pages.

HTML *See* Hypertext Markup Language.

HTTP *See* Hypertext Transport Protocol.

HTTPS A Secure HTTP protocol used for browsers to access a site by typing https:// instead of http:// in front of the URL.

Hyperlink A way of jumping to another place on the Internet. Hyperlinks usually appear in a different format from regular text. Initiate the jump by clicking the link.

Hypertext Markup Language A simple markup language used to create hypertext documents that are portable from one platform to another. HTML files are simple ASCII text files with codes embedded (indicated by markup tags) to indicate formatting and hypertext links. HTML is used for formatting documents on the World Wide Web.

Hypertext Transport Protocol (HTTP)
The underlying protocol by which WWW clients and servers communicate. HTTP is an application-level protocol for distributed, collaborative, hypermedia information systems. It is a generic, stateless, object-oriented protocol. A feature of HTTP is the typing and negotiation of data representation, allowing systems to be built independently of the data being transferred.

I

IDE (Integrated Development Environment)
A visual development interface to rapidly build applications by integrating the variety of tools required to design, develop, debug, and profile a general application.

IIS *See* Internet Information Server.

Inheritance In object-oriented programming, a method for deriving new classes from existing classes. The derived class inherits the description of its base class(es), but can be extended by adding new member variables and functions and by using virtual functions. A class can inherit from a single base class (single inheritance) or from any number of direct base classes (multiple inheritance). A class derived using multiple inheritance has the attributes of all of its base classes.

INI (initialization) file In Windows, a file that an application uses to store information that otherwise would be lost when the application closes. Initialization files typically contain information such as user preferences for the configuration of the application. Initialization files usually have a .INI filename extension.

In-process server A server implemented as a DLL that runs in the process space of the client.

Insertion point The place where text will be inserted when you type. The insertion point usually appears as a flashing vertical bar in a program's window or in a dialog box.

Instance An object created from a particular class.

Instantiate Create an instance of a class.

Interface In the Component Object Model, a set of related functions; a description of an abstract class.

International Standards Organization (ISO)
An international association of member countries, each represented by its leading standard-setting organization-for example, ANSI (American National Standards Institute) for the United States. The ISO works to establish global standards for communications and information exchange.

Internet The global network of networks. *See* also World Wide Web (WWW).

Internet Information Server (IIS) A network file and application server that supports multiple protocols.

Primarily, Internet Information Server transmits information in Hypertext Markup Language (HTML) pages by using the Hypertext Transport Protocol (HTTP).

Internet Protocol (IP)   The messenger protocol of TCP/IP, responsible for addressing and sending TCP packets over the network. IP provides a best-effort, connectionless delivery system that does not guarantee that packets arrive at their destination or that they are received in the sequence in which they were sent. *See* also packet; Transmission Control Protocol (TCP); Transmission Control Protocol/Internet Protocol (TCP/IP).

Internet Server Application Programming Interface (ISAPI)
An API for developing extensions to the Microsoft Internet Information Server and other HTTP servers that support ISAPI. *See* also application programming interface (API).

Internet service provider (ISP)   A company or educational institution that enables remote users to access the Internet by providing dial-up connections or installing leased lines.

Inter-object communication   The COM capability allowing clients to communicate transparently with objects, regardless of where those objects are running - the same process, the same machine, or a different machine. This provides a single programming model for all types of objects, both object clients and object servers.

Interprocess communication (IPC)
The capability, provided by a multitasking operating system, of one task or process to exchange data with another. Common IPC methods include pipes, semaphores, shared memory, queues, signals, and mailboxes.

Intranet   A TCP/IP network that uses Internet technology; a Web site or series of Web sites that belong to an organization and can be accessed only by the organization's members. May be connected to the Internet. *See* also Internet; Transmission Control Protocol/Internet Protocol (TCP/IP).

IP   *See* Internet Protocol.

IP address   Used to identify a node on a network and to specify routing information. Each node on the network must be assigned a unique IP address, which is made up of the network ID, plus a unique host ID assigned by the network administrator. This address is typically represented in dotted-decimal notation, with the decimal value of each octet separated by a period (for example, 138.57.7.27).

IPC   *See* interprocess communication.

ISAM (Indexed Sequential Access Method)
A scheme for decreasing the time necessary to locate a data record within a large database, given a unique key for the record. The key is the field in the record used to reference the record.

ISO   *See* International Organization for Standardization.

ISP   *See* Internet service provider.

IUnknown interface   Lets clients get pointers to other interfaces on a given object through the IUnknown::QueryInterface method, and manage the existence of the object through the IUnknown::AddRef and IUnknown::Release methods. All other Component Object Model (COM) interfaces are inherited, directly or indirectly, from IUnknown. Therefore, the three methods in IUnknown are the first entries in the vtable for every interface.

J

Jet Engine The Microsoft Jet Engine ships with Microsoft Access, the Microsoft Visual Basic programming system, Microsoft Excel, and Microsoft Visual C++. It can not be purchased as a stand-alone product.

K

Key A node in a hierarchically-structured tree in which the Windows Registry stores data. Each key can contain both sub-keys and data entries called values. In a database, a key is a column used as a component of an index.

L

Late binding When a program must determine at run time whether an object will actually have the methods you called using the object variable. Although late binding is the slowest way to invoke the properties and methods of an object, there are times when it is necessary. For example, you may write a function that can act on any of three different objects. The variable that contains the object reference cannot be declared with a specific class type.

Latency The time it takes for a packet of data to travel between two computers.

Linked object A representation or placeholder for an object that is inserted into a destination document. The object still exists in the source file and, when it is changed, the linked object is updated to reflect these changes.

List box In a dialog box, a box that lists available choices-for example, a list of all files in a directory. If all the choices do not fit in the list box, there is a scroll bar.

List view A specialized list control that displays a set of objects. Users can view objects in iconic form (by displaying their large icons or small icons, as listed in the registry), as a list or as a table.

Localization The process of translating software, Help, and online or printed documentation into another language appropriate for other locales, customs, or cultures.

Logical design In the Microsoft Solutions Framework, a structure layout for the solution that is the basis for physical design. Logical design describes the organization of the elements that make up the solution and how they interact. A developer's role is important in this phase.

M

Marshaling In COM, the process of packaging and sending interface parameters across process boundaries. *See* also Remote Procedure Call (RPC).

MDI (Multiple Document Interface) The standard user-interface architecture for Windows-based applications. A multiple document interface application enables the user to work with more than one document at the same time. Each document is displayed within the client area of the application's main window.

Memory A temporary storage area for information and programs.

Menu bar The horizontal bar containing the names of all the program's menus. It appears below the title bar.

Method In object-oriented programming, a procedure that provides access to an object's data.

Modal A window or dialog box that requires the user to take some action before the focus can switch to another form or dialog box.

Modeless A window or dialog box that does not require user action before the focus can be switched to another form or dialog box.

Module A set of declarations and procedures.

MSF The Microsoft Solutions Framework , a flexible, interrelated series of models that guide an organization through the process of assembling the resources, people, and techniques needed to ensure that their technology infrastructure and solutions meet their business objectives

Multiprocessing Execution of multiple threads simultaneously, one thread for each processor in the computer. A multitasking operating system only appears to execute multiple threads at the same time; a multiprocessing operating system actually does so.

Multitasking The capability of a computer to run more than one program, or task, at the same time. Multitasking contrasts with single-tasking, where one process must entirely finish before another can begin.

N

Nested object An object embedded within another object.

Network Two or more computers that are connected together by cables and that are running software enabling them to communicate with one another.

Network protocol Software that enables computers to communicate over a network. TCP/IP is a network protocol, used on the Internet. *See* also

Transmission Control Protocol/Internet Protocol (TCP/IP).

N-tier application A special instance of a three-tier application in which one or more of the tiers are separated into additional tiers, providing better scalability.

Null field A field containing no characters or values. A null field isn't the same as a zero-length string (" ") or a field with a value of 0. A field is set to null when the content of the field is unknown. For example, a Date Completed field in a task table would be left null until a task is completed.

O

Object 1. An entity or component, identifiable by the user, that may be distinguished by its properties, operations, and relationships. 2. Any piece of information, created by using a Windows-based program with COM capabilities that can be linked or embedded into another document.

Object Browser A dialog box that allows examination of the contents of an object library to get information about the objects provided.

Object library Data stored in a .olb file or within an executable (.exe, .dll, or .ocx) that provides information used by Automation controllers (such as Visual Basic) about available Automation objects. You can use the Object Browser to examine the contents of an object library to get information about the objects provided.

OCX control *See* ActiveX control.

ODBC *See* Open Database Connectivity.

OLE The technology and interface for object

interaction. A way to transfer and share information between programs.

OLE DB A specification for a set of data access interfaces designed to enable a multitude of data stores, of all types and sizes, to work seamlessly together. These interfaces comprise an industry standard for data access and manipulation that can ensure consistency and interoperability in a heterogeneous world of data and data types.

OLE Drag and Drop An event that occurs when an OLE object is dragged from one container to another.

OLE object A discrete unit of data that has been supplied by an OLE program-for example, a worksheet, module, chart, cell, or range of cells.

OOP (Object-Oriented Programming) In traditional procedural languages (such as C, Fortran, and COBOL) code and data are separate. In the object-oriented approach, code and data that belong together can be combined into objects. Object-oriented design is further characterized by the use of inheritance (derived classes), polymorphism, encapsulation, and virtual functions (C++) in programming.

Open Database Connectivity (ODBC) An application programming interface that enables applications to access data from a variety of existing data sources.

Out-of-process server A server, implemented as an .EXE application, which runs outside the process of its client, either on the same machine or a remote machine.

P

Path The location of a file within the directory tree.

PC Any personal computer (such as an IBM PC or compatible) using the MS-DOS, OS/2, Windows, Windows for Workgroups, Windows 95, Windows NT Server, or Windows NT Workstation operating systems.

Peer Any of the devices on a layered communications network that operate on the same protocol level.

Peer Web Services A collection of services that enable the user of a computer running Windows NT Workstation to publish a personal Web site from the desktop. The services include the WWW service, the FTP service, and the Gopher service.

Physical design In the Microsoft Solution Framework, a layout that allows developers to construct the solution. Physical design communicates the necessary details of the solution, including organization, structure, technology, and relationships between elements that you will use to create the solution.

Pointer A variable that contains a memory address.

Polymorphism The concept of a single interface for multiple functions. For example, different classes can each contain a function called print that prints data in a format appropriate for objects of that class. The compiler selects the appropriate print function for each call to print.

Pop-up menu *See* context menu.

Preemptive multitasking An operating system scheduling technique that allows the operating system to take control of the processor at any instant, regardless of the state of the currently running program. Preemption guarantees better response to the user and higher data throughput

Private Variables that are available only to the module in which they are declared.

Process An object type which consists of an executable program, a set of virtual memory addresses, and one or more threads.

Program file A file that starts a program. A program file has an EXE, PIF, COM, or BAT filename extension.

ProgressBar control Shows the completion percentage of a particular process by filling from left to right

Property Attribute or characteristic of an object used to define its state, appearance, or value.

Protocol A set of rules and conventions by which two computers pass messages across a network. Networking software usually implements multiple levels of protocols layered one on top of another.

Proxy In COM, an interface-specific object that packages parameters for methods in preparation for a remote method call. A proxy runs in the address space of the sender and communicates with a corresponding stub in the receiver's address space. *See* also stub and marshaling.

Public Variables that are available to all procedures in all modules in all applications unless Option Private Module is in effect. In that case, the variables are public only within the project in which they reside.

R

RAM Random-access memory. RAM can be read from or written to by the computer or other devices. Information stored in RAM is lost when you turn off the computer. *See* also memory.

RDO (Remote Data Objects) A framework for using code to create and manipulate components of a remote ODBC database system. Objects and collections have properties that describe the characteristics of database components and methods that you use to manipulate them. Using the containment framework, you create relationships among objects and collections, and these relationships represent the logical structure of your database system.

Recordset A set of records selected from a data source. The records can be from a table, a query, or a stored procedure that accesses one or more tables. A recordset can join two or more tables from the same data source, but not from different data sources. *See* also result set.

Registry The database repository for information about a computer's configuration. The registry supersedes use of separate INI files for all system components and programs that know how to store values in the registry.

Registry editor A program, provided with Windows 95, that is used to view and edit entries in the registry.

Remote Procedure Call (RPC) A message-passing facility that allows a distributed program to call services available on various computers in a network. Used during remote administration of computers, RPC provides a procedural view, rather than a transport-centered view, of networked operations.

Result set In RDO, the data returned from a query in the form of result sets, which can contain zero or more data rows composed of one or more columns.

Rich-text box Similar to a multi-line edit control, but it adds additional functionality and support for individual character and paragraph formatting

RPC (Remote Procedure Call) A widely used standard defined by the Open Software Foundation (OSF) for distributed computing. RPC enables one process to make calls to functions that are part of another process. The other process can be on the same computer or on a different computer on the network.

S

Scope In programming, the extent to which a given identifier (constant, variable, data type, routine) can be referenced within a program.

Scripting Code that you write in a Web page. The script runs either on the client computer when a user interacts with a control, or on the Web server before the page is returned to the client.

Scroll To move through text or graphics (up, down, left, or right) in order to see parts of the file that cannot fit on the screen.

Scroll bar A bar that appears at the right or bottom edge of a window or list box whose contents are not completely visible. Each scroll bar contains two scroll arrows and a scroll box, which enable you to navigate through the contents of the window or list box.

SDI (Single Document Interface) A user interface architecture that allows a user to work with just one document at a time. Windows Notepad is an example of an SDI application.

Server A computer running administrative software that controls access to all or part of the network and its resources. A computer acting as a server makes resources available to computers acting as workstations on the network. *See* also client.

Server object An object that responds to a request for a service. A given object may be a client for some requests and a server for other requests. *See* also client object.

Server-side cursor Cursors that reside on the server, as opposed to residing on the client computer. While client-side cursors copy the cursor to the workstation, server-side cursors use the resources of the database server to maintain the cursors

Slider control Used to adjust intensity levels such as volume or brightness

SQL Acronym for structured query language, a database programming language used for accessing, querying, and otherwise managing information in a relational database system.

Status bar A line of information related to the program in the window. Usually located at the bottom of a window. Not all windows have a status bar.

Stored procedure A precompiled collection of SQL statements and optional control-of-flow statements stored under a name and processed as a unit. Stored procedures are stored within a database; can be executed with one call from an application; and allow user-declared variables, conditional execution, and other powerful programming features.

String A data structure composed of a sequence of characters, usually representing human-readable text.

Stub An interface-specific object that unpackages the parameters for that interface after they are marshaled across the process boundary, and makes the requested method call. The stub runs in the address space of the receiver and communicates with a corresponding proxy in the sender's address space.

Sub procedure   In programming, a procedure written to perform a specific task. A Sub procedure does not return a value, whereas a Function can return a value.

Swapfile   A special file on your hard disk. With virtual memory under Windows 95, some of the program code and other information is kept in RAM while other information is temporarily swapped to virtual memory. When that information is required again, Windows 95 pulls it back into RAM and, if necessary, swaps other information to virtual memory. Also called a paging file.

Syntax   The order in which you must type a command and the elements that follow the command.

T

TCO (Total Cost of Ownership)   TCO defines the aggregate cost-impact of technology, including the cost of support personnel, user self-management, maintenance, and upgrade costs.

TCP   *See* Transmission Control Protocol.

TCP/IP   *See* Transmission Control Protocol/Internet Protocol.

Text file   A file containing only letters, numbers, and symbols. A text file contains no formatting information, except possibly linefeeds and carriage returns. A text file is an ASCII file.

Thread   An executable entity that belongs to a single process, comprising a program counter, a user-mode stack, a kernel-mode stack, and a set of register values. All threads in a process have equal access to the processor's address space, object

handles, and other resources. Threads are implemented as objects.

Three-tier architecture   An application with presentation, application logic, and data all logically separated. Each element is an independent component that can be changed or replaced without requiring that any other component be rewritten. *See* also n-tier application.

Title bar   The horizontal bar (at the top of a window) that contains the title of the window or dialog box. On many windows, the title bar also contains the program icon and the Maximize, Minimize, and Close buttons.

Toolbar   A standard control that provides a frame for a series of shortcut buttons providing quick access to commands. Usually located directly below the menu bar. Not all windows have a toolbar.

ToolTip   A small label, usually containing a description of the control's function, that is displayed when the mouse pointer is held over a control for a set length of time.

Transaction   A series of changes made to a database's data and schema. Mark the beginning of a transaction with the BeginTrans statement, commit the transaction by using the CommitTrans statement, and undo all your changes since BeginTrans by using the Rollback statement. Transactions are optional and can be nested up to five levels. Transactions increase the speed of operations that change data and enable you to reverse changes easily.

Transmission Control Protocol (TCP)
A connection-based Internet protocol responsible for breaking data into packets, which the IP protocol sends over the network. This protocol

provides a reliable, sequenced communication stream for network communication. *See* also Internet Protocol (IP).

Transmission Control Protocol/Internet Protocol (TCP/IP)
A set of networking protocols that provide communications across interconnected networks made up of computers with diverse hardware architectures and various operating systems. TCP/IP includes standards for how computers communicate and conventions for connecting networks and routing traffic.

Tree control A special list control that displays a set of objects hierarchically using an indented outline format. Plus and minus icons allow the user to expand and collapse the outline.

Trigger A set of conditions that, when met, initiate an action.

TrueType fonts Fonts that are scalable and sometimes generated as bitmaps or soft fonts, depending on the capabilities of your printer. TrueType fonts can be sized to any height, and they print exactly as they appear on the screen.

U

UDA (Universal Data Access) Together ADO and OLE DB form the foundation of the Universal Data Access strategy. OLE DB enables universal access to any data. ADO makes it easy for developers to program. Because ADO is built on top of OLE DB, it benefits from the rich universal data access infrastructure that OLE DB provides.

Uniform Resource Locator (URL) A naming convention that uniquely identifies the location of a computer, directory, or file on the Internet. The URL also specifies the appropriate Internet protocol, such as HTTP, FTP, IRC, or Gopher.

Universally Unique Identifier (UUID)
A unique identification string associated with the remote procedure call interface. Also known as a globally unique identifier (GUID).

URL *See* Uniform Resource Locator.

UUID *See* Universally Unique Identifier.

V

Validation The process of checking whether entered data meets certain conditions or limitations.

Validation properties Properties used to set conditions on table fields and records. Validation properties include ValidationRule, Required and AllowZeroLength.

Validation rule A rule that sets limits or conditions on what can be entered in one or more fields. Validation rules can be set for a field or a table. Validation rules are checked when you update a record containing fields requiring validation. If the rule is violated, a trappable error results.

Variables In programming, a named storage location capable of containing a certain type of data that can be modified during program execution.

VBA (Visual Basic for Applications)
Microsoft's powerful visual programming environment that is seamlessly integrated into another program, known as a "host". With VBA, users can easily extend or customize the behavior of the host by writing code using the popular Visual Basic programming language.

Visual SourceSafe A version control system that enables you to manage your individual and team projects.

W

Web browser A software program, such as Microsoft Internet Explorer, that retrieves a document from a Web server, interprets the HTML codes, and displays the document to the user with as much graphical content as the software can supply.

Web server A computer equipped with the server software to respond to HTTP requests, such as requests from a Web browser. A Web server uses the HTTP protocol to communicate with clients on a TCP/IP network.

What's This Help Provides a link to a pop-up Help topic. It is implemented when the user selects What's This Help and clicks the What's This cursor on a control.

Wildcard A character that represents one or more characters. The question mark (?) wildcard can be used to represent any single character, and the asterisk (*) wildcard can be used to represent any character or group of characters that might match that position in other filenames.

Win32-based API A 32-bit application programming interface for both Windows 95 and Windows NT. It updates earlier versions of the Windows API with sophisticated operating system capabilities, security, and API routines for displaying text-based programs in a window.

Windows NT The portable, secure, 32-bit, preemptive-multitasking member of the Microsoft Windows operating system family. Windows NT Server provides centralized management and security, advanced fault tolerance, and additional connectivity. Windows NT Workstation provides operating system and networking functionality for computers without centralized management.

Wizard A special form of user assistance that guides the user through a difficult or complex task within an application.

Workstation In general, a powerful computer having considerable calculating and graphics capability. 2. A computer that accesses shared network resources provided by another computer (called a server). *See* also client.

World Wide Web (WWW) The software, protocols, conventions, and information that enable hypertext and multimedia publishing of resources on different computers around the world. *See* also Hypertext Markup Language (HTML); Internet.

WYSIWYG An acronym used in Windows terminology: "What you see is what you get."

Index

Tools, blueprints, and *mentoring*
to advance your mastery of
32-bit Windows programming

What's new in Visual Basic® 6.0? Plenty—and these innovations can give you a tremendous edge in Windows® 98 and Windows NT® development. In the MICROSOFT® VISUAL BASIC 6.0 DEVELOPER'S WORKSHOP, you'll find a concise introduction to version 6.0 right up front—you'll learn how these new capabilities can power up projects with greater efficiency and functionality. You'll also discover smart solutions to a wide range of specific, *How do I do that?* questions, along with a toolbox full of ready-to-use source code, projects, forms, and files on CD-ROM. If you've already demonstrated some fluency in Visual Basic, you'll get a major skills upgrade in the MICROSOFT VISUAL BASIC 6.0 DEVELOPER'S WORKSHOP.

U.S.A.	**$49.99**
U.K.	£46.99 [V.A.T. included]
Canada	$71.99
ISBN 1-57231-883-X	

Microsoft®

mspress.microsoft.com

MICROSOFT LICENSE AGREEMENT

Book Companion CD

IMPORTANT—READ CAREFULLY: This Microsoft End-User License Agreement ("EULA") is a legal agreement between you (either an individual or an entity) and Microsoft Corporation for the Microsoft product identified above, which includes computer software and may include associated media, printed materials, and "online" or electronic documentation ("SOFTWARE PRODUCT"). Any component included within the SOFTWARE PRODUCT that is accompanied by a separate End-User License Agreement shall be governed by such agreement and not the terms set forth below. By installing, copying, or otherwise using the SOFTWARE PRODUCT, you agree to be bound by the terms of this EULA. If you do not agree to the terms of this EULA, you are not authorized to install, copy, or otherwise use the SOFTWARE PRODUCT; you may, however, return the SOFTWARE PRODUCT, along with all printed materials and other items that form a part of the Microsoft product that includes the SOFTWARE PRODUCT, to the place you obtained them for a full refund.

SOFTWARE PRODUCT LICENSE

The SOFTWARE PRODUCT is protected by United States copyright laws and international copyright treaties, as well as other intellectual property laws and treaties. The SOFTWARE PRODUCT is licensed, not sold.

1. **GRANT OF LICENSE.** This EULA grants you the following rights:

   a. **Software Product.** You may install and use one copy of the SOFTWARE PRODUCT on a single computer. The primary user of the computer on which the SOFTWARE PRODUCT is installed may make a second copy for his or her exclusive use on a portable computer.

   b. **Storage/Network Use.** You may also store or install a copy of the SOFTWARE PRODUCT on a storage device, such as a network server, used only to install or run the SOFTWARE PRODUCT on your other computers over an internal network; however, you must acquire and dedicate a license for each separate computer on which the SOFTWARE PRODUCT is installed or run from the storage device. A license for the SOFTWARE PRODUCT may not be shared or used concurrently on different computers.

   c. **License Pak.** If you have acquired this EULA in a Microsoft License Pak, you may make the number of additional copies of the computer software portion of the SOFTWARE PRODUCT authorized on the printed copy of this EULA, and you may use each copy in the manner specified above. You are also entitled to make a corresponding number of secondary copies for portable computer use as specified above.

   d. **Sample Code.** Solely with respect to portions, if any, of the SOFTWARE PRODUCT that are identified within the SOFTWARE PRODUCT as sample code (the "SAMPLE CODE"):

      i. **Use and Modification.** Microsoft grants you the right to use and modify the source code version of the SAMPLE CODE, *provided* you comply with subsection (d)(iii) below. You may not distribute the SAMPLE CODE, or any modified version of the SAMPLE CODE, in source code form.

      ii. **Redistributable Files.** Provided you comply with subsection (d)(iii) below, Microsoft grants you a nonexclusive, royalty-free right to reproduce and distribute the object code version of the SAMPLE CODE and of any modified SAMPLE CODE, other than SAMPLE CODE, or any modified version thereof, designated as not redistributable in the Readme file that forms a part of the SOFTWARE PRODUCT (the "Non-Redistributable Sample Code"). All SAMPLE CODE other than the Non-Redistributable Sample Code is collectively referred to as the "REDISTRIBUTABLES."

      iii. **Redistribution Requirements.** If you redistribute the REDISTRIBUTABLES, you agree to: (i) distribute the REDISTRIBUTABLES in object code form only in conjunction with and as a part of your software application product; (ii) not use Microsoft's name, logo, or trademarks to market your software application product; (iii) include a valid copyright notice on your software application product; (iv) indemnify, hold harmless, and defend Microsoft from and against any claims or lawsuits, including attorney's fees, that arise or result from the use or distribution of your software application product; and (v) not permit further distribution of the REDISTRIBUTABLES by your end user. Contact Microsoft for the applicable royalties due and other licensing terms for all other uses and/or distribution of the REDISTRIBUTABLES.

2. **DESCRIPTION OF OTHER RIGHTS AND LIMITATIONS.**

   - **Limitations on Reverse Engineering, Decompilation, and Disassembly.** You may not reverse engineer, decompile, or disassemble the SOFTWARE PRODUCT, except and only to the extent that such activity is expressly permitted by applicable law notwithstanding this limitation.

   - **Separation of Components.** The SOFTWARE PRODUCT is licensed as a single product. Its component parts may not be separated for use on more than one computer.

   - **Rental.** You may not rent, lease, or lend the SOFTWARE PRODUCT.

- **Support Services.** Microsoft may, but is not obligated to, provide you with support services related to the SOFTWARE PRODUCT ("Support Services"). Use of Support Services is governed by the Microsoft policies and programs described in the user manual, in "online" documentation, and/or other Microsoft-provided materials. Any supplemental software code provided to you as part of the Support Services shall be considered part of the SOFTWARE PRODUCT and subject to the terms and conditions of this EULA. With respect to technical information you provide to Microsoft as part of the Support Services, Microsoft may use such information for its business purposes, including for product support and development. Microsoft will not utilize such technical information in a form that personally identifies you.

- **Software Transfer.** You may permanently transfer all of your rights under this EULA, provided you retain no copies, you transfer all of the SOFTWARE PRODUCT (including all component parts, the media and printed materials, any upgrades, this EULA, and, if applicable, the Certificate of Authenticity), **and** the recipient agrees to the terms of this EULA.

- **Termination.** Without prejudice to any other rights, Microsoft may terminate this EULA if you fail to comply with the terms and conditions of this EULA. In such event, you must destroy all copies of the SOFTWARE PRODUCT and all of its component parts.

3. **COPYRIGHT.** All title and copyrights in and to the SOFTWARE PRODUCT (including but not limited to any images, photographs, animations, video, audio, music, text, SAMPLE CODE, REDISTRIBUTABLES, and "applets" incorporated into the SOFTWARE PRODUCT) and any copies of the SOFTWARE PRODUCT are owned by Microsoft or its suppliers. The SOFT-WARE PRODUCT is protected by copyright laws and international treaty provisions. Therefore, you must treat the SOFTWARE PRODUCT like any other copyrighted material **except** that you may install the SOFTWARE PRODUCT on a single computer provided you keep the original solely for backup or archival purposes. You may not copy the printed materials accompanying the SOFTWARE PRODUCT.

4. **U.S. GOVERNMENT RESTRICTED RIGHTS.** The SOFTWARE PRODUCT and documentation are provided with RESTRICTED RIGHTS. Use, duplication, or disclosure by the Government is subject to restrictions as set forth in subparagraph (c)(1)(ii) of the Rights in Technical Data and Computer Software clause at DFARS 252.227-7013 or subparagraphs (c)(1) and (2) of the Commercial Computer Software—Restricted Rights at 48 CFR 52.227-19, as applicable. Manufacturer is Microsoft Corporation/One Microsoft Way/Redmond, WA 98052-6399.

5. **EXPORT RESTRICTIONS.** You agree that you will not export or re-export the SOFTWARE PRODUCT, any part thereof, or any process or service that is the direct product of the SOFTWARE PRODUCT (the foregoing collectively referred to as the "Restricted Components"), to any country, person, entity, or end user subject to U.S. export restrictions. You specifically agree not to export or re-export any of the Restricted Components (i) to any country to which the U.S. has embargoed or restricted the export of goods or services, which currently include, but are not necessarily limited to Cuba, Iran, Iraq, Libya, North Korea, Sudan, and Syria, or to any national of any such country, wherever located, who intends to transmit or transport the Restricted Components back to such country; (ii) to any end-user who you know or have reason to know will utilize the Restricted Components in the design, development, or production of nuclear, chemical, or biological weapons; or (iii) to any end-user who has been prohibited from participating in U.S. export transactions by any federal agency of the U.S. government. You warrant and represent that neither the BXA nor any other U.S. federal agency has suspended, revoked, or denied your export privileges.

DISCLAIMER OF WARRANTY

NO WARRANTIES OR CONDITIONS. MICROSOFT EXPRESSLY DISCLAIMS ANY WARRANTY OR CONDITION FOR THE SOFTWARE PRODUCT. THE SOFTWARE PRODUCT AND ANY RELATED DOCUMENTATION IS PROVIDED "AS IS" WITHOUT WARRANTY OR CONDITION OF ANY KIND, EITHER EXPRESS OR IMPLIED, INCLUDING, WITHOUT LIMITA-TION, THE IMPLIED WARRANTIES OF MERCHANTABILITY, FITNESS FOR A PARTICULAR PURPOSE, OR NONINFRINGEMENT. THE ENTIRE RISK ARISING OUT OF USE OR PERFORMANCE OF THE SOFTWARE PRODUCT REMAINS WITH YOU.

LIMITATION OF LIABILITY. TO THE MAXIMUM EXTENT PERMITTED BY APPLICABLE LAW, IN NO EVENT SHALL MICROSOFT OR ITS SUPPLIERS BE LIABLE FOR ANY SPECIAL, INCIDENTAL, INDIRECT, OR CONSEQUENTIAL DAM-AGES WHATSOEVER (INCLUDING, WITHOUT LIMITATION, DAMAGES FOR LOSS OF BUSINESS PROFITS, BUSINESS INTERRUPTION, LOSS OF BUSINESS INFORMATION, OR ANY OTHER PECUNIARY LOSS) ARISING OUT OF THE USE OF OR INABILITY TO USE THE SOFTWARE PRODUCT OR THE PROVISION OF OR FAILURE TO PROVIDE SUPPORT SERVICES, EVEN IF MICROSOFT HAS BEEN ADVISED OF THE POSSIBILITY OF SUCH DAMAGES. IN ANY CASE, MICROSOFT'S ENTIRE LIABILITY UNDER ANY PROVISION OF THIS EULA SHALL BE LIMITED TO THE GREATER OF THE AMOUNT ACTUALLY PAID BY YOU FOR THE SOFTWARE PRODUCT OR US$5.00; PROVIDED HOWEVER, IF YOU HAVE ENTERED INTO A MICROSOFT SUPPORT SERVICES AGREEMENT, MICROSOFT'S ENTIRE LIABILITY REGARDING SUPPORT SERVICES SHALL BE GOVERNED BY THE TERMS OF THAT AGREEMENT. BECAUSE SOME STATES AND JURISDICTIONS DO NOT ALLOW THE EXCLUSION OR LIMITATION OF LIABILITY, THE ABOVE LIMITATION MAY NOT APPLY TO YOU.

MISCELLANEOUS

This EULA is governed by the laws of the State of Washington USA, except and only to the extent that applicable law mandates governing law of a different jurisdiction.

Should you have any questions concerning this EULA, or if you desire to contact Microsoft for any reason, please contact the Microsoft subsidiary serving your country, or write: Microsoft Sales Information Center/One Microsoft Way/Redmond, WA 98052-6399.

Register Today!

Return this
*Desktop Applications for Microsoft®
Visual Basic® 6.0 MCSD Training Kit*
registration card today

Microsoft®Press

mspress.microsoft.com

OWNER REGISTRATION CARD

0-7356-0620-X

Desktop Applications for Microsoft®
Visual Basic® 6.0 MCSD Training Kit

FIRST NAME   MIDDLE INITIAL   LAST NAME

INSTITUTION OR COMPANY NAME

ADDRESS

CITY   STATE   ZIP

( )

E-MAIL ADDRESS   PHONE NUMBER

U.S. and Canada addresses only. Fill in information above and mail postage-free.
Please mail only the bottom half of this page.

For information about Microsoft Press®

products, visit our Web site at

mspress.microsoft.com

Microsoft®*Press*